The Sporting News

COLLEGE FOOTBALL'S TWENTY-FIVE GREATEST TEAMS

The Sporting News

COLLEGE FOOTBALL'S TWENTY-FIVE GREATEST TEAMS

Editors
JOE HOPPEL
MIKE NAHRSTEDT
STEVE ZESCH

Researcher-Coordinator
JOHN HADLEY

Design
BILL PERRY
MIKE BRUNER

President and Chief Executive Officer
RICHARD WATERS

Editor/The Sporting News
TOM BARNIDGE

Director of Books and Periodicals
RON SMITH

The Sporting News extends a special thank you to the sports information departments at the following universities: Alabama, Louisiana State, Miami (Fla.), Michigan, Michigan State, Minnesota, Nebraska, Notre Dame, Ohio State, Oklahoma, Penn State, Pittsburgh, Princeton, Southern California, Syracuse, Texas, UCLA and the United States Military Academy at West Point. Their cooperation and assistance on this project was very much appreciated. So, too, was the research and information provided by NCAA historian Steve Boda and St. Louisan John Duxbury.

Published in the United States by THE SPORTING NEWS Publishing Co., 1212 North Lindbergh Boulevard, St. Louis, Missouri 63132.

A Times Mirror Company

Library of Congress Catalog Card Number: 88-42855

ISBN: 0-89204-281-8
10 9 8 7 6 5 4 3 2 1

First Edition

Contents

College Football's 25 Greatest Teams

Introduction

When Rutgers players ran off the field November 6, 1869, celebrating their 6-4 triumph over Princeton in the first collegiate football game ever played, not one of them—as far as we know—had an index finger pointed skyward to signify "We're No. 1."

My, how times have changed.

Nowadays, a marginally important victory over a moderately talented opponent seems to produce a rash of finger-pointing, all of which appears to be aimed at the national-television cameras. The claims usually border on the ridiculous.

College football, though, is meant to be good fun for all. Crisp autumn air. Tailgate parties. Homecoming. And if the players get caught up in some frivolous "we're-the-best-in-the-land" activity—despite the fact ol' State U. boasts only a 5-3 record—so be it.

The serious football fan views greatness a little differently, however, and is exceedingly choosy in bestowing No. 1 status. He or she likes nothing better than to take issue with the latest weekly wire-service polls, asserting that top-rated Tech is undeserving of its lofty status because of a soft schedule and that unranked A&M shouldn't be penalized because of a tough early-season loss.

The debate gets hot and heavy every week of the season, year in and year out. Conference rivalries, regional biases and personal favoritism all come into play. Just imagine, then, how much controversy might be created if someone put together a poll of the greatest college football teams of *all time*, not just of one season.

Well, someone—The Sporting News—has done just that.

Using its 1983 poll of leading coaches as the foundation for the all-time rankings, The Sporting News expanded upon its survey in 1988 by asking a TSN panel of football experts to weigh what had transpired over the last five collegiate seasons and incorporate the findings into one, all-encompassing poll.

The task has been completed. The result is The Sporting News' "College Football's 25 Greatest Teams," which examines in narrative and statistical detail the qualities that enabled these squads to ascend to special levels of excellence.

Obviously, it was difficult to compare teams of different eras. Who can say, with any certainty, how the 1924 Notre Dame team—Four Horsemen and all—would fare against intricate modern-day defenses? On the other hand, would the super-quick Oklahoma Sooners of the mid-1950s have the muscle to play with the rough-and-tumble Minnesota Gophers of two decades earlier? How would you rate the free-wheeling Miami Hurricanes of 1986 and 1987 against the powerful and deep Army squads of the mid-1940s? Would the 1971 Nebraska Cornhuskers, as our poll suggests, in fact take the measure of any team from any era?

In-depth analyses of teams' personnel strengths and weaknesses, regardless of the era, shaped our poll decisions. Quality of coaching staffs, toughness of schedules and the always-present intangibles also were key factors.

Clearly, teams making the select list of 25 have earned special prominence among college football's elite. This is one poll where being No. 15, or No. 20, or even No. 25, is an honor. A tribute.

The Sporting News' all-time rankings nevertheless figure to stir debate. That would be in the finest tradition of college football polls. At the same time, we wouldn't be surprised if the ratings inspire another tradition—the raising of an index finger and an accompanying shout of—what else?—"We're No. 1."

'71 Huskers: Best of the Best

Nebraska, 1971
By Mike McKenzie

The 1971 Nebraska Cornhuskers were ranked No. 1 going into their Thanksgiving Day showdown against Oklahoma and their fans were ready to celebrate.

Unlike most contests touted as the Game of the Century, the 1971 Nebraska-Oklahoma game truly lived up to its advance billing. What followed five weeks later was Game of the Century II, and though it failed, as do most sequels, to provide as much excitement as the original, the spectacular result was a national champion that has come to be known as the greatest college football team of all time.

The Nebraska Cornhuskers emerged victorious from both holiday matchups—a Thanksgiving Day skim past Oklahoma, 35-31, and a New Year's Day crushing of Alabama, 38-6, in the Orange Bowl. The first triumph marked the only close call during a season in which the Huskers' slimmest margin of victory in their other games was 24 points, while the second sealed a second consecutive national championship.

"Most of the time, they just toyed with us," said Alabama Coach Paul (Bear) Bryant, whose previously undefeated and No. 2-ranked Crimson Tide was like putty in the hands of the Huskers. "They were one of the greatest (teams), if not the greatest, I have ever seen."

Coming from Bryant, who had played on Alabama's marvelous 1934 team and then coached three Crimson Tide squads to national championships in the 1960s, those words were powerful. They were echoed by Nebraska's coach, Bob Devaney.

"This is one of the greatest teams ever to play football," he said.

Seventeen years later, Devaney was pleased—but not surprised—to hear that his 1971 club had been selected as not just one of the greatest, but *the* greatest, in college gridiron history.

"We dominated every other team except Oklahoma with running, passing and defense," said Devaney, who retired as coach after the 1972 season but still serves as the Huskers' athletic director. "They really didn't have a bad game."

The Huskers hardly broke a sweat while executing almost flawlessly through 12 regular-season games and the Orange Bowl. In fact, the hard-fought battle between the Huskers and the Sooners produced only one penalty flag, a Nebraska offside. "It was a pretty intelligent group that didn't make many mistakes," Devaney said.

The Huskers also arrived at the stadium each week in a positive frame of mind, making Devaney's job that much easier. "One thing I remember so well is that we didn't have to juice 'em up," he said. "They didn't need any hype before games. Oh, if they had a bad half we'd get on their tails a little. But they played up to their capacity often, and most teams can't say that, even the good ones.

"Did we have a weakness? Not really."

Certainly not when it came to athletic ability. "The team wasn't especially big," he said, "but had an unusual amount of talent distributed both ways and a fine combination of passing and running. And then you add to that probably one of the best players who ever played anywhere. . . . It was an exceptional blend of personalities from all stations of life, too."

Indeed, Devaney's memories of his team center more on personalities than statistics, scores and strategies. Ironically, Nebraska's most vivid and controversial personality happened to be "one of the best players who ever played anywhere": Johnny Rodgers.

Rodgers grew up on the north side of Omaha, where violence was a way of life. By the time he was 15 he already had been stabbed and had shot another boy in the stomach. If not for his excellence at sports, he looked like a good bet to wind up in prison—or the morgue.

But a football scholarship to Nebraska offered Rodgers a ticket out of the ghetto. He scored 11 touchdowns as a starting wingback in 1970 and appeared to be on his way to stardom.

After that sophomore season, however, Rodgers ran afoul of the law. It was discovered that a year earlier, he and some friends had robbed a gas station, netting the grand total of $91.

"I didn't need the money," Rodgers later explained. "I had money in my pocket. It was just a challenge to see if we could do it."

Rodgers was sentenced to two years' probation. "He proved to be a good citizen in school on probation," Devaney said. "Credit (assistant coach) Tom Osborne with that, mostly. John hated two things—running and getting up early in the morning. Tom would make John meet him at 6 a.m. and go for a little run if John was late to a meeting or something.

Coach Bob Devaney's revival of a struggling Nebraska program turned the Huskers into a national powerhouse.

That discouraged him, killed him."

Rodgers had additional brushes with the law while at Nebraska, but Devaney stood by him, taking considerable heat from the press in the process.

"John had a knack for being in the wrong place at the wrong time," the coach said, "except when he had a football in his hands."

At those times, Rodgers could take your breath away. As a runner, he juked his way around and sped right past entire defensive units. As a receiver, he had sure hands and an uncanny ability to get open. And as a kick returner, he was sensational. No matter how tightly he appeared to be hemmed in by would-be tacklers, he always seemed to find a way to wriggle free for a few more yards, if not a touchdown. "Probably the best wingback the college game has ever seen," Devaney said.

Rodgers was not averse to the spotlight, which was fortunate for the Huskers. He was driven to reach the end zone.

"We had such a good team," he explained, "that . . . I was desperate. I didn't want to carry it to the 5 or 10 so that someone else could take it in. Every time I got the ball, I wanted to score."

As a junior in 1971, Rodgers led the Huskers in scoring with 17 touchdowns, including three on punt returns, one on a kickoff return and 11 on pass receptions. He earned consensus All-America honors for the first of two years.

"John wasn't big," Devaney said, "but tremendously strong and he carried people along with him. A great competitor, too. I half-kiddingly told him before his junior year he could win the Heisman, and he laughed."

Rodgers did win the Heisman Trophy as a senior, an accomplishment that would have seemed impossible during his troubled teen-age years. Perhaps most surprised by his rise to prominence was Rodgers himself.

"John always pictured himself as a dead-end kid," Devaney said. "We had some dead-end kids, for sure."

Rich Glover, for instance.

"It was bad in Jersey City," recalled Glover, a middle guard from New Jersey. "Not real bad, but bad, and got worse. I always dreamed of getting away from home and seeing some good things, and Nebraska made it possible."

That was just a stroke of luck. Husker coaches, who were forced to recruit nationally because of Nebraska's small population, saw him by chance while scouting offensive tackle Daryl White in East Orange, N.J. Apparently, no other major schools were aware of him,

Though the '71 Cornhuskers were talent rich, the spotlight belonged to the incomparable Johnny Rodgers.

The center of Nebraska's defensive line was rock solid, thanks to the presence of quick, tough middle guard Rich Glover.

either, because Nebraska was the only one that offered Glover a scholarship.

Stardom did not come quickly to Glover. He was a second-string tackle his sophomore season, when the Huskers' Orange Bowl triumph over Louisiana State won them the top spot in the final Associated Press poll. (United Press International, which published its final rankings before New Year's Day upsets of Texas and Ohio State, had the 1970 Huskers rated third.) Entering the '71 season, Glover was lost in a shuffle of defensive linemen. Then one day at practice, Devaney instructed his staff to move Glover to the middle, where the departure of All-Big Eight Conference pick Eddie Periard had created a vacancy. Glover played middle guard with such demonic fury, Devaney left him there.

"I believe he was the best at his position in the '70s," Devaney said. "Some opponents never even knew how tough he was because he was so quick, they never touched him."

Glover earned all-conference honors in 1971, a year before he won both the Outland Trophy and the Lombardi Award. The '71 Outland winner was another Nebraska player, consensus All-America defensive tackle Larry Jacobson.

Like Glover, Jacobson became a much better player than Devaney ever had anticipated. In fact, after Devaney left Jacobson's home in Sioux Falls, S.D., on a recruiting trip, he told his wife, "He looks like a sissy." Jacobson wore horned-rimmed glasses and had a baby face, but his development into a defensive terror taught Devaney a lesson.

"I learned with him not ever to pick a guy on what he looks like," he said. "Jake just had a soft, quiet personality, and on film he looked like he kind of sloughed off, but he was a gamer underneath."

An unassuming gamer. His reaction to the news that he had become Nebraska's first Outland Trophy winner was more confusion than exultation. "Nobody even knew for sure how to spell it," Jacobson said, "let alone what it was."

Nebraska's other consensus All-America in '71 was defensive end Willie Harper, who "belongs in the same class with Jacobson and Glover," Devaney said. The Toledo native made 66 tackles that year, including a team-high 18 behind the line of scrimmage.

Harper, Jacobson and Glover were the big three on a defensive line that was second to none. They and tackle Bill Janssen and end John Adkins combined for 61 tackles for 301 yards in losses.

Nebraska's top linebacker was Bob Terrio, a junior college transfer who, like Glover, found his niche after a position change. He had been tried at fullback, his high school and junior college specialty, before switching to defense. Terrio, the team's leading tackler with 96, and Jim Branch formed a

Defensive end Willie Harper was murder on running backs, as evidenced by his team-leading 18 tackles behind the line of scrimmage.

solid linebacking corps.

One of the strongest but least publicized segments of the Nebraska team was the defensive secondary. The Huskers intercepted 27 passes in '71, compared with only six by their opponents. Largely responsible for that advantage were safety Bill Kosch, cornerbacks Joe Blahak and Jim Anderson and monster back Dave Mason, whom Devaney touted to be "as good as Nebraska has ever had at monster."

Mason and Anderson both hailed from Green Bay, where Devaney got some important help in his recruiting efforts from a man named Henry Atkinson.

"He was a brother to the mayor of Green Bay when we got to know him, a big Packers fan," Devaney said. "He took to Nebraska for some reason and helped us with some recruits out of Green Bay."

Not just any recruits, but future starters: Anderson, the defensive captain, and Mason, plus quarterback Jerry Tagge, an Omaha native who later moved to Green Bay.

Tagge, the offensive captain, had only half of a starting job when the '71 season opened. He and Van Brownson had shared time for two years, and two seniors alternating at quarterback appealed to Devaney. Brownson was the better runner, but Tagge was almost as good, plus he held almost every school passing record after just two years of part-time duty. As the season progressed, Tagge assumed the leading role and rose to No. 1 draft status with his hometown team, the Packers.

Tagge ran the offense beautifully, picking most of the plays himself and often calling audibles at the line of scrimmage. "Devaney and Tom Osborne trained me, and I thought like Bob did," Tagge said. "We would do the same thing in the same situations. He turned it over to me."

Tagge's knack for calling the right play at the right time was a big key to the Huskers' success. "The thing about Jerry," guard Dick Rupert told a reporter that year, "is that he listens to you. He trusts you in the huddle to tell what might work. If I give him a nod, he knows I'm handling my guy and he can run there."

The Huskers lined up in various sets out of the I-formation, making it hard for defenses to get a good read on the play. Even more troublesome than multiple sets were the multiple talents of Tagge's chief ballhandlers—the shifty Rodgers, I-backs Jeff Kinney and Gary Dixon, fullbacks Bill Olds and Maury Damkroger, split end Woody Cox

Playing opposite Willie Harper at the other defensive end spot was Jeff Adkins, pictured above sacking Colorado quarterback Ken Johnson.

and tight end Jerry List. The runners could catch and the receivers could run, lending balance to an already vigorous attack.

The big-play man was Rodgers, but Kinney could do just as much damage. He accumulated more rushing/receiving yards (1,289) than anybody on the team and scored 16 touchdowns while doing everything from line crashes to pass patterns. By season's end he had become the school's career rushing leader and No. 2 career receiver.

Though just a junior, Rodgers already was first in the latter department. He hauled in 53 passes for 872 yards in '71, but opponents who decided to key on Rodgers were in for trouble. Cox (24 catches), Kinney (23) and List (21) made good targets, too.

Less spectacular but even more productive than Nebraska's passing game was its rushing. Kinney led the way with 1,037 yards, while Olds and Dixon combined for 1,001 yards. Tagge and Rodgers chipped in with another 573.

These numbers were of more interest to opponents than they were to the Huskers, who went about their business with level heads and small egos. "We don't have any stars on the team," Tagge said midway through the season. "We just have a lot of good football players who concentrate and carry out their assignments." That may have been the intention, but Tagge, Rodgers, Kinney, Jacobson, Glover and Harper were emerging as stars of the country's strongest team anyway.

The unsung heroes of the Nebraska offense were the linemen. Called "my saviors many times" by Tagge, the line featured White and Carl Johnson at tackle, Rupert and Keith Wortman at guard and Doug Dumler at center. They were "really tight, close, the heart and soul of our team," Tagge said, "the hardest workers but always cutting up, and inseparable. . . . They knew where each other was every minute of the day, and that was mostly in the weight-lifting room."

Two of those linemen were among four recruits who had surprised Devaney by enrolling at Nebraska in the first place. When the prospects, who had played junior college ball in such warm climates as California, Arizona and New Mexico, first visited Lincoln, they had been welcomed by a fierce winter storm.

"It snowed and blowed, and I figured we wasted our money, we'd never see them again," Devaney said. "But all four came and were starters on that '71 team—Dick Rupert, Woody Cox, Carl Johnson and Bob Terrio."

That Devaney wound up as head coach at Nebraska was a bit of a surprise, too. After graduating from Alma (Mich.) College in 1939, he spent 14 years coaching high school football before getting his first taste of the college game as an assistant at Michigan State. Four years later, he was hired as head coach at Wyoming. His Cowboy teams posted a 35-10-5 record in five years, attracting the attention of officials at Nebraska, where fans had cheered only three winning seasons in the previous 21 years. Devaney was hired in 1962.

Devaney was such an unknown when he came to Lincoln that people used a slogan to remind themselves how to pronounce his name: "Get off your fanny and help Devaney." But Nebraskans caught on quickly as his first team went 8-2 and won the Gotham Bowl. When he retired as coach a decade later, none of his teams ever had experienced a losing season and the school had its first two national championships.

The first, in 1970, sent the state into a frenzy. Almost anything in red that featured a "1" displayed prominently was a guaranteed big seller. And with expectations high for a repeat performance in '71, Husker hysteria intensified. The hype even prompted Devaney to declare an official Back-to-Earth Day for his squad. "Overconfidence never became a problem, though," he reflected years later.

Even after squashing their first seven opponents to set up an important Big Eight encounter with once-defeated Colorado, the Huskers stayed cool and worked hard. The ninth-ranked Buffaloes were the first big test for the Huskers, who came through with flying colors in a physical 31-7 victory.

Easy wins the next two weeks boosted Nebraska's record to 10-0. The combined score of those no-contests stood 389-64, including three shutouts, and the Huskers rested comfortably atop the polls. Rated second was Oklahoma, which had overwhelmed all nine of its opponents prior to its November 25 date with Nebraska in Norman. The stage was set for a showdown at the OU Corral.

The media blitz preceding the latest Game of the Century focused on the strengths of the two combatants: Nebraska had the nation's No. 1 defense, but the question was whether it could stop an Oklahoma triple-option offense that was unsurpassed in rushing yards, total yards and scoring. With Jack Mildren at quarterback and the amazing Greg Pruitt, Joe Wylie (or Roy Bell) and Leon Crosswhite behind him, Sooners Coach Chuck Fairbanks had more speed in his backfield than any wishbone coach ever. The Huskers' well-balanced offense was not ignored, but many believed that Oklahoma could simply outscore Nebraska, great defense or not.

All of the prognosticating was somewhat lost on the Huskers, who saw the game as a big one, but nothing monumental.

"We never realized the significance of everything at the time," Tagge said. "Geez, we were all kids who just lived together and played together. There was no big pressure because we were having so much fun.

"It took a lot of work on our part to accomplish all we did, but we never thought of it as work. It was good times. At the time I remember simply thinking it was neat; then, all of a sudden, I find myself a better-than-average player on a great team. A lot of us felt that way.

"I sure never anticipated all the hoopla that

The trigger man for Nebraska's high-powered offense was unspectacular but steady quarterback Jerry Tagge.

would stay with that team. I answer more questions about the 1971 team now than I did in 1971. Especially one game."

That game was watched on national television by more than 55 million people—the largest TV audience ever to watch a college football game—as well as 63,385 fans at Oklahoma Memorial Stadium on a gorgeous autumn afternoon. But the weather didn't keep some of the participants from getting the jitters.

"I remember being very, very cold before the game," Tagge said. "Nothing was going through my mind. I was blanked out."

Until the opening kickoff. "It meant the buildup was over," he said. "Once the game started, we relaxed."

Said Jacobson: "My legs were like rubber at the start, we were so high, and we didn't wake up until the second quarter."

The team as a whole, perhaps, but not Rodgers. Just 3½ minutes into the game, his punt return for a touchdown gave Nebraska the edge it needed in a game in which each side launched four TD drives and Oklahoma added a field goal.

Rodgers ran 72 yards for the score. Some of the yards he covered falling down, some spinning and the last chunk in an all-out sprint. Afterward, on the sideline, he threw up.

"Of all the thousands of plays I've seen in college football," Devaney said, "I probably have to rate that punt return the best. I've watched it so many times on film, I've got it memorized. It's gotten bigger and bigger over the years. . . .

"What I remember most was that Wylie kicked it high and I thought John should have made a fair catch. It never entered his mind."

He fielded the punt and immediately absorbed a hit by Pruitt, who unwittingly spun Rodgers away from the almost certain grasp of teammate Ken Jones. Rodgers nearly went down but steadied himself with one hand on the artificial turf. The return was set up to the right, but Rodgers cut to the left and ran through a horde of would-be tacklers. He motored down the left sideline with only one man left to beat—the punter, Wylie—and Blahak bumped him out of the way.

"John could have crawled in after that," Devaney said.

Rich Sanger's kick made it 7-0. Oklahoma closed the gap to 7-3 on a 30-yard field goal, but the Huskers took a 14-3 lead on Kinney's one-yard plunge after the offense finally started clicking in the second quarter.

"Both teams got better as the game wore on," Tagge said. "I remember us being behind at halftime, and we hadn't been behind at all."

Indeed, Nebraska trailed for the first time all season when the Sooners took a 17-14 lead just before

I-back Jeff Kinney dives over the Oklahoma defense for a touchdown, one of four he scored in Nebraska's 'Game of the Century' victory.

the end of the half. Mildren ran the ball in from two yards out for the first tally and then connected with Jon Harrison, his high school teammate from Abilene, Tex., on a 24-yard scoring toss.

Surprisingly, Nebraska was doing an excellent job controlling the Sooners' running game. The ends, Harper and Adkins, were denying Pruitt and the other backs any chance to sweep outside. But Devaney's preoccupation with stopping that aspect of the triple option left the Huskers vulnerable to the pass.

"They had an outstanding wide receiver (Harrison), and my staff—Warren Powers, Monte Kiffin and John Melton on defense—decided we needed to cover him with our best man," Devaney said. "So we switched Joe Blahak from corner to safety (to defend against the run) and went man for man (with Kosch on Harrison), where we had been in a zone all year.

"It didn't work. We didn't compensate with a good blitz. Every time they needed yards, they threw to that wide receiver. I'm not taking anything away from their offense, but we could handle Jack Mildren and Greg Pruitt, and those passes made the score closer than it should have been. We helped Oklahoma with some erroneous planning, and we were all in on it."

Nebraska regained the lead, 28-17, on a pair of short runs by Kinney in the third quarter. An 11-point lead ordinarily would have been plenty, but the Husker defense continued to bend when pressed by Oklahoma's powerful wishbone. Mildren scored again on a three-yard run, and his 16-yard pass to Harrison gave the Sooners their second lead of the day, 31-28, with 7:10 left in the game.

Time was slipping away, but the Huskers didn't panic. They just took a deep breath and went to work, starting at their own 26-yard line.

"I thought we could score," Devaney said, "because our offense had been moving the ball in the second half."

In this key drive, Nebraska's mover and shaker was Kinney. Tagge kept giving him the ball, and Kinney responded valiantly, thanks to a lesson he had learned in an earlier game.

"I gave Jeff the ball four or five times in a row," Tagge recalled of that previous incident. "He came back and said, 'Give it to somebody else, I'm tired.' I made him run it again. He went 35 yards for a touchdown. When he came to the sideline, I said: 'Now you can rest. If you're going to be in my huddle, you have to be ready.' Jeff never said that again. Against Oklahoma he was, 'Jerry, give me the ball,' and I had to calm him down."

After Rodgers ran four yards on a first-down reverse, Tagge gave the ball to Kinney, who shook off Sooner defenders for gains of five and 17 yards to move inside Oklahoma territory. Dixon then rushed for two yards, pushing Nebraska to the Oklahoma 46, but Tagge's pass to Rodgers on second down went out of bounds. The Huskers needed eight yards for a first down to keep the drive alive.

"When it came to third and eight," Tagge said, "I went to my guy who would give us the big play."

Rodgers.

"He knew me inside out," Tagge said. "He knew

Fullback Bill Olds carries for short yardage in Nebraska's nationally televised matchup with No. 2-ranked Oklahoma.

Alabama was no match for Nebraska in the 1972 Orange Bowl, just as Crimson Tide quarterback Terry Davis was no match (above) for the hard-charging Rich Glover.

just where to slide into their defense. I was scrambling, the play was broken, but Johnny sensed it like always. He had that knack of finding the open spot."

Rodgers found it, slid to his knees as Tagge threw low and gathered in the ball with his fingertips for an 11-yard gain and first down at the Oklahoma 35.

Except for a Rodgers reverse that netted seven yards, Tagge went exclusively with Kinney the rest of the way. The I-back continued to blast through would-be tacklers when given the ball five more times, four of them to the same spot opened by White at left tackle. He accounted for 50 of the 74 yards in the 12-play drive, including the last two for the touchdown with 1:38 remaining. It was the fourth TD of the day for Kinney, who finished with 174 yards rushing on 31 carries.

Oklahoma trailed, 35-31, with one last chance to knock off the top-ranked team in the land. But when Glover deflected Mildren's pass on fourth and 14, the Huskers were free to run out the clock.

"Kinney and Rodgers and Tagge got all the attention, but we never would have stopped Oklahoma that day without Richie," Devaney said. "He smashed their inside game. He had 22 tackles. The TV cameras couldn't help but be on him all day long."

The Game of the Century was over. The Huskers were still No. 1, not to mention Big Eight champions, and the state of Nebraska went wild.

"When we flew back to Lincoln," Jacobson said, "the plane couldn't get us to the terminal because of the people on the runway. It was bedlam."

Nebraska completed its regular season with a trip to Honolulu and a 45-3 romp over Hawaii for its 31st consecutive game without a defeat. The Huskers' last test would come in the Orange Bowl against an 11-0 Alabama team that had risen to second in the polls after the Sooners' loss to Nebraska.

The Game of the Century II matched Devaney, a relative newcomer to the national championship scene, against Paul (Bear) Bryant, who already listed three national crowns on his lengthy resume. Few people realized at the time that Devaney had a better coaching record than Bryant, perhaps because Bryant's Crimson Tide had whipped Nebraska in the 1966 Orange Bowl and 1967 Sugar Bowl.

"A lot of people thought we were psyched out and couldn't beat Bear," Devaney said, "so it was especially satisfying when we found out we could."

Devaney allowed his players to cut loose while visiting Miami. Reports had them horsing around in the pool, betting at the horse and dog tracks and taking in other sights around town.

"We want them to have fun and not impress on them the personal importance I feel about this game," Devaney said at the time. "I've lost twice to Bear, and I don't like to think there's a guy who can just walk out on the field and beat me any time he wants to, even if his team is very good. Fortunately, our players aren't as aware of the stigma as we coaches, because they were only in high school when Bear beat us in the '60s."

Bryant, who kept a tight rein on his players in Miami, had switched to the wishbone in the intervening years. But even with Johnny Musso in the backfield, Alabama's wishbone paled in comparison to Oklahoma's, making Nebraska a strong favorite for the national title.

"We didn't feel like Alabama could push us like Oklahoma did," Devaney said. "We felt Alabama lacked team speed. . . . I was scared going down there, because of the past, and not at all overconfident. But the plain, cold facts were, we were better."

And it showed. Nebraska had no trouble shutting down the wishbone while running roughshod over

The 1971 Cornhuskers: Front row (left to right) —Coaches Carl Selmer, Warren Powers; head Coach Bob Devaney; coaches Cletus Fischer, Mike Corgan, Tom Osborne, Monte Kiffin, Bill Thornton, John Melton, Jim Ross, Jim Walden; trainer Roger Long. Second row—Joe Henderson, Randy Butts, Glen Garson, Woody Cox, Monte Johnson, Larry Jacobson, John Dutton, John Hyland, Van Brownson, Johnny Rodgers, trainer George Sullivan. Third row—Mike Beran, Bill Janssen, Jeff Kinney, Keith Wortman, Doug Dumler, Jim Carstens, Carl Johnson, Dennis Zanrosso, Jerry List, Dick Rupert, trainer Paul Schneider. Fourth row—Bob Pabis, Bill Kosch, Tom Deyke, Stan Hegener, Dan Anderson, Dave Mason, Pat Morell, Bill Olds, Ralph Powell, Bob Wolfe, Joe Duffy, Dale Didur. Fifth row—Tom McClelland, Bruce Hauge, Phil Harvey, Steve Runty, Jon Strong, Don Westbrook, Jeff Moran, John Adkins, Tom Robison, Daryl White, Jim Branch, Bill Sloey. Sixth row—Jerry Tagge, John Kinsel, Brent Longwell, Mike O'Holleran, Marvin Crenshaw, Dan Lynch, Kim McKinley, Steve Wieser, Willie Harper, Rich Glover, Steve Manstedt. Seventh row—John Starkebaum, Bob Terrio, Frosty Anderson, Bob Schmit, Greg Guibord, Tom Alward, Bruce Fuller, Ron Coleman, Max Linder, Tim Lackovic, Randy Butts, Gary Hollstein. Eighth row—Jim Anderson, Bob Thornton, Phil Righetti, John Bell, Chris Nelson, Al Pieratt, Rich Sanger, Pat Fischer, Maury Damkroger, Gary Dixon, John O'Connell. Ninth row—Doug Jamail, Jeff Hughes, Joe Blahak, Dave Goeller, Mike Peetz, Al Austin, Doug Johnson, Randy Borg, David Humm, Bruce Weber, manager Rick Wilson.

a Crimson Tide defense that ranked higher than any the Huskers had faced all season. Rodgers repeated his favorite trick by returning a punt 77 yards for a touchdown on the last play of the first quarter, and Nebraska led, 14-0, on its way to a 28-0 halftime romp. The last 30 minutes were just a formality. "As a matter of fact," Rodgers said, "a few of us talked at the half about a celebration party we were going to have back at the hotel."

Before the celebration, however, came a touching moment in the Nebraska locker room. Moments after the Huskers sealed their second straight national championship with the 38-6 victory, Rodgers jumped up on a bench in the middle of a cluster of reporters, held a ball over his head and shouted, "The game ball should go to one of the greatest guys there is, Rex Lowe."

Lowe was a Husker split end who had contracted Hodgkin's disease. When Rodgers saw Lowe roll into the dressing room in a wheelchair, he gave the ball to his teammate. The two embraced in silence, tears rolling down their cheeks.

Over in the other dressing room, a living legend of a coach, after absorbing his worst beating at Alabama and almost of his career, was saying to all who could decipher his mumbles: "We were just beaten by a great football team.... They just flat whipped our butts in every way known to man."

Great teams have a penchant for doing that—and the Huskers were the best ever.

Nebraska, 1971

ROAD TO GREATNESS

1971 RESULTS (13-0)

Opponent	Score	Opp. Record	Opp. Bowl Game
Oregon	34-7	5-6-0	
Minnesota	35-7	4-7-0	
Texas A&M	34-7	5-6-0	
Utah State	42-6	8-3-0	
at Missouri	36-0	1-10-0	
Kansas	55-0	4-7-0	
at Oklahoma State	41-13	4-6-1	
Colorado	31-7	10-2-0	Bluebonnet (W)
Iowa State	37-0	8-4-0	Sun (L)
at Kansas State	44-17	5-6-0	
at Oklahoma	35-31	11-1-0	Sugar (W)
at Hawaii	45-3	7-4-0	
ORANGE BOWL			
Alabama	**38-6**	**11-1-0**	

FACTS AND FIGURES

The Cornhuskers dominated the collegiate gridiron in 1971. . . . Bob Devaney's troops ranked fifth among the nation's major colleges in total defense, second in rushing defense, eighth in total offense and third in both scoring offense and defense. . . . The Huskers moved the ball effectively both on the ground (258.3 yards per game) and through the air (179.3-yard average). . . . Individually, Johnny Rodgers finished eighth in all-purpose yardage, tied for third in punt-return average and tied for ninth in scoring. . . . Jerry Tagge was 10th in total offense, while kicker Rich Sanger was eighth in kick-scoring. . . . After the first week of the '71 season, Nebraska replaced Notre Dame atop the Associated Press Top 20 poll and held that spot the rest of the way. . . . The Huskers went 4-0 vs. Top 20 competition, defeated six teams with a winning record and beat the teams rated second, third and fourth in the final AP poll. They defeated those three opponents (Oklahoma, Colorado and Alabama) by an average of 20 points per game. . . . Only three foes (Oklahoma State, Kansas State and Oklahoma) managed to score more than a touchdown in a contest. . . . Twelve of Nebraska's 13 victories were by three touchdowns or more. . . . The Huskers' opponents posted a combined record of 83-63-1 (.568 winning percentage). . . . Middle guard Rich Glover, who won the Outland Trophy and Lombardi Award and was named a consensus All-America in 1972, was named Big Eight Defensive Player of the Year in 1971 and 1972. . . . Glover (79) and Rodgers (20) had their jerseys retired after the 1972 campaign. . . . Linebacker Bob Terrio led the Huskers in tackles with 96, monster back Dave Mason had a team-high six interceptions and defensive end Willie Harper led the squad with 18 tackles for loss. . . . Those receiving All-Big Eight honors were Glover, Harper, Rodgers, Tagge, Terrio, offensive tackle Carl Johnson, offensive guard Dick Rupert, Jeff Kinney, Larry Jacobson and defensive backs Joe Blahak, Bill Kosch and Jim Anderson.

STATISTICAL LEADERS

PASSING

	Att.	Comp.	Yards	TD	Pct.	Int.
Jerry Tagge	239	143	2019	17	59.8	4

RUSHING

	Att.	Yards	Avg.	TD	Long
Jeff Kinney	222	1037	4.7	16	66
Gary Dixon	139	501	3.6	6	34
Bill Olds	73	500	6.8	1	67

RECEIVING

	Rec.	Yards	Avg.	TD
Johnny Rodgers	53	872	16.5	11
Woody Cox	24	356	14.8	1
Jeff Kinney	23	252	11.0	0
Jerry List	21	347	16.5	2

SCORING

	TD	FG	PAT	Points
Johnny Rodgers	17	0	0	102
Jeff Kinney	16	0	0	96
Rich Sanger	0	5	60	75

KEY CHARACTERS

The Conductor

COACH: Bob Devaney.

Record: 101-20-2, 11 years at Nebraska.

Devaney ranks among the all-time great coaches and is a member of the College Football Hall of Fame. . . . He coached for five seasons at Wyoming, compiling a 35-10-5 record, before taking the Nebraska job. . . . Devaney gained experience under Biggie Munn and Duffy Daugherty at Michigan State. . . . The Cornhuskers participated in postseason play regularly, playing bowl games in nine of 11 seasons under Devaney while garnering their outright national championship in 1971 and an Associated Press title in 1970. . . . The Cornhuskers also won or shared eight Big Eight titles under Devaney. . . . He retired in 1973 to devote more time to his duties as Nebraska athletic director. . . . He compiled a 33-2-2 record over his final three campaigns and a career mark of 136-30-7 over 16 seasons.

Personal Data:

Born: April 13, 1915, in Saginaw, Mich.
High School: Saginaw High.
College: Alma (Mich.) College.

The Supporting Cast

WINGBACK: Johnny Rodgers.

Rodgers will forever be remembered for 'The Play' in Nebraska's 1971 Game-of-the-Century showdown against Oklahoma—a 72-yard punt return for a touchdown in the Huskers' 35-31 victory, generally regarded as one of the most memorable plays in collegiate football history. . . . He followed that act by returning a punt 77 yards for a touchdown in Nebraska's 38-6 rout of Alabama in the 1972 Orange Bowl. . . . He earned consensus All-America honors in 1971 and 1972 and captured the Heisman Trophy in '72. . . . Rodgers led the Big Eight in receiving and both punt and kickoff returns while breaking numerous school receiving marks in 1971. . . . He combined outstanding speed and elusiveness with an intense desire to succeed. . . . He electrified fans with his scoring ability and crossed the opposing goal line in all but one 1971 game while leading the team with 17 touchdowns.

Personal Data:

Born: July 5, 1951, in Omaha, Neb.
High School: Omaha Tech.

QUARTERBACK: Jerry Tagge.

Tagge was the glue that held together the talented Cornhusker offense. . . . He finished his career holding virtually every Nebraska passing and total offense record. . . . Many still consider Tagge the best quarterback in Cornhusker history. . . . He passed for 17 touchdowns in 1971 while throwing only four interceptions, a passing ratio difficult to top. . . . Though he often was overshadowed by a talented array of teammates, he was the team leader and big-play field general.

Personal Data:

Born: April 12, 1950, in Omaha, Neb.
High School: Green Bay West High in Green Bay, Wis.

I-BACK: Jeff Kinney.

Kinney, a 1,037-yard rusher in '71, finished his career as the Huskers' all-time leading rusher with 2,321 yards. . . . He was a bull-like runner who seemingly battled for each blue-collar yard. . . . He saved his best performance for last, rampaging for 174 yards and four touchdowns in Nebraska's 1971 Thanksgiving Day showdown against Oklahoma. . . . He ran for 50 of the team's 74 yards on the Huskers' game-winning drive. . . . Though his forte was running with the ball, Kinney caught more than 20 passes in each of his three seasons at Lincoln.

Personal Data:

Born: November 1, 1949, in McCook, Neb.
High School: McCook High.

DEFENSIVE TACKLE: Larry Jacobson.

Jacobson was a consensus All-America and winner of the Outland Trophy in 1971. . . . He also was a Lombardi Award finalist. . . . He was a devastating pass rusher, combining deceptive speed and outstanding size.

Personal Data:

Born: December 10, 1949, in Sioux Falls, S. D.
High School: O'Gorman High in Sioux Falls.

FINAL 1971 WIRE SERVICE RANKINGS

ASSOCIATED PRESS		UNITED PRESS	
1. **NEBRASKA**	11. Louisiana State	1. **NEBRASKA**	12. Texas
2. **Oklahoma**	12. Auburn	2. **Alabama**	13. Toledo
3. **Colorado**	13. Notre Dame	3. **Oklahoma**	14. Houston
4. **Alabama**	14. Toledo	4. Michigan	15. Notre Dame
5. Penn State	15. Mississippi	5. Auburn	16. Stanford
6. Michigan	16. Arkansas	6. Arizona State	17. **Iowa State**
7. Georgia	17. Houston	7. **Colorado**	18. North Carolina
8. Arizona State	18. Texas	8. Georgia	19. Florida State
9. Tennessee	19. Washington	9. Tennessee	20. Arkansas
10. Stanford	20. Southern Cal	10. Louisiana State	Mississippi
		11. Penn State	

Bold face indicates Nebraska opponent.

GREATEST

2

TEAMS

Mighty Army Rules Football World

Army, 1944-45
By Ernie Palladino

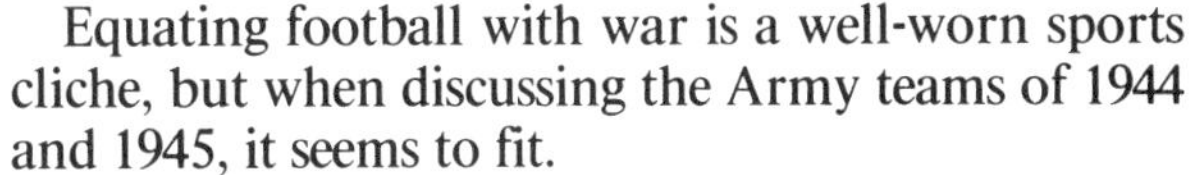

Equating football with war is a well-worn sports cliche, but when discussing the Army teams of 1944 and 1945, it seems to fit.

Mighty armies blend power, speed and a healthy dose of opportunism in battering their opponents in a willful procession across the battlefield. What team better fits that description than the West Point gang of late wartime? The squads combined for an 18-0 record, won consecutive national titles, produced one of the legendary backfields in college gridiron history and didn't play a close game in the bunch while outscoring opponents, 916-81.

Power? Army had it in surplus up front. Guards Joe Stanowicz and John Green, ends Barney Poole and Ed Rafalko, center Bob St. Onge and tackle Tex Coulter rated some All-America recognition in '44, while Coulter, Green, end Hank Foldberg and tackle Al Nemetz made the honor roll a year later.

Speed? Halfback Glenn Davis was one of the fastest players ever to strap on shoulder pads, while bullish fullback Felix (Doc) Blanchard could cover 100 yards in 10 seconds flat.

Opportunism? Army used that, too, without modesty. Because of World War II, Col. Earl (Red) Blaik, the Cadets' coach, was able to recruit active servicemen with prior collegiate experience and offer three more years of eligibility. In exchange, athletes receiving appointments to the U.S. Military Academy were required to complete a four-year education in three years to satisfy the country's demand for officers.

Army Coach Earl (Red) Blaik was a quiet, positive student of football who never afforded himself the luxury of a frivolous joke.

The top guns of Army's 1944-45 offensive machines were speedy halfback Glenn Davis (left) and bullish fullback Felix (Doc) Blanchard.

"You went straight from plebes (freshmen) to sophomore to first class," Blanchard recalled. "There was no junior class."

But Blaik certainly was at no disadvantage. While other colleges struggled to field competitive squads, Blaik stockpiled the country's best football talent and constructed a power at West Point that would have dominated in any year. Spreads as wide as 83-0 and no closer than 23-7—the count by which Navy fell in 1944—highlighted the Cadets' utter superiority.

Blaik had so much talent in 1944 that Blanchard and Davis didn't even start. As plebes, they gave way to upperclassmen.

"We actually had two teams that shared time," said Davis, who in 1987 retired as special events director for the Los Angeles Times. "One was as good as the other. I played more than anybody, and I only averaged 30 minutes, so you can see how good the others were."

The starting backfield in Blaik's T-formation consisted of quarterback Doug Kenna, fullback Bobby Dobbs and halfbacks Max Minor and Dale Hall. These four generally played in the first and third quarters, ostensibly to "soften up" the opposition.

Their jobs done, Blaik then called upon his predominantly underclass unit, which was led by senior quarterback Tom Lombardo. With Blanchard blocking and Davis and halfback Dick Walterhouse providing the bulk of the ground attack, the Cadets rolled up most of their points behind a line that featured plebes Poole, Foldberg, Coulter, Shelton Biles, Herschel (Ug) Fuson, Art Gerometta and Harold Tavzel.

Between the units, Army pulverized opponents by a cumulative 504-35 margin. But its best exhibition came not in its 62-7 beating of Pennsylvania, which opened the season in the Top 10 of the Associated Press poll. Nor was it the Cadets' 59-0 trouncing of defending national champion Notre Dame, which would finish ninth in the national rankings.

It came on a gray Wednesday at West Point. In a November intrasquad scrimmage, Blaik let his A and B squads have at each other for an uncontrolled 30 minutes, during which time the teams traded three touchdowns each.

Blaik later recounted the afternoon in his autobiography "You Have to Pay the Price." The scrimmage "produced what I shall always believe was the best football I ever saw. . . . The speed, power, coordination and ferocity were something I have not seen equaled on a gridiron," he wrote.

Forty-four years later, Davis had a slightly different recollection of the scrimmage—and Blaik's reaction to it.

"I remember that scrimmage very clearly," Davis said. "Especially the way it ended. I carried the ball off tackle and got loose for about a 30-yard gain. Tex Coulter tackled me on the sideline and drove me into a tackling dummy.

"Well, Blaik almost died when he saw me and Coulter go into that tackling dummy. Of course, neither of us were hurt, but that terminated the scrimmage.

"Blaik didn't let those things happen too often anyway because he was afraid of someone getting hurt. Except for that one, I don't remember any scrimmage going over 20 minutes, and there weren't many of them."

Blanchard recalled it simply as a display between a senior squad and a plebe unit.

"That's about the only significance there was to it," said Blanchard, a retired Air Force colonel living in San Antonio. "We'd just gone through Beast Barracks, where they taught us how to be good plebes."

Despite the differing viewpoints—clouded, no doubt, by the passage of time—it can be safely said that the toughest competition the Cadets faced that year came mostly against fellow teammates. The first four games provided no test whatsoever, so Blaik toughened his troops with intense midweek contact drills. By the time they hit their first real test in Duke, the Cadets were ready for anything.

Duke brought a 1-3 record into that game, but all three losses had been inflicted by nationally ranked

Up-front power was generated by such strongmen as Tex Coulter, a fierce competitor who went on to play in the National Football League.

opponents. Blaik termed the game "crucial" to the squad's development.

"They had a pretty good team," Blanchard said. "They kept a lot of good players there in their Navy (V-12) program."

But not enough. After falling behind, 7-6, in the first half, Army came back to win convincingly, 27-7.

That game made believers out of the national media. Army displaced Notre Dame atop the AP poll and from then on, the only question about the Cadets involved the margin of victory.

Army's next big test came against Notre Dame, a team it hadn't beaten since 1931 or scored upon since 1938. No problem. The Cadets handed the Fighting Irish their worst shellacking ever (59-0). Army scored more points in that game than in its last 15 meetings with the Irish combined.

"That was a significant game because of the score," Blanchard said. "But it wasn't that good of a game. Notre Dame got down early and they started doing a lot of foolish things. And we just took advantage of it all."

Said Davis: "I remember that they had more first downs than we did, which tells you a lot about the value of first downs. Every time we got the ball, we scored rapidly."

Actually, Army had 11 first downs to Notre Dame's eight, but Davis' point is irrefutable: When the Cadets got the ball, it didn't take them long to put it in the end zone.

A week later came Army's smashing of Penn. That game was memorable because the contestants almost ran out of footballs. Walterhouse, who set a national record with 47 extra-point conversions that season, kept booting pigskins into the stands, where a couple of fans decided to keep them as souvenirs. As the Cadets' touchdown total mounted, they opted to conserve leather by running and passing the ball for extra points.

Finally, there was Navy.

"I'd say they were our top competition," Davis said. "The Army-Navy game, regardless of the year, is always big. You could lose every game, but if you beat Navy, you've had a good year. But this one was probably a little more significant because we went into it 1-2 in the polls."

That's not how they came out of it. Army was still No. 1, but Navy fell to fourth in the AP poll in the wake of the Cadets' 23-7 triumph at Baltimore's Municipal Stadium, where more than 66,000 fans bought tickets that generated millions of dollars for the country's war bond effort. The game was close for three quarters, but an interception by Davis set up an impressive touchdown drive powered almost entirely by Blanchard, and Davis' 50-yard sprint capped the scoring.

More important than the win itself—if anything can take precedence in a Cadet's heart over beating Navy—was the fact that Army had wrapped up the national championship. The Cadets had dominated all nine opponents while averaging a national-record 56 points per game and leading the nation in rushing offense and scoring defense.

Despite performing on the second team and spending half of each game watching from the bench, Blanchard and Davis were named consensus All-Americas and established themselves as the finest backfield duo in the land. Davis set national records by rushing for 20 touchdowns and averaging 11.5 yards per rush on 58 carries. Blanchard scored nine touchdowns and became known for his crushing blocks as well as his running prowess.

Numerous individual and team awards were lavished on the Cadets, who managed to take everything in stride. Blaik shielded his players from the media as much as possible, thus keeping them from getting carried away with their accomplishments.

"No one was ever out to set any records," Davis said. "And Blaik controlled all that other stuff (newspapers, magazines). We didn't believe half of what we read. He just kept everybody's head on

Glenn Davis, Army's Mr. Outside, breaks away on a 30-yard run in the Cadets' 59-0 thrashing of Notre Dame in 1944.

straight. He wouldn't let anything get out of proportion."

As a result, the character of the Army teams reflected that of the coach—low-key and all business.

"It was a reasonably stable emotional curve," Blanchard said. "Never way up or way down, and we were willing to do whatever it took to win a ball game. But we were never interested in humiliating anyone."

Davis recalls Blaik as a serious student of football who never afforded himself the luxury of a frivolous joke. Whether he was dealing out praise or criticism, the coach did it calmly.

"He wasn't a person to rah-rah or get mad," Davis said. "I never heard him use a swear word or pick one person out to ball him out. He was an outstanding personality—very positive and very quiet."

Coulter, a tackle who went on to a pro career with the National Football League's New York Giants and the Canadian Football League's Montreal Alouettes, remembers Blaik as a trailblazer of sorts.

"I really don't think he's given the credit he deserves as a coach," Coulter said. "He led the way for the modern-day coaches. He emphasized the kicking game, which nobody did at the time, and he organized practices into timed segments. And he was always there if you needed him."

But the line between coach and player was always clear. Blaik may not have yelled, but his words carried as much weight as any tactical commander could.

"The players thought the old man was as smart as

Doc Blanchard, Army's Mr. Inside, bulls over the goal line for a touchdown in Army's 32-13 victory over No. 2 Navy in 1945.

he was, and they respected him for it," Blanchard said. "We never thought of him as our buddy. He was the coach; we were his players. He didn't smoke or drink, but you could trust him.

"Individually, he was more reserved than what I was used to. But if he got out there and said, 'Gosh darn, guys,' you knew something was wrong."

Blaik's demeanor, combined with the rigors of typical cadet life, turned the team into more of a homogeneous unit than the typical college team. Training-table talk centered more around academics than football. Fun and games, if practice can be called that, lasted no more than two hours a day, and then it was back to drilling and studying until lights out. Pranks and rowdy behavior simply didn't fit into the West Point regimen.

"It wasn't an ordinary college team," Davis said. "Other than football, West Point is a serious place. There's not a lot of laughs going on."

There were a few, however. Coulter, a native Texan who still resides in Austin, remembers standing in formation with Poole, a standout end from Mississippi, during their first winter as plebes.

"We plebes had to form up for classes and meals five minutes before everybody else," he said. "Now, for us Southern boys, that first winter was something. It's snowing, the wind's blowing, we're freezing. We're standing at attention, and Barney leans over and says, 'Geez, we're standing here like a bunch of old cows.' We almost got in trouble for that."

Obviously, discipline was strict. The result was a stable team that was aware of, but unswayed by, its own greatness.

"I think we all felt we had a special team," Davis said. "But all we wanted to do was win a game. It didn't matter how big or small the score was."

A team as strong as Army couldn't help but produce big scores, even with the legendary Mr. Inside (Blanchard) and Mr. Outside (Davis) playing just half of each game. "They were so good," Blaik reflected years later, "people couldn't believe it."

Blanchard, who grew up in Bishopville, S.C., began developing his reputation at North Carolina, where he played for the Tar Heels' freshman team in 1942. He quickly gained the tag as one of the best players ever to matriculate at Chapel Hill.

At the end of his freshman year, Blanchard tried

In 1944, Army's starting fullback was Bobby Dobbs, who is shown here picking up 20 yards in the Cadets' lopsided win over North Carolina.

to get into North Carolina's Navy V-12 program for officers training. But deficient eyesight caused by a childhood run-in with a mud pie and an alleged problem with his weight made him ineligible for the program. He was drafted by the Army in 1943 and subsequently gained appointment to West Point in time for the 1944 season.

Blaik was immediately impressed with his new plebe.

"Blanchard was the best-built athlete I ever saw: 6 feet and 208 pounds at his peak, not a suspicion of fat on him, with slim waist, Atlas shoulders, colossal legs," Blaik wrote. "For a big man, Doc was the quickest starter I ever saw, and in the open he ran with the niftiness as well as the speed of a great halfback. He was a terrific tackler and blocker. He could catch passes, punt and kick off exceptionally well."

"Hell," Blanchard said, "I was good at everything."

Coulter learned firsthand just how devastating Blanchard could be.

"In 25 years of playing football, I only took two hits I remember vividly," he said, "and one of them was Doc's. I was blocking and Doc hit me coming off right tackle, and I thought he broke my back."

Davis, a native of Southern California, came to West Point as a legitimate freshman and played for the 1943 Cadets, who went 7-2-1. Academic problems led to his expulsion after one semester, however, and it was only after completing a special four-month math class back home in California that he was granted readmission to the academy. He had to endure a second year as a plebe, but this time he stuck.

At 5-9 and 170 pounds, Davis had a smaller build than Blanchard. But what he lacked in physical strength he made up for in natural speed.

"He was," Blaik wrote, "emphatically the fastest halfback I ever knew. He was not so much a dodger and sidestepper as a blazing runner who had a fourth and even a fifth gear in reserve, could change direction at top speed and fly away from tacklers as if jet-propelled. He could also throw and catch passes and was a superior blocker and tackler."

Davis, an outstanding all-round athlete who also

Halfback Glenn Davis prepares to catch a pass from strong-armed quarterback Arnold Tucker in Army's 1946 victory over Navy.

lettered in baseball, track and basketball at West Point, still ranks as Army's all-time leading rusher with 2,957 yards and scorer with 59 TDs—more than half of which came on plays no shorter than 25 yards. But he bought only some of Blaik's appraisals.

"My big asset was speed," he said, "but of course when you're playing with good players and they open a hole for you, nobody can catch you. I got lucky. I was always surrounded by good players."

Mr. Inside and Mr. Outside were not prone to tooting their own horn.

"Glenn is as bashful as a girl on her first date, even though he is an All-America," Blaik once told a reporter. "It never has given him a big head. Or Doc Blanchard, either."

Blanchard said the sheltering of West Point helped keep him from getting a big head.

"We were a little sequestered up there," he said. "You know, the reporters didn't have access to us directly. But we knew what the people were writing. We got all the newspapers and we could all read. But coming from a small town like I did, I never got carried away with myself anyway."

That modesty was typical of the whole Army team.

"I think we accepted football as a team sport, not an individual sport, back then," Davis said. "Today, a guy scores a touchdown and he's waving his hands and dancing. My God, you'd think he'd just hit the jackpot. In our day, we were much more modest and let the record speak for itself."

The Cadets' impressive record was repeated in 1945 despite the loss of both quarterbacks (Kenna and Lombardo) and seven other members of Blaik's first unit in '44. But Blaik had assembled so much depth the year before that it didn't matter. The overall squad may have been less formidable, but the starting 11 was more of a single, cohesive unit.

"To answer the question, which was greater, 1944 or 1945," Blaik wrote, "I am not fence-straddling when I say '44 was the greater squad, '45 the greater team."

Blanchard and Davis were moved up to the first team in '45, but they still averaged only 32 minutes per contest. Except for the games against Michigan

An interested spectator at the 1945 Army-Navy game was President Harry Truman, who spent half of the game on each team's side of the field.

and Navy—the only two opponents that gave Army even the semblance of a battle—the Touchdown Twins generally spent the second half watching from the bench as Blaik did his best to keep from running up the score.

Blaik's basic backfield consisted of quarterback Arnold Tucker, Blanchard, Davis and Tom (Shorty) McWilliams. Fuson anchored the line at center and was flanked by guards Green and Gerometta, tackles Coulter and Nemetz and ends Foldberg and either Poole or Dick Pitzer. Only Pitzer, Green and Nemetz had been first-teamers the year before, but Blaik was convinced that his starters formed "a dream team."

Blanchard agreed. "In '44," he said, "we had two teams that played alternating quarters. In '45, we had a conglomerate of what was left of those two teams."

The only complete newcomer to that starting conglomerate was McWilliams, who had transferred from Mississippi State to play right halfback. McWilliams was back in Starkville a year later after spending his one season at West Point taking orders from a dictatorial upperclassman bent on shrinking the plebe's ample ego. Decades before the fact, McWilliams had an idea that Anastasio Somoza, then a foreign cadet and the son of Nicaragua's president, would follow in his father's footsteps.

"Shorty was a free spirit," Coulter recalled. "Tremendous sense of humor. But Somoza (who later became president of Nicaragua himself until being forced to flee the country in 1979) was an upperclassman in his company command, and he made Shorty memorize every article—the whole article—in which Shorty's name appeared."

Doing much of the blocking for McWilliams and the Blanchard-Davis duo were Fuson and Coulter, whose appearances could be deceptive.

"Hersch Fuson always made this effort to give this hillbilly impression to everyone," said Blanchard, who was as close to a wild man as could be found on the West Point campus in those days. "He was from (Kentucky), and he was always using these down-home expressions. But he was near the top in English and French. He was a lot smarter than what he let on to."

Coulter's personality was surprising considering the viciousness with which he blasted opponents off the line of scrimmage and around a boxing ring, where he won many a bout at West Point.

"Tex played football wide-open all the time," Blanchard said. "He practiced that way, too. Hell, we were all scared of him. But the contrast of the guy was off the field. He wasn't outgoing and talkative. He was very shy, in fact."

Said Davis: "Tex was a Jekyll-and-Hyde type—very aggressive on the field, very tough, but off the field he was quiet and mild. He never raised his voice. And he was really a fine artist and painter."

In fact, Coulter worked as an artist and sports columnist for newspapers in Dallas and Montreal after completing his pro football career.

"To most people the switch seemed incongruous," he said, "but I had wanted to be an artist since the sixth grade."

The Cadets' new quarterback, Tucker, had thrown 20 passes in mop-up duty as a plebe in '44. Like his predecessors, Tucker was a no-nonsense, classy leader, but his superior arm made opponents respect the Cadets' passing game. Tucker threw for 320 yards that season and Davis chipped in with 253 yards off halfback-option passes. That was just enough to provide extra fuel for the running attack, which increased from 2,687 yards in '44 to 3,238 yards, again the best in the nation. The Cadets also paced the rest of the collegiate field in total offense (4,164 yards) and scoring (45.8 points per game).

Blanchard and Davis, who were named consensus All-Americas again along with Coulter and Green, provided most of the offense. Davis ranked second in the nation with 944 yards rushing, again averag-

The 1945 Cadets: Front row (left to right)—William LaMar, William Webb, Dick Pitzer, Robert Chabot, Al Nemetz, John Green, Roland Caterinella, Robert Wayne, Dick Walterhouse, John Sauer. Second row—Joe Steffy, William West, Arnold Tucker, Harold Tavzel, Robert Kren, Shelton Biles, Albert Joy, Robert Richmond, Glenn Davis, Doc Blanchard. Third row—Tom (Shorty) McWilliams, Robert Stuart, Art Gerometta, Goble Bryant, John Kean, Jack Ray, Tom Hayes, Jim Enos, Elwyn Rowan. Fourth row—Amos Gillette, Jim Rawers, Robert Folsom, John Burckart, Tom Bullock, LeRoy Martin, Tex Coulter, Herschel (Ug) Fuson, Hank Foldberg, Barney Poole. Fifth row—Manager James Ladd, Clyde Grimenstein, R.L. Green, Frank Barnes, Jim Scholtz, Don Goldstrom, William Gustafson, Oscar Smith, Robert Schleiger, equipment manager Stringer.

ing 11.5 yards per carry, and scored 18 touchdowns, but Blanchard got the brass ring. His overall play, which included 718 yards rushing (7.1 average), 19 touchdowns and four interceptions, earned him not only the Heisman Trophy, but also the Sullivan Award for amateur sportsmanship, making him the first football player to win the award.

"Doc was a good competitor," said Davis, who won the Heisman a year later. "He had all the ability in the world and great speed for a big man."

Individual achievements aside, 1945 was marked by continued success against an improved field. Many young men who had been serving in the military in 1944 had returned to college by the beginning of the '45 season, making most teams more competitive.

Including those on the Cadets' schedule. Of Army's nine opponents, six (Wake Forest, Michigan, Duke, Notre Dame, Penn and Navy) finished in the AP Top 20. But none came close to upsetting the Cadets.

It was the third game of the year before anyone scored on Army, and Michigan tallied only once as the Cadets rolled to a 28-7 triumph. Three more foes were shut out, including Notre Dame, 48-0, bringing Army's two-year total against the Irish to an unthinkable 107 points. After blanking Penn, 61-0, Blaik's squad then wrapped up its second consecutive national championship with a 32-13 victory over second-ranked Navy.

"Army never had a better football team," Blaik said after the game. No one argued the point.

Those games, which were notable at the time for their lopsidedness rather than their drama, are distant memories now, as are the records the Cadets set individually and collectively. Only contemporaries and the hard-core younger fans of gridiron history remember the exploits of the wartime Army teams. Most of the nation's younger citizens have never even heard of Mr. Inside and Mr. Outside.

"The old ones remember me," Blanchard said. "Guys often come up and tell me, 'Hey, that kid doesn't know who you are!' And I say: 'Why the hell should he? He wasn't even born when I played.'

"Everybody has a time in life. My time to play football is in the past, and it doesn't bother me a bit."

During that special time, when America was at war and statesiders were looking for something to cheer about, no one dominated like the Cadets of Army.

It wasn't even close.

Army, 1944-45

ROAD TO GREATNESS

1944 RESULTS (9-0)

Opponent	Score	Opp. Record	Opp. Bowl Game
North Carolina	46-0	1-7-1	
Brown	59-7	3-4-1	
Pittsburgh	69-7	4-5-0	
Coast Guard	76-0	6-3-0	
*Duke	27-7	6-4-0	Sugar (W)
Villanova	83-0	4-4-0	
*Notre Dame	59-0	8-2-0	
†Pennsylvania	62-7	5-3-0	
‡Navy	23-7	6-3-0	

*New York †Philadelphia ‡Baltimore

1945 RESULTS (9-0)

Opponent	Score	Opp. Record	Opp. Bowl Game
Louisville AAF	32-0	7-4-0	
Wake Forest	54-0	5-3-1	Gator (W)
*Michigan	28-7	7-3-0	
Melville R.I. (PT Boat)	55-13	4-1-0	
*Duke	48-13	6-2-0	
Villanova	54-0	4-4-0	
*Notre Dame	48-0	7-2-1	
†Pennsylvania	61-0	6-2-0	
†Navy	32-13	7-1-1	

*New York †Philadelphia

FACTS AND FIGURES

Both Doc Blanchard and Glenn Davis garnered All-America honors from The Sporting News in 1944, '45 and '46. They were joined by two teammates, tackle DeWitt (Tex) Coulter and guard John Green, on the '45 team. . . . Blanchard was named Player of the Year by The Sporting News in 1945, and Davis earned the same honor a year later. . . . Each of Army's foes in 1945 finished at or above the .500 mark, and they combined for a record of 53-22-3 for an impressive .699 winning percentage. . . . Army's 1944 opponents went 43-35-2 (.550 winning percentage). . . . The Cadets scored less than 46 points only five times in 1944-45, and their average margin of victory for all 18 games was 46.4 points. . . . They posted nine shutouts in two seasons. . . . Army's 36 interceptions in 1944 tied a national record. . . . The Cadets led the nation in total offense in 1945 after finishing second in 1944, and they were first in rushing offense both seasons. . . . They ranked fourth nationally in passing offense in '44. . . . After ranking fourth in the nation in both total and rushing defense in '44, Army slipped a bit in '45, finishing 10th in overall defense and seventh against the run. . . . Davis was the nation's No. 2 rusher in 1945 with 944 yards, while Blanchard placed eighth with 718 yards. . . . Davis also ranked sixth in total offense that season.

STATISTICAL LEADERS

PASSING

	Att.	Comp.	Yards	TD	Pct.	Int.
Arnold Tucker (1945)	21	12	320	2	57.1	......
Dick Walterhouse (1945)	29	18	259	5	62.1	......
Glenn Davis (1945)	20	11	253	2	55.0	3
Arnold Tucker (1944)	20	8	188	2	40.0	......

RUSHING

	Att.	Yards	Avg.	TD
Glenn Davis (1945)	82	944	11.5	13
Doc Blanchard (1945)	101	718	7.1	13
Glenn Davis (1944)	58	667	11.5	1
Shorty McWilliams (1945)	41	363	8.9	8
Doc Blanchard (1944)	61	335	5.5	9

RECEIVING

	Rec.	Yards	Avg.	TD
Glenn Davis (1945)	5	213	42.6	0
Doc Blanchard (1945)	4	166	41.5	3

SCORING

	TD	FG	PAT	Points
Glenn Davis (1944)	20	0	0	120
Doc Blanchard (1945)	19	0	1	115
Glenn Davis (1945)	18	0	0	108
Doc Blanchard (1944)	9	0	0	54
Shorty McWilliams (1945)	8	0	0	48

KEY CHARACTERS

The Conductor

COACH: Earl (Red) Blaik.

Record: 121-33-10, 18 years at Army.

Blaik, a member of the College Football Hall of Fame, was the architect of Army's postwar football dynasty. . . . Though he was pursued hard and often by such schools as Yale, Harvard, Princeton, Texas, Nebraska, Michigan, Minnesota, Ohio State, Southern California and UCLA, he remained loyal to the academy during good times and bad. . . . He enjoyed six unbeaten seasons as Army coach (1944, '45, '46, '48, '49 and '58) and his teams compiled unbeaten streaks of 32 games (1944-47) and 28 games (1947-50). . . . His Army teams won three national titles and seven Lambert Trophies (emblematic of supremacy in Eastern football) and earned him numerous coaching honors. . . . Blaik began as an assistant at Wisconsin and West Point before accepting the head coaching position at Dartmouth, where he coached from 1934 to 1940. He became the first non-alumnus to coach at Dartmouth, where his teams put together a streak of 22 games without a loss from 1936-38. . . . His coaching career spanned 25 years with a record of 166-48-14.

Personal Data:

Born: February 15, 1897, in Detroit.
High School: Steele High in Dayton, O.
College: Miami of Ohio and U.S. Military Academy.

The Supporting Cast

FULLBACK: Felix (Doc) Blanchard.

Blanchard was a unanimous consensus All-America in 1945 and 1946 and a consensus selection in 1944. . . . He was nicknamed Mr. Inside. . . . Blanchard became the first junior to win the Heisman Trophy, capturing the honor in 1945 after finishing third in the 1944 balloting. He also was named winner that year of the Sullivan Award, given to the year's top amateur athlete. He was the first football player to win that honor. . . . He is a member of the College Football Hall of Fame and he competed in the 1947 College Football All-Star Game. . . . Blanchard earned letters from 1944 to '46 and amassed 1,666 career yards rushing, 535 yards on 19 pass receptions and 38 touchdowns. . . . He also was a good defensive back, intercepting seven career passes, and he averaged 35.5 yards on 32 punts and returned a kickoff 95 yards for a touchdown.

Personal Data:

Born: December 11, 1924, in McColl, S.C.
High School: St. Stanislaus High in Bay St. Louis, Miss.

HALFBACK: Glenn Davis.

Davis was known as Mr. Outside during his stay at the academy. . . . He still holds numerous Army individual records and remains the academy's all-time leading rusher with 2,957 yards. . . . He is a member of the College Football Hall of Fame. . . . He finished second in the Heisman Trophy balloting in 1944 and 1945 before winning the award in 1946. . . . Davis was a consensus All-America from 1944-46, a unanimous selection the last two seasons, and played in the 1947 College Football All-Star Game. . . . He ranks second nationally on the all-time Division I-A scoring (non-kickers) charts with 354 points, trailing only former Pittsburgh star Tony Dorsett by two points. He and Dorsett finished their careers with a record 59 touchdowns. . . . Davis also was proficient at throwing the ball, finishing his career with 57 completions in 126 attempts for 1,172 yards and 12 touchdowns. He amassed 4,129 yards total offense, the second-highest all-time total in Army history.

Personal Data:

Born: December 26, 1924.
High School: Bonita High in La Verne, Calif.

TACKLE: DeWitt (Tex) Coulter.

Coulter, a 6-foot-3, 220-pounder, was a big factor in the success of backs Glenn Davis and Doc Blanchard. . . . He was an accomplished blocker who earned consensus All-America honors in 1945. . . . He played only two years at West Point before going on to a distinguished career with the National Football League's New York Giants and the Montreal Alouettes of the Canadian Football League. . . . He was known for his vicious, attacking style on the football field, and that carried over to his other favorite sport—boxing. His ability to knock unfortunate opponents around the ring was well known around West Point.

Personal Data:

Born: 1925 at Smith County, Tex.

QUARTERBACK: Arnold Tucker.

Tucker finished fifth in the 1946 Heisman Trophy balloting. . . . He lettered in 1945 and '46 and became just the second football player ever to win the Sullivan Award the latter season. Blanchard, his teammate, had been the first. . . . In 1946, Tucker intercepted eight passes, which still stands as an academy record (tied with two other former Cadets).

FINAL WIRE SERVICE RANKINGS

1944 AP

1. **ARMY**	11. **Duke**
2. Ohio State	12. Tennessee
3. Randolph Field	13. Georgia Tech Norman P-F
4. **Navy**	15. Illinois
5. Bainbridge	16. El Toro Marines
6. Iowa Pre-Flight	17. Great Lakes
7. Southern Cal	18. Fort Pierce
8. Michigan	19. St. Mary's P-F
9. **Notre Dame**	20. Second Air Force
10. 4th AAF	

1945 AP

1. **ARMY**	11. Southern Cal
2. **Navy**	12. Ohio State
3. Alabama	13. **Duke**
4. Indiana	14. Tennessee
5. Oklahoma State	15. Louisiana State
6. **Michigan**	16. Holy Cross
7. St. Mary's	17. Tulsa
8. **Pennsylvania**	18. Georgia
9. **Notre Dame**	19. **Wake Forest**
10. Texas	20. Columbia

Bold face indicates Army opponent.

Wilkinson's Winning Tradition

Oklahoma, 1955-56
By Bob Hersom

Oklahoma's unbeaten and untied national championship football teams of 1955 and 1956 had almost everything.

Most of all, they had Coach Bud Wilkinson.

The Sooners also had talent.

"We had guys playing on the third unit that could have started anywhere else in the conference," said Billy Pricer, the No. 1 fullback on the '55 and '56 teams.

Wilkinson's athletes had teamwork, too.

"We had some tremendous athletes, but, really, it was the teamwork, the unselfishness, playing as a team, that made us go," said the quarterback for both national-title winners, Jimmy Harris.

Then there was the matter of confidence.

"We thought we could even move the ball on a professional team," Pricer said. "That's how much confidence we had."

"Johnny Majors (the 1956 Heisman Trophy runner-up from Tennessee) couldn't have made our team," Harris contended.

"I agree, and Paul Hornung (the '56 Heisman recipient) would have had a hard time, too," said Clendon Thomas, a reserve left halfback in 1955 but Oklahoma's starting right halfback in 1956 and 1957.

The Sooners had speed.

"We built everything on speed and quickness," said Bob Burris, the starting right halfback in 1955. "We didn't put much emphasis on size because we just didn't have anybody who was very big. But we could sure run."

Oklahoma's swiftness was apparent even before a play was run. In Wilkinson's scheme to take advantage of other teams' inferior conditioning and at the same time leave the opposition in a constant state of anxiety, the Sooners would sprint from the huddle to the line of scrimmage. And, after completion of the play, they would dash back to the huddle.

Oklahoma had tradition.

"It's the reason everybody goes to Oklahoma right now," Harris said. "The great athletes like to go someplace where there is a winning tradition. If you're used to winning, you want to keep winning, and that just keeps making you a winner.

"I was from Texas and I hadn't been to Oklahoma but one time, and the basic reason I went there was Bud Wilkinson and the winning tradition."

Wilkinson and the Oklahoma football tradition. They were, at the time, one and the same.

Charles (Bud) Wilkinson always had been a winner. He grew up on the same block in Minneapolis as future golf great Patty Berg. He was a blocking back in 1936 for the Minnesota Gophers, the first team to be designated as national champions by the fledgling Associated Press poll.

Wilkinson was, former Sooner players agree, the main reason Oklahoma became the fourth school to win consecutive wire-service national football championships.

Coaching at the Norman, Okla., school from 1947 through 1963, Wilkinson fashioned a 145-29-4 record. His Sooners compiled winning streaks of 31 games from 1948 through 1950 and 47 games, still an NCAA Division I-A record, from 1953 to 1957.

"We would have never won all those ball games in a row without him," Thomas said. "It's one thing to get teams ready to win, but you can never win all those ball games in a row without a brilliant man coaching, knowing when to bear down and when to let up."

Burris maintains that Wilkinson's rivals simply weren't in his class.

"Coach Wilkinson was way ahead of other

coaches and programs in his organization and in his types of offenses and defenses," Burris said. "He was a very articulate organizer and, of course, he knew the game."

"Wilkinson was ahead of his time because he saw talent in every individual and because he was such a good recruiter," said Tommy McDonald, the starting left halfback in '55 and '56. "The minute I met Bud Wilkinson, I knew that's where I wanted to go to school.

"That's the thing about Wilkinson ... once you met him, you knew you wanted to play for him. He is so down to earth and there is not a phony bone in his body. There's no way he's going to try to pull anything on you. You were so overwhelmed by his personality and his honesty and his coaching record that you didn't want to go anywhere else."

Harris shared his teammates' perception of the coach.

"He was by far the sparkplug of the whole thing," Harris said. "He's the one who gave everybody the confidence that they had. I think we can all look back and say we were great athletes for our time, but the spark was that Bud was so well-organized."

Organization. Preparation. They were two of Wilkinson's greatest strengths. "Four hours of preparation for every one hour of practice" was one of his mottoes.

"If you aren't practicing meaningfully, then you're wasting the players' time," Wilkinson said. "So, if you want to maximize their contribution related to their ability to prepare, you don't ask them to do things that they are not totally dedicated to doing. If you're highly, highly organized, then the players realize that you're not wasting any time.

"We prepared for everything we did at practice and knew why we were going to do it. It is a very axiomatic truth that you must, in practice, rehearse every situation that the player will face in a game and then repeat it until the player can react from rote memory rather than having to think. It's visual, and you react to movement."

While 30 years have passed since Thomas last played for Wilkinson, he still remembers one of his mentor's favorite slogans.

" 'The ones who win are the ones who are willing to prepare'—we heard that sermon fairly regularly," Thomas said.

"He would get more out of a two-hour practice than a lot of coaches get out of two or three days of practicing," Harris observed. "He knew exactly how to spend every minute. He certainly inspired me. I feel like he was the most dominant factor in my life, period."

Pricer concurred.

"We were definitely well-prepared for every game. As a matter of fact, sometimes we knew the play that they were going to run before they ran it," Pricer said. "Really, we did. We had scouting reports like that."

"He put the emphasis on, 'We don't play Saturday's ball game on Saturday; we play it starting the Sunday night before,' " Burris said. "And we played it every minute until that Saturday afternoon when we kicked it off.

"His preparation was something else. He had a great ability to know how to keep us ready. It didn't matter who we were playing. Whether it was

Oklahoma Coach Bud Wilkinson, a master of organization, preparation and motivation, was the man behind the Sooners' great winning tradition.

Notre Dame or Texas or Kansas State, we played them the same."

Just as important as Wilkinson's organization and preparation was his use of psychology. He was one of the master psychologists among coaches.

"I was just honest with them," Wilkinson said. "You always can lose. The thought that you automatically win is never true.

"I was just being totally honest, totally sincere and totally straightforward in everything that occurred from the first meeting that we had with the team before spring practice and through the season. I was consistent, I guess you'd say."

"He knew who to criticize and who to praise, to get the most out of each individual," Harris said. "I've seen him cut guys from the squad and they came out singing 'Boomer Sooner' and praising him as the greatest. I don't know anybody who played under him that has anything but the highest regard for him."

"Oh, gosh, he was the greatest psychologist in the world," Pricer said. "He did it by just talking to you. He just had a way with words. He'd talk to you and you felt like going out and playing your heart out for him."

McDonald viewed Wilkinson as a motivator of the first order.

"He knew how to inject little things," McDonald explained. "Like, 'Just remember it's taken a lot of Oklahomas to build up the reputation that that jersey has.' When somebody says something like that and you're 18 or 19 years old, you get goose bumps."

Thomas called Wilkinson "the best motivator that I was ever around," adding that "there isn't any question that he's the best coach I ever played for."

Thomas gave two examples. Each incident occurred during a subpar practice session. Wilkinson reacted differently each time, but each result was the same. In the first example, Thomas was having a bad day.

"When a young guy wasn't playing full speed," Thomas said, "the coach would take him aside and ask him if he was having trouble with his school work, or at home, or if anything was bothering him. The whole time, the kid was simply loafing.

"He pulled that on me one day. I wasn't having a good practice and he took me aside and simply talked to me and asked me a lot of those questions. None of them was the reason I was having a bad practice. He knew it, and I knew it. But he had that tremendous ability to motivate kids."

In Thomas' second example, the entire Oklaho-

Halfback Tommy McDonald was an adept passer and runner with a knack for getting the ball into the end zone.

ma squad was having a poor practice. This time, Wilkinson reacted quite differently—but, again, calmly.

"He let us off the field when any other coach would have driven us into the ground," Thomas recalled. "He had a keen sense of where we were going and what was wrong.

"We were having a bad practice in the first 10 minutes and he whistled us up and said: 'We're going to stop. Go down and have a Coke, do whatever you need to do, and let's come out tomorrow and have a good practice. You're all tired.'

"He didn't want to create any bad habits. Now, how many coaches on a Tuesday or a Wednesday, when you usually work the hardest, would do that?

"We were getting ready to get beat because we were just getting tired of the same thing over and over again. I don't know how to explain it. You want to, but you can't do it. But he knew how to handle that.

"I look back on that practice and remember that we killed the team we played in the next game. That one day off made the difference."

Wilkinson also was a master strategist, devising innovations in the split-T offense and founding the "Oklahoma 72" defense. Of course, Wilkinson didn't do it all by himself. The Sooners had remarkable talent in 1955 and 1956.

Left guard Bo Bolinger was a consensus All-America in '55, while center Jerry Tubbs and the fleet McDonald were accorded the same status in '56. Thomas and guard Bill Krisher, prominent players as sophomores in '55, also attained All-America recognition by the end of their careers.

Of the 17 players listed on the All-Big Seven Conference team in '55, eight were Sooners. Making the squad besides Bolinger, Tubbs, McDonald, Burris and Harris were guard Cecil Morris and tackles Cal Woodworth and Ed Gray, the latter being the only player on the team daring enough to call Wilkinson "Bud."

Seven Sooners won all-league honors the next season. New Oklahoma names on the select team were end John Bell and tackle Tom Emerson.

These Sooner teams clearly had one of the finest backfields in college football history.

Harris, described by Wilkinson as "the most underrated athlete who ever played," merely compiled a 24-0 won-lost record as an Oklahoma starter.

Pricer, despite seven knee operations, had a career rushing average of 5.5 yards per attempt in a Sooner uniform.

McDonald gained 6.8 per carry in 1955 and 7.2 yards every time he lugged the ball the following season. Over those two years, the speedster from Albuquerque, N.M., scored a total of 33 touchdowns.

Thomas, a fifth-teamer on the freshman squad in 1954, was Oklahoma's career ground-gaining leader by 1957. His rushing averages in the Sooners' wonder years of '55 and '56 exceeded even those rung up by McDonald. The Oklahoma City product covered 6.9 and 7.9 yards per carry in those seasons.

Center Jerry Tubbs was an intense competitor who would do just about anything for the good of the team.

McDonald and Thomas were rivals on the NCAA statistical charts but very unselfish on the field.

Thomas, in fact, clinched the 1956 NCAA touchdown title—he finished with 18 TDs, compared with McDonald's 17—on an eight-yard pass from, of all people, McDonald. The touchdown came in Oklahoma's final game, a 53-0 romp at Oklahoma A&M (now Oklahoma State) that increased the Sooners' winning streak to 40 games, breaking the record established by Washington from 1908 to 1914.

"I've never let Tommy forget that touchdown, either," Thomas said with a laugh. "Really, finishing first and second (nationally in scoring) was great. It was an amazing statement for that football team . . . . "

After notching his 18th touchdown, Thomas gave up an opportunity for another by switching positions with lineman Gray, who then scored his first and last college TD on a two-yard run.

"In the huddle, Ed said, 'I want to score.' I laughed and we changed places," Thomas said. "He went over my block. It was the only time I ever played offensive tackle in college.

"Ed went off the field with the ball under his arm. I remember Wilkinson laughing. It was a hysterical moment."

The Oklahoma football team had more than its share of laughs—and laughers—in the mid-1950s. In fact, the seniors on the '56 squad, playing in the days when freshmen weren't eligible for varsity competition, concluded their careers with 31-0 records. As part of 10-0, 11-0 and 10-0 teams, they helped the Sooners outscore their opponents, 1,155 points to 173, an average of 37.3 to 5.6.

"Down through the years," McDonald said, "I have found out what really made those teams click. I found out two things that make a team or a company, any type of organization that's trying to be successful, click.

"You not only have to have intelligent, competitive people, but personalities—the charisma that each individual person adds. And if you look back at those teams, we really had some great personalities."

Six Oklahoma players were starters in both 1955 and 1956: Tubbs, Gray, Bell, Harris, McDonald and Pricer.

"Jerry had such a competitive fire," McDonald said in praise of Tubbs, "that he'd just do anything to help the team and he was, of course, a captain."

Tubbs, from Breckenridge, Tex., was such a fine athlete that he was used at fullback, a position he had never played before, in 1954 and averaged 6.1 yards per carry.

The Sooners' other co-captain in '56 was Gray, the team's top comedian. One of Gray's hobbies was tropical fish. When he cleaned his fish tanks, Gray would plug the shower drain at Jefferson House, then the football players' dormitory, and empty the fish onto the shower-room floor. Sooner players occasionally showered with the fish.

"Ed was a real cut-up," McDonald said. "He would pull jokes on everybody all the time. He was really lively, very enthusiastic . . . . "

Gray also was the only player on the '55 and '56 teams to start every game of his three-year college career.

Bell was a quiet, intelligent son of an Arkansas preacher who loved to read, as subscriptions to five magazines would attest. He also was the most immaculate dresser on the team. His teammates, with respect for his hustle and determination, called him "Mad John."

Harris' leadership qualities and winning ways served him well on the football field—and continue to benefit him. Long after running the Sooners' offense, Harris is running Harris Oil and Land Co. in Shreveport, La. He's company president.

"Here was a guy," said McDonald, a company president in his own right in King of Prussia, Pa.,

Oklahoma's only consensus All-America in 1955 was Bo Bolinger, a big guard who made life easier for the Sooners' swift and talented backfield.

"who wasn't hung up on himself. The team was the most important thing to him." And Harris' importance to the team was evident, too. Besides inspiring teammates, the man could play. In '56, Harris wound up with eight touchdown passes despite throwing the ball only 37 times and finished as the team's No. 3 rusher.

McDonald, who would go on to an outstanding 12-year career in the National Football League, "was constantly chattering, like a parrot," Thomas said, chuckling. "In the huddle, he was always wanting the ball, saying, 'Give it to me, give it to me.' " The Sooners did just that in '55 and '56, with electrifying results. The 5-foot-9, 169-pound McDonald rushed for a total of 1,555 yards in those seasons and scored touchdowns in 20 of the Sooners' 21 games.

McDonald wasn't too shabby at defensive back, either, as shown by his 1956 total of six interceptions, which he returned for 136 yards.

Coming out of high school, McDonald wanted to play for Notre Dame. But the Fighting Irish indicated by letter that he was too small for them and that he should try playing for a small college.

Pricer "hardly ever got to carry the ball," McDonald said in an overstatement, "yet he'd sacrifice his body throwing blocks for me and Clendon Thomas and Bob Burris. And even though Billy Pricer was real dedicated to the team, he was a cut-up, too."

As an Oklahoma freshman recovering from surgery on both knees, Pricer may have "cut up" once too often. Near dinner time one day, teammates stole his crutches. No problem. Pricer simply crawled downstairs to the dining hall.

Occasional high jinks aside, the Oklahoma football players took their roles seriously and were cognizant of their good fortune. Most were homegrown, with 44 of the 61 squad members in '55 and 43 of the next season's 65 players being from the Sooner State.

"Most of us had hoped and dreamed of just getting a chance to be a part of OU football," Thomas said. "In my wildest dreams I would have never even imagined, as a young kid, even getting a chance to go do what I did. I was one of the lucky ones that got to live out those dreams.

"I think a great many of us who were there felt like that . . . .

"If anything, it was a big group of guys, not individuals, that stands out in my mind. It was a unique group because everyone was so unselfish."

That unselfishness still shows in conversations today.

"They could have done it without me," said Harris, the 24-0 quarterback. "Then again, I think we probably could have done it without Tommy McDonald or Clendon Thomas. I think we had that kind of depth and that kind of teamwork and camaraderie.

"I don't think any one person was by far the best. We didn't have any Paul Hornungs. But don't get me wrong. McDonald and Thomas both were just

The quarterback of Oklahoma's 1955 and '56 undefeated national-championship teams was Texan Jimmy Harris.

The locker-room sign above Oklahoma halfback Bob Burris serves as a testimonial to Bud Wilkinson's motivational tactics.

phenomenal athletes."

"We were," Pricer said, "just one, big, happy family. I'll tell you, we had unity down there. Talk about being unselfish—we had Tommy and Clendon and they were really unselfish. Back in our day, we never went for the 100-yard game. They didn't care if they gained 100 yards or not, just as long as we won the ball game."

"The team always came first, which is only right as far as I'm concerned," McDonald said. "Back then, the slogan was, 'What can you do for the team?'

" . . . I mean, a guy didn't sit and pout after a game. It just didn't happen that way. The most important thing wasn't who was going to score, but how were we going to get the ball down there."

There was a twist, however, to all this esprit de corps. Ironically, it involved the main man, Wilkinson.

"He kept a distance from his players," McDonald said. "You didn't really get to know Bud like a father or anything like that because (assistant coach) Gomer Jones more or less handled that.

"The only time you had dealings with Bud would be on the field and on a road trip, and then maybe if he called you into his office to make a point or something like that.

" . . . If you had problems with class, or if your parents wanted to try to come to the game, or if after the game was played it was all right to go home with Mom and Dad . . . Gomer handled all of that.

"Bud handled the coaching aspect. Other than that, you have no other dealings with him. So there was really no way in the world for you to get close to Bud at all."

There was, for the longest time in college football history, no way for opponents to come very close to beating Oklahoma, either.

Oklahoma's 47-game winning streak is widely recognized as one of sport's "unbreakable" records. Then again, Babe Ruth's home run records once were considered unbeatable, too.

"Oh, yeah, I think our record could be broken," Wilkinson said. "Every record is made to be broken. It will be difficult, but that doesn't mean it won't happen."

The winning streak, in which Oklahoma averaged 34.5 points per game compared with the opposition's mark of 5.9, began in the third week of the 1953 season after the Sooners had opened the campaign with a 28-21 loss to Notre Dame and followed with a 7-7 tie with Pittsburgh. The streak ended in 1957 with a 7-0 loss to Notre Dame in the eighth game, played on November 16 at Norman. It was Statehood Day—Oklahoma had been admitted to the Union 50 years earlier—but the Fighting Irish put a damper on the celebration.

The loss to Notre Dame came 55 weeks after the Sooners had pounded the Irish in one of the more memorable games of the streak.

Playing at South Bend, Ind., on October 27, 1956, the Sooners harassed Notre Dame quarterback sensation Hornung all afternoon and embarrassed the Irish, 40-0.

Despite a miserable performance that day and the fact Notre Dame would win only two of 10 games in '56, Hornung captured the Heisman Trophy that year. McDonald and Tubbs, meanwhile, finished third and fourth in the balloting.

Part of Hornung's all-around ineffectiveness against the Sooners no doubt could be traced to a thumb injury he had suffered the previous week against Michigan State.

Oklahoma knew about the injury.

"Bud came in that morning, at our pregame meal, and said he had heard that Hornung would probably go to some sort of single-wing (alignment) because he'd hurt his hand and he wasn't going to be able to take the snap from center," Pricer recalled. "Bud said if he did that we were going into a certain defense.

"On the first play, Notre Dame shifted into that thing and they rolled out to the right and old Tubby (Jerry Tubbs) was just going along with Hornung. Hornung decided to turn upfield and old Tubbs hit him so hard. . . .

Oklahoma Coach Bud Wilkinson, assistant Gomer Jones and the Sooner bench celebrate a touchdown during the Sooners' 1955 national-championship season.

The 1956 Oklahoma Sooners: Front row (left to right) —Dennit Morris, Hugh Ballard, Jerry Tubbs, Carl Dodd, Bill Brown, Dale DePue, Clendon Thomas, Billy Pricer, Jimmy Harris, Ken Nothcutt, J. Henry Broyles, Fred Hood, Joseph Oujesky, Byron Searcy. Second row—Dick Carpenter, Benton O'Neal, Wayne Greenlee, Bill Krisher, David Baker, Ken Hallum, George Talbott, Benton Ladd, Bob Timberlake, Tom Emerson, Doyle Jennings. Third row—Bill Harris, Victor Hayes, Kenny Crossland, Lonnie Holland, Ken Fitch, Roland Powell, Cloyd Shilling, Don Nelson, Dick Evans, Ernie Day, Lyle Burris, Joe Rector, Gerald McPhail. Fourth row—John Bell, Steve Jennings, David Rolle, Ross Coyle, Jim Lawrence, Lynn Burris, Dick Gwinn, John Pellow, Dick Corbitt, David Loop, Don Stiller, Rodger Taylor. Fifth row—Henry Bonney, Delbert Long, Chuck Bowman, Bob Martin, Galen Young, Jakie Sandefer, Bob Harrison, B.W. Scott, Mickey Johnson, Tommy McDonald, Ed Gray, Robert Derrick, Jay O'Neal, Dale Sherrod.

"I was standing over Hornung, and he had to grab his helmet to stop his head from shaking. And, boy, he went back into the split-T and never did come out in a single-wing the rest of the ball game."

"Tubbs hit Hornung with as hard a lick as I've ever seen," Harris said. "Tubbs met him at the line with one of those beautiful tackles, driving him back about five yards. Hornung's helmet cut into his nose and he came up bleeding. I'm sure Paul remembers that."

Another landmark game in Oklahoma's winning streak came the very next week at Boulder, Colo. That contest, unlike most, was not a showcase for the Sooners' speed, power and verve. Instead, it demonstrated the team's resolve. Down 19-6 at half-time against a Colorado Buffaloes team hellbent on ending the Sooners' skein at 35 victories, Wilkinson's charges rebounded for a pulsating 27-19 triumph.

Wilkinson considers the '55 and '56 teams as his best—along with the undefeated team of 1949.

"The '49 team was a totally different team, but it was an awfully good team," Wilkinson said. "When I say totally different, 1949 was the senior year after World War II, which meant that you compressed everybody that graduated during the war years into one freshman class in 1946.

"So you had three or four years of accumulated talent and they were older people, chronologically, and much more experienced.

"In '55 and '56, there was the normal sequence related to high school and then to college. So, I would say that '55 and '56 were my best teams, along with '49. We were a good team in 1950, but not as good."

The '50 Sooners were named national champions by the Associated Press and poll newcomer United Press—before a 13-7 Sugar Bowl loss to Kentucky ended Oklahoma's 31-game victory streak.

Make no mistake, though, the mid-'50s Sooners were something special. In more than 50 years of NCAA official statistics-keeping, only one school has led Division I-A in scoring, rushing and total offense in consecutive seasons: Oklahoma, 1955 and 1956.

"My proudest accomplishment in coaching," said Wilkinson, looking beyond victories and records, "is the quality of the individuals that went to school at the university and what they've done since they graduated from OU." Of the lettermen Wilkinson coached in his 17 seasons at Norman, 87.2 percent earned college degrees.

The quality of the athletes he coached, particularly in 1955 and 1956, was pretty impressive, too.

Oklahoma, 1955-56

ROAD TO GREATNESS

1955 RESULTS (11-0)

Opponent	Score	Opp. Record	Opp. Bowl Game
at North Carolina	13-6	3-7-0	
Pittsburgh	26-14	7-4-0	Sugar (L)
*Texas	20-0	5-5-0	
Kansas	44-6	3-6-1	
Colorado	56-21	6-4-0	
at Kansas State	40-7	4-6-0	
at Missouri	20-0	1-9-0	
Iowa State	52-0	1-7-1	
at Nebraska	41-0	5-5-0	
Oklahoma A&M	53-0	2-8-0	
ORANGE BOWL			
Maryland	**20-6**	**10-1-0**	

*Dallas

1956 RESULTS (10-0)

Opponent	Score	Opp. Record	Opp. Bowl Game
North Carolina	36-0	2-7-1	
Kansas State	66-0	3-7	
*Texas	45-0	1-9	
at Kansas	34-12	3-6-1	
at Notre Dame	40-0	2-8	
at Colorado	27-19	8-2-1	Orange (W)
at Iowa State	44-0	2-8	
Missouri	67-14	4-5-1	
Nebraska	54-6	4-6	
at Oklahoma A&M	53-0	3-5-2	

*Dallas

FACTS AND FIGURES

Oklahoma juggernauts of 1955-56 hardly needed help in building perfect records, but they received boost nonetheless in inferior quality of opposition. Sooners' 1955 opponents combined for 47-62-2 mark, a winning percentage of .432. The 1956 OU squad faced an even lighter load; its foes went 32-63-6, .347., and only one team, Colorado, posted a winning record . . . Biggest test of two-year period, at least on paper, came in the 1956 Orange Bowl when No. 1-ranked Sooners were matched against No. 3 Maryland. Sooners trailed, 6-0, at halftime, but rebounded for 20-6 triumph. Carl Dodd's 82-yard interception return for a touchdown sealed the victory. . . . Oklahoma shut out 11 opponents over the two years and really beat up on rival Oklahoma A&M. Sooners pounded A&M to the tune of 53-0 in '55. What to do for an encore? Would you believe 53-0 again in '56?. . . . After a close call at Colorado (27-19) in sixth game of '56 campaign, Oklahoma averaged 54.5 points in last four contests. . . . Sooners gained representation on consensus All-America team for sixth consecutive season when guard Bo Bolinger made the squad in '55. Streak was extended the next year when center Jerry Tubbs and halfback Tommy McDonald made the select team.

STATISTICAL LEADERS

PASSING

	Att.	Comp.	Yards	TD	Pct.	Int.
Jim Harris (1956)	37	23	482	8	62.2	1
Tommy McDonald (1955)	24	17	265	0	70.8	0
Tommy McDonald (1956)	12	8	183	3	66.7	1

RUSHING

	Att.	Yards	Avg.	TD	Long
Tommy McDonald (1956)	119	853	7.2	13	58
Clendon Thomas (1956)	104	817	7.9	14	......
Tommy McDonald (1955)	103	702	6.8	14	......
Clendon Thomas (1955)	71	487	6.9	8	58

RECEIVING

	Rec.	Yards	Avg.	TD	Long
Tommy McDonald (1956)	12	282	23.5	4	65
Clendon Thomas (1956)	12	241	20.1	4	49
Robert Burris (1955)	8	104	13.0	0	19

SCORING

	TD	FG	PAT	Points
Clendon Thomas (1956)	18	0	0	108
Tommy McDonald (1956)	17	0	0	102
Tommy McDonald (1955)	16	0	0	96
Robert Burris (1955)	11	0	0	66

KEY CHARACTERS

The Conductor

COACH: Charles (Bud) Wilkinson.

Record: 145-29-4, 17 years at Oklahoma.

Wilkinson was a member of three national championship teams while playing for Coach Bernie Bierman at Minnesota from 1934-36. . . . He then coached the Sooners to three undisputed national titles during his tenure from 1947-63. . . . He is a member of the College Football Hall of Fame. . . . Oklahoma still holds the NCAA record (47 games) for the longest winning streak in college football history, compiled from 1953-57 under Wilkinson. . . . His coaching style was less harsh than many of his contemporaries and he was considered an offensive genius and a master of preparation and motivation. . . . He served as an assistant at Syracuse, Minnesota, Iowa Pre-Flight and Oklahoma before becoming coach of the Sooners. . . . He coached 15 consensus All-Americas at Oklahoma, including at least one at every position but quarterback. Yet three of his quarterbacks—Eddie Crowder, Jack Mitchell and Darrell Royal—later became head coaches. . . . He remained at Oklahoma despite numerous major-college offers. . . . He captained Minnesota's golf team and was goalie for the Gophers' hockey team during his college days. . . . While coaching at Syracuse, he also coached the Orangemen's golf team.

Personal Data:

Born: April 23, 1916, in Minneapolis.
High School: Shattuck Military Academy in Faribault, Minn.
College: Minnesota.

The Supporting Cast

HALFBACK: Tommy McDonald.

Jack Gallagher of the Houston Post describing McDonald in 1955: "A back whose fire and desire burn so intense he once fell down running back to the huddle.". . . . He was selected as The Sporting News Player of the Year and a consensus All-America in 1956 and is a member of the College Football Hall of Fame. . . . McDonald was a versatile halfback and an alert, fierce-hitting defensive back. . . . He scored in each of Oklahoma's 1955 regular-season contests and produced the winning score in the Sooners' Orange Bowl victory over Maryland. . . . He led the 1955 Sooners in five offensive categories and completed an amazing 70.6 percent (17 of 25) of his halfback passes. . . . He averaged 7.2 yards per rush and completed eight of 12 pass attempts for 571 yards in 1956. . . . He finished his career with 1,683 yards rushing and a 6.8-yard average. He also scored 35 touchdowns, intercepted nine passes and averaged 15.8 yards on 31 punt returns. . . . He led the Big Seven in punt returns in 1954 and finished second in '55. . . . His 210 career points still are tied for ninth on Oklahoma's all-time list.

Personal Data:

Born: July 26, 1934, in Roy, N.M.
High School: Highland High in Albuquerque, N.M.

CENTER: Jerry Tubbs.

Tubbs was a unanimous consensus All-America and winner of the Walter Camp Trophy, which signified him as 1956 Player of the Year. . . . He attained All-America status as a center, but was a tenacious linebacker as well. . . . He finished fourth in the 1956 Heisman Trophy balloting. . . . He was switched to fullback temporarily in 1954 to fill a void and responded by gaining 387 yards while averaging 6.1 yards per carry. . . . Tubbs' finest collegiate performance may have come against archrival Texas in 1955 when he intercepted three passes and made numerous big defensive plays in Oklahoma's 20-0 victory. . . . He was co-captain of the 1956 Sooner squad. . . . He also excelled in the classroom, earning the second-highest grade-point average among Oklahoma's freshman football players in 1953.

Personal Data:

Born: January 23, 1935, at Throckmorton, Tex.
High School: Breckenridge High in Breckenridge, Tex.

FINAL 1955 WIRE SERVICE RANKINGS

ASSOCIATED PRESS

1. **OKLAHOMA**
2. Michigan State
3. **Maryland**
4. UCLA
5. Ohio State
6. TCU
7. Georgia Tech
8. Auburn
9. Notre Dame
10. Mississippi
11. **Pittsburgh**
12. Michigan
13. Southern Cal
14. Miami (Fla.)
15. Miami (Ohio)
16. Stanford
17. Texas A&M
18. Navy
19. West Virginia
20. Army

UNITED PRESS

1. **OKLAHOMA**
2. Michigan State
3. **Maryland**
4. UCLA
5. Ohio State
6. TCU
7. Georgia Tech
8. Auburn
9. Mississippi
10. Notre Dame
11. **Pittsburgh**
12. Southern Cal
13. Michigan
14. Texas A&M
15. Army
16. Duke
17. West Virginia
18. Miami (Fla.)
19. Iowa
20. Navy
    Stanford
    Miami (Ohio)

FINAL 1956 WIRE SERVICE RANKINGS

ASSOCIATED PRESS

1. **OKLAHOMA**
2. Tennessee
3. Iowa
4. Georgia Tech
5. Texas A&M
6. Miami (Fla.)
7. Michigan
8. Syracuse
9. Michigan State
10. Oregon State
11. Baylor
12. Minnesota
13. Pittsburgh
14. TCU
15. Ohio State
16. Navy
17. George Washington
18. Southern Cal
19. Clemson
20. **Colorado**

UNITED PRESS

1. **OKLAHOMA**
2. Tennessee
3. Iowa
4. Georgia Tech
5. Texas A&M
6. Miami (Fla.)
7. Michigan
8. Syracuse
9. Minnesota
10. Michigan State
11. Baylor
12. Pittsburgh
13. Oregon State
14. TCU
15. Southern Cal
16. Wyoming
17. Yale
18. **Colorado**
19. Navy
20. Duke

Bold face indicates Oklahoma opponent.

GREATEST 4 TEAMS

Still No. 1 In Trojan Country

Southern Cal, 1972
By Dave Newhouse

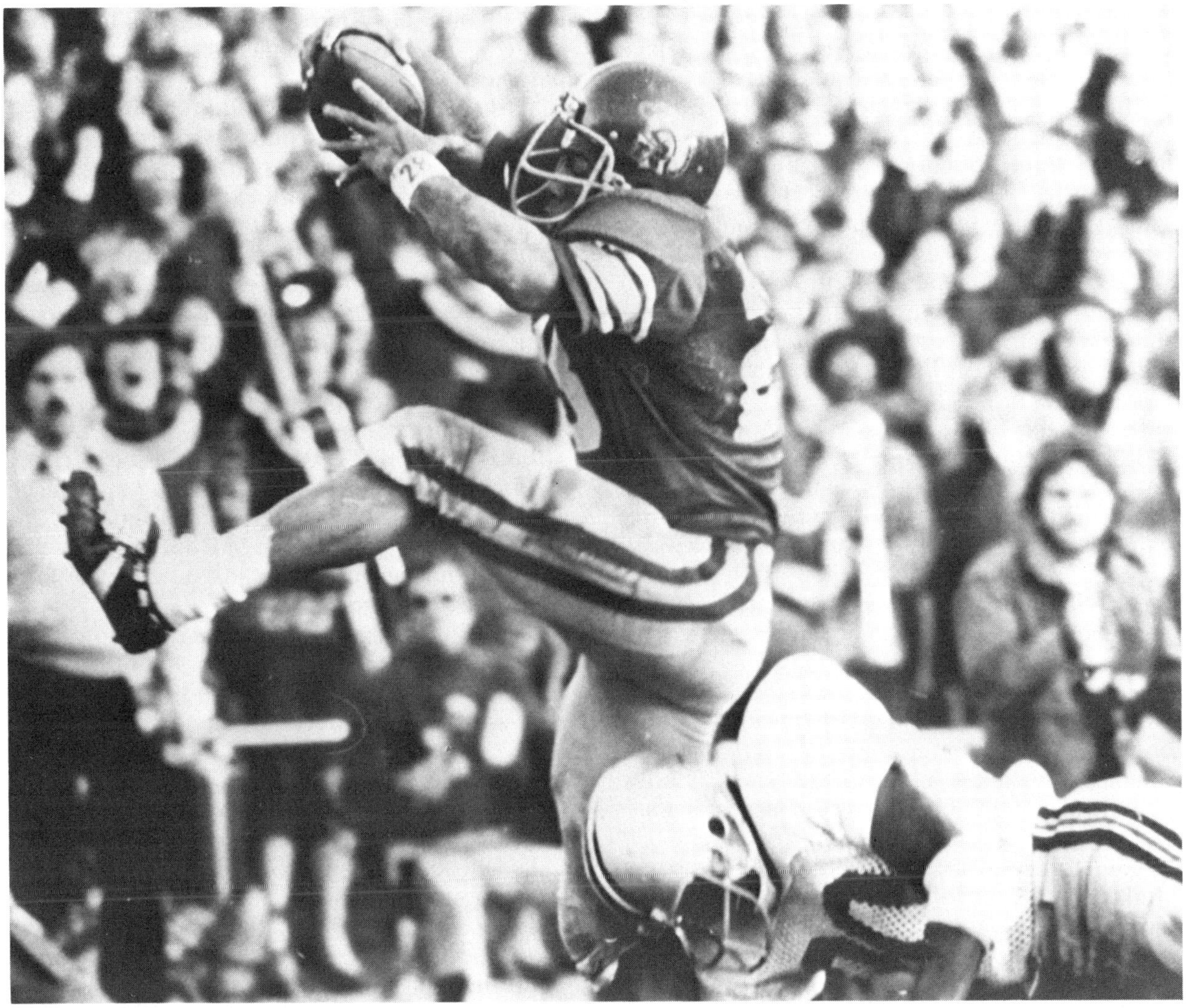

Colorful Anthony Davis was at his high-stepping best as he crossed the goal line against Ohio State in the 1973 Rose Bowl.

"Davis! Davis! Davis! Davis! Davis! Davis!"

The banner headline across the front page of the Los Angeles Times' sports section captured the magnificence of one player and the dominance of one team.

With flashing feet and dancing knees, tailback Anthony Davis had scored six touchdowns in perhaps the greatest single-game performance in Southern California football history, much less in a USC-Notre Dame football series that took root in 1926, when a legend named Rockne coached in South Bend and a budding cinematic giant known as the Duke was a reserve Trojan lineman.

Inspired by Davis' heroics that December 2 in Los Angeles, Southern Cal knocked the fight out of the 10th-ranked Fighting Irish, 45-23, for its 11th victory in an unblemished 1972 season.

"USC has had a lot of good football teams in the past, but this is probably the best-balanced team they've ever had," Notre Dame Coach Ara Parseghian said.

"Yes, they are the best college football team I have ever seen," Ohio State Coach Woody Hayes conceded after USC bludgeoned his Buckeyes, 42-17, in the Rose Bowl to complete a perfect 12-0 campaign. His massive tackle, John Hicks, stood in the doorway of the USC locker room after the mayhem and told the Trojans, "We just wanted you guys to know that you're the best team we've ever played at Ohio State."

"Some people," reflected John McKay, the Trojans' coach from 1960 through 1975, "have called it the best-balanced, best all-around football team there has ever been. I'm inclined to agree. It's the best I've ever seen."

Indeed, the 1972 Trojans were the first college football team to receive every first-place vote in both the Associated Press and United Press International final polls that determine the wire services' national champion. And in The Sporting News' selection of its 25 greatest college football teams of all time, USC trails only the 1971 Nebraska, 1944-45 Army and 1955-56 Oklahoma squads. That's not bad company.

"I think it's an insult," said Charles Young, the outstanding, and outspoken, All-America tight end on that 1972 USC powerhouse. "Nebraska had outstanding individuals. Johnny Rodgers was an unbelievable player. But for USC to be Number 4, that's ridiculous. They had 12 months to compare."

Young alluded to Hayes and others who had studied the '71 Cornhuskers and '72 Trojans, up close or from afar, and decided at that time that USC was better. But not all of the Trojans are as vociferous as Young.

"It's kind of a mythical thing anyway, right?" quarterback Mike Rae reacted. "In SC country, we would be Number 1. It's all opinions. There's no real way to tell. Nebraska had that big game with Oklahoma. That stuck out in people's minds. We didn't have any games like that. They were mostly blowouts."

USC's narrowest victory margin was nine points; its average spread was 28 points. The men of Troy scored more than 50 points three straight weekends without being accused of pouring it on. They couldn't help themselves. They had so much talent that Davis started the season as the third-string tailback.

The Pacific-8 Conference champions finished in the top seven nationally in scoring (third), total offense (sixth), total defense (seventh), rushing defense (third) and scoring defense (seventh).

"We didn't have a single particular weakness," McKay said.

Often a measure of the greatness of a college team is how it is perceived by the National Football League. The NFL drafted 30 players from that 1972 USC team. The Trojans were so formidable that, even if you could put together a football team from scratch, you couldn't do much better than with this particular bunch.

Start at quarterback—and the Trojans had two. Rae, a senior (and the school's record-setting placekicker with 49 extra points and eight field goals in 1972) set a USC mark with 2,001 yards in total offense—and he was rarely on the field in the fourth quarter. That's because he was pushed by sophomore Pat Haden, the future Rhodes scholar who would set a school record as a junior with 137 completions. Both had the mental capacity to succeed in the McKay system, a school of thought that opposed the developing trend in which coaches called each play for their quarterback.

"I've believed for years that if the game is what it is supposed to be, to develop character and leadership in young men, then you should train them and then go out and see what has developed," said McKay, a former halfback and teammate of Norm Van Brocklin at Oregon.

"I'm going to train our quarterbacks to call the play. If he doesn't like it, he is going to change it and try something else, whether it's right or wrong. He's still going to have the right of leadership and change the plays.

"If I call every play, he doesn't have to know anything except how to take the snap from center and throw a forward pass."

At fullback was senior Sam (Bam) Cunningham, a fast, powerful 6-foot-3, 220-pound bruiser who had been an outstanding shot-putter in high school and competed in the decathlon as a USC freshman. "Cunningham has the potential," Southern Cal track Coach Vern Wolfe had said, "to be the greatest decathlon performer ever."

Cunningham made an impact on college football

in two ways: He popularized leaping over the line of scrimmage on short-yardage situations, and he broke the "color line" in Alabama.

In Cunningham's varsity debut in 1970, he rumbled for 135 yards on 12 carries and scored two touchdowns as USC crushed Alabama, 42-21, in Birmingham. The game was the first in which Alabama played an extensively integrated team. Afterward, Coach Paul (Bear) Bryant began recruiting more blacks for the Crimson Tide.

"That guy Cunningham did more for integration in 60 minutes than anybody else had done in 60 years," Bryant said a few years later.

USC started the '72 season with four promising tailbacks—Rod McNeill, Manfred Moore, Allen Carter and Davis, all of whom would be drafted by pro teams. It wasn't until the eighth game, against Oregon, that the world of college football would learn of Davis, who combined the speed of O.J. Simpson with the moves of Mike Garrett, two Trojan greats who had won the Heisman Trophy in the 1960s.

"I just wanted to break in," Davis said, "get a little playing time and contribute to a winning team." He became a starter only after injuries to McNeill and Carter, then rushed for 678 yards and scored 12 touchdowns in the final four games of the regular season and became the first USC sophomore to gain 1,000 yards.

"I coach him not to get tackled," McKay explained.

Davis, or "A.D." (his preferred handle), was simply too adroit and explosive to get a hand on, much less a line on. "The hardest thing with Davis is figur-

Southern Cal Coach John McKay gives sideline instruction to Pat Haden, the Trojans' backup quarterback and a future Rhodes scholar.

ing what he's going to do," said Notre Dame's Jim O'Malley. "He's got speed to go outside, but he's also got power to jolt you on the inside. He's quick, and he's built low to the ground so you can't get under him to tackle him."

Or, more often than not, around his blockers to even see him. Davis, only 5-9 but 190 pounds, was an expert at tailgating blockers before blasting through a hole. "I try to explode as quick as I can and follow close behind the block," he said. "When they hit a defender, I'm right there and I can veer off one way or the other. Running is instinct as well as ability."

Lynn Swann, the flanker, combined those qualities as well, but his immense talents were somewhat overshadowed at USC, where the tailback was the big man on campus. The Trojan offense scored 53 touchdowns during the 1972 season, 42 on the ground. Swann, who caught 21 passes, finished his Trojan career in 1973 as the USC career reception leader, but not once did he rank among the NCAA receiving leaders. He, Young and Cunningham all would be first-round NFL picks without having stood out statistically at USC.

"I struggled with that," Young said of his diminished role as a receiver in college. "Not only me, but Sam. He was an outstanding runner, but they made him a blocker. Lynn was an outstanding receiver. But the thing that was special about our team was our relationships with one another. Everyone on the team came together. We put aside our individual goals."

Young, nicknamed "Tree" because he was built like one (6-4, 230 pounds), caught 55 passes for the Philadelphia Eagles in 1973, only 13 fewer than he grabbed in his entire career at Southern Cal.

The Trojan split ends were Edesel Garrison—perhaps the nation's fastest receiver with clockings of 45.4 seconds in the 440-yard dash and 9.5 in the 100—and J.K. McKay, the coach's son, who led the ground-oriented Trojans with four touchdown catches.

The offensive interior had two more first-round NFL picks at tackle: Steve Riley and Pete Adams. Guards Allan Graf and Mike Ryan and center Dave Brown completed a line that was explosive off the ball. McKay, in fact, traced the Trojans' improvement over their 6-4-1 season in 1971 to his offensive line. Ultimately, USC had the publicized tailbacks because of its unpublicized but physical linemen opening holes the width of Frank Sinatra's Lear jet.

Defensively, the Trojans yielded only 15 touchdowns during the '72 season. The longest run against them was 29 yards, the longest pass 45 yards.

"Our defense was the quickest I've ever watched, college or pro," said McKay, who later coached the Tampa Bay Buccaneers. "Richard Wood could run the 40-yard dash in 4.5 seconds; he caught everybody from behind."

As a senior at Thomas Jefferson High School in Elizabeth, N.J., Wood saw a photograph in his coach's office of Simpson scoring a touchdown against UCLA. Wood, an offensive guard then, asked his coach, Frank Cicarell, "Is there a possibility of my going to USC?"

Was there! McKay pursued Wood as tenaciously as he would a Heisman tailback. Wood became a full-time linebacker and USC's first three-time All-America.

Tight end Charles Young was an outstanding pass receiver who played second fiddle to Southern Cal's vast stable of running backs.

"At USC, you know all about tradition," Wood said. "Howard Jones, O.J., John Wayne, who used to be Marion Motley. . . . Being a three-time All-America put me on the same plane as those guys."

Not Marion Motley, Richard. Marion Morrison. Or the Duke. However, at USC there is no mistaking the tradition. Not for a moment.

"You're expected to win every week," Rae stressed. "It's like the Raiders when I played for them. Nothing is good enough. It's a cocksure, confident attitude."

The Trojans were 6-4-1 in both 1970 and '71, and for seniors such as Cunningham, Young, Adams, Grant and Rae, this was their final chance to catch the freeway to Pasadena and the Rose Bowl. "We were kind of prime to do something, but nobody knew what that was," Rae remembered. "We knew we had a lot of talent, a lot of depth."

The Trojans were two deep with future pros at several positions. "We had a dozen linebackers who were all excellent,' McKay said. Wood and Charles Anthony were the two official starting linebackers, although USC's ends, Dale Mitchell and James Sims, most often were stand-up linebackers. Both were blessed with speed (Sims ran the 40 in 4.6 seconds, Mitchell in 4.7) quickness and agility, qualities that endeared them to McKay, who had sensed the impact the wishbone formation would have on defensive strategy.

"You can't play with big, heavy linemen," he said. "You must have speed on the outside, speed on the corners. The front makes the tackles because you get a one-on-one situation so often.

"You must have very agile people who can play somebody one-on-one and make the tackle in the open field. We've gone to three down linemen and everybody else has to run very fast."

That defensive interior was composed of John Grant, Monte Doris and Jeff Winans. In the secondary, Charles (Sugar Bear) Hinton, Artimus Parker and Charles Phillips proved capable leaders. Parker finished his career at USC in 1973 with a school-record 20 interceptions, which tied a conference mark. Phillips, a Trojan from 1972 through 1974, would set a conference record with 365 career return yards on 13 interceptions.

The 1972 Trojans had all physical and mental components working together. There was a real togetherness, a unity of mind and spirit, that team members still talk about today, almost with reverence. "It was probably the most unselfish team I've played on," Cunningham said.

Southern Cal would receive a quick reading of its

Lynn Swann, a graceful receiver who went on to fame in professional football, caught only 21 passes in the 1972 Trojans' ground-oriented offense.

potential with fourth-ranked Arkansas as its first opponent. Led by quarterback Joe Ferguson, the Razorbacks were talking national championship. And the game was in Little Rock.

But at halftime, the underdog Trojans found themselves tied, 3-3. They told themselves, "Hey, if these guys are supposed to be good, how good are we?" They soon found out. USC won going away, 31-10, rushing for 208 yards and passing for 269 more against a supposedly formidable foe.

"They kept us off balance all night, run or pass," Arkansas Coach Frank Broyles said. "Their offense was as strong physically as any we've faced."

Ferguson sensed perfectly what had taken place. "If USC doesn't go undefeated," he said prophetically, "then something's wrong."

The Trojans buried their next three opponents—Oregon State (51-6), Illinois (55-20) and Michigan State (51-6)—and took over the No. 1 ranking in the polls. In the first four games, 14 different Trojans had scored touchdowns. Next up was unbeaten Stanford, which McKay referred to as "the Radcliffe of the West." McKay had a sarcastic wit; some saw it as biting. But he genuinely disliked Stanford, viewing the school as snobbish and mocking.

USC defeated Stanford by only nine points, 30-21, but McKay raised eyebrows when he tried for a last-second touchdown pass from the Stanford 10-yard line with the victory already in hand. "I'd liked to have won by 2,000 points," McKay snapped in defense.

"They're the worst winners I've ever gone up against," he said in reference to Stanford's victories over USC in 1970 and '71. "They have no class."

When McKay's 2,000-point comment was mentioned to Cardinals Coach Jack Christiansen, he mentioned something about getting into a urinating match with a skunk.

The relationship between the two private schools was dragged to its lowest depths in the final hours before kickoff at Stanford. Walking the quarter-mile from the locker room to the stadium that day, racial epithets were directed at the Trojan players from tailgating Stanford fans.

"I couldn't believe it that a major institution would say things like that," said Wood, who is black, 16 years later. "There's no place for that in sports. I won't forget it. It leaves a scar on my mind."

The fact that USC missed by 1,991 points of reaching the victory margin McKay would have preferred upset his players as well.

"It was the worst game we've played," Swann said afterward. "I still don't think we've paid Stanford what we owe them. Two years ago up here their fans and players made very snide remarks, degrading us and our school. They did it again this year. . . ."

From that point on, whenever a McKay-coached team played at Stanford, the Trojans put on their uniforms at the hotel, bused to the stadium gate, played the game, bused to the hotel, showered, changed clothes and flew home.

USC hardly broke a sweat against its next two opponents, trouncing California, 42-14, and Washington, 34-7, before heading north to play Oregon—the game that would showcase little Anthony and the imperials. Well, Davis was 5-9 and the Trojans certainly were imperial that autumn.

Davis hadn't exactly been mopping out the locker room prior to that rainy Saturday in Eugene. He had scored six touchdowns in seven games as a backup to McNeill, including scoring runs of 44 and 14 yards against Washington.

Davis was clearly emerging, although he had effected a noticeable swagger as a sophomore that annoyed some Trojans.

"At times, A.D. would get under your skin," Cunningham said. "He had a cockiness about him that rubbed the other players wrong. He got under McKay's skin, too. But the coach put him in a spring scrimmage and he got beat up pretty good. He showed he could take it."

Young, demonstrating the bond of the '72 Trojans, defended Davis. "Most people don't understand Anthony Davis and the way he carried himself," Young said. "Everyone on that team had confidence; they just carried it inside. USC was a conservative school, but Anthony was flashy. He'd sell copies, advertise . . . nothing that General Motors wouldn't have done. Where in history has anyone scored six touchdowns against Notre Dame?"

Oregon wasn't Notre Dame, but the Ducks managed to forge a scoreless tie at halftime. Enter Davis, whose touchdown runs of 48 and 55 yards on a slick field helped deflate Oregon, 18-0, as the Trojans' defense intercepted four passes and held Oregon's passing game to a net 11 yards. The Ducks' quarterback was a pretty good passer, too. Fellow named Dan Fouts.

Davis' 206 yards rushing that day gave him the starting job. He responded with 195 yards and three touchdowns the following week as USC pummeled Washington State, 44-3. Cougars Coach Jim Sweeney then informed McKay: "John, you're not the Number 1 team in the country. The Miami Dolphins are better."

Following a practice session before USC's next game against chief rival UCLA, Davis showed a funny little dance to Trojan assistant coach Wayne Fontes. It was kind of a jitterbug on knees and Davis said he might perform it against the Bruins. Fontes laughed.

"Well, I scored against the Bruins (on a 23-yard run)," said Davis, reliving that day, "and actually slipped to my knees in the end zone. I did the dance, even though I had forgotten about it. I walked into the sports information office the following Monday. The guys in there told me: 'A.D., you can't stop that dance now. It's nationwide.' "

The Trojans stymied UCLA, 24-7, to clinch a Rose Bowl berth, their fifth in seven years after a two-year interruption by Stanford. "I guess USC is the best team I've ever seen, period," said Bruins Coach Pepper Rodgers, who watched his outside running game forced inside after a first-quarter touchdown drive and his passing attack net 38 yards all afternoon. "There isn't anything they don't do well on offense or defense," he said, "and they know they can do it. . . ."

"The I-Bone is back," joked McKay, whose I-formation worked like a well-oiled machine while UCLA's wishbone was effectively splintered by the Trojan defense. Davis rushed for 178 yards, but he had barely begun to fill his dance card.

"Never in my wildest dreams did I anticipate a game like this," said Davis of Notre Dame, which made him a national star.

He received the Irish's opening kickoff and scooted 97 yards through a forest of larger bodies for a touchdown. He scored twice more in the first quarter on runs of one and five yards. Blanked in the second quarter, he scored twice in the third on a four-yard run and another kickoff return of 96 yards. On the first play of the fourth quarter, he had his sixth score of the game on an eight-yard run.

"Davis! Davis! Davis! Davis! Davis! Davis!"

Six Trojan records fell by the wayside that afternoon as A.D. established single-game marks for most touchdowns, most touchdowns in one quarter, most points, longest scoring kickoff return and most touchdowns on kickoff returns. He increased his season kickoff return yardage to a record 468 yards.

Parseghian praised Davis as the best kick returner he had ever coached against. "We knew he was good, but we thought we could handle it," he said. "And we've got to look at him for the next couple of years."

Davis, who had 368 all-purpose yards that game, told the amused media afterward, "I have three accelerations: One when I get the ball, one when I get to the line and one when I get into the open."

And a fourth when he gets to the press room.

Although the Trojans' No. 1 ranking could hardly be disputed, they obliterated any remote chance of being unseated by second-ranked Oklahoma by trouncing Ohio State in the Rose Bowl.

"All right, is there anybody else they (Associated Press) want us to play?" McKay asked testily after his 100th career victory.

"If you can't pick (your No. 1) at the end of the regular season because you've got two undefeated teams, OK. But when the season was over, we were the only one. I understand that. The UPI understands it. But I was very willing to play this game for the national championship."

Linebacker Richard Wood was the class of a quick and deep Southern Cal defense that yielded only 15 touchdowns during the 1972 season.

USC flattened Ohio State, 42-17. Hayes had never given up that many points. Davis scored once, on a 20-yard run, but this time the spotlight belonged to Cunningham, who catapulted himself four times over the Buckeyes' goal-line defense. Four touchdown runs (a Rose Bowl record), or leaps, amounting to five yards. Economical. Sky-walking running backs weren't faddish until Sam the Bam sprouted

John McKay, the coach and father figure of Southern Cal's 1972 'family,' provided guidance for such youngsters as Charles (Sugar Bear) Hinton (26), a defensive back.

wings.

"It was spontaneous," he said. "My junior year, the line didn't get off the ball well. It seemed like the natural thing to do. But I couldn't levitate like people today."

Cunningham was named the Rose Bowl Player of the Game, which especially pleased his coach. "I owe Sam something," said McKay, who was making his sixth Rose Bowl appearance. "He was a great runner, but I made him a blocker for three years. He's the best runner I ever ruined."

Hayes wasn't given to lavish compliments, but he certified the Trojans as the best his old eyes had seen "because of their enormous balance. You can run on them some, but they passed us out of the park."

Rae completed 18 of 25 passes for 229 yards, in-

The 1972 Trojans: Front row (left to right)—Coach Dave Levy, Mike Rae, Dave Boulware, Rob Adolph, Pat Haden, Eddie Johnson, Ken Randle, Head Coach John McKay, Artimus Parker, Chris Chaney, John Cantwell, Phil Cantwell, Edesel Garrison, Allen Carter, coach Marv Goux. Second row—Coach Willie Brown, Lynn Swann, Marvin Cobb, J.K. McKay, Charles Hinton, Rod McNeill, Anthony Davis, Ray Washmera, Sam Cunningham, Jim Lucas, Manfred Moore, Danny Reece, coach Craig Fertig. Third row—Coach Wayne Fontes, Steve Fate, Al Pekarcik, Charles Phillips, Kevin Bruce, Ray Rodriguez, Cliff Culbreath, Charles Anthony, Mike Smith, Dave Brown, Bob McCaffrey, Eugene Lawyrk, coach Don Lindsey. Fourth row—Coach Skip Husbands, Allan Graf, Bob Shaputis, Booker Brown, Mike Ryan, Tom Bohlinger, George Follett, Mike Cordell, Monte Doris, Allen Gallaher, Pete Adams, Steve Riley, coach John Robinson. Fifth row—Ronnie Miller, Chris Vella, Glenn Byrd, Richard Wood, Dale Mitchell, Dean Lingenfelter, Ed Powell, Charles Young, George Stewart, Jeff Winans, John Grant, Mike Hancock, Jim Lee. Sixth row—Managers Bill Sutton, George Yablonsky, Bob Perkiss, Brian Hufford; assistant trainers Jerry Meins, Paul Williams; trainer Jack Ward; managers Bill Bristow, Ross Boylan; coaches Ray George, Joe Margucci, head manager Steve Belton.

cluding 12 straight completions in the second half as USC scored on five consecutive possessions.

"...Their passing game, it was very good," Hayes said. "We could not stop it, but 11 other teams couldn't either."

Southern Cal simply had too many weapons: speed, size, skill, strength and depth.

"We lived up to what I had said before the game," Davis said. "We have Swann, Charlie Young, Mike Rae, Sam. You can't play us without worrying about everybody. We took it away from them mentally. They had so much to think about—our kickoff and punt returns, our outside and inside games . . . everything."

Interestingly, even though the 1972 Trojans had five players earn All-America recognition (Cunningham, Wood, Grant, Adams and Young, a unanimous selection), Rae was voted by his coaches as the team's most valuable player. With all those tailbacks, a quarterback as MVP?

"If I had called the plays," Rae said, chuckling, "we would have been a passing team."

McKay would produce four national champions at USC—1962, 1967, 1972 and 1974. Besides his '72 team, the '67 Trojans are ranked ninth among The Sporting News' all-time best 25. USC and McKay are the only school and coach represented twice in the Top 10.

"We were like a family," Wood said of the '72 Trojans. "There wasn't one bad guy on the team to me. I think about Sam Bam, John Grant and all the guys a lot. Those were good times. My wife, Karen, was a Trojan. I met her when I was a freshman. My son Marlon has his Trojan uniform, and my daughter Rochelle her SC cheerleader uniform."

Only one thing is missing from Wood's family picture. The statue of Tommy Trojan. Wood's dream is to one day coach at USC. Once a Trojan, always a Trojan.

Memories run clear and free as stream water for the 1972 team.

"It's a feeling that no matter what you do in your lives," Cunningham said, "you can look back and say that in 1972, we were the best. Maybe you can say that in 1988, too."

It's all mythical, right?

Southern Cal, 1972

ROAD TO GREATNESS

1972 RESULTS (12-0)

Opponent	Score	Opp. Record	Opp. Bowl Game
*Arkansas	31-10	6-5-0	
Oregon State	51-6	2-9-0	
at Illinois	55-20	3-8-0	
Michigan State	51-6	5-5-1	
at Stanford	30-21	6-5-0	
California	42-14	3-8-0	
Washington	34-7	8-3-0	
at Oregon	18-0	4-7-0	
†Washington State	44-3	7-4-0	
at UCLA	24-7	8-3-0	
Notre Dame	45-23	8-3-0	Orange (L)
ROSE BOWL			
Ohio State	**42-17**	**9-2-0**	

*Little Rock. †Seattle.

FACTS AND FIGURES

The explosive Trojans scored more than 40 points in seven of their 12 games in 1972. . . . They won nine games by three touchdowns or more and defeated four teams listed in the final Top 20 rankings by an average margin of 26.3 points. . . . USC's opponents posted a combined record of 69-62-1, a .527 winning percentage. . . . It was the Trojans' second (and last) perfect season under Coach John McKay, who posted an 11-0 mark in 1962, and only their second unbeaten, untied campaign since 1932. . . . The Trojans ranked among the country's top seven teams in total offense, total defense, scoring offense, scoring defense and rushing defense. . . . Tailback Anthony Davis ranked 10th in the nation in all-purpose yardage and tied for fourth in scoring. . . . Davis led the Trojans in rushing, scoring and kickoff return yardage from 1972 through 1974. . . . Mike Rae, the team's quarterback and place-kicker, tied for sixth in the nation in scoring by kickers and set a single-season school record with 49 extra points, including bowl games. . . . Flanker Lynn Swann ranked among the nation's top five punt returners. . . . Team leaders on defense included safety Artimus Parker and linebacker Richard Wood, who intercepted six and five passes, respectively. Parker is the Trojans' all-time leader with 20 career interceptions, including bowl games. . . . Tight end Charles Young was named to The Sporting News' 1972 All-America squad. . . . Trojans named to the Pacific Eight all-conference team were offensive tackle Pete Adams, center Dave Brown, defensive tackle John Grant, defensive end James Sims, Wood and Young. . . . Three players—Young, Sam Cunningham and Adams—were first-round picks in the 1973 National Football League draft and among 10 Trojans chosen overall. Swann and offensive tackle Steve Riley were first-round picks the following year. . . . Rae was selected the team's most valuable player, Cunningham as its back of the year, and Grant and Young as linemen of the year.

STATISTICAL LEADERS

PASSING

	Att.	Comp.	Yards	TD	Pct.	Int.
Mike Rae	174	96	1525	4	55.2	12
Pat Haden	70	33	453	7	47.1	3

RUSHING

	Att.	Yards	Avg.	TD	Long
Anthony Davis	184	1034	5.6	16	64
Rod McNeill	127	535	4.2	7	18
Sam Cunningham	91	311	3.4	9	17
Mike Rae	79	276	3.5	5	30

RECEIVING

	Rec.	Yards	Avg.	TD	Long
J.K. McKay	25	328	13.1	4	33
Charles Young	23	388	16.9	3	40
Lynn Swann	21	435	20.7	2	50
Anthony Davis	15	115	7.7	0	38

SCORING

	TD	FG	PAT	Points
Anthony Davis	18	0	0	108
Mike Rae	5	8	43	97
Sam Cunningham	9	0	0	54
Rod McNeill	7	0	0	42

KEY CHARACTERS

The Conductor

COACH: John McKay.

Record: 127-40-8, 16 years at Southern Cal.

McKay has the fourth-best winning percentage among all-time Trojan coaches. Many attribute the early success enjoyed by his successor, John Robinson (ranked second on the all-time list), to players recruited by McKay. . . . The Trojans finished among the nation's Top 10 on nine occasions under McKay, and his Southern Cal teams won four United Press International national championships and three Associated Press crowns during his 16-year stay. . . . Three of his teams were unbeaten, while three others suffered only one loss. . . . McKay posted an 18-11-3 record against archrivals Notre Dame and UCLA. . . . He also compiled a 5-3 mark in Rose Bowl play and a 6-3 overall bowl record at USC. Seven of his last 10 teams played in the Rose Bowl. . . . McKay coached 19 consensus All-Americas. . . . Among McKay's assistants at USC were such notables as Don Coryell, Dick Coury, Joe Gibbs, Robinson, Bruce Snyder and Ted Tollner.

Personal Data:

Born: July 5, 1923, in Everettville, W.Va.
High School: Shinnston High in Shinnston, W.Va.
College: Purdue and Oregon.

The Supporting Cast

FULLBACK: Sam Cunningham.

Cunningham is considered among the finest collegiate fullbacks ever to play the game. . . . He was a superb athlete with superior speed for his size (6-3, 220 pounds), a point driven home by the fact that he competed in the decathlon as a sophomore at USC. . . . He was co-captain of USC's 1972 national championship squad. . . . He was the third-leading rusher (742 yards) in the Pacific Eight Conference as a junior in 1971, despite missing the final two games with a knee injury. . . . Cunningham, known for his acrobatic dives over the line on short-yardage situations, lettered from 1970-72.

Personal Data:

Born: August 15, 1950, in Santa Barbara, Calif.
High School: Santa Barbara High.

TAILBACK: Anthony Davis.

Davis finished second to Ohio State's Archie Griffin in the 1974 Heisman Trophy balloting after finishing 13th the previous season. . . . He was a unanimous consensus All-America selection in 1974. . . . He and Charles White (1977-79) are the only USC backs ever to gain 1,000 yards in three different seasons. . . . A.D., who lettered from 1972-74, helped the Trojans throttle Notre Dame in 1972 with what many consider the greatest individual performance in college football history. He scored six touchdowns (including two on 96- and 97-yard kickoff returns) against the Irish and compiled 368 yards in total offense. . . . Davis still holds the school record for career kickoff return yardage (1,361 yards) and ranks as the third-leading career rusher with 3,724 yards. . . . He also played baseball at USC and was selected in both the June 1971 and June 1974 major league drafts by the Baltimore Orioles' organization and in January 1975 by the Minnesota Twins.

Personal Data:

Born: September 8, 1952, at San Fernando, Calif.
High School: San Fernando High.

FLANKER: Lynn Swann.

Including bowl statistics, Swann caught 27 passes and averaged 20.1 yards per catch in 1972. . . . Swann lettered from 1971-73 and was a consensus All-America in 1973. . . . He saw action as a defensive back as a freshman. . . . Swann led the Trojans in receiving in 1971 (his sophomore campaign) with 27 receptions and in 1973 with 41 catches for 714 yards and six touchdowns.

Personal Data:

Born: March 7, 1952, at Alcoa, Tenn.
High School: Serra High in Foster City, Calif.

TIGHT END: Charles Young.

Young lettered from 1970-72 and was a unanimous consensus All-America his senior season. . . . He was one of the best tight ends of the decade. . . . He still ranks as the Trojans' all-time reception leader at tight end with 68 catches for 1,090 yards and 10 touchdowns. . . . Young was an excellent blocker, a top-notch receiver and a deep threat in USC's offense.

Personal Data:

Born: February 5, 1951, in Fresno, Calif.
High School: Edison High in Fresno.

FINAL 1972 WIRE SERVICE RANKINGS

ASSOCIATED PRESS		UNITED PRESS	
1. **SOUTHERN CAL**	11. Louisiana State	1. **SOUTHERN CAL**	11. Tennessee
2. Oklahoma	12. North Carolina	2. Oklahoma	12. **Notre Dame**
3. Texas	13. Arizona State	3. **Ohio State**	13. Arizona State
4. Nebraska	14. **Notre Dame**	4. Alabama	14. Colorado
5. Auburn	15. **UCLA**	5. Texas	North Carolina
6. Michigan	16. Colorado	6. Michigan	16. Louisville
7. Alabama	17. N.C. State	7. Auburn	17. **UCLA**
8. Tennessee	18. Louisville	8. Penn State	**Washington St.**
9. **Ohio State**	19. **Washington St.**	9. Nebraska	19. Utah State
10. Penn State	20. Georgia Tech	10. Louisiana State	20. San Diego State

Bold face indicates Southern Cal opponent.

The Beginning Of a Dynasty

Notre Dame, 1946
By Bill Bilinski

At a Notre Dame football banquet following a particularly disappointing season a few years ago, the university's vice president, the Rev. Edmund P. Joyce, was offering the senior class as much consolation as he could muster. Defeat, Joyce was saying, was character's building block.

When Joyce was finished with his comments, master of ceremonies John Lujack took the podium.

"Father," he said, "I must not have much character then because I was on the losing side only once when I played at Notre Dame."

For a few others who played with Lujack, there were no losses at all. None. The run began in 1946, and it never ended for the freshmen who entered Notre Dame that year. In that incredible four-year span, the Fighting Irish fashioned a 36-0-2 mark and claimed three national championships.

The pieces fell in place quickly as the end of World War II triggered the beginning of the dynasty. Many of the players that year were returning after a couple of years away, hardened in body and spirit by military service. Among the returning veterans was Lujack, who had played on the 9-1 1943 team that won the national crown. After Heisman Trophy winner Angelo Bertelli joined the Marines six games into that season, Lujack finished the year as the starting quarterback. He then spent the better part of three years in the Navy before returning to South Bend.

Left over from the 7-2-1 1945 team was a solid group of players that included halfback Terry Brennan and linemen Bill Walsh, Bill Fischer and John Mastrangelo. There were a few transfers, including the great tackle George Connor and center George Strohmeyer, who came over from Holy Cross and Texas A&M, respectively, after Navy hitches. There were guys who had joined the service

Coach Frank Leahy (left) was the driving force behind Notre Dame's 1946 machine, while lineman Bill Fischer was one of its key cogs.

After serving nearly three years in the Navy, John Lujack took Notre Dame's quarterback reins in 1946 and won the Heisman Trophy a year later.

before beginning varsity careers, such as end Jim Martin and halfback Emil (Red) Sitko. There were some outstanding freshman recruits such as end Leon Hart. And joining Lujack on the list of Irish veterans whose careers had been interrupted by the war were such 1946 starters as tackle Zygmont (Ziggy) Czarobski, end Jack Zilly and fullback Jim Mello.

"It was just so great to have the war over and everyone coming back healthy," Lujack said. "It was so much fun to get out there and have everyone into sports rather than war."

The talented crew had behind it the ultimate driving force in Coach Frank Leahy. Like many of his players, the man who ruled with an iron fist (if not a magic wand) also was returning after a couple of years in the service.

Leahy, who instituted the powerful T-formation at Notre Dame in 1942, was a brilliant football technician, but there was nothing fancy about his style. His discipline and strict demands on his coaching staff and players had a military flavor at times. Without question, no one outworked him—or the Irish.

Leahy played under Notre Dame's first and college football's foremost legendary figure, Knute Rockne. The Nebraska native inherited some of Rockne's traits, the most obvious of which was his passion for the game. He was so devoted to his job that he drove himself into the ground with worry and work, eventually forcing a premature exit from the game he so loved.

But while he coached, he was usually on top. He had taken over for Elmer Layden in 1941 at the age of 32 and led the Irish to an 8-0-1 mark in his first year. Leahy had his first national championship in '43, then took off the next two years to assist the war effort. He resumed control of the club in '46 and coached through the 1953 season, by which time his health was deteriorating and he decided to resign. In 11 seasons he won more than 85 percent of his games (87-11-9) and captured four top rankings in the final wire-service polls.

Notre Dame was not just promoting one of its own when it named Leahy coach. After graduating from Notre Dame in 1931, he had distinguished himself as a line coach at Georgetown, Michigan State and Fordham, where he helped build the famed Seven Blocks of Granite line. He then went to Boston College, where he fashioned a 20-2 mark in his first head coaching stint. When Notre Dame beckoned after his second season in Boston, he returned to the Midwest.

Coaching the Irish was a dream come true for Leahy, a devout Catholic who often interspersed religious references with his halftime tirades against players who failed to produce as expected. He got results, as evidenced by a tongue-lashing he inflicted on his troops between halves of a 1949 game in which the Irish went to the locker room tied with North Carolina, 6-6.

"Leon Hart. Oh, Leon Hart," Leahy barked. "Some day you will cause the Pope himself to leave the church. Oh, you do not deserve to represent Our Lady. Perhaps somebody else should take your place. . . . Give Leon Hart 75 cents for meal money and let him start hitchhiking home right now. I see absolutely no hope for his immortal soul. Let us now bow our heads and pray to Our Lady for forgiveness, for we have disgraced her terribly."

Led by a supercharged Hart, Notre Dame came out breathing fire in the second half and whipped the Tar Heels, 42-6.

Leahy's methods weren't always easy to live with, and it's no small wonder, especially given the age of many of the players coming out of the service, that he maintained his tight control.

He could make football a year-round sport in some years and take his players right to the edge.

The spring of '46, Brennan recalled, was one of those years when spring practice began in February and ended in June. "I almost quit after that spring, but my father talked me into going back out," he said.

Generally, the players hung on because they "sure liked the feeling on Saturday nights," said Ed (Moose) Krause, an assistant under Leahy who later became athletic director. And they hung on because Notre Dame attracted the players and students who knew what they were getting into.

"That discipline stuff was right up my alley," said Connor, a consensus All-America along with Lujack in both '46 and '47.

"Notre Dame had great spirit," Lujack said. "And if we were told we had to pay the price, we bought it. But I just loved to play. If it was practice, that was swell because you knew you were always improving under Leahy."

The players improved not only because of Leahy's discipline and brutal conditioning programs, but also his close scrutiny of their performance in practice.

"The players thought he had four eyes," Krause said. "He could be on the other side of the field and see a mistake and start bawling someone out."

Leahy, who could be a charmer on the recruiting trail, had stockpiled enough talent by 1946 that there was little difference between the Irish first and second teams. Though he would present a weekly mask of worry and concern to the press—overconfidence never became an issue with Leahy teams—he had such strength in numbers that he could take a lot of chances in practice. He scrimmaged daily, and it took some luck to stay healthy and keep a job.

"I think he was such a fundamentalist," Lujack said, "that he probably knew what weaknesses we had and that if another team exploited them, we could lose."

Lujack, however, couldn't think of any weaknesses. And if the Irish were healthy on Saturday, they certainly knew they were in excellent condition. "Saturday games were a picnic compared to practice," Connor said.

The daily team-on-team drills were so intense, Brennan said, that "it was like survival of the fittest."

Leahy's coaches also were a strong and healthy lot. They had to be because they coached by example, actually going against players in practice.

By the time Saturday rolled around, Leahy had two teams of players ready to go. That gave Notre Dame a great edge in those days of single-platoon football. Leahy substituted freely, often en masse, and if the Irish talent didn't get to the opposition, fatigue often did. "We just wore down a lot of teams," Connor said.

Halfback Terry Brennan was one of Notre Dame's many talented running backs who ran roughshod over opposing defenses after World War II.

One of Notre Dame's backfield combinations featured (left to right) halfback Emil (Red) Sitko, quarterback John Lujack, fullback John Panelli and halfback Bob Livingstone.

Some of the stars played only the first and third quarters in many games, even the rare close ones, and it didn't matter. In '46, 13 different players rushed for more than 100 yards, led by Sitko's 346 and Brennan's 329. The Irish rolled up 3,061 yards on the ground (tops in the nation) and another 911 in the air.

"We pretty much crunched people," Brennan said. "We didn't really fool anyone. . . . Sometimes it was more fun to be on the second team because the first team got beat up trying to wear the other guys down."

With the war over, football's popularity had another growth spurt and Notre Dame packed them in on Saturday—at home and on the road. More than half a million people saw the Irish play in '46, including 75,119 in the opener at Illinois, which went on to win the Western (now the Big Ten) Conference title that year but fell to the Irish, 26-6.

Sitko got it all started that day with an 83-yard run that set up the first Irish touchdown. To understand what the war meant to the shuffling of players, it was Sitko, a Notre Dame student for one semester before joining the service, who had helped beat the Irish in 1943 while playing for Great Lakes.

As the season wore on it became obvious that only one other team—Army—was in a class with Notre Dame. But before the Cadets came up, the Irish routed five opponents in what could be considered a challenging schedule of Illinois, Pittsburgh, Purdue, Iowa and Navy. Notre Dame was so good and the games were so bad that some of the players started sympathizing with the other side.

"I always thought I'd like to go into the other team's locker room before a game and meet the other players," said Connor, whom Leahy tabbed in later years as one of his best defensive players, "just to tell them: 'We're the same as you. Let's go out and play football and have some fun.' I think other teams were awed by Notre Dame. We'd blow teams out in the first half, then things settled down and they usually played us even."

Offensively, the T-formation helped exploit Lujack's many talents. Besides completing 49 of 100 passes for 778 yards, he rushed for another 108. "Lujack could do everything," Krause said.

As potent as the offense was that year, the Irish defense was even better—perhaps the best ever for a Notre Dame team. Leahy's lads led the nation in total defense (141.7 yards allowed per game) and scoring defense (2.7 points per game) as only Illinois, Purdue, Iowa and Southern California scored on the Irish. While the offense was racking up 271 points against nine opponents, the defense held the opposition to 24 points.

Those school defensive records are all the more

remarkable considering that defense was emphasized less than offense during Leahy's practices.

"We didn't really practice defense," Connor said. "We played defense as a necessity against our own team. The main emphasis was always on offense."

Leahy's instructions on defense were simple: Be quick and aggressive. "The theory was to always be on the attack," Krause said. "You had to attack and assume authority. And we were always going after the ball."

Said Lujack: "Leahy reviewed the film and set up the defense accordingly. And not much got by that line."

Leahy preferred speed over bulk and was always cognizant of the balance, weighing in his players daily. One hefty player in particular, Czarobski, had trouble with that rule and was always trying to alter the weigh-in results. Particularly concerned one day, he arranged to be first up on the scale. Of course, he had rigged the scale the night before.

Czarobski had a way of keeping the club relaxed and having his fun without wearing thin on Leahy. It didn't hurt that he also was a great tackle.

Czarobski was at his comedic best one afternoon just before the Iowa game. Iowa was a heavy underdog, but Leahy expressed concern that the Irish were taking the Hawkeyes too lightly. Czarobski, always eager to help, asked permission to give the Irish freshmen a pep talk, and Leahy said sure.

Ziggy delivered an eloquent, tearful speech in which he lauded the Notre Dame tradition. He impressed upon the awed freshmen how important it was for them not to let Notre Dame down. A victory against the Hawkeyes, he advised, was critical.

"The point I wish to make," Ziggy said in his falsetto voice, wiping away a tear, "is that soon we are going to New York to play Army, a great team, in Yankee Stadium. Army hasn't lost in two years. Think of the price we'll be able to get for our Army tickets if we go to New York unbeaten!"

A few weeks later, Czarobski got wound up as a practice was running late. He reportedly started the chant "We wanna eat, we wanna eat."

When Leahy heard what was going on, he marched down from the other end of the field. The chant became "We wanna eat, we wanna eat . . . the Wildcats."

Everyone knew how far they could go with Leahy, and Czarobski probably went the farthest. The coach had little tolerance for nonsense, especially when he thought his team was not giving 100 percent. Winning wasn't necessarily enough; Leahy wanted perfection.

Krause recalled a game in which the Irish had buried their opponent but had failed on one occasion to score from the 1-yard line. Leahy couldn't live with that, so he got the team back on the field on Sunday and immediately set the ball on the 1-

Tackle George Connor transferred to Notre Dame from Holy Cross and won the first Outland Trophy for his performance in the trenches in 1946.

One of the big games in college football history occurred in 1946 when exuberant fans filled Yankee Stadium and watched Notre Dame battle Army to a 0-0 tie.

yard line. Practice began there.

"He never let them be content," Krause said. "He'd always find something wrong."

One would imagine that Leahy had to look pretty hard at times. The Irish coasted through their first five games, blanking Navy to set up the battle against Army, which was ranked No. 1 in the Associated Press poll.

Army, coached by the great Earl (Red) Blaik, featured Doc Blanchard and Glenn Davis in the backfield. The Cadets had won two straight national titles and 25 straight games. Included in the streak were consecutive poundings of Notre Dame by a combined 107-0 score. The pregame buildup reached Super Bowl proportion as 74,121 fans jammed Yankee Stadium for the November 9 battle.

Offensively, the game was a bust. Caution was the rule as both coaches avoided making the first mistake. The Irish got as far as the Army 4-yard line in the second quarter for the day's best scoring threat, but the Cadets held on downs. Lujack's game-saving, open-field tackle of Blanchard, who appeared to have a clear shot to the end zone after getting

Notre Dame Coach Frank Leahy was a master tactician who roamed the Irish sideline for 11 seasons and produced four wire-service national champions.

past Notre Dame's line, salvaged a 0-0 tie.

Years later, Brennan had lunch with Blaik. "He (Blaik) told me, 'We both choked in that game,'" Brennan recalled. "Of course, Leahy never would admit to that."

Neither club cared much for the tie, which allowed Army to retain its No. 1 ranking. But Notre Dame came back to rout its final three opponents, including Southern Cal, while Army narrowly escaped with a victory over Navy. In the final AP poll, the Irish were named national champions. And they were just getting started.

After that season, Leahy took nothing for granted regarding his 1947 team. He kept working his players hard and even issued an ultimatum to Czarobski, who had put on about 30 pounds in the months prior to spring practice.

"If you go to work this summer and take off 30 pounds," the coach wrote in a note to Ziggy, "we will be very happy to have you back. If not, do not bother to report. We are not interested in funny fat men."

Czarobski returned for fall drills looking strong and tough—and about 30 pounds lighter.

"Well, Zygmont," Leahy said, "you look as if you had been working, as I suggested. Where were you?"

"In Wisconsin, Coach," Ziggy answered.

"Working on a road gang?"

"I guess you could call it that," Ziggy replied, shrugging.

"Splendid," the coach said. "We are happy to see you back, looking so well."

Czarobski decided that what Leahy didn't know wouldn't hurt him.

"I didn't have the heart to tell him the truth," he said later. "I worked as a bouncer at a roadhouse in Wisconsin, and between brawls, I got in a lot of dancing. That's how I got the weight off."

Czarobski was one of eight returning starters for the 1947 Irish. Mello, Mastrangelo and Zilly were gone, but fullback John Panelli, guard Marty Wendell and Hart were experienced replacements. Bill Walsh moved ahead of Strohmeyer to become the full-time center. The backfield had Brennan and Sitko returning under Lujack's cagey direction. Lujack's backup was Frank Tripucka, who went on to become a fine quarterback in his own right.

But it was not all smooth sailing from the start. "At one point there was a lot of dissension," Brennan said.

The dissension came early in the year when

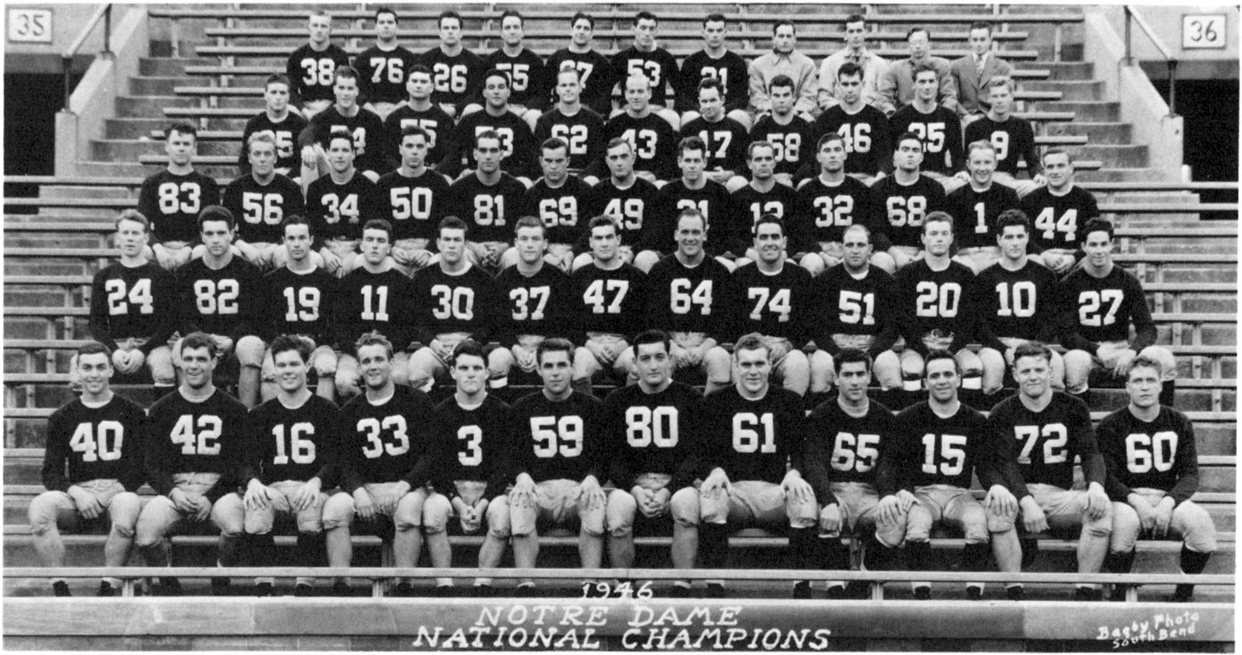

The 1946 Fighting Irish: Front row (left to right) —Bob Livingstone, Fred Rovai, Bob Skoglund, Frank Kosikowski, Roger Brown, Al Zmijewski, Gus Cifelli, Bill Russell, Jim Mello, John Agnone, Bill Fischer, George Strohmeyer. Second row—Larry Coutre, Leon Hart, Coy McGee, Jim Brennan, Bill Gompers, Terry Brennan, Bob McBride, Gasper Urban, Joe Signaigo, Vince Scott, Lancaster Smith, Bill Heywood, Ray Espenan. Third row—Bill Wightkin, Jack Zilly, Paul Limont, Bob Walsh, George Connor, Corwin Clatt, Bernie Meter, Jim McGurk, Russell Ashbaugh, John Lujack, Jack Fallon, Fred Earley, Len LeCluyse. Fourth row—Ernie Zalejski, George Sullivan, John Mastrangelo, Marty Brutz, Floyd Simmons, Tom Potter, George Tobin, Marty Wendell, Bill Walsh, Bill O'Connor, George Ratterman. Fifth row—Jim Martin, Zygmont Czarobski, Ralph McGehee, Mike Swistowicz, John Panelli, Gerry Cowhig, Art Statuto; managers Bill Boss, Bill Flaherty, Tom Earls, John Kelly.

Leahy's intense daily scrimmages began to take their toll. The bruises were adding up, the level of intensity was dropping and the Irish chemistry was in limbo.

According to Brennan, sportswriter Warren Brown provided a big helping hand.

"When he was talking to Leahy," Brennan explained, "he just told him, 'I don't know if you know this or not, but you've almost got a revolt on your hands.' "

Leahy wasn't one to take advice from a sportswriter, but the practice intensity eased and "he became more judicious with the workouts," Brennan said.

The team finally was able to relax a little. Some remember Leahy standing in front of the team soon after that, saying: "We're going to start over with the basics. Lads, this is a football."

Czarobski piped in, "Coach, not so fast."

It was business as usual.

Notre Dame whipped Pitt, 40-6, to start its season and never slowed down. The Irish went 9-0 and won their second consecutive national title. Twenty-nine lettermen from that team went on to the pros, including Lujack, who completed 61 of 109 passes, ran for 139 yards, played excellent defense and was named the Heisman winner. Sitko rushed for 426 yards, Brennan 404 (with 11 touchdowns) as the Irish rolled up a 291-52 scoring margin.

Among the losses to graduation the next spring were Connor, Czarobski and Lujack, but the ball was rolling and quarterback Tripucka still had Brennan, Sitko and Panelli behind him. The Irish won their first nine games in 1948, but a season-ending 14-14 tie with USC—a game in which they scored with 35 seconds to play—squeezed them out of their third straight national championship as Michigan was voted in.

There was no stopping the Irish in '49, when Martin and Hart captained the team to a 10-0 mark. Consensus All-America quarterback Bob Williams guided one of Leahy's best all-around backfields in Frank Spaniel, Larry Coutre and Sitko as the Irish tallied 360 points to their opponents' 86. Hart and Sitko were consensus All-Americas for the second year in a row, and Hart also won the Heisman, becoming Notre Dame's third winner of the 1940s. The Irish also earned their third national crown in four years, capping an incredible span of dominant postwar football.

Notre Dame, 1946

ROAD TO GREATNESS

1946 RESULTS (8-0-1)

Opponent	Score	Opp. Record	Opp. Bowl Game
at Illinois	26-6	8-2-0	Rose (W)
Pittsburgh	33-0	3-5-1	
Purdue	49-6	2-6-1	
at Iowa	41-6	5-4-0	
*Navy	28-0	1-8-0	
†Army	0-0	9-0-1	
Northwestern	27-0	4-4-1	
at Tulane	41-0	3-7-0	
Southern California	26-6	6-4-0	

*Baltimore. †New York City.

FACTS AND FIGURES

The 1946 Fighting Irish went 1-0-1 against teams ranked in the final Associated Press Top 20 poll, tying second-ranked Army and beating Rose Bowl champion Illinois. . . . Only four of nine Irish opponents finished with winning records, but the overall record of Irish foes just inched above .500 (41-40-4, .506 winning percentage). . . . Notre Dame posted five shutouts, including four in the final five contests. . . . No opponent scored more than six points against the rock-solid Notre Dame defense. . . . The 1946 team was the second unbeaten squad under Frank Leahy—and the first of four in a row. . . . After the 0-0 tie with Army, the Irish won 21 consecutive games. And beginning with the season-opening triumph over the Illini, Notre Dame went 39 games without suffering defeat. . . . The Irish led the nation's major colleges in total offense, rushing offense, total defense and scoring defense. . . . The Irish also finished third in pass defense, fifth in rushing defense and seventh in scoring offense. . . . John Lujack ranked 15th in passing among the nation's major-college players and finished third in the 1946 Heisman Trophy voting. . . . Lujack, George Connor, guard John Mastrangelo and center George Strohmeyer were named to The Sporting News' 1946 All-America team. . . . The '46 team owns several modern school records, including offensive rushing yards per attempt (5.4), fewest points allowed in a season (24) and fewest yards allowed per game (141.7). . . . In addition to Coach Frank Leahy, six players on the '46 team are members of the College Football Hall of Fame—Connor, Lujack, Emil (Red) Sitko, tackle Ziggy Czarobski, guard Bill Fischer and end Leon Hart. . . . Halfback Terry Brennan led the Irish in receiving, scoring (tied with Jim Mello) and interceptions made (tied with Strohmeyer) in 1946. . . . Twenty-nine different players carried or caught the ball for the '46 Irish.

STATISTICAL LEADERS

PASSING

	Att.	Comp.	Yards	TD	Pct.	Int.
John Lujack	100	49	778	5	49.0	8
George Ratterman	18	8	114	1	44.4	2

RUSHING

	Att.	Yards	Avg.	TD
Emil (Red) Sitko	54	346	6.4	3
Terry Brennan	74	329	4.4	4
Jim Mello	61	307	5.0	5
Bill Gompers	51	279	5.3	3
John Panelli	58	265	4.6	4
Coy McGee	21	250	11.9	3

RECEIVING

	Rec.	Yards	Avg.	TD
Terry Brennan	10	154	15.4	2
Jack Zilly	8	152	19.0	1
Bob Skoglund	6	76	12.7	0
Leon Hart	5	107	21.4	1

SCORING

	TD	FG	PAT	Points
Terry Brennan	6	0	0	36
Jim Mello	6	0	0	36
Fred Earley	0	0	31	31
John Panelli	4	0	0	24
Bill Gompers	3	0	0	18
Coy McGee	3	0	0	18
Emil (Red) Sitko	3	0	0	18

KEY CHARACTERS

The Conductor

COACH: Frank Leahy.

Record: 87-11-9, 11 years at Notre Dame.

Leahy has the second-best career winning percentage (.864) in collegiate football history, trailing only his former mentor, Knute Rockne. . . . His overall career record is 107-13-9 in 13 years. . . . He lettered at Notre Dame in 1928 and 1929 as a tackle playing for Rockne. . . . He is a member of the College Football Hall of Fame. . . . Leahy was an assistant at Georgetown, Michigan State and Fordham before accepting the head coaching position at Boston College and then moving on to South Bend. . . . At Fordham, he served as line coach and tutored the famous Seven Blocks of Granite. . . . Nine of his 11 Irish teams finished in the Top 10 and four captured national championships. Six were unbeaten, and the Leahy-coached Irish compiled an unbeaten streak of 39 games from 1946-50. . . . The 1946 squad battled the mighty Army team, featuring Doc Blanchard and Glenn Davis, to a 0-0 tie and stopped the Cadets' 25-game winning streak. . . . He coached 22 consensus All-Americas at Notre Dame and produced four Heisman Trophy winners—Angelo Bertelli (1943), John Lujack (1947), Leon Hart (1949) and John Lattner (1953). . . . He entered the Navy in 1944 and returned to coaching in 1946. . . . He compiled a 20-2 mark at Boston College, including a 1941 Sugar Bowl victory over Tennessee.

Personal Data:

Born: August 21, 1908, at O'Neill, Neb.
High School: Winner High in Winner, S.D.
College: Notre Dame.

The Supporting Cast

TACKLE: George Connor.

Connor is a member of both the college and pro football Halls of Fame. . . . He won the Outland Trophy in 1946, the first year the award honoring interior linemen was presented. . . . He was a two-time consensus All-America (1946 and '47). . . . Connor started his career at Holy Cross, where he won numerous regional honors before entering the Navy in 1944 and transferring to Notre Dame. . . . He was a physical player who punished opposing runners. . . . He lettered in 1946 and '47.

Personal Data:

Born: January 21, 1925, at Chicago.
High School: De La Salle High in Chicago.

END: Leon Hart.

Hart won the Heisman in 1949 and was a unanimous consensus All-America as well. He also earned consensus All-America honors in 1948. . . . Hart and Yale's Larry Kelley (1936) are the only linemen ever to win the Heisman. . . . He lettered from 1946-49 and never played in an Irish loss. Hart, a member of the College Football Hall of Fame, helped Notre Dame compile a 36-0-2 record and win three national championships during his stay.

Personal Data:

Born: November 2, 1928, in Turtle Creek, Pa.
High School: Turtle Creek High.

QUARTERBACK: John Lujack.

Lujack won the Heisman Trophy in 1947 after finishing third in the 1946 balloting. . . . He is a member of the College Football Hall of Fame. . . . He was a unanimous consensus All-America in 1946 and 1947. . . . He was an honorable mention selection to The Sporting News All-Time All-America Team picked in 1983. . . . He took over as quarterback in 1943 when that year's Heisman Trophy winner, Angelo Bertelli, joined the Marines. Lujack led the Irish to national championships in 1943, 1946 and 1947. . . . He was extremely versatile, whether throwing, running or stopping opposing runners from his defensive back position. . . . His leadership qualities were demonstrated by Notre Dame's 26-1-1 record in the three seasons Lujack lettered. . . . He also is remembered for his game-saving tackle of Army's Doc Blanchard to preserve a scoreless tie in 1946. . . . He went on to play four seasons with the National Football League's Chicago Bears before returning to Notre Dame for two seasons as an offensive backfield coach.

Personal Data:

Born: January 4, 1925, at Connellsville, Pa.
High School: Connellsville High.

HALFBACK: Emil (Red) Sitko.

Sitko finished seventh in the 1948 Heisman Trophy balloting and eighth in 1949. . . . He was a consensus All-America both years and a unanimous pick in '49. . . . He is a member of the College Football Hall of Fame. . . . He holds the Notre Dame record for longest run from scrimmage without scoring (an 83-yard burst against Illinois in 1946). . . . He led the Irish in rushing four consecutive seasons (1946-49) and ranks sixth on the Irish all-time rushing charts with 2,226 yards. He also scored 25 touchdowns and averaged 6.1 yards per rushing attempt. . . . He lettered from 1946-49.

Personal Data:

Born: May 5, 1929, at Connellsville, Pa.
High School: Immaculate Conception High in Connellsville.

FINAL 1946 WIRE SERVICE RANKINGS

ASSOCIATED PRESS

1. NOTRE DAME	6. Michigan	11. Georgia Tech	16. Arkansas
2. Army	7. Tennessee	12. Yale	17. Tulsa
3. Georgia	8. Louisiana State	13. Pennsylvania	18. N.C. State
4. UCLA	9. North Carolina	14. Oklahoma	19. Delaware
5. Illinois	10. Rice	15. Texas	20. Indiana

Bold face indicates Notre Dame opponent.

GREATEST 6 TEAMS

Paying the Price In Bear Country

Alabama, 1979
By Al Browning

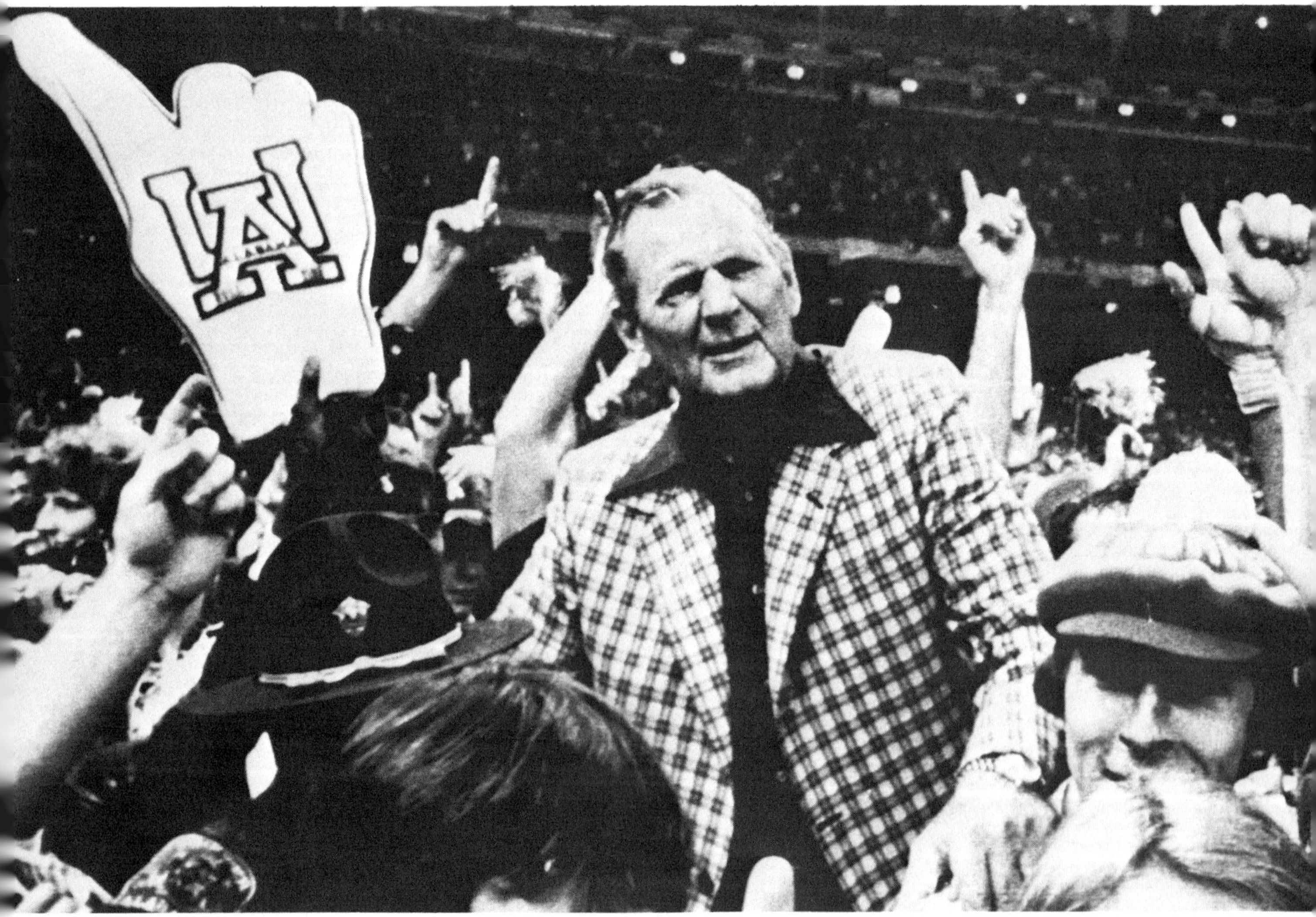

Excited fans set the stage for a perfect 1979 season by escorting Coach Bear Bryant from the field after Alabama's 1979 Sugar Bowl win over Penn State.

Paul (Bear) Bryant was less than a month away from his 66th birthday, seemingly too old to cause a commotion, yet definitely too experienced building championship football teams to let a subpar performance go unnoticed. And what he saw on the practice field below him on that muggy afternoon in August 1979 was not even close to meeting the high standards he had set for his Alabama football players.

Standing atop his 30-foot observation tower, Bryant growled and reached for a bullhorn that was never more than a quick yank away. Bringing the amplifier to his lips, the coach ordered his players to stop what they were doing on the steamy artificial surface.

The heat and humidity that day made Tuscaloosa feel like hell on earth, which was reflected in the expressions the Crimson Tide players had on their faces at that moment. The veterans had come to expect fire-and-brimstone sermons when Bryant stopped practices, and the rookies had heard enough about such orations to dread experiencing one.

But shortly after the activity had ceased, when the only sound that could be heard was a gentle breeze rustling through the bushes surrounding Thomas Field, it became apparent that Bryant, while obviously irritated, was going to inspire his troops, not rake them over the coals.

"Let's get off the headgear and take a knee," Bryant said, which was his way of commanding his players to form a military-like line in front of him.

Thus assembled, the players looked up at the living legend who was on his way to winning more college football games than anybody in history.

"Gentlemen," Bryant began, "a day like this is the reason you're Alabama football players, while others are somewhere else. I know it's hot. Hell, I'm hot. I know you're tired. I'm tired, too. I know it's tough. But it's supposed to be. If I didn't think you were up to this type challenge, I wouldn't have invited you to join this team, wouldn't have recruited you for Alabama. So you don't have to prove yourselves to me. I already know you're capable. But I'm asking you to prove something to yourselves, to let yourselves know you've got what it takes to be a championship team.

"Frankly, you're a helluva lot better than you're showing today. You're wallowing around, feeling sorry for yourselves. You aren't paying the price, not even coming close, and you're the ones who'll be disappointed because of it. Believe me, when it gets down to nut-cracking time, when it's tough in the fourth quarter, you'll be glad you didn't quit out here in this heat.

"Now let's get back to work."

That pep talk, which had all the earmarks of a lecture, was not followed by predictable cheering and chanting, the false enthusiasm often seen on a practice field. Instead, it led to one of the most glorious seasons in Crimson Tide history, which has produced more than a few.

That 1979 Alabama team went 11-0 in the regular season. Most of the victories came without the Crimson Tide breaking much of a sweat, certainly nothing like it did that day in August. But three of them came as Bryant predicted they would—in the fourth quarter, when the toil of preparation enabled the team to come from behind against one threatening opponent and to hold off two others.

Alabama then proceeded to defeat Arkansas in the Sugar Bowl, wrapping up its second consecutive national championship. That gave the Crimson Tide six national crowns under the direction of Bryant—unanimous Associated Press-United Press International verdicts in 1961, 1964 and 1979 and split decisions in 1965, 1973 and 1978. The coach went to his grave in January 1983 claiming another such title, one his unbeaten and untied 1966 team barely lost to Notre Dame and Michigan State.

Alabama reached a peak in 1979, not only because it represented Bryant's last national champion, but also because he closed out the '70s with a national record for victories in a decade. Like fine wine, Bryant improved with age, and his basic theory about how to develop winners maintained its magic.

"You see, there's a difference in being a player and a football player," Bryant said when asked to explain his practice-field remarks that summer day in 1979. "A player just puts on a uniform and shows up for games, while a football player works to be a winner. A winner takes his victories and leaves it at that. A champion pays an extra price to be better than everybody else. It's working for the rewards, that's all, doing what it takes to reach potential.

"We've had great teams at Alabama, like that unbeaten and uncrowned bunch, and this could be another one if these young men understand what's in front of them. It's hard for them to realize that on a day like this, when it's hot and miserable. But it'd be a shame for them to let their chance to reach greatness slip away because they didn't work hard enough."

Bryant became agitated when many of his enthusiastic thoughts about his 1979 team appeared in the local newspaper the following afternoon.

"That's not the kind of talk our players should hear or our fans should read at this point of the season," said Bryant, who had filled trophy cases by challenging his players, not praising them. He feared that the heavenly confidence associated with being the defending national champion would be transformed into deadly cockiness.

But the uncharacteristic optimism Bryant exhib-

Two of Alabama's most talented defenders were intimidating cornerback Don McNeal and defensive end E.J. Junior, who combined brains with brawn.

ited in August set the stage for an unusual year at Alabama. The coach further broke with tradition by lavishly praising his team in the middle of its season. On October 21, the day after Alabama overcame a 17-0 deficit to defeat bitter Southeastern Conference rival Tennessee, 27-17, he vowed for the first time to vote the Crimson Tide first in the UPI poll, a position it had claimed in that poll and the AP poll one week earlier.

"We've had some good ones at Alabama, obviously, like in 1961 and 1966, plus several in more recent years," Bryant said, "but I've never been prouder of one than I am this one. Against Tennessee our players hung in there and fought and fought and fought. When they had to have it, they reached down and got it. We've got some kind of team. Our players have character, pride and class. I think we can beat anybody. If not, somebody will have to prove me wrong, which isn't gonna be easy to do based on what I've seen."

Bryant was impressed by Alabama's performance in the second half against Tennessee, which fell to 4-2. But it was what his players did not do at halftime—panic in the wake of a 17-7 deficit—that prompted an uncharacteristic display of optimism by the man who gave pessimism a more profound meaning, if he did not coin the word himself.

"They impressed me at halftime," Bryant said after his team's sixth victory in six tries. "They didn't come into the dressing room with their heads bowed like dogs that'd been whipped with a stick. Instead, they were composed. They weren't rattled. They knew their mettle would be tested. They knew their courage was on the line. They seemed to like the situation. It was as if they were thinking, 'Well, if we're going to be national champions, now is the time to prove it.' "

If the Tide players were upbeat, their coach was positively exuberant during the intermission. In fact, some of the players were wondering whether Bryant had read the scoreboard correctly.

"I thought Coach Bryant had lost it," recalled Steve Whitman, the fullback in Alabama's wishbone offense. "I honestly thought he thought we had 17 points and Tennessee had seven. He acted like we were ahead.

"He came into the dressing room clapping his hands, like he always did after a good play or a victory, and he said: 'Men, we've got Tennessee right where we want them. If you come back and win this game, nobody in the country will doubt that you deserve to be Number 1. If you come back and win, I'll believe that you've got what it takes to be the national champion. I'm telling you that a victory over Tennessee under these circumstances will be something you'll be able to tell your grandchildren about.'

"We tore down the door to get back onto the field for the second half. Coach Bryant had challenged us. That's how it was with that team. He'd issue a challenge and we'd answer it."

Actually, a few players paused to do something else before leaving the dressing room for the second half.

"Just before we went back out there, (defensive end) E.J. Junior, (middle guard) Warren Lyles and I got together and prayed," said defensive tackle David Hannah, whose brother John had been a consensus All-America guard at Alabama and then an All-Pro with the New England Patriots. "It was a spontaneous thing that happened just after (cornerback) Don McNeal jumped up and screamed: 'Don't anybody on this team quit. That's not the Alabama way. We're going back out there and prove ourselves by whipping their tails.' We did that, for sure. But it was through God that we won, which is something else worth remembering about that team. It was a spiritually strong team, a together team and a talented team."

Byron Braggs (47), Robbie Jones (97) and Warren Lyles (91) were part of a swarming Alabama defense that considered it a sin to let the opposition score.

Indeed, the Tide's starting quarterback was senior Steadman Shealy, a lay minister with a choirboy face who was active in the Fellowship of Christian Athletes. Shealy suffered a career-threatening knee injury in the spring of 1978 but worked his way back to the No. 2 spot behind Jeff Rutledge that fall. He continued to rehabilitate his knee and emerged as the starter in 1979. He ran the wishbone beautifully, rushing for a team-high 791 yards and completing 55.6 percent of his passes for 717 yards en route to a 10th-place finish in the Heisman Trophy voting.

The star against Tennessee, however, was Shealy's replacement, Don Jacobs, a tobacco-chewing, tart-talking junior who always thought he should be on the first team. Jacobs tried to blend in with the other squeaky-clean Alabama quarterbacks, but he remembers one time when he showed up for a team meeting with a light beard and long hair. Seated near him in the first row were Shealy and another quarterback, Alan Gray.

"I stood out like a sore thumb when Coach Bryant came in," Jacobs said, "because those guys couldn't grow a beard if they had to. Coach said, 'Alabama quarterbacks don't look like that.' I went right down to the training room and got the clippers. Everybody else was laughing. I failed to see the humor because I knew he was serious as a heart attack."

When Shealy struggled against the Volunteers, Bryant inserted Jacobs, who rushed 17 times for 45 yards, including a 13-yard run for the Tide's final touchdown.

"We showed some class and guts," Jacobs said in the dressing room after the game. "We just licked our wounded pride, went back out there and whipped their butts."

By that point in the season, behind-the-woodshed behavior was old hat. In fact, Alabama fans, who were becoming increasingly spoiled, considered the 10-point victory over Tennessee as little more than a near miss. They had watched their beloved Crimson Tide secure previous victories over Georgia Tech, Baylor, Vanderbilt, Wichita State and Florida by a combined score of 219-9.

The fans were not ignorant. They could look down the roster and see strength at every position. They could count, too, so they knew Bryant had played everybody dressed in some games, an amazing 45 in the first quarter at Florida.

There were nine future National Football League players among the top two dozen, led by a couple of defensive stalwarts—McNeal, who went on to start in the Miami Dolphins' secondary, and Junior, who later represented the St. Louis Cardinals in the Pro Bowl.

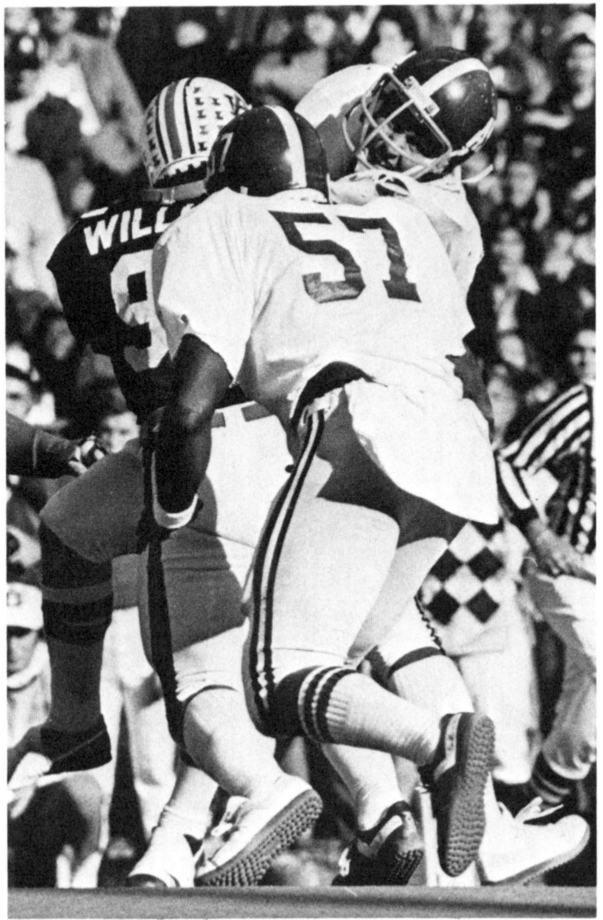

Alabama's Bear Bryant called Dwight Stephenson (57) the greatest center he had ever coached.

McNeal, Alabama's only All-America pick on defense in 1979, was the most intimidating force in a backfield that helped set a school record with 25 interceptions. The safeties were a couple of youngsters who had come to Tuscaloosa from out of state as highly touted quarterbacks—Tommy Wilcox, a redshirt freshman from a suburb of New Orleans, and Jim Bob Harris, a sophomore from Athens, Ga. The switch to defense proved wise as McNeal, Harris and Wilcox combined to break up 27 passes in '79, while cornerbacks Ricky Tucker and Mike Clements added nine more deflections.

One of the Tide's most interesting and talented players was Junior, who almost went to school in his hometown of Nashville. Along with his father, the vice president of business affairs at Tennessee State, and his mother, a high school principal, Junior devised a rating system that helped him select the college that was right for him. Alabama edged out Vanderbilt and Tennessee State, for which Crimson Tide fans are eternally grateful. Junior became an outstanding defensive end, leading the team in sacks, tackles for loss and fumbles caused as a junior in '79. He also was a good student (he earned his degree in public relations) and had a flair for music.

"I play a little bit of everything but country and western," he said. "I've played at clubs a couple of times when people recognized me and dragged me up there, but mostly I just play with my family. It's fun because all of us play at least one or two instruments."

Junior and Wayne Hamilton, who was hampered by injuries until midway through the '79 season, formed a strong defensive end tandem. The middle of Alabama's imposing front wall was anchored by Lyles and Curtis McGriff, who shared the starting job, with standout tackles Byron Braggs and Hannah on either side.

Hannah was a well-known name on the Alabama campus long before David arrived, and not just because of his brother John. Another brother, Charley, and their father, Herb, all played for the Tide before moving on to the NFL. But David said he never felt overly pressured by the situation. If anything, his family's legacy made him more competitive.

"There has always been a rivalry among the Hannah brothers," he said. "That's just competition. I don't think there's been a set of brothers born that hasn't had a rivalry between each other. That's healthy."

Hannah, who overcame two knee operations, became a leader on a defense that also featured Randy Scott and Thomas Boyd, the Tide's top two tacklers, at linebacker. Bryant's squad was feisty, limiting opponents to 5.3 points per game, the best figure in NCAA Division I-A. Alabama recorded five shutouts, one of which was preserved when Wichita State failed to score after securing a first down inside the 1-yard line. After being held to no gain on each of the first three plays, the Shockers coughed up a fumble on the 4-yard line on fourth down. "We do things like that for our pride," McGriff explained.

The Alabama philosophy was simple: "It's a sin to let somebody score," Braggs said.

Offensively, Alabama attacked opponents with players who seemed to be moving toward defenses in droves. Armed with depth, Bryant kept fresh players on the field in every game, regardless of the score. He used 13 runners against Florida, eight in the first half. His team was so deep in talent that it was easy to move Harris and Wilcox from quarterback to the defensive secondary, where they became All-SEC picks. The Tide mastered the thought-to-be-boring wishbone so well that offensive coordinator Mal Moore spent much of practice time innovating, inserting all manner of new wrinkles.

'Bama's 'bone was powered by a talented backfield and an awesome line. The Tide hammered away for 428.6 yards per game, with 80 percent of

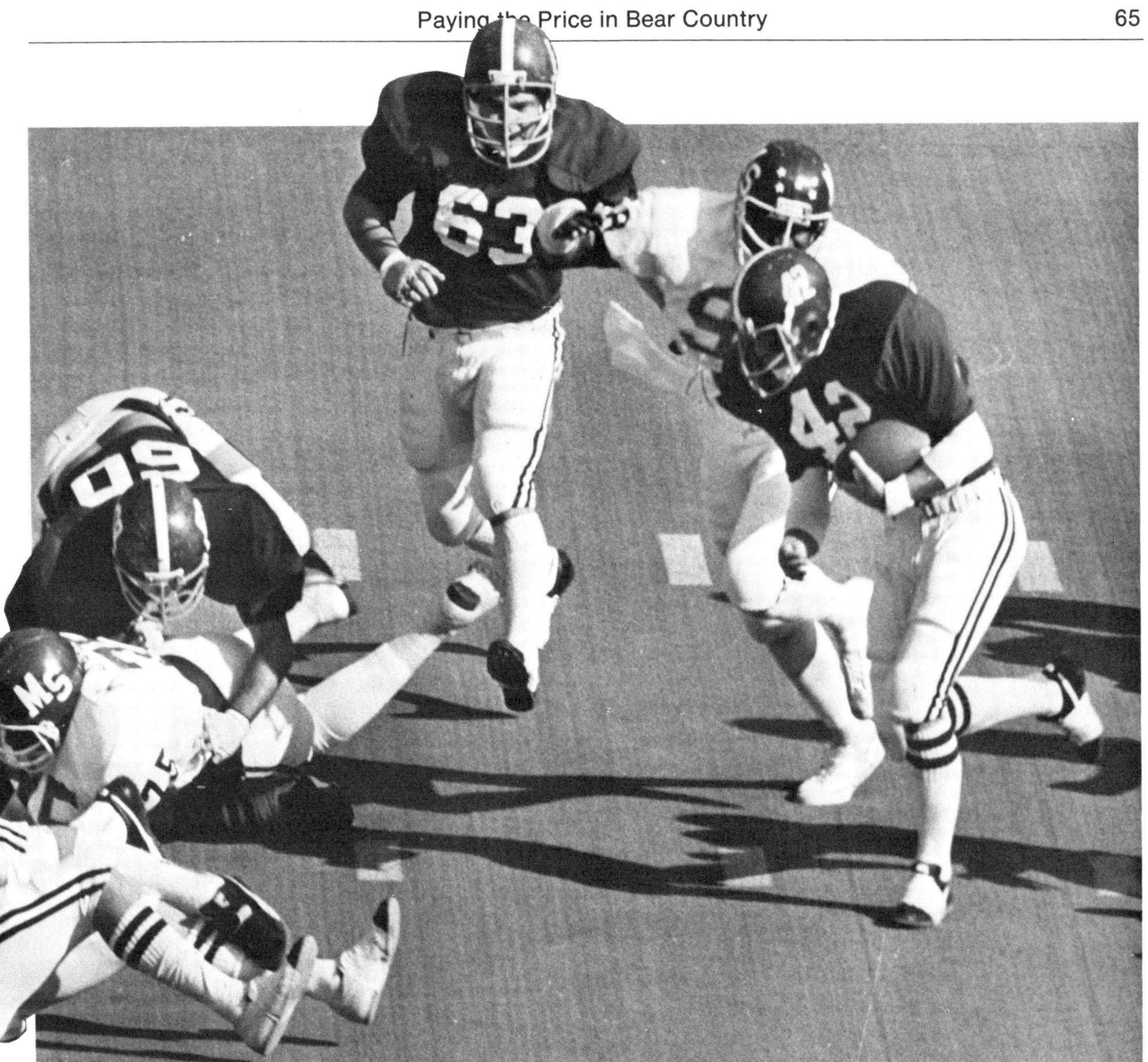

The heart of Alabama's offense was Major Ogilvie (42), who ran behind the blocking of guard Vince Boothe (60) and tackle Jim Bunch (63).

that yardage coming on the ground. Bryant always contended that the triple-option attack requires a quality center, two strong guards, a crafty quarterback and a bullish fullback. He had that and more with Dwight Stephenson at center, Mike Brock and Vince Boothe at the guards, Shealy and Jacobs at quarterback and Whitman at fullback.

Bryant called Stephenson, who went on to greatness with the Dolphins, "the greatest center I've ever coached." The quiet, unassuming senior destroyed middle guards and linebackers with strength, quickness and determination. His powerful performances must have surprised the neighborhood kids back in Hampton, Va., where a lack of money for food among his parents and six siblings had left Dwight skinny and vulnerable. "Even the girls pushed me around," he recalled.

Stephenson finally started bulking up when he was 14. He was hired at a supermarket and devoured everything his paycheck could cover. A healthy diet and plenty of basketball converted the added sustenance to muscle, and by his senior year in high school—only his second on the football team—he was all-state. After coming to Alabama as a defensive end, Stephenson was switched to center as a freshman and quickly established himself as the greatest center in Crimson Tide history.

"Stephenson was a man among children," Bryant said. "He didn't say very much, but he didn't have to."

Stephenson was flanked by tremendous blockers on both sides. Boothe and Brock, a former 190-pound walk-on who put on 50 pounds of muscle and became a two-time all-conference pick, helped Stephenson open up the middle, while consensus All-America Jim Bunch and Buddy Aydelette were explosive at the tackle spots.

Running was easy behind that overpowering

front wall, but Shealy had a couple of good targets when Bryant decided to mix it up with an occasional pass. Split end Keith Pugh had a team-high 25 receptions for 433 yards despite missing three games with a shoulder injury, and tight end Tim Travis, a solid blocker, chalked up 150 yards on seven catches.

The heart of the offense, however, was running back Major Ogilvie, who could run inside and outside, catch passes and return punts and kickoffs. Born Morgan Oslin Ogilvie Jr., he was like the dream boy next door—handsome, articulate, personable and gritty to the point that he almost made the San Francisco 49ers' roster despite limited physical gifts.

"I'm not real fast," Ogilvie said. "I'm slow as Christmas, in fact. I'm not real big, either (6-foot, 187 pounds). I guess I'm not exactly what the pros are after, but that's all right. I'm not real interested in the pros."

Ogilvie, the team's third-leading rusher with 512 yards behind Shealy and Whitman (653 yards), also was unselfish. He never failed to compliment his blockers or to point out that the skills of his backfield mates—the darting moves of Shealy and Jacobs, the outside running of numerous other halfbacks and the constant pounding of Whitman and fullback/halfback Billy Jackson—made it easy for him to operate.

With all this talent and versatility, the Tide's wishbone attack kept opposing defenses so befuddled, they didn't know what to expect. And with their own offenses stalled by Alabama's rock-hard defense, opposing coaches were left scratching their heads as they tried to explain devastating defeats. By the middle of the season, the losing coaches were making the Crimson Tide, which had opened the season ranked second in the nation behind Southern California, sound invincible.

- Georgia Tech's Pepper Rodgers: "I've never felt so small. Hell, they were too strong for us. They would've beat 99 percent of the teams in the country the way they played today."
- Baylor's Grant Teaff: "I've got one vote in the UPI poll, and you know who's gonna get mine for Number 1. We couldn't make a first down."
- Vanderbilt's George MacIntyre: "I thought before the game that they were the best team I had ever seen. I didn't see anything during the game to change my mind about that."
- Wichita State's Willie Jeffries: "This is the best team we're going to play for a long time."
- Florida's Charley Pell: "There's your national champion. The season is only five weeks old and we've already got the champ. It's Alabama, gentlemen, a team with no weaknesses. Not one."
- Tennessee's John Majors: "We just played shoe to shoe with the best team in the nation. It isn't a moral victory by any stretch of the imagination because there's no such thing in this rivalry, but there's consolation in knowing we had a great team on the ropes for three quarters."

Four days after Alabama disposed of the 18th-ranked Vols, comedian Bob Hope visited Tuscaloosa. With the Tide almost methodically building what would become a 28-game winning streak, Hope, a close friend and golfing companion of Bryant's, picked a good time to visit the Deep South. The fact that Joe Namath, a former Alabama and New York Jets star quarterback, accompanied him for the filming of a segment for a television special made his appearance even more special for Alabama fans.

"Tell my friend Bear there's Hope on the way," Hope said in a newspaper interview before his arrival. "Tell him there's a 75-year-old kicker named Thunder Foot coming to town. Tell him he has to take a look at this guy."

That was the theme of the skit Bryant, Hope and Namath did for an NBC-TV special titled "Homecoming U.S.A." Namath, who was cast as a former player, brought Thunder Foot, a prize prospect played by Hope, to meet the Alabama coach, played by Bryant, of course. Bryant muffed numerous lines provided for him on cue cards while making a most unimpressive acting debut. Ultimately, he decided to ad-lib, which worked much better, gruffy drawl and all.

"That's not how I'd say it," Bryant said when taking charge and changing the script.

Hope, who was appropriately attired in an Alabama jersey with the number "1" on its front, threw a football toward Bryant to signal his arrival. The errant toss broke the stone figure of a Crimson Tide player being used as a prop. "I'm a kicker, not a quarterback," Hope said with a laugh.

Namath showed up late for the filming because of a flight delay from New York. Still, he paused outside the door long enough to kiss an admiring coed.

"Why don't comedians and coaches get that kind of treatment?" Hope said to Bryant after the Namath smooch, proving that some enlightening scenes never even make it far enough to be swept away on the cutting room floor.

Actually, Bryant was being treated more royally than Hope suspected, particularly by members of the news media. The coach's dogged pursuit of Amos Alonzo Stagg's collegiate record of 314 coaching victories (Bryant had 290 after beating Tennessee) made him a big national story. Combine that individual achievement with the Tide's standing atop the polls and it was hard to imagine anyone not knowing about the Bear.

To test that theory, one sportswriter asked kindergarten students at an elementary school in Savannah, Ga., if they knew who Bear Bryant was. Some of the answers were as delightful as expected:

"Somebody who makes you live."

"He works bringing in tubs."

"He eats fish and honey."

"He chops wood."

"A man who paints houses."

The kindergartners at a Tuscaloosa school did somewhat better:

"Plays at the football game."

"He's a mean bat."

"I heard his name at the lake."

"He coaches Alabama."

The last description was the only one that mattered to Virginia Tech Coach Bill Dooley, whose team was next on the Alabama schedule. And foremost on his mind was not who was coaching the Tide, but rather the impressive players Bryant had at his disposal.

"I've seen the films," Dooley said, "and I'll be realistic about it. We're building a program at Virginia Tech. They're established at Alabama, more so than any other program in the nation. I don't anticipate us winning."

Dooley was correct. Even with numerous starters injured, five of whom watched the game from the sideline, the Tide defeated Virginia Tech, 31-7. "They showed me they definitely deserve their Number 1 ranking," Dooley said.

The following week, Bryant watched his team in action and said, "We're like a car running with a plug missing or on a flat tire." But Shealy looked like a Mercedes Benz, rushing for 190 yards, the most ever for an Alabama quarterback, and the Crimson Tide defeated Mississippi State, 24-7.

Watching from the opposite sideline was Emory Bellard, who had invented the wishbone formation when he was an assistant coach at Texas. "We played a dadgum great game and lost by 17 points," he said. "What does that tell you? It tells me we played a dadgum great game against a dadgum great team."

Bryant was concerned that his team was not winning by greater margins. The Tide was in a mild slump.

"We're struggling like somebody trying to hit a Bob Gibson fastball," said Bryant, a baseball fan. "I think we've got to pick up the pace, do some hitting during the week. I don't care how great a hitter is, Rod Carew or whomever, he has to take a little batting practice from time to time."

The Tide's next big test was Louisiana State, always a tough opponent in Baton Rouge. It was rainy, windy and cold when the Alabama players arrived at Tiger Stadium, where they got anything but a warm reception. The chanting LSU fans formed an unruly tunnel through which the players had to walk from the buses to the dressing room.

Halfback/fullback Billy Jackson (33) pounded opposing defenders, opening the door for Alabama's many elusive running backs.

"It's just like Wilcox said it'd be," Lyles said. "They're surly and rude. They're wanting our hides."

Most of the 73,708 fans were in high spirits after a scoreless first half that saw Alabama placekicker Alan McElroy miss two field goals. But with its offense stymied by a wicked weather-aided LSU defense, Alabama turned up its own defense a few extra notches. LSU managed only 67 yards rushing and 97 yards passing. Only twice did the Tigers cross the 50-yard line, never getting beyond the 42, as Alabama posted its fourth shutout of the year.

"That's the night we proved an old fact," Braggs said. "If a team doesn't score against you, it can't beat you."

The decisive points came in the third quarter, when McElroy showed that the third time is the charm by booting a 27-yard field goal.

At halftime, the other guys told me not to get down on myself," McElroy reflected on what became a national championship-saving field goal. "The offensive guys said they'd get me another chance. When it came, well, I was determined to get that darn football through the uprights. I knew three points would be enough the way our defense was playing."

The defense refused to buckle and Alabama im-

Alabama was already well on its way to a national title when former Tide quarterback Joe Namath (left) and comedian Bob Hope (center) visited Tuscaloosa to film a segment of an upcoming television special with Coach Bear Bryant.

proved to 9-0.

"I'm proud of them again," Bryant said after the game. "It's hard to understand how I feel unless you've played or tried to coach in Tiger Stadium. It's a different world, one I wish every player and coach could experience at least once. It's loud. It's hostile. When you're Alabama and you're ranked Number 1 and haven't been whipped in a while, it's a frightening thing.

"I'm old and tired. And wet and cold. I'm ready to get back to Tuscaloosa."

After returning home, Alabama coasted to a 30-0 victory over Miami (Fla.), which had upset Penn State in its previous outing. The pass-happy Hurricanes surrendered five interceptions to a defense that seemed to be getting better by the moment.

"I remember reading a press clipping in the dressing room before the game," McNeal said. "Their pass receivers said they could beat our secondary deep all afternoon. Well, they didn't even score."

That same day, Auburn whipped Georgia, leaving Alabama as the only undefeated team in the SEC race. With only its season-ending showdown with intrastate rival Auburn remaining, the Tide had a clear shot at the league title and automatic Sugar Bowl berth—unless it lost to the Tigers. In that event, 'Bama would finish in a three-way tie with Georgia and Auburn, and the Sugar Bowl bid would go to Georgia. The Bulldogs had four nonconference losses, but an SEC-Sugar Bowl rule required the co-champion that had played in the bowl most recently ('Bama) to step aside. NCAA probation removed Auburn from the bowl picture.

So, the defending Sugar Bowl-champion and No. 1-ranked Tide could return to New Orleans only by beating Auburn. The intricacies of the bowl-selection process, however, were of little interest to Bryant.

"If we don't beat Auburn," he said about an 8-2 team, "we don't deserve to go to a bowl." As if that jab at the Tigers wasn't enough, Bryant later said, "If we can't beat Auburn, I'd just as soon stay home (from the bowl game) and plow." Auburn fans, who hadn't had an "Iron Bowl" victory to celebrate since 1972 and were sensitive to remarks about their school's agricultural heritage, weren't amused.

Bryant continued his whimsical ways just before the game. As he walked around the playing field with his players, who were still in street clothes, the coach was greeted by Auburn students seated in their cheering section at Legion Field in Birmingham. "Plow, Bear, plow," they chanted. "Plow, Bear, plow." Hearing that, the coach instructed Charley Thornton, the Tide's assistant athletic director for sports information, to get in front of

The 1979 Crimson Tide: Front row (left to right) —Buddy Holt, Woody Umphrey, Keith Pugh, Don Jacobs, Alan McElroy, Jerrill Sprinkle, Jim Bob Harris, Steadman Shealy, Ken Coley, Michael Landrum, Alan Gray, Tommy Wilcox, David Reeves, Ricky Tucker, Jeremiah Castille, Ken Simon. Second row—Jim Haney, Benny Perrin, Joe Jones, Tom Spencer, Don McNeal, Ben Orcutt, Darryl White, Billy Jackson, Al Blue, Jeff Fagan, Ricky Rozzell, Earl Collins, Charley Williams, E.J. Junior, Mitch Ferguson, Major Ogilvie, Mike Clements, John Hill, Steve Whitman, trainer Chip Miller. Third row—Manager Tom Connor, Byron Braggs, Mark Nix, Bobby Smith, Randy Scott, Gary DeNiro, Barry Smith, Wiley Barnes, Steve Mott, Bob Dasher, Joe Robbins, Scott Allison, Jim Bunch, Danny Holcombe, Vince Cowell, Gary Bramblett, Bill Searcey, Mike Brock, Bob Cayavec, Eddie McCombs, David Hannah, manager Danny Cates. Fourth row—Doug Collins, Buddy Aydelette, Tim Clark, Mike Pitts, Keith Marks, Larry Brown, John Mauro, Joe Beazley, Ry Ogilvie, Bart Krout, Tim Travis, Russ Wood, Thomas Boyd, Warren Lyles, Scott Homan, Curtis McGriff, Robbie Jones, Jackie Cline, John Lancaster.

him and lean forward. Then he took Thornton by the hands, making him a figurative mule, and acted as if he were plowing. The rival fans cheered wildly.

Before long, it was time to get down to business. After the Tide established a 14-3 halftime lead, the Tigers took advantage of four Alabama fumbles to take the lead, 18-17, early in the fourth quarter. Sugar Bowl officials were nervous.

Alabama players, on the other hand, were composed when they looked at an unfriendly scoreboard with 11:31 remaining in the game and studied the end zone 82 yards away. Despite its ineffectiveness in the third quarter, the Tide offense was confident.

"When Auburn took the lead, I had the greatest feeling in the world," said Bunch, the tackle from Virginia who starred in an all-senior offensive line. "I knew then we had the challenge we needed. I never thought about losing. None of us did. In the huddle we looked at each other with confident expressions. We knew we could drive the ball down their throats. When adversity presents itself, a champion fights back."

It took Alabama only seven plays to steady its national championship course. A 15-yard unnecessary roughness penalty against suddenly reeling Auburn helped the cause, and Shealy scored the decisive touchdown on an eight-yard run. The quarterback capped the scoring with another run for a two-point conversion.

"They're good folks," Bryant said about his players before accepting an invitation from the Sugar Bowl to play sixth-ranked Arkansas. "They've got class. They've been down some this season, but they've fought back."

The next day, Bryant taped his weekly TV highlights show in Birmingham. He sang "Love Lifted Me" between takes. He looked tired but happy. "I swear, this team makes me feel young and spry again," he said.

Bryant definitely had reason to feel that way after a 24-9 victory over Arkansas in the Sugar Bowl. The Tide, which won its 21st consecutive game in New Orleans, threw the figurative kitchen sink at the Razorbacks, including two quick kicks, and left no doubt about its superiority. Alabama was the national champion—again.

"I'm pleased we successfully defended our national championship," Bryant said. "But I'm not surprised. It's a team that proved itself all season. It's a team that had its back to the wall a few times and fought back. It's a team of character. It's a team that paid the price for the accomplishment."

Bryant was asked in his office that early January afternoon if paying the price included that blistering day in August when his players received a lecture on the practice field from their troubled leader.

"That's where they came together," Bryant said. "That's when they became real football players."

Alabama, 1979

ROAD TO GREATNESS

1979 RESULTS (12-0)

Opponent	Score	Opp. Record	Opp. Bowl Game
at Georgia Tech	30-6	4-6-1	
*Baylor	45-0	8-4-0	Peach (W)
at Vanderbilt	66-3	1-10-0	
Wichita State	38-0	1-10-0	
at Florida	40-0	0-10-1	
*Tennessee	27-17	7-5-0	Bluebonnet (L)
Virginia Tech	31-7	5-6-0	
Mississippi State	24-7	3-8-0	
at LSU	3-0	7-5-0	Tangerine (W)
Miami (Fla.)	30-0	5-6-0	
*Auburn	25-18	8-3-0	
SUGAR BOWL			
Arkansas	**24-9**	**10-2-0**	

*At Birmingham, Ala.

FACTS AND FIGURES

The Crimson Tide was dominant in 1979, albeit against many less-than-formidable foes. The combined record of the opposition was 59-75-2 for a weak .441 winning percentage. . . . Three Alabama opponents combined for two wins, 30 losses and one tie that season, and the Tide rolled over them by a combined score of 144-3. . . . 'Bama blanked five teams in 1979. . . . The Tide won seven of 12 contests by three touchdowns or more. . . . 'Bama's average margin of victory over its five opponents with winning records (four of which went to bowl games) was 16 points. . . . The Tide went 3-0 against teams that finished in the final Top 20 poll of either the Associated Press or United Press International. . . . The '79 Tide was the last Alabama team to go undefeated. . . . Offensively, the Tide ranked fourth in rushing and eighth in scoring among the nation's Division I-A schools. . . . The key to Alabama's success was its tough defense, which ranked first in scoring defense, second in total and passing defense and fifth in rushing defense. . . . Don McNeal was named to The Sporting News' 1979 All-America team. . . . Offensive tackle Jim Bunch was a consensus All-America. . . . Bear Bryant once called Bunch the "quickest, most forceful offensive lineman" he had ever coached. . . . Those receiving All-Southeastern Conference honors were McNeal, Bunch, Major Ogilvie, Dwight Stephenson, E.J. Junior, guard Mike Brock, quarterback Steadman Shealy, linebacker Thomas Boyd, defensive tackles David Hannah and Byron Braggs and safeties Jim Bob Harris and Tommy Wilcox. . . . Ogilvie was an academic All-America. . . . Shealy finished 10th in the 1979 Heisman Trophy balloting. . . . Junior and Stephenson were later named to the All-SEC 25-Year Team (1961-85). . . . Boyd led the '79 Tide in tackles with 92. . . . Alan McElroy, the team's placekicker and leading scorer, came to Tuscaloosa as a walk-on. . . . The '79 team produced 11 National Football League draft picks over the next two years, including first-rounders McNeal (1980) and Junior ('81).

STATISTICAL LEADERS

PASSING

	Att.	Comp.	Yards	TD	Pct.	Int.
Steadman Shealy	81	45	717	4	55.6	5

RUSHING

	Att.	Yards	Avg.	TD	Long
Steadman Shealy	152	791	5.2	11	64
Steve Whitman	126	653	5.2	3	22
Major Ogilvie	97	512	5.3	9	26
Don Jacobs	73	448	6.1	3	73

RECEIVING

	Rec.	Yards	Avg.	TD	Long
Keith Pugh	25	433	17.3	2	38

SCORING

	TD	FG	PAT	Points
Alan McElroy	0	15	32	77
Steadman Shealy	11	0	*1	68
Major Ogilvie	9	0	*2	58

*Two-point conversion.

KEY CHARACTERS

The Conductor

COACH: Paul (Bear) Bryant.

Record: 232-46-9, 25 years at Alabama.

Bryant may have been the finest coach ever to stalk the college football sidelines. . . . He won more games than any Division I-A coach in history, and his 38-season combined career record was 323-85-17, which computes to a .780 winning percentage. . . . Both the Associated Press and United Press International rated 19 of his 25 teams in the Top 10 of their final polls. . . . His teams finished No. 1 five times in AP polls and four times in UPI's final rankings. He won consensus national championships in 1961, 1964 and 1979. . . . Bryant is the only coach in college football history to win 100 games in a decade, compiling a 103-16-1 record during the 1970s. . . . He played end on Alabama's undefeated 1934 team with the great Don Hutson and later served as an assistant at both Alabama and Vanderbilt. . . . He got his first head coaching job in 1945 at Maryland, where he compiled a 6-2-1 mark in one season before moving to Kentucky. He finished with a 60-23-5 mark at Kentucky, guiding the 1950 Wildcats to their only Southeastern Conference title in history, and a 25-14-2 record at Texas A&M, his last stop before returning to Tuscaloosa. . . . At Alabama, Bryant was the SEC's Coach of the Year seven times. . . . The list of former Bryant assistants who later coached at major universities reads like a Who's Who: Bill Arnsparger, Jerry Claiborne, Paul Dietzel, Pat Dye, Danny Ford, Charley McClendon, Jack Pardee, Ray Perkins, Bum Phillips, Howard Schnellenberger, Jackie Sherrill and Gene Stallings, to name a few. . . . His last 24 teams played in postseason bowls, a record that likely will hold up for years. . . . He is a member of the College Football Hall of Fame. . . . Bryant died of a heart attack in 1983.

Personal Data:

Born: September 11, 1913, in Fordyce, Ark.
High School: Fordyce High.
College: Alabama.

The Supporting Cast

DEFENSIVE END: E.J. Junior.

Junior was a dominant force, ranging from sideline to sideline when playing linebacker and putting on a big pass rush when playing end. . . . He lettered from 1977-80 and was a unanimous consensus All-America his senior year. . . . Junior also was known as an excellent special-teams player, whether blocking kicks or opposing defenders on runbacks.

Personal Data:

Born: December 8, 1959, in Sallsburg, N.C.
High School: Maplewood High in Nashville.

CORNERBACK: Don McNeal.

McNeal played the game of his career in helping the Tide win the 1979 Sugar Bowl, breaking up two Penn State passes (one in the end zone), intercepting another pass in the end zone, recording four tackles and making a game-saving tackle at the Tide 1-yard line that set up an Alabama goal-line stand. . . . McNeal, who lettered from 1977-79, was considered an excellent man-to-man coverage defender and, like Junior, excelled as a special-teams player.

Personal Data:

Born: May 6, 1958, in Atmore, Ala.
High School: Escambia County High in Atmore.

RUNNING BACK: Major Ogilvie.

While his forte was running with the ball, he was considered an excellent blocker. . . . His seven-yard touchdown run was the game-winner in Alabama's 14-7 victory over Penn State in the 1979 Sugar Bowl. . . . He was a big-play man, as evidenced by his selection as 'Bama's most valuable player in both the '80 Sugar Bowl and '81 Cotton Bowl. . . . He ranks as the school's ninth all-time leading rusher with 1,725 career yards. . . . He lettered from 1977-80.

Personal Data:

Born: December 12, 1958, in Birmingham, Ala.
High School: Mountain Brook High in Birmingham.

CENTER: Dwight Stephenson.

Stephenson, who began his career as a defensive end, switched to center to take advantage of his size and speed. . . . He ranked among the best centers in the game and went on to a distinguished All-Pro career with the Miami Dolphins of the National Football League. . . . He won the 1979 Jacobs Award, given annually to the best blocker in the SEC. . . . He lettered from 1977-79.

Personal Data:

Born: November 20, 1957, in Murfreesboro, N.C.
High School: Hampton High in Hampton, Va.

FINAL 1979 WIRE SERVICE RANKINGS

ASSOCIATED PRESS		UNITED PRESS	
1. **ALABAMA**	11. Washington	1. **ALABAMA**	11. Washington
2. Southern Cal	12. Texas	2. Southern Cal	12. Brigham Young
3. Oklahoma	13. Brigham Young	3. Oklahoma	13. Texas
4. Ohio State	14. **Baylor**	4. Ohio State	14. North Carolina
5. Houston	15. North Carolina	5. Houston	15. **Baylor**
6. Florida State	16. **Auburn**	6. Pittsburgh	16. Indiana
7. Pittsburgh	17. Temple	7. Nebraska	17. Temple
8. **Arkansas**	18. Michigan	8. Florida State	18. Penn State
9. Nebraska	19. Indiana	9. **Arkansas**	19. Michigan
10. Purdue	20. Penn State	10. Purdue	20. Missouri

Bold face indicates Alabama opponent.

A Royal Party In Texas

Texas, 1969
By Mark Wangrin

When you visit the building in which James Street conducts his insurance business, you never have to ask which office belongs to the former University of Texas quarterback. All you need to do is glance inside the doorway and look at the walls. There are pictures of Street's children dressed in the burnt-orange color of the Texas Longhorns. There are plaques telling of his collegiate football and baseball heroics. There is a framed Sports Illustrated cover of Street running past an Arkansas lineman. And there is a painting.

A large painting.

Done in oil, the painting hangs right behind Street's desk and above the big chair with the burnt-orange upholstery. It depicts one of the biggest moments in Texas football history. Street, wearing number 16 as well as one of the most intense expressions imaginable, is looking straight at Longhorns Coach Darrell Royal. Over Street's head, almost as a label, is the Cotton Bowl scoreboard. It reads: ND 17, Texas 14. Texas is facing a fourth-and-two situation on the Notre Dame 10-yard line in the closing minutes of the 1970 Cotton Bowl game. The unbeaten and No. 1-ranked Longhorns are, in fact, 2 minutes and 26 seconds from losing.

Street, as was his trademark, pulled that one out. Eschewing a possible tying field goal from the reliable leg of Happy Feller, Royal called for a pass play and Street delivered with an eight-yard completion to split end Cotton Speyrer. The play, on which Speyrer made a desperate grass-level catch, set up Billy Dale's one-yard touchdown run that

Texas Coach Darrell Royal (right), blessed with a strong 1969 cast that included bruising fullback Steve Worster, had reason to smile.

preserved Texas' perfect season and clinched the national championship for the Longhorns.

A few years later, Street was pitching advertisements for Orange Power, his now-defunct Longhorn sports newsletter, to a big Texas alumnus in Houston. The alum asked Street if he owned a copy of that famous Cotton Bowl scene. Street thought he meant a photograph. Instead, the businessman handed over the giant painting. "I think you'll enjoy this more than I have," he said.

Now a successful insurance agent, Street sat in front of that painting in his West Austin office and talked about yesteryear. It was immediately apparent that the traits that had served Street so well on the gridiron were proving just as crucial to his post-football life. He remains personable, charismatic and tremendously confident. You can picture him selling an annuity to a bus driver as deftly as he sold a play to a Longhorn teammate.

Street finds his current situation ironic, recalling times when he was a student/athlete and insurance men would call him. He'd make appointments just to get the agents off his back and then not show up. The James Street of today is the prototypical salesman. Among his many attributes is an ability to talk. Boy, can he talk. And he gets people to listen.

"Our team personality probably took on Street's," said Speyrer, now a securities broker. "He was a dedicated, never-say-die type with a flamboyant flair. He was kind of an overachiever. James wasn't big or fast or didn't have a great arm. All he did was beat people."

All Texas did in 1969 was beat people—often and badly. For a while, starting halfback Ted Koy recalled, the Longhorns' second-teamers ranked higher in the national statistical tables because they got more playing time. The Horns' defense never allowed more than 17 points in a game and the offense, confounding the opposition with the innovative wishbone attack, scored 45 or more points six times.

Texas had all the necessary ingredients in 1969. First, the Longhorns had Street at quarterback. What you mainly need to know about Street, as Royal was quick to point out, was that he started 20 football games for Texas and the Longhorns won all 20 of them. Behind Street were Koy and Jim Bertelsen at the halfback slots and Steve Worster at fullback. They ran behind an offensive line anchored by All-America tackle Bob McKay and also featuring All-Southwest Conference tackle Bobby Wuensch. When defenses ganged up to stop the run, Street passed to big-play receivers Speyrer and Randy Peschel, the tight end.

Defensively, Texas boasted exceptional players in end Bill Atessis, tackle Leo Brooks and linebacker Glen Halsell. Also a cut above were linebacker Scott Henderson and defensive backs Tom Campbell, Danny Lester and Freddie Steinmark.

Most of all, Texas had Darrell Royal.

Ask his former players what stands out about Royal and they'll reflect on how the coach could remember names of players' family members long after the athletes' football careers had ended and how he never had to tell his players to quiet down when he entered a room.

"Even if you weren't looking at him, you could hear the quietness come through the room," Street recalled. "It sounds funny, but you could. You knew 'Daddy' was in the room."

Reared in Hollis, Okla., a town of 3,000 just across the Texas border, Royal endured a childhood filled with the poverty and misfortune of the Dust Bowl. Athletics proved his diversion and he excelled in football, leading Hollis High School to an undefeated season.

After a stint in the Army Air Corps during World War II, Royal played for Oklahoma, Texas' bitter rival from across the Red River, starring as a 160-pound quarterback. He set—and still holds—the record for the longest punt return (96 yards) in Sooners' history. After graduation, Royal moved around as a coach, serving one-year stints as an assistant at North Carolina State, Tulsa and Mississippi State before taking over in 1953 as coach of the Edmonton Eskimos of the Canadian Football League.

In 1954, Royal accepted the top job at Mississippi State. He stayed in Starkville for two years before moving on to Washington and coaching the Huskies for one season. Then, when Texas Coach Ed Price was released after directing the Longhorns to a 1-9 season in 1956, Royal was poised to take his seventh coaching job in eight seasons.

Royal, though, wasn't Texas' first pick. Bobby Dodd of Georgia Tech turned down the job after giving the post serious consideration, and Duffy Daugherty's name also was bandied about.

Royal supposedly was on the outside looking in until given a chance to make his pitch to University of Texas officials. A convincing pitch it was. Four-hours after landing in Austin on December 18, 1956, Royal became the 24th coach in Texas' fabled football history.

Royal was an immediate success. In his first five seasons as the Longhorns' man in charge, he guided the Steers to four bowl appearances and an overall 39-13-2 record. Then adversity struck.

In August 1962, a fourth-team sophomore guard named Reggie Grob and two other Longhorns collapsed from heat exhaustion during workouts. A refrigerated suit helped Grob through the first night, but doctors discovered that his liver and kidneys had suffered irreversible damage. Eighteen days later, after being flown to a Dallas hospital for a specialized operation, Grob died.

The Longhorns' offensive line was well manned by the likes of tackles Bobby Wuensch (50) and Bob McKay (center) and guard Randy Stout.

Steve Worster used his superior size to run over defenders and averaged 4.8 yards per carry in 1969 while scoring nine touchdowns.

For those few days when Royal wasn't coaching his football team, he was spending time with Grob and his family at the hospital. He came to the conclusion that coaching wasn't worth such a catastrophe and almost quit. Almost.

"All those things go through your mind," Royal said. "If we hadn't run wind sprints. If we hadn't done this or done that. If we hadn't been practicing football. Then you get back to thinking realistically and take the percentages and see the good that's done. You think about quitting it, but then you start thinking about driving cars, thinking about the people hurt driving cars. Do you quit? No matter what you quit, you can't stop the process. The process of life."

The car-driving analogy is a particularly personal and chilling one for Royal. Two of his children have been killed in motor-vehicle accidents.

Royal stayed on, and soon things were upbeat on the Austin campus. Very upbeat. In 1963, the Longhorns, sparked by the play of All-America lineman Scott Appleton, Tommy Ford, future Texas mentor David McWilliams and rising star Tommy Nobis, rolled to an undefeated season and their first national championship.

After a 9-1 regular-season mark in 1964, Texas stumbled to the first of three consecutive four-loss seasons. Not horrendous, but not good enough for Longhorn standards. Still, when the Oklahoma athletics council recommended that Royal take over the Sooners' struggling program after the 1965 season, Texas backers were worried. Royal finally withdrew, and Oklahoma hired Jim Mackenzie.

After Texas' three sub-par years, Royal's offensive backfield coach, Emory Bellard, tinkered with Texas' wing-T offense in an attempt to come up with a scheme that would make use of the Longhorns' stable of quality backs without allowing defenses to load up on one side of the formation.

Bellard's concoction combined the Houston veer and the triple-option that Texas A&M had been running from the I-formation. Bellard rounded up some of his son's high school buddies to put the concept into action. He liked what he saw. Now all the Longhorns had to do was put the as-yet-unnamed formation to work.

Texas proceeded to battle Houston to a 20-20 tie in the 1968 season opener, after which Houston Post sportswriter Mickey Herskowitz, duly noting the shape of the Longhorns' formation, dubbed the alignment the "wishbone." It was more than a wish. It quickly became hard reality for defenders, who had to stop the options skills of the Horns' quarterback, senior Bill Bradley at the outset of the season, and at the same time contain the hard running of Chris Gilbert, also a senior, and underclassmen Koy and Worster.

Texas rolled to a 8-1-1 regular-season mark in '68, losing only to Texas Tech in the second game of the year. It was during that loss to the Red Raiders that Bradley lost his quarterback job to a brash junior named James Street. Two weeks later, in a 26-20 come-from-behind triumph over archrival Oklahoma, Street secured his position by leading Texas on a game-winning, 85-yard touchdown drive.

"You've seen that shot of him (Street) on the sideline when I'm talking to him before that crucial play in the Cotton Bowl?" Royal wondered aloud almost 20 years later. "If you want an insight into James Street, look at that photograph and look at his eyes and see where they're focused. He's not wandering into space. His eyes were glued onto me and every word I said and always were.

"James was a chatterbox and he'd b.s. around. But the seconds before snapping the football, when it got down to the meat of the thing, it was no-nonsense. His eyes would get wide and he'd focus on the job at hand. You know, (golfer Lee) Trevino has that. Trevino laughs and jokes with people, but when Lee approaches the ball, he's able to block out all that chatter."

Speyrer, recalling Street's intensity, remembered an incident when he played golf with the Texas signal-caller. Speyrer's ball was 120 yards from the pin and he needed to hole his next shot to beat Street.

Halfback Jim Bertelsen (35) was Texas' main man on the ground, picking up 740 yards while averaging 7.1 per carry in '69.

Considering the odds, Cotton bent over to pick up the ball. Street was appalled.

"If you don't want me to hit you over the head with my 2-iron, you'll play it out," Speyrer recalled Street as saying. "It might go in the hole."

There was the other side of Street, the one the coaching staff seldom witnessed. Gung-ho around the coaches, he was the team comic who could get away with saying anything and ripping teammates about subjects others wouldn't touch.

On one preseason press day, Street pulled a fast one on the gathered sportswriters. One of the writers, looking for a good angle or at least some hard news, asked Street about a bandage on his leg. Street didn't miss a beat.

"A dog bit me," he offered. "I was a mail carrier in Boulder (Colo.) this summer. They're still checking me for rabies. They think I've been acting a little crazy."

The writers bought it. Street milked it for a few seconds. "Aw, I was just kidding," he conceded. "I got it hurt in practice yesterday."

One writer confessed that his notes had read "dog," "mail carrier," "Boulder"—and then "phooey."

That fun-loving nature stayed with Street. After his Texas career, he had a brief fling as a sportscaster. He'd mispronounce names and once, after a Texas victory over Texas Tech, he forgot the score. So he made one up.

"He'd give scores like '3-2, 8-5, 7-5,' " Speyrer said. "He wouldn't give the teams or who was ahead. I hope he did it as a joke."

When it came to football, there was no joking around. Any description of Street—nicknamed "Slick"—alluded to his standing as a consummate leader. He often would guess the next play in the huddle before it was sent in from the coaching staff. He would ride McKay—"I was all the time on his ass"—while at the same time taking the back-patting approach with Speyrer. "I'd say, 'It's my fault, buddy, I'll get it down next time,' " Street reminisced about his relationship with Speyrer. "It may have been a pass he could have caught. But the next time I'd throw him one, he'd make a circus catch."

In the huddle, Street projected himself as more than a quarterback to his teammates.

"I'd try to sell them on the play," Street said. " 'It's going to work because you're going to block, McKay. It's going to work because you're going to hang on to the ball, Woo (Worster). Right 54. Break.' "

Sometimes Street delivered his sales pitch without mentioning the product.

"One time against Oklahoma State, James called the formation we were going to use, then he got wrapped up giving us a pep talk," Koy said. "Finally, he gave us the snap count and we broke the

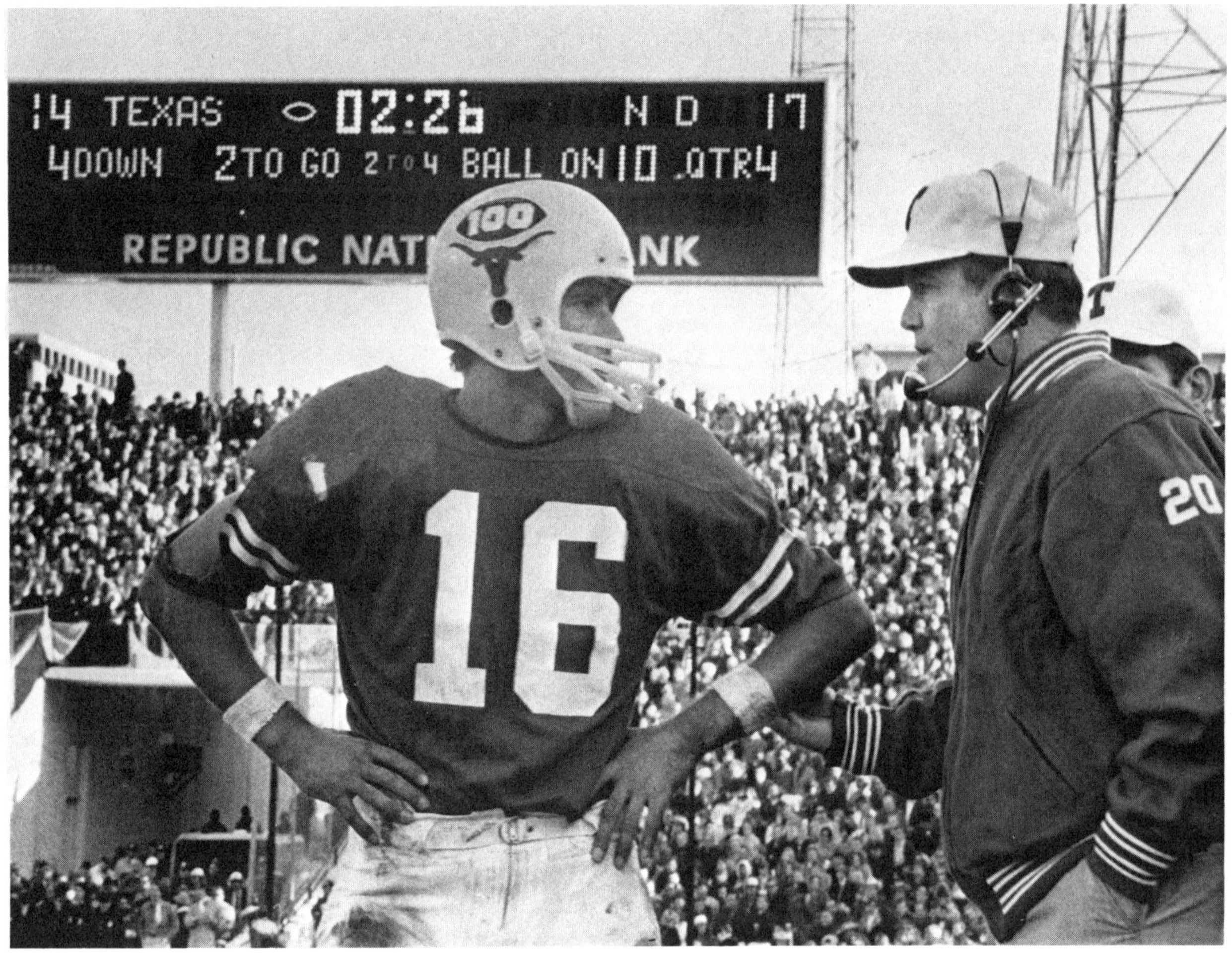

Quarterback James Street, the Longhorns' Mr. Clutch, talks with Coach Darrell Royal as the scoreboard reflects their late-game plight in the 1970 Cotton Bowl.

huddle. We all took a step and then remembered he hadn't called the play we were going to run. That's James for you."

Not everyone was in the mood for sermonizing, however.

"Sometimes Bob McKay threatened to punch him in the mouth if he didn't shut up and call the play," Speyrer said.

Street wasn't just a football star. In the spring, he pitched for the Texas baseball team, for whom he was a strikeout specialist. His career average of 10.39 strikeouts per game ranks fourth behind Longhorn leader Burt Hooton and ahead of a Texas alum by the name of Roger Clemens. Street, who fashioned a 1.86 earned-run average over three seasons at Texas, threw two no-hitters, including a seven-inning perfect game against Texas Tech a little more than three months after the January 1, 1970, Cotton Bowl triumph over Notre Dame.

If Street had a counterpart on the Texas defense, it had to be Glen Halsell. The moon-faced linebacker with the prematurely receding hairline probably was the focus of as many stories as he was tackles. Everyone on the team seemed to have a yarn about Halsell. After all, Halsell allegedly was the guy who:

- Fulfilled a date's request that he drop her off at the door of her dormitory by driving his car up the steps of the front entrance before letting her out.
- At a time when it was stylish to wear animal pins, pinned a dead bird to his shirt and wore it to class.
- Bit the heads off frogs. Such behavior no doubt resulted from a dare, teammates believe, although Halsell apparently didn't need much reason for such antics.
- Was terrified of armadillos. Armed with that knowledge, teammates would put live armadillos in the drawers under his bed. "He'd go crazy," Brooks said. "It would scare the hell out of him."

Today, Halsell is a lawyer in Odessa, Texas.

There was, in fact, no shortage of characters on the 1969 Texas team. Center Forrest Wiegand, for example, was acknowledged as the team hypochondriac.

"I always used to say, 'I'll tape an aspirin on your

head, Wiegand, and you'll be OK,' " Street remembered. "Then we'd drag him back to the huddle."

There were the Campbell twins, Mike and Tom, sons of head defensive coach Mike Campbell, of whom Brooks remembers, "If they weren't fighting someone else, they were fighting each other."

Also in the forefront were Speyrer, who liked to drive golf balls down the hall of his dorm; Happy Feller, whose name described his personality and whose naivete was legendary, and Bob McKay, who was so adept at finding "activities" to keep the players busy that Street dubbed him the Longhorns' "recreational director."

"I remember assistant coach Bill Ellington once told us someone asked him what type of team we were going to have," said lineman Brooks, reflecting on his rambunctious teammates, "and he told them, 'Not worth a damn. They haven't torn anything up yet.' "

Bertelsen and Koy had their moments, too. Recalling his first meeting with the quiet Bertelsen, Speyrer said that "for the first 30 minutes, I thought he was a mute." Street remembers another side of the Hudson, Wis., product. Bertelsen once fumbled without being hit on a sure touchdown run, which would have been his fourth TD of the game. For a long time, Bertelsen lay on the turf. Street, thinking he was injured, rushed to his side. Bertelsen looked up and said, "How's the crowd taking it?" And there was the night that Bertelsen and Speyrer, finding the gate to the stadium open, drove onto the brand-new artificial surface and did "doughnuts" with a truck.

Koy was the straight arrow. Seemingly. "He just did it (felt his oats) at 3 o'clock in the morning," McKay cracked, "and nobody got caught."

Still, it was discipline that saw the Texas Longhorns through. The success for the 1969 season was germinated in the spring of 1968 after the third straight subpar season, when Royal implemented a set of new and strict rules, ranging from a curfew to grooming standards. He also accelerated the Medina Sessions, an incredibly demanding series of drills named after trainer Frank Medina and performed principally while wearing sweat clothes in a heated room. For 45 minutes, the Longhorns jumped rope, ran sprints, climbed rope, hit the punching bag and ran stadium steps. For members of the "Fat Man Club," there was an extra session with 20-pound vests.

"I remember walking through the 'Fat Man' workout once and they were doing situps," Koy recalled. "Frank was sitting there saying, 'Up 499, up 500, (Tommy) Matula's not doing it right, 10 more. Up 501, up 502 . . . . '

"The only reason we're laughing now is that we don't have to go through it," Koy said with a smile. "If I was 20 years old again, I'd be turning white now."

By 1969, Street had developed into a quarterback capable of taking his team to a national title.

The Longhorns parlayed discipline, conditioning and Street's emergence into a banner 1968 season, one capped with a Cotton Bowl rout of Tennessee. Still, Royal had mixed feelings as the Horns prepared for 1969.

"I think we'll be one of those to contend with, but I sure don't feel real good that we're going to be an outstanding football team," Royal said in September. "I think it would be wishful thinking to think we could pick right up and be the same type of offensive football team that we were last year." (The '68 Longhorns ranked second nationally in rushing and sixth in total offense.)

At the same time, Royal liked what the success of 1968 meant. "We've got the swagger back in our walk and that means a lot," Royal said. "You know what I mean by that, don't you? That 9-1-1 last year just kind of helps you. You take a salesman who's made nine straight sales and he feels pretty good when he goes after the 10th one. It's not cockiness,

Freddie Steinmark, the Longhorn who had a leg amputated late in the 1969 season, toured the Astrodome 11 days after the operation was performed in Houston. The Astrodome message board saluted the honored guest.

it's confidence."

Texas opened its 1969 season with a 17-0 conquest of California and then avenged its only loss of 1968 with a 49-7 dismantling of Texas Tech. A rout of Navy, a come-from-behind victory over Oklahoma and cakewalks against Rice, Southern Methodist, Baylor and Texas Christian followed. Then came an off week. And some great news.

Heading into the collegiate schedule of Saturday, November 22, the Associated Press' football poll listed Ohio State, Texas and Arkansas, all unbeaten in eight games, as 1-2-3. United Press International had the same top two teams, but listed Arkansas fourth behind Penn State.

"Ohio State had to lose," said Royal, pointing to the Buckeyes' November 22 game at Michigan, a contest that would conclude the regular season for Coach Woody Hayes' team. "They were ranked No. 1 (and had held the top spot since the beginning of the season). People forget that. They just think we walked on through. Prior to that Ohio State-Michigan game, Ohio State had the hammer."

The defending national champion Buckeyes, whose smallest margin of victory to that juncture of the '69 season had been 27 points, had their 22-game winning streak snapped by Michigan on a day in which Texas and Arkansas rested in anticipation of Thanksgiving Day games against Texas A&M and Texas Tech, respectively. After Michigan's 24-12 upset of the Buckeyes, the next AP poll had Texas No. 1 and Arkansas No. 2, with Ohio State tumbling to fourth behind Penn State; UPI rated Texas No. 1, but placed Arkansas at No. 3 behind Penn State.

Texas and Arkansas responded well to their ascent up the rankings ladder. A 63-yard run on the fourth play of the game by sophomore Bertelsen sent Texas winging to a 49-12 victory over Texas A&M at College Station, while Arkansas blitzed Texas Tech, 33-0, in Little Rock. Now, in the final regular-season game for each club, the Longhorns and Razorbacks would square off December 6 in Fayetteville.

Before the season, ABC-TV had approached Texas and Arkansas about moving their game, scheduled for October 18, to the end of the season, after everyone else had played. While both teams had been projected as strong contenders for national honors, no one could have conceived of ABC's master stroke. When the teams got together in December at Razorback Stadium, Texas was No. 1 in both polls and Arkansas was No. 2 in the AP ratings (and still No. 3 in UPI's rankings).

"It makes them look wiser than a tree full of owls," Royal said of ABC officials and their rescheduling request, which obviously had been met with approval from both universities.

Thirty-thousand people turned out for a Longhorns pep rally that included taped messages from newsman Walter Cronkite, astronaut Alan Bean and actor Fess Parker, all of whom had attended the Austin school. As the tension mounted, Arkansas Coach Frank Broyles, who would retire from the coaching ranks on the same night as Royal in 1976, said, "Frankly, I don't believe the fellow who invented football ever intended it to be that big."

Texas fell behind early in the big game and trailed 14-0 entering the fourth quarter. On the first play of the final period, Street broke loose on a 42-yard touchdown run. He then ran for two points. "We felt that was the time for the two-point conversion," said Royal, who had called for extra-point kicks after every other Longhorn TD of the '69 season. "If we had missed it, we could have still gone for two again and gotten a tie. . . . "

On a fourth-and-three play at the Horns' 43 with 4 minutes, 47 seconds remaining in the game, Royal called a pass. "Every now and then you have to . . . pick a number," Royal philosophized. "You don't use logic and reason. You just play a hunch. I never considered punting." The Texas coach had picked the right number. Street and Peschel hooked up on a 44-yard completion that carried to the Arkansas 13. An 11-yard run by Koy and Bertelsen's two-yard burst tied the score, and Feller's conversion kick moved Texas into a 15-14 lead. Tom Campbell's interception of a Bill Montgomery pass in the final minute and a half of the game wrapped up the contest for Texas.

After the game, President Richard Nixon congratulated the Longhorns in the locker room. Billy Graham was there, too.

With the runs by Street and Bertelsen accounting for both of Texas' touchdowns against the Razorbacks, the Longhorns finished the regular season with 51 touchdowns on the ground. The Horns' average of 5.1 rushing TDs per game tied an NCAA Division I-A record established by Oklahoma in 1956. Royal's team gained a nation-leading 363 yards per game rushing in 1969, ranked fifth in total offense with 472.1 yards per contest and finished third in scoring offense with 41.4 points per outing.

Bertelsen was Texas' main man on the ground, rushing for 740 yards, gaining 7.1 yards per carry and running for 13 touchdowns. Worster averaged 4.8 yards a crack and scored nine TDs rushing while netting 649 ground yards. As proof positive of the Steers' depth, nine Longhorns in all rushed for more than 200 yards.

Street ranked fourth on Texas' rushing chart, following Koy's 441-yard total with a 412-yard figure. Additionally, he completed 40 of 81 pass attempts for 699 yards and three scores (all of his TD throws going to Speyrer).

Feller was indeed Mr. Reliable, converting on 43 of 45 extra-point kicks and hitting on six of eight field-goal attempts.

Texas was almost as good defending against the rush as it was grinding out yards on the ground. The Longhorns allowed only 90 yards per game rushing, the eighth lowest figure in the nation. In the total-defense charts for the 1969 season, the Horns ranked sixth nationally with 226 yards allowed overall per game. And Texas finished sixth in scoring defense by permitting an average of just 10.2 points.

The glow emanating from the Arkansas game and the entire regular season didn't last long. On the Tuesday after the momentous game in Fayetteville, Royal was in New York City with tri-captains Koy, Street and Halsell to accept the National Football Foundation's MacArthur Trophy (awarded to the nation's top team) when he heard the news about Freddie Steinmark. The small Longhorn safety, who had been slowed up because of what was believed to be a bruised thigh, had bone cancer. That Friday, Steinmark's left leg was amputated.

Royal said he'll never forget seeing the purple lines drawn on Steinmark's leg to guide the X-ray technicians. "When we found out, we were flabbergasted," Mike Campbell Sr. said. "They said there was just muscle holding the bone together."

Steinmark never indicated that the disease was getting the better of him. When his hair fell out, he got an earring and teammates began calling him "The Jolly Green Giant."

When the Campbells played golf with Steinmark several months after his surgery, Mike Sr. recalled how Steinmark could balance on one leg and still smack the ball great distances. "He'd get very upset if he couldn't hit a golf shot," Tom said. "That's the only time I ever saw him show emotion." (On June 6, 1971, Steinmark died. Two years later, in September, defensive backfield mate Danny Lester was killed in a crash on a rain-slick Texas freeway.)

Texas, shaken by the Steinmark situation but showing tremendous resolve, followed up its memorable triumph over Arkansas by rallying from a 10-point deficit—the Street-to-Speyrer pass play with 2:26 to play turned the tide—and knocking off Notre Dame, 21-17, in the Cotton Bowl. The Fighting Irish were playing in their first bowl game in 45 years.

The national championship that the Longhorns locked up in the Cotton Bowl was the second in the school's history, the '63 team having accounted for the other title. The 1970 team added half-a-loaf, going undefeated in the regular season and thereby earning the No. 1 spot in UPI's final rankings, which at the time were released before bowl games. AP was now in its third consecutive year of waiting until after the bowl competition to take a final poll, and while Texas was atop AP's ratings entering a

The 1969 Longhorns: Front row (left to right) : Coaches Leon Manley, Fred Akers, Willie Zapalac; Head Coach Darrell Royal; Coaches R.M. Patterson, Emory Bellard, Mike Campbell. Second row—Manager Jim Lemmon, Dean Campbell, Donnie Wigginton, Rob Schultz, Raymond Fontenot, Billy Dale, Steve Worster, Ted Koy, Tom Campbell, Sam McBrierty, Johnny Otahal, Will Wilson, Terry Collins, trainer Spanky Stephens. Third row—Manager Paul Hobbs, Jimmy Gunn, George Cobb, David Arledge, Mike Hutchings, Mike Campbell, Chris Young, Jay Cormier, Mike Dean, Bobby Mitchell, Greg Ploetz, Ronnie Tyler, David Keeton, Scooter Monzingo, manager Bill Hall. Fourth row—Manager James Cooke, Mike Speer, Jeff Zapalac, Travis Roach, Randy Stout, Dickie Johnston, Eddie Phillips, Ken Ehrig, Randy Peschel, James Street, Freddie Steinmark, David Richardson, Paul Kristynik, Dan Terwelp, Steve Adger, manager Bubba Simpson. Fifth row—Manager Mike Cave, Bo Anders, Rick Troberman, Randy Braband, Bob Huffman, Rick Martin, Bobby Callison, Jimmy Hull, Pat Macha, Jim Bertelsen, Stan Mauldin, Robert Paine, Rick Nabors, Happy Feller, trainer Roy Baldwin. Sixth row—Manager David Fox, Mack McKinney, Gary Rike, Jim Williamson, Leo Brooks, Bob McKay, Bill Zapalac, Scott Palmer, Carl White, Cotton Speyrer, Tommy Lee, Rob Layne, Danny Lester, trainer Jim Pippin. Seventh row—Johnny Robinson, Scott Henderson, Kevin Hutson, Donny Windham, Tommy Asaff, Bud Hudgins, Forrest Wiegand, Glen Halsell, Larry Webb, Sam Lawless, George McIngvale, Jack Rushing, David Ballew, manager Jimmy Kay. Eighth row—Tommy Woodard, Jerrell Bolton, Wayne Kirk, Bill Atessis, Bobby Wuensch, Charles Crawford, Tommy Matula, Sid Keasler, Jim Achilles, Paul Robichau, Robbie Patman, Bill Catlett, Tex Alshouse.

Cotton Bowl rematch against Notre Dame, the Horns slipped to No. 3 after falling to the Irish on January 1, 1971.

When people reminisce about the Texas Longhorns of this era, they focus on the 1969 team and its titanic struggle against Arkansas. A public television station in Austin still replays the game during fund-raising drives. "I wish they'd show a game we played well in," McKay said wistfully.

Street remembers visiting Las Vegas a few years after the Fayetteville thriller and being invited backstage to talk about the game with Elvis Presley. "Here's Bill Medley thinking Arkansas should have won and Elvis saying Texas should have won," Street said.

The impact of the game continues to astound Street.

"It seems to me when people talk about the Arkansas game, they always have a story to tell," he said. "I have people write who had heart attacks during the game and the first thing they asked when they came to in the hospital was, 'Who won?' It amazes me that people got that involved in it."

Nearly two decades later, fans are still involved in—and caught up with—the exploits of the 1969 Texas Longhorns.

Texas, 1969

ROAD TO GREATNESS

1969 RESULTS (11-0)

Opponent	Score	Opp. Record	Opp. Bowl Game
at California	17-0	5-5-0	
Texas Tech	49-7	5-5-0	
Navy	56-17	1-9-0	
*Oklahoma	27-17	6-4-0	
Rice	31-0	3-7-0	
at Southern Methodist	45-14	3-7-0	
Baylor	56-14	0-10-0	
Texas Christian	69-7	4-6-0	
at Texas A&M	49-12	3-7-1	
at Arkansas	15-14	9-2-0	Sugar (L)
COTTON BOWL			
Notre Dame	**21-17**	**8-2-1**	

*Dallas.

FACTS AND FIGURES

Coach Darrell Royal was named The Sporting News' 1969 Coach of the Year. . . . Offensive tackle Bob McKay won consensus All-America honors in '69. . . . Besides McKay, Longhorns receiving All-Southwest Conference designation were split end Cotton Speyrer, offensive tackle Bobby Wuensch, quarterback James Street, fullback Steve Worster, defensive end Bill Atessis, defensive tackle Leo Brooks and linebacker Glen Halsell. . . . Only two of Texas' regular-season opponents wound up with winning records. Including Cotton Bowl foe Notre Dame, the Longhorns' opposition put together a 47-64-2 record, which computes to a .425 winning percentage. . . . In only one stretch—its regular-season finale against Arkansas and the ensuing bowl date with the Fighting Irish—did Texas play consecutive games against teams that finished the season with winning marks. Fittingly, those games proved the stiffest tests for the Steers, who slipped past the Razorbacks by one point and emerged as four-point winners against the Irish. . . . The Longhorns' efficient offense rated among the most potent of the decade. Steers scored 45 or more points in six games en route to their first unbeaten season since 1963. Team averaged a nation-leading 363 yards on the ground and was fifth-best in the country in total offense. . . . Defense did its part, too. The Longhorns ranked sixth in both scoring defense and total defense and were No. 8 in rushing defense. . . . Tough everywhere, Texas was downright belligerent on its home turf in Austin. In the five games played at Memorial Stadium, the Longhorns averaged 52.2 points compared with the opposition's 9.0 mark. Closest call—so to speak—was a 31-point verdict against Rice.

STATISTICAL LEADERS

PASSING

	Att.	Comp.	Yards	TD	Pct.	Int.
James Street	81	40	699	3	49.4	10
Eddie Phillips	29	14	217	1	48.3	1

RUSHING

	Att.	Yards	Avg.	TD
Jim Bertelsen	104	740	7.1	13
Steve Worster	136	649	4.8	9
Ted Koy	84	441	5.3	4
James Street	76	412	5.4	5
Eddie Phillips	50	271	6.4	5

RECEIVING

	Rec.	Yards	Avg.	TD	Long
Cotton Speyrer	30	492	16.4	3	49
Randy Peschel	14	228	16.3	1	44
Ken Ehrig	10	167	16.7	1	51

SCORING

	TD	FG	PAT	Points
Jim Bertelsen	13	0	0	78
Happy Feller	0	6	43	61
Steve Worster	9	0	0	54
James Street	5	0	*1	32
Billy Dale	5	0	0	30
Eddie Phillips	5	0	0	30

*Two-point conversion.

KEY CHARACTERS

The Conductor

COACH: Darrell Royal.

Record: 167-47-5, 20 years at Texas.

Royal replaced Ed Price in 1957. . . . Seven of his teams won 10 or more games, 11 won or shared Southwest Conference championships and two (1963 and '69) captured consensus national championships. His 1970 Longhorns finished first in United Press International's final rankings. . . . Ten of his teams finished among the Top 10 in the final Associated Press poll and 11 in UPI's Top 10. . . . He coached 14 consensus All-Americas, including Longhorn greats Earl Campbell and Tommy Nobis, and guided Texas to 16 bowl games, including 10 Cotton Bowls, one Sugar Bowl and one Orange Bowl. . . . His Longhorns compiled a 5-5 record in Cotton Bowl games and played in the classic six consecutive seasons (1968-73). . . . He was named Coach of the Decade (1960s) by an ABC-TV poll conducted in 1970. . . . He began his football career as a player under Coach Bud Wilkinson at Oklahoma. . . . He served as an assistant at North Carolina State, Tulsa and Mississippi State before becoming head coach of the Edmonton team in the Canadian Football League in 1953. He became coach at Mississippi State in 1954 and took over at Washington two years later before moving to Austin after the 1956 season. . . . Among his Texas assistants was Emory Bellard, who is credited with inventing the wishbone formation. . . . Royal teams compiled a 17-3 mark against archrival Texas A&M, including a 10-game winning streak from 1957-66.

Personal Data:

Born: July 6, 1924, in Hollis, Okla.
High School: Hollis High.
College: Oklahoma.

The Supporting Cast

PLACEKICKER: Happy Feller.

Feller ranks as one of the Longhorns' finest kickers of all time. . . . He set a number of kicking records, many of which have since been broken, and was known as Mr. Reliable. . . . A long-distance threat, he set a Longhorn record (since broken) when he kicked a 53-yard field goal against Oklahoma in 1968. . . . He lettered from 1968-70.

Personal Data:

Born: June 13, 1949, in Fredericksburg, Tex.
High School: Fredericksburg High.

SPLIT END: Cotton Speyrer.

Speyrer's dramatic fourth-and-two catch of an eight-yard pass at the Notre Dame 10-yard line kept alive the Longhorns' winning drive in the 1970 Cotton Bowl, a victory that sealed the No. 1 spot in the final AP poll. . . . He led the Longhorns in receiving in both 1968 (26 catches) and 1969 (30). . . . He caught eight passes in a 1969 game against Oklahoma, tying him with three other players in the Longhorn record book. . . . Speyrer, who lettered from 1968-70, showed big-play ability as a sophomore when he caught touchdown passes of 78 and 79 yards against Tennessee in the 1969 Cotton Bowl, a 36-13 Texas victory.

Personal Data:

Born: April 29, 1949, in Port Arthur, Tex.
High School: Port Arthur High.

QUARTERBACK: James Street.

Street was a fiery leader who dominated the huddle and led by example. . . . He was 20-0 as a starter and closed his career by leading the Longhorns to their dramatic victory over Notre Dame in the 1970 Cotton Bowl and a consensus national championship. . . . He was known for his intense style and his ability to lead Texas to come-from-behind victories. . . . Street, who lettered in 1968 and '69, also pitched for the Longhorn baseball team and threw two no-hitters.

Personal Data:

Born: August 2, 1948, in Longview, Tex.
High School: Longview High.

FULLBACK: Steve Worster.

Worster was a consensus All-America in 1970. . . . He was a feared blocker out of Texas' wishbone formation, and his surprising speed allowed him to break the big play occasionally. . . . He finished fourth in the 1970 Heisman Trophy balloting. . . . Worster, who lettered from 1968-70, made a name for himself in 1968, his sophomore season, when he scored the winning touchdown in the Longhorns' 26-20 win over rival Oklahoma. . . . He rushed for 155 yards in the 1970 Cotton Bowl.

Personal Data:

Born: July 8, 1949, in Bridge City, Tex.
High School: Bridge City High.

FINAL 1969 WIRE SERVICE RANKINGS

ASSOCIATED PRESS		UNITED PRESS	
1. **TEXAS**	11. Nebraska	1. **TEXAS**	11. Tennessee
2. Penn State	12. Houston	2. Penn State	12. Nebraska
3. Southern Cal	13. UCLA	3. **Arkansas**	13. Mississippi
4. Ohio State	14. Florida	4. Southern Cal	14. Stanford
5. **Notre Dame**	15. Tennessee	5. Ohio State	15. Auburn
6. Missouri	16. Colorado	6. Missouri	16. Houston
7. **Arkansas**	17. West Virginia	7. Louisiana State	17. Florida
8. Mississippi	18. Purdue	8. Michigan	18. Purdue
9. Michigan	19. Stanford	9. **Notre Dame**	San Diego State
10. Louisiana State	20. Auburn	10. UCLA	West Virginia

Bold face indicates Texas opponent.

Woody and His Super Sophomores

Ohio State, 1968
By Paul Hornung

A Columbus, O., restaurant once sponsored a campus-area billboard featuring a picture of Woody Hayes with the caption: "In All The World, There's Only One!"

That generally applauded proclamation still serves as an appropriate salute to the colorful, complex and unique football coach who, in 28 rarely-a-dull-moment years, brought Ohio State four outright or shared national championships, 13 outright or shared Big Ten Conference titles and 205 victories (61 losses, 10 ties) while stamping himself as a beloved legend and hated foe—depending on one's college football affiliation.

After Hayes was relieved of his command in 1978 for punching a Clemson player in a startling Gator Bowl incident, former players organized a banquet exclusively for those who had played for or coached under him. More than 450 persons attended from all over the country. And to further demonstrate the feeling Hayes generated among his former players, Ohio State's greatest team, the national champions of 1968, put together a sizable endowment pledge to the university's scholarship fund in his name. The gesture only serves to punctuate an oft-repeated Hayes axiom: "You can't pay back, but you can pay forward."

Of course, the then-55-year-old Hayes was not the only one responsible for the Buckeyes' glorious 10-0 season of '68, which was climaxed by a 27-16 win over Southern California in the first battle of unbeaten teams in the 22 years that Big Ten and Pacific Eight Conference teams had been meeting in the Rose Bowl.

As with any "greatest team," there was a happy combination of ingredients. In addition to Hayes, the '68 Buckeyes had an exceptional staff of assistants, five of whom later would become head coaches; a sophomore class that Hayes termed "unquestionably the best we had ever recruited, and perhaps the best college team ever recruited"; a framework of solid upperclassmen who provided leadership and stability, and a "team concept" that defined the term.

But any analysis of 1968 begins with Hayes, the man behind the legend.

Wayne Woodrow Hayes, a native of Clifton, O., was a hard-nosed, tell-it-like-it-is individual who believed he could succeed only by outworking the opposition—14 to 16 hours a day, virtually 365 days a year. Football was the consuming centerpiece of his life and he expected similar, if not identical, dedication from the rest of his staff and players.

Yet he was amazingly well-read and impressively literate on a wide range of subjects. His specialty was history, specifically military history, which influenced his philosophies and coaching maneuvers on the football field. He was well-versed in current events and frequented Ohio State's faculty club, talking with professors from different fields. He also found time to sit in on class lectures, once even attending an operatic workshop in the School of Music.

Hayes, who left Miami of Ohio in 1951 to take the Ohio State coaching job, liked to point out that his teams didn't get "fatheaded, because they've got a mean old coach." And he often suggested that "anytime people start saying, 'Good old Woody,' it's all over." But, in reality, this self-styled curmudgeon image was merely a smokescreen for the soft-hearted Hayes who was a goodwill ambassador above and beyond the call of duty. He had immeasurable influence on his football players, but also helped numerous non-athletic students with personal advice, loans and outright gifts. The number of hospi-

Whether raising a ruckus on the sideline (left) or graciously posing for a photographer, Ohio State Coach Woody Hayes was a formidable presence.

tal visits he made, sometimes to people he did not even know, was staggering, and if a former player, coach or acquaintance had a death or crisis in the family, Woody would be there.

At work, he was intense, demanding, a taskmaster bordering on tyrant. His practice-field explosions would rattle headgear and could be measured in megatons. He had a volatile temper, was impatient with mistakes and intolerant of less than 100 percent effort by anyone. In exasperation, he would sometimes rip up his ever-present baseball cap or fling his wrist watch (a purposely inexpensive model) to the ground and stomp on it. Even his most-ardent supporters conceded that he sometimes went overboard. But while some of these outbursts erupted naturally, others were sprinkled with a psychological undertone—they tended to have greater impact on an offender than the usual yelling.

Afterward, the offender would be summoned to Hayes' quarters for a discussion of the transgression and a pep talk. But Woody never criticized a player in the media or in public. He once ordered the Big Ten commissioner and a large group of visiting sportswriters out of the practice compound because things were going badly and he didn't want to discipline his players in front of strangers.

Hayes' coaching style was vintage Midwest—conservative, minimal risks, no frills, meticulous preparation, three yards and a cloud of dust.

His vocabulary could be salty on the practice field or in the locker room, but it was always quite proper in other circumstances. He had been an English major (and football player) at Denison College, which he clearly demonstrated in public appearances, speeches, in writing four books, on his popular television show, in social gatherings, at university settings, etc. He was an engrossing conversationalist and a willing practitioner. He frequently dropped by players' dormitory rooms just to chat—and listen. With a retentive mind, he sprinkled talk and writing with quotations from myriad sources. And he made most of his hundreds of

Ohio State quarterback Rex Kern was a competent passer and dangerous runner, as he showed (above) during the 1968 Michigan game.

speeches and public appearances for free.

More than anything else, however, Woody Hayes was the embodiment of law and order, patriotism, loyalty, the work ethic—all the so-called old-fashioned values.

At no time in his storied career was the strength of Hayes' personality and the success of his system and philosophy more evident than in 1968.

"I don't know what the magic was," said 1968 halfback Larry Zelina. "It was an intangible relationship between the team and Woody. You could feel the man's presence. He was a winner."

Some of the intangibles were subtly touched by other former Buckeyes.

"Woody Hayes had the ability to make a good player great, a great player a superstar and a superstar the greatest," said two-time consensus All-America middle guard Jim Stillwagon.

"He might yell at you and scream at you and chew you out, but he really cared about you as a person," said tight end Jan White. "He wanted you to succeed, on and off the field, and it meant a lot to him when you did."

"Woody gave you confidence and leadership," said defensive back Jack Tatum, another two-time consensus All-America. "The way he taught basic fundamentals, making sure you could block and tackle, be in good shape, hustle all the time . . . by the time you got in the game, you actually believed nobody could outhit you. Another thing I liked about Woody, when he told you something this week, it was going to be the same next week. People who let you know where you stand, you can work with."

His players realized Hayes' intense loyalty and personal interest at the time, but they appreciate it more today.

"He cared about you before you went there (Ohio State), while you were there and after you left," said Zelina. "There wasn't anything he wouldn't do for you. When my mom was dying of cancer, I stopped in to see Woody and he dropped everything he was doing and helped me do everything I could for my mom. This was 15 years after I got out of school! The man was a humanitarian."

"The thing I liked about Woody, he would see me 10 years after my last year of football (at OSU) and he'd ask about every member of my family and call them by name," said Tatum. "He did that with all the players' families. That impressed me, with all the players he's had."

But 1968 wasn't all intangibles.

"We had great coaching by Woody Hayes and very talented football players," said Earle Bruce, who coached the offensive line in 1968 and later succeeded Hayes as head coach at Ohio State.

"The whole thing was a meld of unusual, really talented football players," said Esco Sarkkinen, an Ohio State coach from 1946 through 1977.

Actually, the foundation for the team's 1968 championship was laid in 1967. Hayes was a master recruiter and on this occasion, he succeeded beyond his wildest dreams.

"When he came to recruit me," White recalled, "my father and mother were there and by the time Woody got done, my father was so keyed up he said, 'Where do I sign?' My father wanted that scholarship. Woody had charisma; he was a salesman, but he was honest and sincere."

"He talked less about football than anybody that recruited me," Zelina said. "He talked grades, family, history. . . ."

Hayes' recruiting philosophy was simple: "If we bring a young man to our university and don't make sure he gets an education, we're cheating him," he insisted. Buckeye players were goaded to earn their degrees and Hayes' campaign didn't end with their final football game.

After he had become a star defensive back with the Oakland Raiders, Tatum attended a speech Hayes made in Charlotte, N.C., where Tatum's parents lived. Afterward, Hayes insisted on visiting the

Tatum home.

"Woody made me promise my mother that I would go back to Ohio State and finish," Tatum said. "I couldn't turn either of them down. I went back and got my degree."

A few statistics confirm how extraordinary that talent bonanza of 1967 was:

• Thirteen of the 28 recruits played their way into the starting offensive and defensive lineups as sophomores in 1968 (freshmen were not eligible at the time), three others started games and 20 earned letters.

• During their college careers, Ohio State captured one undisputed national championship, two outright Big Ten titles and one co-championship. They posted a 27-2 overall record (26-1 in the regular season with two 9-0 marks) and never finished lower than fifth in the Associated Press and United Press International final rankings. The 1969 Buckeyes were undefeated until they suffered a 24-12 loss to Michigan in their season-ending game.

• Two players (Stillwagon and Tatum) earned consensus All-America recognition twice during their varsity service, and 13 were drafted by National Football League teams, four in the first round.

But the "Super Sophomores" didn't do it alone. The upperclassmen contributed mightily as the Buckeyes charged through the regular season unbeaten and untied, capped by a devastating 50-14 romp over archrival Michigan in the Big Ten championship playoff that set up the dream pairing of 9-0 Ohio State and 9-0-1 Southern Cal in the Rose Bowl.

The potential for major morale problems had existed at the outset.

Fourteen starters returned from a 1967 team that finished 6-3 and won its last four games. The heralded rookies moved in, shunting aside upperclassmen. Not that it wasn't expected. As Sarkkinen pointed out, "Their freshman year, when we matched them up with the varsity in scrimmages and practices, they beat the stuffings out of the varsity."

But squad spirit in 1968 could not have been healthier or more unifying.

Lou Holtz, the team's defensive backfield coach and current Notre Dame head coach, explained. "It was one of those years when the chemistry and leadership were as important as the talent we had," he said. "We had great chemistry on the team. The sophomores were really talented and they didn't play like sophomores, or act like sophomores, yet the upperclassmen maintained leadership of the team."

"The biggest factor was the blending of the new guys with the guys who had been there a year or two," said tackle Dave Foley, a co-captain and consensus All-America in 1968. "The sophomores were

A quick start and good body balance were the qualities that made fullback Jim Otis one of the top short-yardage backs in the country.

a really talented group and they all grew during the season. The whole team grew together."

"A few weeks before Woody passed away (in 1987), we were talking about 1968," said quarterback Rex Kern, "and he said: 'I've never seen a team that really enjoyed being around one another more than your team.' It was true. We had a great deal of respect and admiration for each other and what each could do."

The attitude of the sophomores helped.

"I don't think we were ever cocky," insisted Stillwagon.

"We were very confident, but we didn't have a bunch of cocky guys; no showboats or anything," said backup quarterback Ron Maciejowski.

"It was more a real confidence level," Kern said. "It gave us a lot of confidence going into the Big Ten knowing that as freshmen we had done so well against the varsity."

"We thought we were pretty hot stuff," White

said. "We didn't know any better."

"We didn't understand big pressure, we were just having fun," said Tatum.

"The guys who showed cockiness had reason to be," Foley added. "They were *players!*"

Confidence was not lacking among the daring, freewheeling sophomores. Sarkkinen recalls visiting the freshman dressing room after a 1967 victory at Indiana "and they were asking me, 'When we go to the Rose Bowl next year, where do we stay?' That was amazing."

Hayes' most difficult problem was fitting all those stars into the proper positions and keeping everybody happy.

"That was one of the greatest jobs of leading a group of young men I've ever seen," said Lou McCullough, Ohio State's defensive coordinator in 1968. "We had to have great leadership from Woody to make sure we got the best out of all those sophomores. He did just an outstanding job of coordinating the whole thing."

"Everybody on that team was used to being *the man* in high school," Zelina said. "But Woody had the ability to get them to play together, to be cohesive, to keep their heads on straight and realize that whatever he asked them to do or wherever he asked them to play was for the good of the team. He was not just a football coach, he was a mentor."

"We feel every senior gave us his greatest season," Hayes said in a season-ending summary, "and when you combine that with the enthusiasm of the sophomores and the know-how of the juniors, you've got yourself a great football team."

Camaraderie and mutual respect existed between the offensive and defensive units, which relied on—and complemented—each other.

When Illinois staged a 24-point second-half rally to tie the Buckeyes, nobody panicked. "Tatum came up to me along the sidelines," Kern said, "and said: 'Rex, you guys are going to have to pull something off. We're doing the best we can, but they're stretching us out (the Illini had gone into wide splits in the line and rushed effectively).'

"He was saying we're counting on you and that's the way we on offense felt. We knew Tate or 'Wagon or Tim Anderson or Doug Adams or one of the other (defensive) guys would come up with a big play to get us the ball."

Hayes' run-oriented offense was more freewheeling than usual. When all was said and done, it had amassed 4,402 yards (including the Rose Bowl game), and counted 323 points, the second-highest total in OSU history (to that time).

The Buckeyes still ground down the opposition with Hayes' traditional fullback-oriented power running attack (3,018 yards and 36 touchdowns), but launched, by previous standards, about

John Brockington, one of Ohio State's 'Super Sophomores' in 1968, was slowed part of the season by an ankle sprain.

two-seasons-worth of passes (188) and fully embraced the option play.

The key reason was Kern, an exceptional athlete who had been an all-Ohio high school star in football, basketball and baseball and had so impressed Hayes as a freshman that he was immediately installed as the starting quarterback when he came to the varsity, even though he had undergone spinal disc surgery in mid-June and though returning senior Bill Long had been the starter in 1966 and '67.

The 6-foot, 180-pound Kern justified Hayes' decision with a flair and competence that quickly established him as an all-time favorite with Buckeye followers.

Kern proved to be a competent passer and dangerous runner. He also was a clutch player and a heady field leader who carried 27 classroom hours in one quarter, almost twice the average student's load, and made straight A's. He also delivered speeches nationally for the Fellowship of Christian Athletes and later earned a master's degree on a graduate fellowship and a Ph.D.

"Rex was the master of the broken play," Hayes said. "At faking, he was in a class by himself." After the 1969 Rose Bowl, Los Angeles Times columnist Jim Murray wrote: "They (the Buckeyes) have a quarterback who may have passed up a promising career picking pockets. Rex Kern had the USC line tackling the wrong guy all afternoon."

Hayes also had exceptional depth at quarterback, with Long and sophomore Maciejowski, who became known as "Super Sub" for his high-level performance in relief of the occasionally injured Kern. The talent pool at the other backfield spots was equally impressive.

Fullback Jim Otis and halfback Dave Brungard, 1967 starters, and their backups, Paul Huff and Ray Gillian, returned as juniors, joined by talented sophomores John Brockington and Leo Hayden, two future first-round NFL draft picks, and Zelina, tabbed by Hayes as "the most versatile Ohio State back since Vic Janowicz."

Otis, a 6-foot, 208-pounder, fit the traditional mold of Ohio State fullbacks.

"He had an extremely quick start, amazing body balance and was without a doubt one of the best short-yardage backs I have ever seen," Hayes said after his graduation, adding that Otis' boyhood experience as a diver and trampolinist probably accounted for some acrobatic moves on the football field.

Otis held his starting spot, leading the Buckeyes in rushing (985 yards including a 101-yard Rose Bowl performance) and scoring and going on to consensus All-America recognition a year later.

As the season progressed, Brungard gave way to the two big, fast, hard-running sophomores.

Hayden, a 6-2, 204-pound Ohio product, finished the season brilliantly, rushing for 90 yards and catching a touchdown pass in the Rose Bowl.

Whether playing noseguard or middle linebacker, sophomore Jim Stillwagon stepped in and made the Buckeyes' defense click.

Brockington, a 6-1, 210-pounder from Brooklyn, distinguished by a high-knee-action running style, was slowed part of the season by an ankle sprain, but started at both left and right halfback and played some fullback. He went on to become the first-round NFL draft pick of the Green Bay Packers in 1971 and was named NFC rookie of the year by The Sporting News.

The 6-foot, 195-pound Zelina, another Ohioan, demonstrated his versatility, running with a swift, gliding gait from the halfback, wingback or slot positions as well as returning kickoffs and punts and serving as the backup placekicker.

The Buckeyes' top two receivers also were sophomores: Bruce Jankowski, a converted halfback from New Jersey, and the 6-2 White, a prototype tight end who was devastating whether catching passes or blocking.

All this talent enjoyed tremendous support from an experienced interior line, featuring bookend senior tackles Foley, a 6-5, 246-pounder, and Rufus Mayes, 6-5 and 250. Both hailed from Ohio and had been starters since 1966. And both were first-round NFL draft picks following the 1968 season.

Senior center John Muhlbach and junior guard Alan Jack were returning starters while junior Tom Backhus and sophomore Brian Donovan shared the other guard spot.

"The offense didn't make many mistakes," said Bruce, who pointed out that it lost only nine fumbles and threw only 11 interceptions. But care of the football was a Hayes trademark—and fetish.

Ohio State's defense was even more sophomoric than the offense, but, as Sarkkinen noted, "Each side was a cohesive group with great leaders and great, explosive players."

McCullough said of his unit: "They were young and eager, a very intense group. We had a lot of stars, but really no stars. One would be a star one week, one the next week."

"What made the defense great," Stillwagon suggested, "was that we were very aggressive, constantly putting the (opposition) offense under pressure, and every player in our lineup had the potential of making the big play. Also, we had about 62 or 72 different looks off the basic 5-3, 5-4 and 4-3."

Knee injuries sidelined end Nick Roman before the season and linebacker Dirk Worden, a co-captain, in the third game, leaving linebacker Mark Stier as the lone senior starter. End Dave Whitfield, tackles Paul Schmidlin and Brad Nielsen and cornerback Ted Provost had been 1967 regulars.

But the new talent made the difference. And if there were no stars on this Buckeye defense, Stillwagon and Tatum came close enough.

Stillwagon was a native Ohioan who won honors as a center and linebacker at a military school in Virginia. He played noseguard on some Ohio State defenses, middle linebacker on others. He was a standout from the first game in both roles and went on to win the Outland (the nation's outstanding interior lineman) and Lombardi (top lineman) awards (he was the first recipient of the latter), and to become an all-star in the Canadian Football League.

Tatum had been a rugged fullback on the Ohio State freshman team, but said he preferred "to hit rather than being hit." Hayes accommodated the youngster, switching him to defensive roverback. It was a master stroke.

With his sprinter speed, jarring tackles and uncanny field sense, Tatum quickly gained national attention, especially when he totally frustrated Heisman candidate Leroy Keyes in the Buckeyes' upset of then-No. 1 Purdue in the season's third game.

Tatum, always covering the wide side of the field, harnessed a succession of other star backs with persistent man-to-man coverage en route to consensus All-America honors in 1969 and '70 as well as a place in the Ohio State University Hall of Fame.

Jack Tatum, another sophomore in 1968, switched from offense to defense and became a two-time consensus All-America.

Two other offensive converts, sophomores Anderson and Mike Sensibaugh, moved into the open cornerback and safety spots with conspicuous success, with Sensibaugh also handling the Buckeyes' punting chores.

Sophomore Mark Debevc replaced the injured Roman and another sophomore, Doug Adams, took over for Worden.

"We weren't very big," Holtz said, and that point was graphically illustrated when the Ohio State and Southern Cal squads met at Disneyland before the Rose Bowl. "It was like the rich and the poor physically and that worried us as coaches," Sarkkinen said. "But fortunately, we had our hitters, too."

Every win, the narrowest by five points, counted equally in the 10-0 record, but four loom largest in appreciating the 1968 Buckeyes.

In the third game, Big Ten preseason favorite Purdue arrived in Ohio Stadium as the top-ranked team in both major polls and averaging 41 points. Keyes, quarterback Mike Phipps and a huge line had devastated the Buckeyes, 41-6, in their 1967 Ohio Stadium visit.

The Buckeyes missed two field goals, had another one blocked and lost Brockington and Worden on injuries in the first half, but the score was 0-0 at intermission. As Holtz told it, "We said before if they threw the outcut, Tatum would be the hero; if they threw the curl, Provost would be the hero. On the third play of the second half, they threw the outcut and Jack had it, but dropped it."

"Jack and I would switch off taking the inside or the outside guy," Provost explained. "The play before Jack had taken the outside and I'd taken the inside guy. We switched off the next time."

"I went to Teddy's spot," Tatum agreed, "and Mike Phipps came back with the same pattern and he read me and threw the outcut. Teddy was sitting right there waiting."

"I took it (interception) on the dead run," Provost said, "and it was so wide open down the sideline, all I had to do was catch the ball and run it in."

As it turned out, Provost's 35-yard touchdown sprint would have been enough. But, when the conversion try missed, tension remained heavy. Long supplied the insurance later in the quarter, after Stillwagon had intercepted another Phipps pass. Four plays moved the ball to Purdue's 14. On the fourth, Kern was hurt and Hayes dispatched Long to replace him because "I felt the man with experience should enter the game at that time." Some in the crowd booed, obviously wanting Maciejowski.

The play called was "a hitch pass to Jan White," Long said, "but as soon as I got back in my drop, I knew I was in trouble. Suddenly there was this hole a Mack truck could have run through." Long took off. With a Purdue defender bearing down, he said, "I remember leaping as far as I could to get into the end zone."

That 13-0 victory was the catalyst for a glorious season. "Provost's interception might have been one of the all-time great plays," McCullough said.

Two weeks later, at Illinois, the favored Buckeyes went to the dressing room leading 24-0, and Stillwagon confessed, "We thought we had it made." In the second half, the Illini sprang a revised offense that produced three touchdowns and three two-point conversions (all three by rushing) for a shocking tie.

With less than five minutes remaining and the ball on the Ohio State 30, Kern started to drive, but was knocked out on a scramble. This time Hayes sent in Maciejowski—to the latter's surprise.

"I was sitting on the bench and when Woody called me, I ran up without my helmet," he recalled. "It was under the bench with helmets of about 30 other guys who weren't playing and I had to run back and look for it."

Mike Sensibaugh moved into Ohio State's starting safety spot and also handled the Buckeyes' punting duties.

Maciejowski passed to Zelina for 10 yards, scrambled for 12 and lofted a 44-yarder to Zelina to set up a touchdown plunge by Otis. The winning streak had been saved, 31-24.

To Hayes, the annual regular-season-ending joust with Michigan always represented more than a game. It was war. He considered it "the greatest rivalry in football." The Big Ten championship often hung in the balance, as it did in 1968. Both teams were unbeaten.

The Buckeyes broke a 14-14 tie late in the second quarter to lead 21-14 at intermission and turned it into a 50-14 rout in the second half. Otis smashed into the end zone four times.

"The way we dominated them in the second half was the greatest feeling in my athletic career," Foley said.

That set up the Rose Bowl as a national championship-deciding match. Each team was ranked

The 1968 Buckeyes: Front row (left to right)—Jim Roman, Gary Roush, Jay Bombach, Gerald Ehrsam, John Muhlbach, Mark Stier, Dirk Worden, Nick Roman, Rufus Mayes, Dave Foley, Victor Stottlemyer, Bill Long, Bob Smith, John Stowe, Ed Bender, John Sobolewski. Second row—Head Coach Woody Hayes, Dan Aston, Butch Smith, Mike Polaski, Alan Jack, Dave Whitfield, Paul Schmidlin, Charles Hutchison, Ted Provost, Bill Urbanik, Brad Nielsen, Paul Huff, Jim Otis, Arthur Burton, David Brungard, Kevin Rusnak. Third row—Bruce Jankowski, William Hackett, Jim Gentile, Ray Gillian, Michael Radtke, Steve Crapser, Tom Backhus, Randy Hart, Harry Pollitt, Jan White, Leo Hayden, Ted Kurz, Horatius Greene, Robert Trapuzzano. Fourth row—Jim Stillwagon, Mike Sensibaugh, Larry Zelina, Larry Qualls, Rex Kern, James Conroy, David Cheney, Charles Aldrin, Brian Donovan, Richard Kuhn, Jim Oppermann, Richard Troha, Gerald King, John Brockington, Tom Ecrement. Fifth row—Page, Michael Dale, Suber, Bruce Smith, Ralph Holloway, Tim Anderson, Charles Waugh, Ron Maciejowski, Lapuh, Hausman, James Marsh, Mark Debevc, James Coburn, Paul Johnston. Sixth row—Wells, Jack Tatum, Phil Strickland, Doug Adams, Tim Wagner, coaches Hugh Hindman, Bill Mallory, Esco Sarkkinen, Lou McCullough, Earle Bruce, George Chaump, Lou Holtz, Rudy Hubbard, Tiger Ellison.

No. 1 in one of the major polls and the pregame hype was both fun and unnerving. The colorful Hayes, a favorite target of the Los Angeles media, was there to guide his exciting young Buckeyes against the experienced and talented Trojans, led by one of the greatest backs of all time, O.J. Simpson.

Ohio State's game plan called for shutting off Simpson's wide sweeps. It did that effectively on one play in the second quarter, but the cornered O.J. cut back against the grain and passed up a half a dozen futile defenders on an 80-yard touchdown sprint.

Suddenly, the Buckeyes trailed, 10-0. But there was no panic.

"There was concern," admits Kern. "The concentration level went up a few octaves. I went into the huddle and told the guys, 'We better start playing football.' We knew if we played our game, we'd be all right. I think O.J.'s run did more to wake us up than excite his teammates."

"He made us go to work," said Foley. Mayes agreed. "He lit the fire."

Even Hayes later said he wasn't worried, contending, "I knew we'd win, sure. Because I felt we could move the ball on them and I knew O.J. wasn't going to be able to cut back again."

"I thought Woody did a great job by not coming out of our game plan after O.J. scored," Kern said.

Kern guided the Buckeyes 84 yards to a touchdown, passed to Gillian (Zelina exited with a cracked rib early in the game) to set up another score and to Gillian again for a touchdown. It was 27-10 and the national championship had been emphatically decided before the Trojans posted a disputed last-minute TD.

Before taking off after the Rose Bowl for one of his four trips to Vietnam to talk with, and show football films to, U.S. servicemen, Hayes summarized 1968: "I thought before the season this team had great potential, but might be a year away. It came along faster than I thought."

Perhaps the most-appreciated of all the accolades heaped on the Buckeyes, at the time and since, came from an unexpected visitor to the Ohio State locker room after the Rose Bowl. After its traditional post-game prayer, the Buckeye squad erupted in wild celebration. Suddenly, the dressing room door flung open and a handsome Gold and Maroon-clad young man entered.

"Quiet, guys! It's O.J.!" several Buckeyes shouted, and the room went silent.

"You're the greatest football team in the country," said an emotional Simpson, "and don't let anybody tell you you aren't!"

Ohio State, 1968

ROAD TO GREATNESS

1968 RESULTS (10-0)

Opponent	Score	Opp. Record	Opp. Bowl Game
Southern Methodist	35-14	8-3-0	Bluebonnet (W)
Oregon	21-6	4-6-0	
Purdue	13-0	8-2-0	
Northwestern	45-21	1-9-0	
at Illinois	31-24	1-9-0	
Michigan State	25-20	5-5-0	
at Wisconsin	43-8	0-10-0	
at Iowa	33-27	5-5-0	
Michigan	50-14	8-2-0	
ROSE BOWL			
Southern Cal	**27-16**	**9-0-1**	

FACTS AND FIGURES

Coach Woody Hayes was named The Sporting News' 1968 Coach of the Year, and offensive tackle Rufus Mayes was a member of The Sporting News' 1968 All-America team. . . . The Buckeyes finished the season with a 4-0 record against opponents that ranked among the nation's final Top 20 in the Associated Press and United Press International polls. . . . The combined record of Ohio State's 1968 opponents was 49-51-1. While the Buckeyes faced just four teams with winning records, they impressed skeptics with the way they manhandled those teams, defeating them by an average of 20 points per game. . . . Buckeyes who were named to the '68 All-Big Ten team were offensive tackles Dave Foley and Mayes, roverback Jack Tatum and defensive back Ted Provost. . . . Both Foley and Mayes were first-round selections in the 1969 National Football League draft and 18 players from the '68 team eventually were drafted by NFL clubs. Halfback John Brockington, halfback Leo Hayden, cornerback Tim Anderson and Tatum were first-round selections in the 1971 draft. . . . The Buckeyes, 27-16 winners over Southern Cal in the 1969 Rose Bowl, are just 1-6 in Rose Bowl competition since. . . . The Buckeyes' explosive 1968 offense ranked highly among major-college leaders nationally in several categories. Ohio State finished fifth in the nation with an average of 449 yards per game and third in rushing offense (306.4 yards per game). The Buckeyes also were 10th nationally in scoring offense, averaging 32.9 points. . . . The potent Buckeyes scored 30 or more points in six contests. . . . Safety Mike Sensibaugh remains Ohio State's all-time leader with 22 career interceptions, and Provost is third with 16. . . Jim Otis' 102-point total in 1968 (including one touchdown in the Rose Bowl) is tied for sixth on Ohio State's all-time scoring list. . . . The 50-14 devastation inflicted on archrival Michigan in 1968 represented the second-largest margin of victory ever for an Ohio State team over the hated Wolverines. The 1935 Buckeyes defeated Michigan, 38-0. . . . Ohio State's 1968 Big Ten championship began a string of three straight seasons and nine out of 10 in which the Buckeyes won or shared league titles.

STATISTICAL LEADERS

PASSING

	Att.	Comp.	Yards	TD	Pct.	Int.
Rex Kern	116	66	871	5	56.9	6

RUSHING

	Att.	Yards	Avg.	TD
Jim Otis	189	884	4.7	16
Rex Kern	119	499	4.2	8
Larry Zelina	38	329	8.7	1

RECEIVING

	Rec.	Yards	Avg.	TD
Bruce Jankowski	30	326	10.9	3
Jan White	20	266	13.3	1
Larry Zelina	17	322	18.9	1
Jim Otis	10	82	8.2	0

SCORING

	TD	FG	PAT	Points
Jim Otis	16	0	0	96
Rex Kern	8	0	0	48
Jim Roman	0	3	18	27

KEY CHARACTERS

The Conductor

COACH: Wayne Woodrow (Woody) Hayes.

Record: 205-61-10, 28 years at Ohio State.

Hayes was a legend in the world of college football. . . . He was a demanding taskmaster whose disciplinary tactics were both feared and respected. . . . He built a powerhouse program known for its rough and rugged style, mirroring the personality of its leader. . . . He is a member of the College Football Hall of Fame. . . . His 1968 team was a consensus national champion, and the final 1954 Associated Press and 1957 United Press International polls also ranked the Buckeyes No. 1. . . . His teams finished second in three AP polls (1957, '61 and '73) and three UPI polls (1957, '61 and '70). . . . Fifteen of his teams ranked among the Top 10 in each of the polls. . . . He led the Buckeyes to eight Rose Bowls, including four straight from 1972-75, compiling a 4-4 record. . . . His teams posted a 16-11-1 record against archrival Michigan. . . . Hayes' previous head coaching experience came at Denison (O.) College and Miami of Ohio. . . . A history buff, he was particularly interested in military strategy, which often influenced his maneuvers on the football field. . . . Among Hayes' proteges were Earle Bruce, George Chaump, Lou Holtz, Rudy Hubbard, Bill Mallory and Bo Schembechler. . . . He posted an overall career mark of 238-72-10 in 33 seasons and ranks fourth on the all-time victory list. . . . He died in 1987 at the age of 74.

Personal Data:

Born: February 14, 1913, in Clifton, O.
High School: Newcomerstown High in Newcomerstown, O.
College: Denison.

The Supporting Cast

QUARTERBACK: Rex Kern.

Kern was an exciting passer and runner who took charge when he was on the field. . . . He finished third in the 1969 Heisman Trophy balloting and fifth the next season. . . . He ranks fifth among Ohio State's all-time leading passers (2,444 yards) and sixth in total offense (4,158 yards). . . . Kern, who lettered from 1968-70, also ran for 1,714 career yards.

Personal Data:

Born: May 28, 1949, in Lancaster, O.
High School: Lancaster High.

FULLBACK: Jim Otis.

Otis was the backbone of the Buckeye attack with his workmanlike style of punishing opposing defenders. . . . He was a consensus All-America in 1969 and placed seventh in the 1969 Heisman voting. . . . He ranks fifth on the Buckeyes' career rushing list with 2,542 yards and eighth in scoring with 210 points. . . . Otis, who went on to a long but unspectacular pro football career, lettered from 1967-69.

Personal Data:

Born: April 29, 1948, in Celina, O.
High School: Celina Senior High.

MIDDLE GUARD: Jim Stillwagon.

Stillwagon became the first-ever winner of the Lombardi Award in 1970 and captured the Outland Trophy the same year. He was the first middle guard to win the Outland and the first of seven players to win both awards in the same season. . . . He was a consensus All-America in 1969 and '70, a unanimous selection in the latter. . . . Of all the defensive linemen with whom he was associated, Hayes called Stillwagon the best. . . . He lettered from 1968-70.

Personal Data:

Born: February 11, 1949, in Mount Vernon, O.
High School: Mount Vernon High and Augusta Military Academy in Fort Defiance, Va.

ROVERBACK: Jack Tatum.

Tatum was a consensus All-America in 1969 and a unanimous consensus pick in 1970. . . . He began his career as a halfback but requested a switch and became one of the best defenders in Ohio State history. . . . He was a master of one-on-one coverage and a vicious hitter who drew enough attention to finish 10th in the 1969 Heisman voting and seventh in 1970. . . . He lettered from 1968-70.

Personal Data:

Born: November 18, 1948, in Cherryville, N.C.
High School: Passaic High in Passaic, N.J.

FINAL 1968 WIRE SERVICE RANKINGS

ASSOCIATED PRESS

1. **OHIO STATE**	11. Oklahoma
2. Penn State	12. **Michigan**
3. Texas	13. Tennessee
4. **Southern Cal**	14. **SMU**
5. Notre Dame	15. Oregon State
6. Arkansas	16. Auburn
7. Kansas	17. Alabama
8. Georgia	18. Houston
9. Missouri	19. Louisiana State
10. **Purdue**	20. Ohio University

UNITED PRESS

1. **OHIO STATE**	12. Alabama
2. **Southern Cal**	13. Oregon State
3. Penn State	14. Florida State
4. Georgia	15. **Michigan**
5. Texas	16. **SMU**
6. Kansas	17. Missouri
7. Tennessee	18. Ohio University
8. Notre Dame	Minnesota
9. Arkansas	20. Houston
10. Oklahoma	Stanford
11. **Purdue**	

Bold face indicates Ohio State opponent.

Determination And a Shot of O.J.

Southern Cal, 1967
By Nick Peters

Bringing Orenthal James Simpson to campus was the best thing Southern California did to build a great team in 1967. The second-best thing was losing its last three games the year before.

In 1966, while Simpson was shattering junior college records at City College of San Francisco, the Trojans were winning their first six games and inching close to the top of the polls. But the season ended on a sour note with consecutive losses to UCLA, Notre Dame and Purdue (in the Rose Bowl). Moreover, the loss to UCLA was USC's second straight, creating the impression that the Trojans weren't even No. 1 in Los Angeles. That burden weighed heavily on the shoulders of USC's returning veterans.

"The ('67) season was like a mission to seniors like Tim Rossovich, Adrian Young and myself," consensus All-America tackle Ron Yary said. "We'd lost to UCLA and Notre Dame as juniors and were knocked off by (both teams) as sophomores. Playing those teams for the last time in 1967 made the season a lot more significant to us."

The Trojans had plenty of motivation to excel in 1967. All they lacked was a star tailback—until O.J. Simpson arrived.

Simpson, a 6-foot-1, 202-pound speedster who could run the 100-yard dash in 9.4 seconds and the 40 in 4.5 (wearing football shoes, no less), participated in only seven football practices in the spring of '67 because he was running with the USC track team. But his performances were memorable.

"I'll never forget O.J.'s first day of practice," recalled Craig Fertig, an assistant under Coach John McKay. "He started at flanker, so everyone was watching the first pass thrown his way. He caught it, juked a defender and ran for a TD.

"Coach McKay asked me to put him at tailback and run a pitch. He carried the ball like a loaf of bread, the way you're not supposed to do it, but he took it 78 yards for a TD. We knew right then and there we had something special."

Simpson always knew he had talent, but it went unnoticed for quite some time. He was outstanding at Galileo High School in San Francisco, but his team's perennial poor record and his own poor grades kept most of the scouts away. He got no scholarship offers. After two junior college All-America seasons, however, every major college in the country was drooling over him. He opted for USC, the team he had cheered as a youngster, where his much-ballyhooed arrival made him somewhat apprehensive.

"I was confident in my ability from the start, but I'd never played four-year ball," Simpson said. "It obviously was the most exciting year in my life, more so than when I rushed for 2,000 yards with the (National Football League's Buffalo) Bills. All I had to do was go back 18 months prior to the 1967 season and I was a kid out of high school nobody wanted."

Everybody, it seemed, wanted a piece of Simpson as he worked his way toward 1,415 yards rushing (tops in NCAA Division I) and consensus All-America honors in his rookie season as a major-college back. But he handled the publicity glut with class and in the process became one of the most popular athletes ever to wear the cardinal and gold. O.J., who already bore the nickname Orange Juice when he arrived at USC, was famous for his winning smile and sincere friendliness.

"I like people, and that evidently comes across," said Simpson, who was well liked by his teammates as well as his fans.

"There was no animosity toward O.J. because he

It didn't take long for the Trojans of Southern California to realize that speedy and elusive tailback O.J. Simpson was something special.

It was under the tutelage of Coach John McKay that Southern Cal's tradition of great tailbacks, a la O.J. Simpson, was born.

didn't act like a star," Fertig said. "He was one of the guys, and he set an example by finishing off every play in practice, going 60 yards instead of stopping after 20. He was something else."

And not just in football. Before gaining his first yard as a Trojan, Simpson helped USC win the first of two consecutive Division I track championships. He ran one leg of USC's 440-yard relay squad, which established a world record of 38.6 seconds at the 1967 meet.

Running the first leg of that relay team was another Trojan football player, split end Earl McCullouch, who won the 120-yard high hurdles with a 13.4 clocking. He then equaled the world record in the 110-meter high hurdles (13.2 seconds) at the trials for the Pan American Games, where he won a gold medal.

McCullouch had been a backup in 1966, but McKay made him the starting split end in '67 when his tremendous speed became apparent. McCullouch credited the hurdles with making him a better football player, saying it lengthened his stride. But his greatest asset was his explosive start.

"I do come off the line quick. . . . It gives me an edge over the defensive backs," he said.

The Pan Am Games featured another USC player, Steve Sogge, who batted .410 and powered a U.S. championship over Cuba in baseball. Though Sogge entered the '67 football season as the backup to quarterback Toby Page, he was one of many talented athletes who made Trojan fans optimistic.

"Once the football season started, we knew we were good," Simpson said. "You could sense it. We had great balance. We could run and pass and play great defense. There was a lot of enthusiasm going in because we had a lot of guys back on defense and our offense was supposed to be improved. Unlike some USC teams, we had the passing to go with a dominant running game."

Besides having the horses, the Trojans also had team spirit. The players got along well and believed in each other.

"We had unbelievable rapport on that team," Yary said. "It was a small school, a great school, so there was a family feeling. We really cared about each other."

But the Trojans were not a bunch of clones. "It was a team which probably was ahead of its time," tight end Bob Klein said. "The team was made up of quite a diverse group of guys. Rossovich, (Mike) Battle and Young were typical defensive players, aggressive and boisterous."

Especially Rossovich. "The harder I hit people, the better I like it," the consensus All-America defensive end once said. "When you hit a guy and he hits the ground hard, and his eyeballs roll, and you see it, and he looks up at you and knows you see it, then you've conquered him. It's a great feeling."

Rossovich played his position like he was possessed, but some of his off-the-field adventures were even wilder. A free spirit, he specialized in the outrageous. As a freshman, he attracted the attention of school authorities (not to mention other students) by standing on the ledge outside his dormitory stark naked, in broad daylight, after taking a shower. "It was a windy day," he explained. "It seemed like a good way to dry off." He also was known for playing Christmas carols year-round, running down the street wearing nothing but shaving cream from head to toe, falling off sorority house rooftops, eating glass and denting every locker in the USC dressing room with his head.

"He was a legend," Fertig said.

Joining Rossovich in many of these extracurricular activities was Battle, the Trojans' starting safety.

"We used to set fire to cars," Rossovich said. "We'd buy these old cars for $25, Mike Battle and a few of us, and we'd set them on fire or we'd drive one to a big intersection and everybody would jump out and pound it with sledgehammers and saws and things."

Battle also enjoyed rolling old cars. "I rolled one over six times once," he said.

Battle's daring nature extended to the playing field. As the Trojans' primary kick returner, he hated calling for a fair catch, even if it meant getting the tar knocked out of him. He wound up leading the nation in punt returns in '67, averaging 12.1 yards on 47 runbacks.

Rossovich and Battle were the most notorious characters on a defense that was as dangerous as it was bizarre. Playing opposite Rossovich up front was end Jim Gunn, with middle guard Ralph Oliver and tackles Willard Scott and Gary Magner in between. In the secondary, Battle got help from rover back Jerry Shaw and cornerbacks Pat Cashman and Bill Jaroncyk. The linebacking was handled by Young, a consensus All-America, and Jim Snow.

"Then," said Klein, describing another aspect of the team's personality, "we had calculating offensive linemen like Yary, guys who were quiet, big and strong."

Yary, a 6-5, 245-pounder who won the 1967 Outland Trophy, is considered one of college football's best tackles ever. Whether pass-blocking or opening holes for Simpson, he overwhelmed opponents. Klein (who shared time at tight end with Bob Miller), tackle Mike Taylor, center Dick Allmon and guards Mike Scarpace and Steve Lehmer teamed with Yary to provide a solid front wall for the USC offense, which got additional firepower from flanker Jim Lawrence and fullbacks Dan Scott and Mike Hull.

"And then there was O.J.," Klein said. "We'd all heard about him when spring ball started, but none of us realized how truly great he was."

Before the '67 season was a month old, it seemed as if the whole world was talking about The Juice, who rushed for 94 yards in the Trojans' season-opening shutout of Washington State and then tallied no less than 158 yards in each of the next three games.

"I hope that we don't see anybody with more capabilities, and I don't think we will," Texas Coach Darrell Royal said of Simpson after USC posted a 17-13 victory over the Longhorns in a battle between two highly ranked powers. With Sogge calling the signals—he had become the starting quarterback when Page was sidelined with bruised ribs in the opener—the Trojans went on to defeat Michigan State and Stanford, rising to No. 1 in both the Associated Press and United Press International polls.

The stage was set for a Poll Bowl against Notre Dame in South Bend, where USC hadn't won since 1939. The Trojans had dropped eight of their last 10 games to the Fighting Irish, including a 51-0 drubbing at home in 1966. Though Notre Dame, the preseason No. 1 pick, had been upset by Purdue two weeks earlier, the fifth-ranked Irish still were favored by as many as 12 points.

McKay was determined to avenge for past losses—particularly that 51-0 score—and retain the top ranking. "For all of us at USC it was a very emotional week," the coach wrote in "McKay, A Coach's Story," his 1974 autobiography. "For a year there wasn't a night I went to bed or morning that I awoke when I hadn't thought about 51-0. It was still stuck in my throat."

Opening big holes for Simpson and other USC running backs was tackle Ron Yary, winner of the 1967 Outland Trophy.

McKay, a flamboyant 44-year-old who hobnobbed with Hollywood's celebrity crowd, was as sharp strategically as he was socially. He used multiple offenses and defenses that confused technologically inferior teams. He attacked opponents with everything from the I-formation to the shifting T, and his defensive alignments had about a dozen variations. Fertig recalls how McKay dreamed up a new defensive scheme to spring on the Irish in '67.

"We came out of a meeting one night and we were standing near the statue of Tommy Trojan," Fertig said. "Coach McKay had me pose as (Notre Dame quarterback) Terry Hanratty, and we used a bottle of champagne someone had given us as a football. The coach devised a defense where we used man-to-man coverage underneath and a two-deep zone. We called it, for the lack of something more imaginative, the Trojan Defense. It's a 4-5-2 alignment we first used that week at Notre Dame. We're

Trojans defensive end Tim Rossovich was a free spirit who wreaked havoc on opposing ballcarriers as well as life in general.

still using it."

McKay wasn't big on pep talks, so without overstating the point, he also reminded his troops how they had been humiliated by the Irish the year before. Everyone got the message, including players such as Simpson who had not been around in '66. With Young, a native of Ireland, enthusiastically leading them in calisthenics, the Trojans prepared feverishly.

"The preparation that week was much more intense," Simpson recalled. "When we got on that plane in L.A., it was like we were going on a crusade."

McKay resorted to a psychological ploy to increase the intensity. On the Trojans' last visit to South Bend in 1965, they had been left standing on the field for 20 minutes prior to Notre Dame's appearance for the opening kickoff. McKay simmered over the tactic for the next two years.

"I'll never forget it," Simpson said. "The coaches had finished their pregame talk and there was a knock on the clubhouse door. We were invited to take the field, but Coach McKay told us not to go because Notre Dame wasn't on the field.

"He remembered the last time USC was there and how the team had to stand around on the field while the emotion built up. Coach McKay said he would never allow that to happen again, that we'd forfeit if Notre Dame didn't come out first.

"He actually told us to put our street clothes back on. He was serious, and we were all wondering what was going on. Then we were told Notre Dame was on the field. It was like a victory before the game had started.

"You could sense we weren't going to take any crap from anybody. They had a great team, but we were ready. We went out and physically beat them up. It was a heavyweight fight for a half, and then we pulled away."

Notre Dame took a 7-0 halftime lead, but the second-half kickoff proved to be the turning point. Notre Dame's Chuck Landolfi fumbled it, and USC recovered on the Irish 18-yard line. The Trojans ran the ball seven straight times, the last five by Simpson, who plunged over from the 1-yard line for the touchdown.

"O.J. is not in a union—he can carry the ball as many times as we want him to," McKay pointed out on a day in which his torrid tailback turned a season-high 38 attempts into 150 yards and three TDs.

"I'd hear Sogge call my number," Simpson recalled, "and I'd say to myself, 'Lord, not again.' But once I got the ball, instinct would take over and somehow my legs would move."

With the game tied, 7-7, and the Trojans on the Irish 36, Simpson provided the back-breaker. Sogge rolled left on an option play before flipping to Simpson. Scott made a key block and O.J. exploded into a gap for the go-ahead score.

Despite Simpson's great performance, the Trojans' 24-7 victory was sparked by the defense, which held the Irish to only 15 completions in 40 attempts and picked off seven passes. Young led the way with four interceptions.

"I was here two years ago when we lost, 28-7," Young said after the game. "I was only a sophomore and I was in awe of Notre Dame. The fans waved those big handkerchiefs at us then. I told the guys before the game today that if they (fans) were going to be using their hankies again, it would be to wipe their faces off, not to make fun of us."

Three of Young's interceptions came at the expense of Hanratty, whose dismal performance concluded when he was knocked out cold while trying to tackle Battle after another interception.

"We had them figured and our people were able to get in the right places," McKay explained.

Quarterback Steve Sogge listens to instructions from Trojans Coach John McKay during a 1967 game.

"Hanratty was off, and we got him to throw impatiently on a couple of occasions. We also made some defensive adjustments that paid off."

The Trojans kept rolling with victories over Washington, Oregon and California. Simpson rushed for a season-high 235 yards, scored twice and fired a touchdown pass to McCullouch against the Huskies, but he and his teammates were slowed to a crawl by a fired-up Oregon defense. Simpson sprained his right foot early in the third quarter and was replaced by Steve Grady, who rushed for 108 yards. USC's 28-6 triumph was less impressive than the score indicated.

"They knocked the hell out of us," McKay lamented. "And we just stood there and took it, like we were reading our press clippings instead of playing football. I think O.J. got it because we were just standing around. I hope we learned a lesson today."

With Simpson sidelined the next week, USC's vaunted defense took charge and limited Cal to one yard rushing in a 31-12 win. The Trojans were unblemished at 8-0, but they weren't firing on all cylinders, a poor sign heading into the mud at Oregon State.

Mike Haggard's 30-yard field goal in the second quarter accounted for all of the scoring in a 3-0 Oregon State upset. The Beavers weren't slouches, having stunned highly ranked Purdue and tied UCLA, and so it was apparent the top-rated Trojans had to beware of Greeks bearing mud.

"I feel like we've just conquered the Roman Empire," said a grinning Demosthenes (Dee) Andros, coach of the Beavers. "O.J. is a great runner. He's all that everybody says. But our defense rose to the occasion. We stopped them every time we had to."

Simpson showed no ill effects from his injury, sloshing for 188 yards in the Corvallis quagmire. But the day belonged to the Oregon State defense and Haggard. "If I never kick another field goal the rest of my life, I'll still be happy," he said.

Gunn wasn't so sure that Haggard's kick was a legitimate game-winner. "The mud was knee deep," the defensive end recalled. "When they kicked the winning field goal, I had a good angle because I was face-down in the mud, looking up at the goal posts. The kick was high above one of the posts, and it looked wide to me. I've always felt it should have been a 0-0 tie."

Adrian Young was the outstanding linebacker who keyed the Trojans' 24-7 victory over Notre Dame with four interceptions.

McKay would have none of that. He accepted the referee's decision and added, "Yes, the field was wet, but if we had been the better team, we would have won on a muddy field."

McKay was philosophical in defeat, praising the Beavers for a great effort and looking ahead to the next game. "It's a 10-game schedule," he said, "and we've got a big one coming up against a really fine team. We're going to see whether we're really good or just another football team."

Looming on the horizon was UCLA, which had moved to No. 1 in both wire-service polls while USC slipped to fourth in AP, third in UPI. If the Trojans were to be national champions, the schedule couldn't have been better planned.

"If you have to lose, you'd want it to happen the week before you had a chance to play a Number 1 team and redeem yourself," Fertig said. "It was an upset at Oregon State, but they had a great team. We hated losing up there, but it wasn't an embarrassment considering the mud and their ability."

The annual USC-UCLA contest doesn't require added hype to produce a great game, but this one had extra elements to make it memorable. Like so many others, it was for an Athletic Association of Western Universities championship and a Rose Bowl berth. But it also was for a national crown (AP and UPI conducted their final polls before bowl games in '67), and it provided national TV exposure for the one-two entries in the Heisman Trophy race, with newcomer Simpson facing off against Heisman favorite Gary Beban.

Beban, the Bruins' outstanding quarterback, had guided his team to a 7-0-1 record that included the tie with Oregon State and narrow victories over Tennessee, Penn State and Stanford.

"We've been good when we had to," said Bruins Coach Tommy Prothro.

"We've had to be good," retorted McKay, pointing to the Trojans' tougher schedule.

Prothro had beaten McKay's USC teams three times in four tries (once at Oregon State and the last two years at UCLA), and it was said that he had McKay's number. That notion became the central theme of Marv Goux's locker-room speech the day before the game.

"The worst thing in life is to be a prisoner.... I would rather die," the fiery Trojan assistant howled. "We've been prisoners to those bleeps over there for two years. Today's the day we go free!"

The players got the message. Everything was on the line, so the past was forgotten. The Trojans focused on UCLA with an intensity that exceeded that entering the Notre Dame game. It was time to put up or shut up.

"I still don't understand to this day what happened at Oregon State, but it really didn't matter," Yary said. "We could have come out of that one 0-9 and it wouldn't have made a difference. UCLA was next, and that's always a one-game season.

"It was a season in which we really took it one game at a time. Our only thought was on the next game. I remember coach Dave Levy writing on the blackboard: 'Death awaits for those who stray, dreaming of victories won yesterday.' He was right. The past meant nothing."

More than 90,000 spectators packed the Los Angeles Memorial Coliseum for a classic confrontation that justified its advance billing. The scoring was opened in the first quarter by UCLA, which was a three-point underdog despite its No. 1 ranking. Beban directed a superb drive, and the Bruins nursed a 7-0 lead while Simpson struggled to get going.

As was the case in previous games, the USC defense provided a much-needed spark. Cashman intercepted a Beban pass and returned it 55 yards for a touchdown. With Rikki Aldridge's extra point, the game was tied.

McCullouch bolted 52 yards on a reverse and caught a 13-yard pass as the Trojans reached the UCLA 13-yard line in the second period. At this point, Simpson provided the first of two incredible runs that afternoon. After bursting through a hole at the line of scrimmage, he chugged 13 grueling yards entirely on his own, breaking tackle after tackle. The only defenders he didn't shake were the two he dragged to the end zone for the tie-breaking touchdown. The amazing run through almost the entire UCLA defensive unit was to be immortalized as the "Run to Daylight" that was part of an art series commemorating the centennial celebration of college football in 1969.

"We were in trouble," The Juice recalled. "It was a broken play, so the main thing on my mind was not to lose ground. I got the ball and thought about making it to the line of scrimmage. I got past it and cut upfield on the left side. All I could think about was doing a drill—keep the legs churning and run like hell."

Undaunted, Beban drove the Bruins back within field-goal range. But Zenon Andrusyshyn, whose strong toe was supposed to give UCLA an edge, saw his 44-yard field-goal attempt blocked by defensive end Bill Hayhoe. USC went into the half with a 14-7 lead.

The Trojans had trouble moving the ball in the second half. Meanwhile, Beban rallied the Bruins to a pair of touchdowns and a 20-14 lead. Between those scores, however, Hayhoe blocked another Andrusyshyn field-goal try, and he barely tipped his extra-point attempt after UCLA's last touchdown. The kick went just outside the goal post, preventing the Bruins from taking a seven-point lead. The soccer-style kicker was shaping up as the goat of the game—assuming USC found a way to put the ball in the end zone one more time.

The Trojans found a way: O.J. It all came down to one exhilarating play that Simpson regards as his greatest collegiate run. USC faced a third and eight at its own 36-yard line when Page, who had replaced Sogge at quarterback, called a pass play in the huddle. But he changed his mind at the line of scrimmage and called Simpson's number—23-Blast. Sixty-four yards and an extra-point kick later, Southern Cal had a 21-20 lead that the defense protected for the last 10 minutes of the game.

"After running the kickoff back, I could hardly move," Simpson recalled. "In the huddle, I told Toby to give me a play, meaning a rest. So he called a pass, and I felt a lot better already because all I had to do was fake. Then we get to the line and he audibilizes.

"I'm thinking one, there's no way I can do this, and two, it's a horrible call with eight yards to go for a first down. But when I got the ball, I could see

Tight end Bob Miller signals touchdown as O.J. Simpson scores in the Trojans' 1967 victory over Notre Dame.

Split end Earl McCullouch was a world-class track star who also found success in college football.

the linebackers had dropped into a zone, expecting a pass. I got great early blocks from Lehmer and Taylor. Then Danny (Scott) took out a linebacker. I leaped for a first down and there was nobody there. I was at the left sideline and I got a couple more blocks, including one from (split end Ron) Drake.

"The pursuit was coming toward me, so I knew I had to get going. I just cut to my right and took off. I always prided myself on having stamina, on being the best-conditioned guy on the field. That's why runners like Payton, Brown, Dickerson and Allen have an edge. For the great runners, the fourth quarter is theirs. I was pooped, but I still had something left."

McKay thought he had seen Simpson do it all, but this run took the cake. "O.J. always gives his blockers the credit," the coach said, "but I don't think the blocking was good on that particular play. He turned five-yard blocking into a 64-yard run. I believe it was the most exciting college run I've ever seen."

If anyone harbored doubts about Simpson's greatness and the special edge he had given the Trojans that year, his performance against UCLA erased them. Simpson finished with 30 carries for 177 yards and two remarkable touchdowns in the game for all the marbles.

"The UCLA game will always remind me of O.J.," Klein said. "He was such an exciting guy to play with and such a nice guy. It felt great to block for him because you always felt you could spring him."

Yary realized that fact a few years later. "As an offensive lineman, you're so focused on what you're doing, so you engulf yourself with your assignment," he said. "There's really no time to appreciate what's going on around you. I didn't fully appreciate O.J.'s talent until I played against him. When I got to the NFL with the (Minnesota) Vikings and played against him, watching him blow past defenders, then I realized how truly great he was."

The other hero of the day was Hayhoe, who had a hand on three kick blocks. "We'd been working on it in practice all week," said Hayhoe, a 6-8 junior. "We knew he (Andrusyshyn) kicked low, so the coaches put me in for (5-10) Jim Snow and told me to jump. I just made contact."

Added McKay: "I was told by 10 million people during the week that he kicks the ball low. We had to put in somebody bigger than Snow, so Hayhoe was in there."

Whereas the weary Simpson's foot was throbbing and Beban overcame bruised ribs to complete 16 of 24 passes for 301 yards and two TDs, it was Gunn who epitomized courage that afternoon.

Gunn, whose forte was speed and quickness, was knocked out of the game in the first period when he tore ligaments in his knee. But when he was needed late in the game, Gunn charged off the bench and kept the pressure on Beban, who was smothered for 59 yards in losses that day.

"I was hurting, but I was too pumped up to feel great pain," Gunn explained. "We needed to put more pressure on Beban, and I had a job to do. . . . I didn't take any shots for the knee before I came back in. They just taped a padded armband around the knee. I tackled Beban for a couple of big losses. I'll never forget that game. Rossovich told me I'd make All-America the next year because of what I did, and he was right."

It was actually two years later that Gunn was named an All-America, but Rossovich's point was well taken. Gunn's gutsy play had sparked the USC defense to protect a narrow lead.

"His defensive performance was one of the keys to our victory," McKay said. "We asked him if he could go back in and do the job. Jim told us he

The 1967 Trojans: Front row (left to right)—Mike Holmgren, Steve Sogge, Toby Page, Sandy Durko, head Coach John McKay, Athletic Director Jess Hill, Mike Battle, Kendall Nungesser, Steve Grady, Earl McCullouch. Second row—Coach Craig Fertig, Mike Hull, Rikki Aldridge, Jim Lawrence, Pat Cashman, Wilson Bowie, O.J. Simpson, Steve Dale, Dan Scott, Bill Jaroncyk, coach Marv Goux. Third row—Coach Dave Levy, Jerry Shaw, Terrel Ray, Adrian Young, Bob Jensen, Bill Adams, Ralph Oliver, Jim Snow, Jim Gunn, coach Rod Humenuik. Fourth row—Scout Joe Margucci, John Coleman, Steve Swanson, Steve McConnell, Reg Fielder, John Blanche, Fred Khasigian, Dick Allmon, Steve Lehmer, Willard Scott, coach Phil Krueger. Fifth row—Coach Dick Coury, manager Bob Stuber, Sid Smith, Jack O'Malley, Mike Taylor, Gary Magner, Mike Scarpace, Ron Yary, Dennis Born, Dennis Crane, coach Jim Strangeland. Sixth row—Managers Pete Trapp, Bill Loadvine; Ty Salness, Tony Terry, Ron Drake, Bob Klein, Bill Hayhoe, Bob Miller, Tim Rossovich, Joe Obbema, managers Bill Rakow, Bill Tormey, Mike Green.

could, and he did exactly what we wanted."

Gunn required knee surgery the next day and was unable to play in the Trojans' 14-3 Rose Bowl victory over Indiana. Following such emotionally and physically draining triumphs over Notre Dame and UCLA, the trip to Pasadena almost was anticlimactic. The Trojans, who had given McKay his second unanimous national championship, already had proven their greatness.

"The UCLA game was one of the greatest of all time," Fertig said. "O.J.'s runs were unforgettable. On the 13-yarder, at least nine guys had a hand on him. And how can you forget what Hayhoe and Gunn did?"

You can't, of course, yet the Trojans' success story was much more than one great play or one great game. It was the sum of its parts, a blending of diverse talents into a winning combination that ranks with the finest in history.

"You never know how good you are, but we knew we had talent," Gunn said. "We also had the aura of a Heisman contender and several All-Americas. O.J. was great, but he had complementary talent."

Simpson, who finished second to Beban in the '67 Heisman derby before winning it the next year, concurred. "The outstanding characteristic was raw talent," he said. "We had guys who could play rock-em, sock-em football. We were a physical team, whereas the 1972 Trojans were more athletic.

"If we were to play the 1972 club, it would have been a great game. I'd match our defense with theirs, but they had better athletes and more weapons with guys like Lynn Swann at flanker and Anthony Davis running back kicks."

Even if the '72 Trojans did have the edge, O.J. was being modest. He came out of nowhere, setting a standard for Southern Cal tailbacks and producing a memorable '67 season—with a little help from his friends.

Southern Cal, 1967

ROAD TO GREATNESS

1967 RESULTS (10-1)

Opponent	Score	Opp. Record	Opp. Bowl Game
Washington State	49-0	2-8-0	
Texas	17-13	6-4-0	
at Michigan State	21-17	3-7-0	
Stanford	30-0	5-5-0	
at Notre Dame	24-7	8-2-0	
at Washington	23-6	5-5-0	
Oregon	28-6	2-8-0	
at California	31-12	5-5-0	
at Oregon State	0-3	7-2-1	
UCLA	21-20	7-2-1	
ROSE BOWL			
Indiana	**14-3**	**9-2-0**	

FACTS AND FIGURES

The 1967 Trojans played four teams (Notre Dame, Oregon State, UCLA and Indiana) that received Top 10 mention in either the final Associated Press or United Press International poll, emerging victorious three times. . . . Their only defeat—a 3-0 upset by Oregon State—was inflicted by the same team that had beaten John McKay in his first game as USC coach in 1960. . . . The Trojans have not lost to Oregon State since 1967. . . . After that loss, the Trojans were not shut out again until 1983, a stretch of 186 games that stands as an NCAA Division I-A record. . . . None of USC's 1967 regular-season opponents participated in postseason play, but eight of 11 opponents (including Rose Bowl foe Indiana) posted non-losing marks. The 11 teams' combined record was 59-50-2 (.541 winning percentage). . . . In 1967, USC ranked eighth among the nation's major colleges in total defense, fifth in scoring defense and eighth in rushing offense. . . . Safety Mike Battle, who had a team-high five interceptions in 1967, led the nation in punt returns (12.1-yard average) that year. He led the Trojans in punt-return average in each of his three varsity seasons (1966-68). . . . O.J. Simpson paced all major-college players in rushing with 1,415 yards in 1967 and 1,709 yards in 1968. . . . He led the team in total offense in both years. . . . In addition to winning the 1968 Heisman Trophy, Simpson won the Walter Camp Award in 1967 and 1968 and the Maxwell Award in '68. Each award denotes a particular organization's selection as the college football player of the year. . . . Southern Cal retired jersey number 32 in Simpson's honor. . . . Those receiving all-conference honors were Battle, Simpson, Ron Yary, Adrian Young, Tim Rossovich and split end Earl McCullouch. . . . Eleven Trojans were selected in the 1968 National Football League draft, including five first-round picks—Yary, Rossovich, McCullouch, offensive tackle Mike Taylor and fullback Mike Hull. . . . Simpson and tight end Bob Klein were first-round selections in 1969.

STATISTICAL LEADERS

PASSING

	Att.	Comp.	Yards	TD	Pct.	Int.
Steve Sogge	144	71	975	7	49.3	6

RUSHING

	Att.	Yards	Avg.	TD	Long
O.J. Simpson	266	1415	5.3	11	86
Steve Grady	69	279	4.0	1	18
Dan Scott	66	264	4.0	4	32

RECEIVING

	Rec.	Yards	Avg.	TD	Long
Earl McCullouch	28	517	18.5	5	50
Jim Lawrence	20	319	16.0	1	45
O.J. Simpson	10	109	10.9	0	33

SCORING

	TD	FG	PAT	Points
O.J. Simpson	11	0	0	66
Rikki Aldridge	0	4	32	44
Earl McCullouch	5	0	0	30

KEY CHARACTERS

The Conductor

COACH: John McKay.

Record: 127-40-8, 16 years at Southern Cal.

McKay, who had been an assistant at Southern Cal for less than a year, replaced Don Clark after the 1959 season. . . . He revamped the program and led the Trojans to a 10-0 regular-season record and a victory over Wisconsin in the Rose Bowl that followed the 1962 campaign. It was USC's first perfect season in 30 years and the first of McKay's undisputed national championships. . . . He went on to lead USC to two more undisputed championships (1967 and '72) and one partial crown (1974). . . . He is a member of the College Football Hall of Fame. . . . He coached the Trojans' first Heisman Trophy winner (Mike Garrett in 1965) and their only Outland Trophy winner (Ron Yary in 1967). . . . He also produced an impressive line of Trojan tailbacks that includes Garrett, O.J. Simpson, Clarence Davis, Anthony Davis and Ricky Bell, as well as fullback Sam Cunningham. . . . He was a teammate of Norm Van Brocklin's at Oregon.

Personal Data:

Born: July 5, 1923, in Everettville, W.Va.
High School: Shinnston High in Shinnston, W.Va.
College: Purdue and Oregon.

The Supporting Cast

DEFENSIVE END: Tim Rossovich.

Rossovich was a consensus All-America in 1967. . . . His speed and size (6-5, 230 pounds) allowed him to make the switch from the offensive line to the defensive line after his sophomore season (1965). . . . He handled some placekicking duties for the Trojans, booting three extra points and a field goal during the 1966 showdown against Texas. . . . Rossovich, who lettered from 1965-67, also served as the Trojans' full-time kickoff man.

Personal Data:

Born: March 14, 1946, at Palo Alto, Calif.
High School: St. Francis High in Mountain View, Calif.

HALFBACK: O.J. Simpson.

Orenthal James Simpson is a member of both the college and pro football Halls of Fame. . . . He won the 1968 Heisman Trophy after finishing second in the balloting the previous season. . . . Though he played only two seasons, he ranks high on the Trojans' all-time rushing charts with 3,123 yards and holds the Pacific-10 record with a career average of 164.4 yards per game. . . . He was a unanimous consensus All-America pick in both 1967 and 1968 and a member of The Sporting News All-Time All-America Team, picked in 1983. . . . Simpson and Marcus Allen share the school record for most points (138, including bowls) and most touchdowns (23) in a single season. . . . He was twice named junior college All-America while attending City College of San Francisco in 1965 and 1966. . . . He set numerous national junior college rushing and scoring marks, finishing his two years with 54 touchdowns (including postseason action). . . . He ran a leg for USC's 440-yard relay team that set a world record in 1967.

Personal Data:

Born: July 9, 1947, in San Francisco.
High School: Galileo High in San Francisco.

OFFENSIVE TACKLE: Ron Yary.

Yary, a member of the College Football Hall of Fame, was the 1967 recipient of the Outland Trophy. . . . He was a two-time consensus All-America, earning his selection unanimously in 1967, and was a member of The Sporting News All-Time All-America Team selected in 1983. . . . Yary, an outstanding drive blocker, was switched from defense to offense after his sophomore season and earned letters from 1965-67. . . . He attended Cerritos Junior College in 1964.

Personal Data:

Born: August 16, 1946, in Chicago.
High School: Bellflower High in Bellflower, Calif.

LINEBACKER: Adrian Young.

Young, a consensus All-America in 1967, was the Trojans' defensive captain his junior and senior seasons. . . . He lettered from 1965-67. . . . He holds the Trojan record for most interceptions (four) in one game, burning Notre Dame in 1967. . . . Young's strengths were his outstanding athletic ability, instinct and knack for being in the right place at the right time.

Personal Data:

Born: January 31, 1946, in Dublin, Ireland.
High School: Bishop Amat High in La Puente, Calif.

FINAL 1967 WIRE SERVICE RANKINGS

ASSOCIATED PRESS

1. SOUTHERN CAL	6. Wyoming
2. Tennessee	**7. Oregon State**
3. Oklahoma	8. Alabama
4. Indiana	9. Purdue
5. Notre Dame	10. Penn State

Only Top 10 ranked.

UNITED PRESS

1. SOUTHERN CAL	11. Penn State
2. Tennessee	12. Syracuse
3. Oklahoma	13. Colorado
4. Notre Dame	14. Minnesota
5. Wyoming	15. Florida State
6. Indiana	16. Miami (Fla.)
7. Oklahoma	17. North Carolina St.
8. Oregon State	18. Georgia
9. Purdue	19. Houston
10. UCLA	20. Arizona State

Bold face indicates Southern Cal opponent.

The Gospel According To Schwartzwalder

Syracuse, 1959
By Joe Gergen

For Syracuse, the 1959 national college football championship did not fall from a clear blue sky. However, the man most responsible for the achievement did. Frequently, in fact.

An explanation is in order.

After many years of producing top teams, outstanding players and such future coaching legends as Chick Meehan, Pappy Waldorf and Duffy Daugherty, the Syracuse program fell on hard times in the wake of World War II. For five seasons following the resumption of football on Piety Hill after a suspension of play in 1943, the Orangemen majored in losing, with an overall record of 11-29-1 compiled under three coaches. Clearly, new leadership was required.

Enter Floyd Burdette Schwartzwalder, a tough former lineman who had been a starting center and captain at West Virginia despite a playing weight that failed to exceed 152 pounds. If there had ever been any doubt about his leadership ability, it had been answered during the war when he served as a company commander in the 82nd Airborne Division. Maj. "Ben" Schwartzwalder (the nickname had been provided by his brother and eagerly accepted) was a paratrooper who led the 507th Parachute Infantry into battle. When he told his troops to jump, they jumped.

True story: On D-Day, the man fell asleep on the flight across the English Channel and had to be awakened as the plane approached Normandy. "Well," he explained, "I'd been up for 24 hours getting my outfit ready, and I figured I needed some

Coach Ben Schwartzwalder hands off the ball to the pride of Syracuse, Ernie Davis. A star sophomore in 1959, Davis would win the Heisman Trophy in 1961.

A happy group of Orangemen, led by Gerhard Schwedes (16) and Ernie Davis (44), celebrate their 23-14 Cotton Bowl triumph over the Texas Longhorns.

rest, because I wouldn't get it when I hit the ground."

Schwartzwalder returned from the service with a chestful of ribbons and a GI haircut he never bothered to update, and eagerly threw himself into a less lethal form of combat. A high school coach before the war, he landed the position of football coach at Muhlenberg College in time for the 1946 season. In his first year at the Pennsylvania school, he took a team that had been winless in five games the previous season and won eight of nine games, plus the Tobacco Bowl against St. Bonvaventure.

Ironically, his teams were too successful for Muhlenberg, causing officials embarrassment at the prospect of dominating the competition indefinitely. After three seasons, Schwartzwalder needed a challenge. Syracuse offered one of the largest challenges in the profession.

Not only had the Orangemen lost their last eight games in 1948 after winning the season opener against Niagara (which soon dropped football), but the enthusiasm for the sport on campus also had diminished. The administration had imposed limitations on recruiting and the schedule was dotted with other private schools for whom national honors were never a consideration. If Schwartzwalder had reservations about Syracuse, some Syracuse football supporters had reservations about him.

After all, Muhlenberg was not Penn State. And the man was less than a prominent national figure. "The alumni wanted a big-name coach," Schwartzwalder once said with wry humor that often was overlooked, "and got a long-name coach."

The name would not be his biggest contribution to Syracuse. He brought with him some strong opinions of how the game should be played and schemes that distinguished the Orangemen from opponents. "We wanted to be original," he said.

So he took the unbalanced line from the single-wing attack of his playing days and merged it with the "T" formation that swept through football in the 1940s. "I grew up with the unbalanced line," he said. " But we ran it both right and left. We always had a good short-side attack."

Schwartzwalder wanted the other team to spend extra time preparing for Syracuse. And if the defense had done its homework and overshifted to the strong side, the Orangemen would run the "scissors" play, a counter to the weak side that became a Syracuse trademark. Despite his experience with the airborne, the coach preferred to stay close to the ground on the football field. Yet, he insisted that both his halfbacks be able to throw and used option passes to discourage aggressive behavior on the part of opponents.

He also was ahead of his time in employing multiple defenses. Syracuse lined up in a five-man line before each play, then jumped into a four-, a six- and even, upon occasion, an eight-man line. This created momentary confusion. Frequently, it enabled his defense "to meet them on the other side of the fence," as he put it.

With Schwartzwalder's system, his dedication to football and his insistence upon toughness and conditioning, Syracuse became respectable immediately. The Orangemen won four of nine games in 1949, and that would be the coach's only losing season until 1972. His fourth team, in 1952, even received Syracuse's first bowl invitation, although Alabama's 61-6 victory in the Orange Bowl didn't do much for the New York school's reputation.

Despite the man's coaching and the administration's gradual relaxation of the scholarship restrictions, it took the arrival of a remarkable athlete from Long Island to push the program to the next plateau. There was virtually no sport in which Jimmy Brown did not excel. He was a fine track athlete, an accomplished basketball player and perhaps the most gifted player in the history of college lacrosse. If it took him a while to emerge as a star in football, it was the combination of inexperience and an offensive system that was not designed, according to Schwartzwalder, to revolve around a single player of astonishing ability.

Brown first attracted considerable notice in the sixth game of his varsity career, rushing for 151 yards and playing admirably on defense in a loss to Cornell. He wore jersey 44 because no accomplished varsity player had requested it and he was no better than fifth on the depth chart at the start of practice in his sophomore year. But as he began to dominate games against powerful teams in his junior season, the number took on a special significance. As a senior, he finished third in the nation in rushing and virtually carried Syracuse into the national spotlight.

The Orangemen won seven of eight regular-season games in 1956 and earned another major bowl invitation. And while Syracuse was a loser in the Cotton Bowl by a 28-27 score to Texas Christian, Brown's performance was nothing short of brilliant. He rushed for 132 yards, scored three touchdowns and kicked three extra points. He also brought the school to the attention of many outstanding athletes who would make up the 1959

End Fred Mautino, shown catching a pass in the Cotton Bowl against Texas, was an important two-way performer for the '59 Orangemen.

The only blot on Syracuse's season was a Cotton Bowl brawl that started as a fight between Texas tackle Larry Stephens (84) and John Brown (76).

team.

Among them was an outstanding running back from Elmira, N.Y., named Ernie Davis. Although Davis was pointed in the direction of Syracuse by alumnus Marty Harrigan, his high school coach, and adviser Tony DeFilippo (another Syracuse alum), he also had the benefit of a personal visit by Brown. Not only did he decide to follow in Brown's footsteps, but he even wore the same number. Thus did one of the great traditions in college sports take hold.

In time, Davis would become the most honored athlete in school history as well as the first black to receive the Heisman Memorial Trophy. He also would be cut down, by leukemia, before he had a chance to play his first professional game, alongside Brown, for the Cleveland Browns. To his older teammates and his coach on the 1959 Syracuse team, the effect of the player on the program was secondary to that of the person.

"Ernie was unique," Schwartzwalder said years later in a moving tribute. "He was like a saint. He was so kind and so good, you couldn't believe it." That's not ordinary coach talk, but then Davis was an extraordinary individual.

As a high-profile sophomore on a veteran squad that had won eight of nine regular-season games and played in the Orange Bowl at the conclusion of the 1958 season, Davis might have engendered resentment. But his presence was so understated, his spirit so infectious that he became a major source of team unity. There wasn't a better running back on the field as long as he was in the game and there wasn't a more enthusiastic cheerleader in ancient Archbold Stadium whenever he was on the sideline.

"Even though he has it made, he's still in there working as if he were trying to make the squad," said Bill Bell, an aide to Schwartzwalder. "He's the first man on the field and the last to leave. When the team does laps, he leads the pack. Barring physical trouble, Ernie will be a great football player . . . . "

Davis was the least of the worries for Old Ben (the coach had a habit of referring to himself in the third person) as Syracuse prepared for its opening game against Kansas. He was more concerned about the quarterback position, where senior Bob Thomas, an understudy the previous year, was lost for the season because of a back injury. Reluctant to start either of two promising sophomores, Dave Sarette or Dick Easterly, Schwartzwalder nominated German-born Gerhard Schwedes for the assignment.

When Schwartzwalder arrived on the Syracuse campus a decade earlier, Schwedes was an 11-year-old kid kicking around a soccer ball in Germany. "The first football game I ever saw was between GI teams in Germany," said Schwedes, who accompanied his family to the United States shortly thereafter. "I wondered what they were doing, why they weren't playing with a round ball . . . . "

Schwedes was a senior and the captain of the 1959 Syracuse team. The coach as well as Gerhard's teammates recognized his leadership qualities and his dedication to football. But Schwedes also was a halfback whose throwing ability was enhanced by the surprise factor. He was less a threat as a dropback passer.

Nevertheless, Schwartzwalder reasoned that Syracuse could run the ball consistently well enough to control Kansas. The Jayhawks did indeed allow 308 yards on the ground, but they jammed the line of scrimmage at key junctures and thereby prevented the Orangemen from mounting successful drives. And, bolstered by an explosive offensive talent in John Hadl, Kansas jumped to an early lead.

Reluctantly, Schwartzwalder was forced to go to the air. In doing so, the coach made what would become the most important tactical adjustment of the season: He called upon Sarette. Alternating with Schwedes as the Orange's signal-caller against Kansas, Sarette proceeded to complete nine of 13 passes for 117 yards and one touchdown. Syracuse won handily, 35-21. More typical of the season than Sarette's rescue effort was Syracuse's overall statistical edge. The Orangemen outgained the Jayhawks, 493 yards to 67.

As the season progressed with a series of one-sided victories, it became evident that despite the outstanding halfback tandem of Davis and Schwedes (reinstalled at right halfback), the powerful thrusts of fullback Art Baker and a passing attack that was more than adequate, the true strength of the team was in the line. The forward wall was unusually big for its time, averaging 6-foot-3 and 216 pounds per man. In addition, it was remarkably agile for the simple reason that only one member of what the media began calling the "Sizable Seven" had been a down lineman in high school.

"That was part of Ben's genius in recruiting," Sarette said. All but tackle Bob Yates, who doubled as a placekicker, had played a so-called skill position (end or back) before arriving at Syracuse. The linemen were powerful but never ponderous.

"The way those lineman get into your backfield, they could be called the 'Sinister Seven' as well as the 'Sizable Seven,'" Navy Coach Wayne Hardin cracked.

Center Al Bemiller, guards Roger Davis and Bruce Tarbox, tackles Yates and Maury Youmans and ends Fred Mautino and Gerry Skonieczki were a force on both offense and defense in the era of two-way football. Week after week, they thoroughly dominated the line of scrimmage.

Roger Davis, who would be the lone consensus All-America on the 1959 Syracuse team, was in top form in the second game of the season, against Maryland. The man called "Hound Dog"—so named because of his harassment of the opposition and his hobby of training dogs—threw the Terrapins' quarterback for a loss on one play and blocked a punt on the next, setting the tempo for a Syracuse runaway. Maryland was limited to eight yards rushing, 29 yards overall. Holy Cross lost yardage on the ground against Syracuse, as did three other opponents—Pittsburgh, Boston University and UCLA. Syracuse, getting 141 yards rushing from Ernie Davis, outgained West Virginia, 589 yards to 109 in total offense, and the Orangemen posted a total of five shutouts in '59. The Orange would have had a sixth shutout but, in a matchup of unbeaten teams, a Holy Cross player intercepted a lateral from Sarette and scored the game's first touchdown. Syracuse, whose only regular-season defeat the previous season had been administered by the Crusaders, retaliated with 42 points.

Not only did the Orangemen boast an outstanding first unit, but they had a talented second team. And Schwartzwalder made maximum use of the reserves, devising a rotation system for each quarter. Although the unit's forte was defense, the group had an impact whenever and however it was deployed.

The unsung players were known as Gerlick's Gorillas, in honor of senior Al Gerlick, who played inside tackle on offense and interior guard on defense. "I always wanted to be 6 feet," Gerlick said. Unfortunately, fate had consigned him to battle through life at approximately 5-9 (although he was listed at 5-10). "It gave me extra incentive," he said. That incentive was evident in the play of the entire unit, which featured a lineman with vast potential in 220-pound John Brown and the massive (6-5, 250 pounds) Gene Grabosky.

Although the Gorillas left their mark on earlier games, most notably against Navy when Mark Weber (an understudy to Ernie Davis) stole a pass and ran 30 yards for a touchdown, it was the Penn State game that established the reputation of the second team. For the first time since the opening game, 6-0 Syracuse was challenged—and this contest would decide Eastern supremacy.

The outcome appeared in doubt until the Orangemen boosted their lead to 20-6 in the fourth quarter. Their relief was momentary. Roger Kochman, Penn State's star halfback, returned a kickoff for a touchdown and the Nittany Lions—also unbeaten—scored again after blocking a punt deep in Syracuse territory. Almost before the Orangemen could gather themselves, Penn State was lining up for a two-point conversion that could have tied the score.

The first unit had been on the field for both Penn State touchdowns. In desperation, Schwartzwalder sent the second team into the game in time for the conversion attempt. As was its habit, the defensive line shifted just before the snap. Linebacker Bob Stem moved up and Gerlick bounced over, leaving him in a gap and with a clean shot at the ballcarrier.

"It was a counter play to Kochman," Gerlick said. "I went for his legs but he gave a juke. I grabbed one leg and he managed to shake loose. I thought, 'Oh, no, I missed him,' but I turned around and there was John Brown and Gene Grabosky. They saved the day for me."

Grabosky made the tackle at the 3-yard line. Ironically, the man had transferred from Penn State because he felt unwanted. With that one play, he justified his decision.

Still, there were more than five minutes remaining in the game, plenty of time for Penn State to regain possession. Taking no chances, Schwartzwalder sent the chastened first unit back into the

Syracuse defenders Gerry Skonieczki (88) and Maury Youmans (78) close the hole on Texas running back Jack Collins.

game with orders to run out the clock and the Orangemen did just that, grounding out 48 yards against a defense rigged to stop the running attack.

"I'd actually point to the spot," Sarette said of the grind-it-out strategy that clinched a 20-18 triumph. "I'd say, 'We're coming here,' and that's where we'd go. Those guys probably didn't know if I was trying to trick them or not, but I was serious. It was them or us. That was the kind of mettle that team had."

Mautino was a key performer against the Nittany Lions, putting constant pressure on All-America quarterback Richie Lucas and also catching a 20-yard pass that set up Syracuse's first touchdown.

"I can't ever remember seeing another end who gets on top of a passer any quicker and still remains under control," Orangeman assistant coach Joe Szombathy said of Mautino. "This is the secret. On top of that, he has extremely long arms and this permits him to block more passes just as they're leaving the thrower's hand.

"Offensively, he's a fine receiver. His big hands make him a sure catch, and his height (6-3) makes him a grand target. In addition, he's a great blocker."

The victory over Penn State was the major hurdle of the '59 season for the Orangemen and Syracuse found itself atop the wire-service polls the next week, giving Eastern football its highest prestige since the great West Point clubs of Doc Blanchard and Glenn Davis ran roughshod over the opposition in the mid-1940s. Before routs of traditional rival Colgate and Boston University, the Orangemen had a decision to make. They were courted by the Orange, Sugar and Cotton bowls and were in the position of naming their holiday destination.

"Ben said he was going to let us vote," Youmans said. He also informed the players that Texas was the highest-ranked available opponent. "We all wanted to go to Miami," Youmans said. "We had a terrific time there the year before. So we voted for the Orange Bowl. We didn't care who was Number 2."

But the coach cared. After being apprised of the vote, he addressed his team. Peering over his glasses, Schwartzwalder said in a calm but forceful voice, "Boys, I think you better vote again." On second thought, the Orangemen selected the Cotton Bowl and the matchup against the next highest-ranked team. The official acceptance of a bid to the Dallas classic was disclosed after the Orangemen had destroyed Colgate, 71-0.

After throttling BU, 46-0, the next week, there was one game yet to play in the regular season. Syracuse was scheduled to meet UCLA in Los Angeles, and the coach made certain that his team understood what was at stake. The Orangemen had the opportunity to defeat an intersectional opponent on national television, and this wasn't just any opponent. The Bruins were 5-3-1 and had upset a Southern California team that had boasted an 8-0 record. Schwartzwalder transformed the game into a crusade for Eastern football.

"They always called us the 'effete East,' " the coach said. "Well, I looked that up in the dictionary, so I knew what it meant. And I made sure the players knew, too."

Whatever the reason, Syracuse responded with a superior effort, perhaps its best of the season. Not even 82-degree heat and smog could slow the Orangemen's drive to the first unbeaten season in school history. Using its 20-pound per man advantage along the line, Syracuse raced to a 21-0 lead and romped to a 36-8 victory, gaining 456 yards and substituting freely in the process. As well as the first unit played, the reserves were even more effective, eliciting good-natured speculation that perhaps Syracuse's second group should be ranked No. 2 in the nation.

Although Ernie Davis was Syracuse's big man in the backfield in 1959, Schwedes and Baker were forces, too. Schwedes averaged 6.3 yards per carry and Baker bulled his way for 5.1 yards each time he lugged the ball. Sarette threw for touchdowns on 10 of his 49 completions. And Schwedes scored 16 touchdowns overall.

So formidable did the Orangemen appear that Life magazine sent a team of reporters to Houston, where the team held preliminary practice for the New Year's Day bowl game in Dallas. The magazine was prepared to crown Syracuse as the best college football team of the decade. Surely, Syracuse had the statistics to underwrite such a claim. The Orangemen led the nation in scoring, rushing, total offense, rushing defense, total defense and, praise the Lord and pass the ammunition, touchdown aerials.

As a result, Syracuse was installed as a two-touchdown favorite over a good Texas team that had won nine of 10 regular-season games. The large spread presented the Longhorns with an emotional edge. Roger Davis noted tears in the eyes of the opposing players when the band struck up "The Eyes of Texas" and told his teammates, "Boys, we're in for a game."

More accurately, they were in for a fight. Schwartzwalder was concerned about the condition of Ernie Davis after the halfback, who had led the team in rushing with 686 yards and a seven-yard average per carry, suffered a leg injury while practicing kickoffs four days before the game. Although Davis did limp while walking, his running was not impaired. He proved that in the opening minute and a half of the game when he circled out of the backfield, broke into the clear down the middle of the field and caught a halfback pass from Schwedes. The connection covered 87 yards, a Cotton Bowl pass-play record that still stands, and demonstrated Syracuse's resourcefulness. As a Penn State assistant coach named Joe Paterno had remarked eight weeks earlier, "If you make just one little mistake on Davis, it's goodbye. He's the kind of runner you hate to coach against. You can't instruct a boy to tackle a man if he can't catch him."

The Orangemen boosted their lead to 15-0 in the second quarter when Davis completed an 80-yard drive with a fourth-down thrust from inside the one-yard line, then caught a two-point conversion pass from Sarette. It was the second unit that threatened to break open the game late in the first half, but an apparent 41-yard scoring pass from Easterly to Ken Ericson was nullified, one of several controversial calls that infuriated Schwartzwalder and his team. One official ruled that Ericson had lost control of the ball at the goal line. Another signaled holding on Gerlick.

While arguments raged, Texas tackle Larry Stephens and John Brown almost came to blows. Later, teammates charged that the Longhorn lineman had been harassing Brown, one of three blacks on the Syracuse team, with racial taunts. Players from both teams jumped in and the coaches, Schwartzwalder and Darrell Royal of Texas, raced onto the field.

After the game, Stephens denied allegations that he had baited Brown and the Syracuse lineman, a quiet sophomore, declined to repeat the names he had been called. "A guy gets excited in a game," he said, "and sometimes he says things he doesn't really mean. It doesn't bother me anymore."

The unfortunate incident, however, produced an undercurrent of bitterness that was felt in every block and tackle for the remainder of the game. Texas threatened briefly in the third quarter after scoring on a 69-yard pass play from Bobby Lackey to Jack Collins, but Syracuse matched that touchdown on a three-yard run by Schwedes after Ernie Davis had intercepted a Longhorn pass. A second conversion pass from Sarette to Davis padded the lead to 23-6. Texas added a touchdown and two-point conversion in a fourth quarter otherwise distinguished by hard hitting and minor injuries. The final score was Syracuse 23, Texas 14.

In its issue of January 11, 1960, Life ran a photo essay on the game entitled "A Brawling Battle of the Hard-Noses," and did say Syracuse "maybe was the best team in a decade." But it offset the pictures of

The 1959 Orangemen: Front row (left to right) —Trainer Neil Pratt, assistant coaches Joe Szombathy, Dick Beyer, Jim Shreve, Bill Bell, Coach Ben Schwartzwalder, assistant coaches Ted Dailey, Rocco Pirro, trainer Jules Reichel, team physician Dr. Clyde Barney, equipment manager Al Zak. Second row—Ken Ericson, Danny Sullivan, Mark Weber, Danny Rackiewicz, Dave Applehof, Johnny Nichols, Jim Anderson, Gerry Skonieczki. Third row—Maury Youmans, Fred Mautino, Dave Baker, Bob Yates, Al Bemiller, Bruce Tarbox, Jim Lamey, Frank Mambuca. Fourth row—Glenn Gill, Dave Sarette, Ed Bowers, Joe Caramanna, Bob Hart, Bill Sproule, George Brazel, Charlie Heck. Fifth row—Vince Moran, Norm Lemieux, Tommy Gilburg, Art Baker, Brian Howard, Don Brace, Sam Colella, Ernie Davis, Gary Fallon. Sixth row—Dick Feidler, Jim Laffey, Bill Fitzgerald, Frank Santoli, Jerry Sobul, Dick Reimer, Bob Thomas, Gerhard Schwedes, Pete Brokaw. Seventh row—George Francovitch, Tom Spillett, John Brown, Leon Cholakis, John Howell, Fred Hilliard, Mike Neary, Jim Saylor, Ron Bartlett. Eighth row—Manager Bruce Hoag, Bob Stem, Jim Bennett, Otis Godfrey, Dick Easterly, Stan Sokol, Gene Grabosky, Al Gerlick, Jon Beckom.

aggression with those from a special event staged in the chapel at Southern Methodist University on January 2. Schwedes, the captain, and Yates, the tackle, were married in a double wedding ceremony on the day following the game.

There's a postscript to the story, one that underlines that particular team's enduring influence. Twenty-five years after their perfect season, the players returned to the school for a reunion. They attended a dinner party on Friday night and then sat in the modern Carrier Dome, constructed on the site of old Archbold Stadium, and watched the 1984 Orangemen, prohibitive underdogs, upset No. 1-ranked Nebraska, 17-9. One of the standout players on that '84 Syracuse team was wide receiver Scott Schwedes, the captain's son.

Syracuse, 1959

ROAD TO GREATNESS

1959 RESULTS (11-0)

Opponent	Score	Opp. Record	Opp. Bowl Game
Kansas	35-21	5-5-0	
Maryland	29-0	5-5-0	
*Navy	32-6	5-4-1	
Holy Cross	42-6	6-4-0	
West Virginia	44-0	3-7-0	
at Pittsburgh	35-0	6-4-0	
at Penn State	20-18	9-2-0	Liberty (W)
Colgate	71-0	2-7-0	
at Boston University	46-0	4-5-0	
at UCLA	36-8	5-4-1	
COTTON BOWL			
Texas	**23-14**	**9-2-0**	

*Norfolk, Va.

FACTS AND FIGURES

Syracuse placed two players on The Sporting News' All-America team for 1959—guard Roger Davis and tackle Bob Yates. . . . The Orangemen rolled to an unbeaten season against opposition that played creditably overall. Orange's 11 opponents won 59 games, lost 49 and tied 2 for a winning percentage of .545. . . . Lesser lights on schedule—the three teams that concluded the season with losing records—never had a chance, though, falling to Syracuse by a combined score of 161-0. . . . The Orange posted five shutouts in '59, four of them coming in a five-game span. . . . After beating Penn State by two points in their toughest game of the season, the Orangemen went out and won by 71 points the next week (against Colgate). . . . Syracuse's domination of the national statistical charts showed the brute force of Coach Ben Schwartzwalder's team. Orangemen led the country in total offense and in total defense, a winning combination if there ever was one. That, however, was just for starters. Syracuse also was No. 1 in rushing offense, scoring offense and rushing defense. . . .While the Orange didn't make the top 10 in passing offense, Schwartzwalder's troops showed their aerial prowess by topping the nation in touchdown passes. . . . Syracuse averaged 6.1 yards every time it handled the ball from scrimmage in 1959; its opponents managed a mere two yards per play. . . . Incredibly, as reflected by the total-offense tables, the Orangeman outgained the opposition by an average of 355.3 yards per game. . . . Cotton Bowl triumph that capped the season was the first postseason victory in school's history. In its three previous bowl appearances, Syracuse had lost twice in the Orange Bowl (1953, 1959) and once in the Cotton Bowl (1957). . . . From the seventh game of the 1955 season through the Liberty Bowl victory that wrapped up the 1961 campaign (and also ended Ernie Davis' career in an Orange uniform), Syracuse—fueled by its 11-0 squad of '59—fashioned a 48-12-1 record.

STATISTICAL LEADERS

PASSING

	Att.	Comp.	Yards	TD	Pct.	Int.
Dave Sarette	83	49	763	10	59.0	5
Dick Easterly	39	21	353	7	53.8	5

RUSHING

	Att.	Yards	Avg.	TD
Ernie Davis	98	686	7.0	9
Gerhard Schwedes	90	567	6.3	11
Art Baker	100	507	5.1	2

RECEIVING

	Rec.	Yards	Avg.	TD
Fred Mautino	17	215	12.6	2
Gerhard Schwedes	15	231	15.4	5
Gerry Skonieczki	13	256	19.7	3
Ernie Davis	11	94	8.5	0

SCORING

	TD	FG	PAT	Points
Gerhard Schwedes	16	0	*2	100
Ernie Davis	10	0	*2	64
Mark Weber	6	0	0	36
Art Baker	5	0	0	30

*Two-point conversion.

KEY CHARACTERS

The Conductor

COACH: Floyd (Ben) Schwartzwalder.

Record: 153-91-3, 25 years at Syracuse.

Schwartzwalder succeeded Reaves Baysinger as Syracuse coach in 1949 and proceeded to build a strong football program. . . . The 1951 Orangemen finished 5-4, the school's first winning season since 1942. . . . His teams would not suffer another losing season until 1972, his second to last season as Syracuse coach. . . . Two of his teams lost one game and his 1959 national championship team was undefeated. . . . From 1958-60, the Orangemen won 21 consecutive regular-season games. . . . Four Schwartzwalder-coached teams won the Lambert Trophy, symbolic of Eastern college football supremacy, and his 1952 unit played in the Orangemen's first-ever bowl game—a disappointing 61-6 loss to Alabama. . . . He guided the Orangemen into seven bowl games, in which they compiled a 2-5 record. . . . He produced five consensus All-Americas, including three of the game's top running backs—Jim Brown, Ernie Davis and Larry Csonka. . . . He coached the Orangemen to a 20-18 victory over Penn State in 1959 in what was considered an Eastern football classic. . . . He ranks as the 20th all-time winningest Division I-A coach with 178 victories and is a member of the College Football Hall of Fame. . . . His first collegiate coaching job was at Muhlenberg (Pa.) College, where his teams compiled a 25-5 record. . . . Schwartzwalder's Syracuse program suffered through lean times in the early 1970s when black athletes boycotted the Orangemen, accusing Schwartzwalder and his staff of racism, and former Syracuse player Dave Meggyesy wrote a book charging the university with medical abuses and payoffs to players.

Personal Data:

Born: June 7, 1909, at Point Pleasant, W. Va.
College: West Virginia.

The Supporting Cast

HALFBACK: Ernie Davis.

Davis was among the finest talents ever to grace college football. . . . He was a leader on and off the field and one of the most admired athletes of his time. . . . Davis won the 1961 Heisman Trophy and is a member of the College Football Hall of Fame. . . . He was a consensus All-America in 1960 and a unanimous consensus pick in '61. . . . Davis, who lettered from 1959-61, shattered almost every Syracuse rushing record and was primed for a professional career when it was discovered that he was suffering from leukemia, which proved fatal. . . . His tragic death came May 18, 1963.

Personal Data:

Born: December 14, 1939, at New Salem, Pa.
High School: Elmira Free Academy in Elmira, N.Y.

OFFENSIVE GUARD: Roger Davis.

Davis was named Syracuse's most valuable player in 1959, the same season he was named unanimous consensus All-America. . . . He also was named United Press International's Lineman of the Year that season. . . . He opened the holes for Ernie Davis and shut them as a top-notch guard on defense. . . . He made five consecutive tackles in Syracuse's key 1959 victory over Penn State. . . . Davis, who was nicknamed "Hound Dog" by teammates, lettered from 1957-59.

Personal Data:

Born: June 23, 1938, at Cleveland, O.

QUARTERBACK: Dave Sarette.

Sarette was the sophomore quarterback who guided the Orangemen to their national championship. . . . He led the Orangemen in total offense with 879 yards and completed 47 of 83 passes for 763 yards and 10 touchdowns. . . . He lettered from 1959-61.

HALFBACK: Gerhard Schwedes.

Schwedes was co-captain of the 1959 team and the Orangemen's leading scorer with 16 touchdowns and 100 points. . . . He was the second-leading rusher (567 yards) and second-leading receiver (15 catches, 231 yards) in Syracuse's championship season. . . . He was a quarterback in 1957 before switching to halfback and lettering from 1957-59 for the Orangemen. . . . His father was a prisoner of war during World War II in Germany, where Gerhard was born. . . . His son, Scott, later played at Syracuse (1983-86) and became the Orangemen's all-time leading receiver.

Personal Data:

Born: 1938 at Ulm, Germany.
High School: Hunterdon Central High in Flemington, N.J.

FINAL 1959 WIRE SERVICE RANKINGS

ASSOCIATED PRESS		UNITED PRESS	
1. SYRACUSE	11. Clemson	**1. SYRACUSE**	11. Illinois
2. Mississippi	**12. Penn State**	2. Mississippi	12. Southern Cal
3. Louisiana State	13. Illinois	3. Louisiana State	13. Alabama
4. Texas	14. Southern Cal	**4. Texas**	**14. Penn State**
5. Georgia	15. Oklahoma	5. Georgia	15. Oklahoma
6. Wisconsin	16. Wyoming	6. Wisconsin	16. Northwestern
7. TCU	17. Notre Dame	7. Washington	Michigan State
8. Washington	18. Missouri	8. TCU	18. Wyoming
9. Arkansas	19. Florida	9. Arkansas	19. Auburn
10. Alabama	**20. Pittsburgh**	10. Clemson	Missouri

Bold face indicates Syracuse opponent.

Irish Tie Down Another Title

Notre Dame, 1966
By Bill Bilinski

For the first nine games of 1966, chemistry and confidence made Notre Dame the best team in the country. Its character in Game 10 made it official.

"Our biggest moment of the year was when we played Southern Cal," recalled Alan Page, a consensus All-America defensive end on the 1966 team. "We were beat up. It had been a long season, and there was some concern whether we could stay on the field with them."

One week after The Game against Michigan State ended in a numbing 10-10 tie, Notre Dame went west and somehow decimated the Rose Bowl-bound Trojans, 51-0. The Irish were missing starters at quarterback and center, but a casual observer wouldn't have noticed.

"How it happened is absolutely beyond me," recalled Jim Lynch, a consensus All-America linebacker and the Irish captain that year. "I know I was there physically.... It was one of those fluky situations, one of those games that come along once in a decade."

The triumph, which marked Notre Dame's sixth shutout and Coach Ara Parseghian's 100th collegiate victory, gave the school its fifth national title since the Associated Press began certifying the winner of the national crown in 1936. United Press International concurred in its poll of college coaches.

The architect of this team was Parseghian, who had come to South Bend from Northwestern in 1964 and immediately restored Notre Dame to national prominence following a decade in the doldrums. After Frank Leahy's last team finished sec-

The architect of Notre Dame's 1966 championship was Ara Parseghian, who installed intensity and dedication as part of the Fighting Irish work ethic.

Parseghian entrusted Notre Dame's offense to strong-armed quarterback Terry Hanratty (5) and backup Coley O'Brien.

ond in both wire-service polls in 1953, the Irish posted a modest 51-48 record in 10 years under Terry Brennan, Joe Kuharich and Hugh Devore. But Parseghian directed his first squad to a 9-1 record and a No. 3 ranking in the polls, and Irish spirits again were flying high.

Parseghian's psychological ploys and emotional leadership resurrected memories of Knute Rockne, whose innovative strategy and famous halftime speeches had sparked the great Notre Dame teams of the 1920s. Parseghian believed that proper motivational techniques could help his players reach "emotional peaks—the ability to do things you just wouldn't realize you could do." The mind games seemed to work, as evidenced by a game against Ohio State when he was at Northwestern. For a week preceding the game, Parseghian reminded his players again and again how the Buckeyes had run up the score on them the year before. "Dirt! Dirt! That's how Ohio State treats you!" he screamed. The Wildcats responded with a 21-0 victory, handing the Buckeyes their only loss of the year.

Parseghian, however, was the first to admit that psychology could go only so far. "The game is not won by a pep talk on Saturday," he said. "It's won by preparation of your club from Monday until game time." That preparation included vigorous physical conditioning and the assimilation of volumes of information from playbooks and scouting reports. Parseghian knew the game inside out and was attentive to the smallest details.

"You always went into a game knowing you wouldn't be outcoached," Lynch said.

Despite Parseghian's heavy doses of discipline, his

Quarterback Terry Hanratty plugged a big Notre Dame hole and served as the trigger man for the Fighting Irish's high-scoring offense.

former players describe him as "fair" and, as Page put it, "a great communicator of football." His whole personality was electric. And intense? "You can underline that three or four times," quarterback Terry Hanratty said.

Hanratty manned one of the few positions that had loomed as potential trouble spots for the 1966 Irish. Notre Dame had graduated 21 lettermen from a 7-2-1 team in 1965, but 36 returned, leaving only a few spots uncertain.

"The big question marks at that time were at the 'skill' positions," Lynch said. "But then Hanratty and (split end Jim) Seymour turned out to be the golden boys."

If not golden boys, they certainly had the golden touch. They were both sophomores, still untested because freshmen were ineligible for varsity action in those days, but Parseghian was anxious. He had seen their potential as a passing combination in practice.

Hanratty and Seymour had begun working together the previous winter. "In the winter we'd go into the old field house," Hanratty said. "It was old, had the dirt track and bad lighting. All it had was Rockne's echoes."

It was there that the two teen-agers practiced their timing, moves and mechanics night after night. They memorized each other's habits so that little guesswork would be necessary under fire. "I can almost tell how he's going to go, in what direction, as soon as he decides," Hanratty told a reporter midway through his sophomore season.

Seymour was a good bet to fill one of the vacant end slots, but Hanratty was no shoo-in for a starting job. Another sophomore, Coley O'Brien, had quarterbacked the freshman fodder against the varsity the previous fall, and their competition was fierce. Parseghian had to choose between Hanratty's great passing potential and the smaller, quick-footed O'Brien. Bearing in mind that he already had a solid running game in place from the previous year with the swift Nick Eddy at left halfback, Larry Conjar at fullback and 1965 backup Rocky Bleier at right halfback, he opted for a passing quarterback to balance the offense. Hanratty got the nod.

The highly recruited Hanratty, who had given serious thought to attending Michigan State or Penn State before settling on Notre Dame, was only 17 when he arrived in South Bend, but he came packaged with poise.

"I never really felt that much pressure going into a game," he said. "I never got that nervous. My philosophy always was to prepare as best you could and have fun on Saturday. Obviously I was out there to win, but it really is only a game."

In the first game of his collegiate career, Hanratty displayed the poise of a veteran. He connected 13 times with Seymour, who set school single-game records for receptions, yards receiving (276) and touchdown catches (three, tying the previous mark). By comparison, end Leon Hart had only 257 yards receiving in his entire Heisman Trophy-winning 1949 season. Hanratty finished with 304 yards passing in a 26-14 victory over Purdue.

"It was just one of those days," Seymour said. "You get up, feel good, get to the stadium and just know it's going to be your day. I think we caught (Purdue, which was ranked No. 7 in the final AP poll) by surprise."

The "Baby Bombers" were the talk of the town, but the Irish coaching staff wasn't about to let success go to the youngsters' heads.

"I went into the film room that Sunday feeling pretty good," Hanratty recalled. "I had thrown for 300 yards, we beat (Bob) Griese and all that. And then (assistant coach) Tom Pagna started in on me, and by the time we were done looking at the film, I thought I had played a horrible game."

Parseghian allowed little room for swelled egos. But he admitted that "the greatest thing to happen to them (Seymour and Hanratty) was that first game. It gave them great confidence that they could compete at that level."

Before long, many National Football League and American Football League experts believed that the sophomores were ready to compete at an even higher level. Gil Brandt of the Dallas Cowboys said both players would be certain first-round draft picks, while the Baltimore Colts' Upton Bell praised Hanratty's "on-the-mark, 50-yard bullets" and Seymour's ability to "stop a missile and hold on to it." And Don Klosterman of the Houston Oilers called Seymour "the best pro prospect I've ever seen at any position. I believe he could make any professional team in the country right now."

Hanratty still credits Seymour with much of his success. "He (Seymour) had that great height, about 6-4, that was unheard of for an end back then," he said. "He'd get out there on a 5-9 defensive back and I'd sit back and throw it up in the air."

Overshadowed by the Hanratty-Seymour show in the opener was a defensive performance that made it clear Notre Dame never would be out of a game. Purdue's offense scored only once, the other touchdown coming on Leroy Keyes' 94-yard return of a fumble. The Irish never allowed more than one touchdown in any game the rest of that season, and it would be almost two months before they were tested again.

John Ray, Parseghian's defensive coach, said it took some shuffling before they hit upon the right

Hanratty's fellow golden boy and big-play receiver was Jim Seymour, a living nightmare for opposing defensive backs.

The backbone of Notre Dame's 1966 defense was a linebacking corps manned by (left to right) Dave Martin, John Pergine, Jim Lynch and Mike McGill.

combination of players for the '66 defense.

"If a player wasn't locked into a spot, Ara would say (to staff members), 'OK, who wants to try him somewhere else?' " Ray recalled. "Ara had great foresight to see that (flexibility) in people."

Seymour, for instance, had been recruited as a defensive back and punter. But he caught the ball so well while giving the quarterbacks a practice target as a freshman that Parseghian knew he had a keeper at end.

Most of the changes involved offensive players moving to defense. Lynch had been a tight end and fullback as well as a linebacker in high school. He stayed put at linebacker at Notre Dame, where he started for three years and won the 1966 Maxwell Award as the nation's top college player.

Not everyone was so cooperative. It took some convincing to get Tom Schoen, who had been the No. 2 quarterback in 1965, to move to the secondary. Ray even had to discuss the matter with Schoen's father. Shoen eventually gave in and became one of the team's top all-around performers as the starting safety in Notre Dame's three-man backfield. He led the '66 Irish in interceptions (seven) and punt returns (29 for 253 yards) and scored three touchdowns on runbacks (two interceptions and a punt).

Another former quarterback, John Pergine, became a great inside linebacker, and tackle Pete Duranko had been an Irish fullback nicknamed "Diesel" before moving to the defensive line. Duranko became one of a dozen Notre Dame players to be named to somebody's All-America team in '66.

Mike McGill, a fullback/linebacker in high school, fit in well at outside linebacker, joining Lynch, Pergine and Dave Martin. But McGill was lost for the season in the sixth game, forcing Pergine to move to the outside and his backup, John Horney, to take over inside.

Parseghian's entire starting secondary from 1965 graduated, but previous position changes made it easy for him to fill the void. Schoen was joined by Jim Smithberger, a high school halfback, and Tom O'Leary. Smithberger's backup was Dan Harshman, a halfback who earned most of his playing time on defense.

The line was big and powerful. Duranko and 6-foot-5, 270-pound tackle Kevin Hardy were flanked by ends Tom Rhoads and Page. Together they presented an intimidating front wall.

Page, a 6-5, 238-pound senior from Canton, O.,

was the only black on the team, not to mention one of the few blacks attending Notre Dame. But Page said the situation was not troublesome, even during that turbulent decade of civil rights activities.

"If you were a football player back in the '60s, you sort of had blinders on," he said. "You were totally isolated from that. I don't recall any particular problems."

Especially on the field. Page went on to a great professional career with the Minnesota Vikings and Chicago Bears, and in 1988 he became the first Canton native to be enshrined there in the Pro Football Hall of Fame.

"A defensive player should think of himself more as an aggressor, not as a defender," Page once said in explanation of his defensive philosophy. "I've got a job to do, and my job is not to sit back and wait and then react to what the offense does. My job is to go after them. If you are going to make a mistake, make it aggressively."

His defensive mates approached their jobs the same way. "I know it's a cliche," Page said, "but everyone on that defense was a hitter."

Said Parseghian: "It was a defense that had excellent chemistry. It was aggressive with a lot of quickness and speed, just a bunch of good football players. And you can't say enough about Jim Lynch's leadership."

Lynch "had a real sense of keeping the guys together," Harshman said. "He was a visible, vocal leader, plus the way he played was such an example."

Joe Doyle, then sports editor of the South Bend Tribune, said simply: "You knew from the minute Lynch started playing, he was going to be the captain."

Lynch was one of the key reasons Notre Dame's 4-4-3 defense worked so well. "It was kind of complicated at the time," Ray said, "but the kids really liked it."

With their quickness and size, the tackles could control the line of scrimmage and funnel the action to the linebackers. Lynch and Pergine were ready and waiting inside. They led the team with a combined 204 tackles.

The defensive players were dedicated and disciplined, what Lynch called "a perfection thing. They took it very personally." Ray even schooled them at length on proper decorum during timeouts.

Notre Dame's defense produced a lot of long days for the opposition. The Irish recorded shutouts against Army, North Carolina, Oklahoma, Pittsburgh, Duke and Southern Cal and should have been credited with one against Navy, which scored off a blocked punt. In allowing only 38 points in 10 games, Notre Dame ranked second in the nation in scoring defense.

Meanwhile, the offense was tallying an average of 36.2 points per game, tops in the country. The squad was well balanced, averaging 210.6 yards on the ground and 180.9 yards in the air to compile the nation's third-best overall offense.

The focal points of the offense were, of course, Hanratty and Seymour, who were gracing the cover of Time magazine before Halloween. Hanratty completed 78 of 147 passes for 1,247 yards, with Seymour on the receiving end of most of his tosses. Seymour gathered in 48 passes for 862 yards and eight touchdowns.

But they couldn't do it all themselves. Offering pass protection was a solid line that seemed to play beyond its potential. Consensus All-America guard Tom Regner was the standout, but tackles Paul Seiler and Bob Kuechenberg, center George Goeddeke, guard Dick Swatland and tight end Don Gmitter more than held their own.

The linemen were dedicated to protecting Hanratty. "If anything happens to Terry," Goeddeke explained, "Coach will kill us."

The ground game was sparked by Eddy, who earned consensus All-America honors and led the team with 553 yards rushing. Conjar, a workhorse back, followed with 521 yards, and Bleier, who doubled as a punter, was effective as both a runner and receiver.

Bleier had neither remarkable speed nor power,

Defensive end Alan Page, the only black on Notre Dame's 1966 team, was a big, powerful youngster who performed his job aggressively.

Linebacker Jim Lynch was the captain, locker-room coach and spiritual leader of the 1966 Fighting Irish.

but he got the job done. That he later did so as a longtime member of the Pittsburgh Steelers was amazing considering his tragic war experience. Bleier, who had been Notre Dame's captain in 1967 and was drafted by Pittsburgh the next spring, was serving in Vietnam in August 1969 when his platoon was ambushed. After taking a bullet in his left leg, a grenade exploded under his right foot. Doctors spent several hours cleaning the shrapnel out of his limbs, and they said he was lucky not to become an amputee.

Bleier came home but could not play football in 1970, and over the next three years he carried the ball only four times. But he fought his way back, became a star in the Steelers' backfield with Franco Harris and won four Super Bowl rings.

The Irish were hitting on all cylinders by the fifth game of the season. That was a trip to Norman, Okla., where No. 1-ranked Notre Dame took on undefeated, 10th-ranked Oklahoma. It was supposed to be a toss-up.

Lynch remembers the game being billed as a matchup of "all these strong, quick guys going against us slow, big, fat guys." But the little guys were out of their league. Despite losing Seymour to an ankle injury (he missed the next two games), Notre Dame rolled, 38-0.

"I thought that our speed and quickness would overcome our lack of size," Sooners Coach Jim Mackenzie said. "But they were much bigger and, as far as I could tell, just as quick and fast. There's just no comparison between the teams."

The Irish coasted through their next three games to raise their record to 8-0 and set the stage for a showdown in East Lansing, Mich. Michigan State, which had gone 9-0 en route to its second consecutive Big Ten Conference title, would host Notre Dame in its season finale. It was No. 1 vs. No. 2 with the national championship on the line. Not surprisingly, the pregame hype was tremendous.

"I walked into a press conference in South Bend and there were 15 microphones in my face," said Lynch, who later was a key member of the Kansas City Chiefs' Super Bowl IV championship team. "There was more buildup to that than the Super Bowl."

The heated rivalry between the two schools merely escalated the hype. The Spartans had won nine of their last 10 games against the Irish, who had come up on the short end of a 12-3 score a year earlier. "We hated MSU and they hated us," Lynch said.

"There certainly was no love lost," Seymour added.

The Notre Dame campus was buzzing with nightly pep rallies. Radio interviews, complete with comments from Spartan players picked up on distant East Lansing stations, were even piped into the students' dining hall. "It was crazy," Seymour said.

Emotions were running high November 19 as the teams took the field at Spartan Stadium, where enough talent was assembled to form an NFL franchise. Playing that day were nine future first-round draft choices—defensive end Bubba Smith, roverback George Webster, split end Gene Washington and halfback Clint Jones of Michigan State, plus Notre Dame's Seymour, Regner, Seiler, Page and Hardy. The aggressiveness on the field reflected the caliber of the players involved.

"The hitting in that game was tremendous," Seymour said. "If you had to characterize it, you'd call it brutal. You could hear the hits, and the intensity never let down."

It didn't take long to build, either. Before the end of a scoreless first quarter, the Spartans already had knocked out Hanratty and Goeddeke, who joined

Eddy on the sideline. The halfback missed the entire game after aggravating a shoulder injury when he slipped getting off the train in East Lansing. Goeddeke (ankle) and Hanratty (shoulder separation) went down under fire.

Tim Monty, who at 198 weighed 30 pounds less than Goeddeke, took over at center. And Hanratty's backup, O'Brien, had been diagnosed with diabetes only a few weeks earlier and was still adjusting, requiring two insulin shots a day. As the game wound down, so did his energy.

But O'Brien led the Irish back after they fell behind, 10-0, in the second quarter. His 34-yard toss to Eddy's backup, sophomore Bob Gladieux, put the Irish on the board, and Joe Azzaro's 28-yard field goal on the first play of the last quarter tied it up.

That was as much offense as Notre Dame could muster that day. But the Irish defense wouldn't budge. In 16 second-half running plays, the Spartans didn't gain a yard. And late in the fourth quarter, Schoen intercepted a pass and ran it back to the Spartan 18-yard line. That was the break Notre Dame needed, but three plays netted minus-six yards, and Azzaro's 41-yard field-goal attempt sailed wide to the right.

After the defense held again, Michigan State punted. Schoen fielded it, dropped it and fell on it in time. Notre Dame had the ball on its own 30 with 1:24 on the clock—time enough to throw about four passes and try to set up a game-winning field goal.

Parseghian, however, opted for a safer strategy. With O'Brien tiring, Notre Dame ran the ball six straight times—including once for a first down on fourth-and-one—and the clock ran out. Though the next-to-last play was supposed to be a pass (Smith sacked O'Brien for a seven-yard loss), Parseghian took considerable heat for what was considered his conservative play selection, which allowed the game to end in a tie.

"It was a hard-fought battle, and I wasn't going to let the kids blow it by throwing down there," Parseghian told reporters after the game. "I know how good a placekicker (Michigan State's) Dick Kenney is. We were trying to get to midfield running and then throw. But I wasn't going to do a jackass thing like letting them get an interception on us and cost us the game after 60 minutes of football like our boys played."

More than two decades later, Parseghian still stands by his decision. "I've always felt that was a helluva comeback," he said. "It was amazing to me how they (writers) could make the decision like that for me when I knew my club. I lived with them 24 hours a day. I didn't go for a tie. That game ended in a tie."

His players agreed.

"If you looked at that game play-by-play, you'd understand Ara was guilty of playing intelligent football," Lynch said.

All-America guard Tom Regner (76) anchored an offensive line that seemed to perform beyond its potential for Coach Ara Parseghian.

It took a few days for the result to sink in.

"It was such a strange feeling the way it ended," Harshman said. "The tie was disappointing at first. But we thought we had really come back, and we didn't feel the intensity of the controversy at that time."

Said Hanratty: "I never knew what that game was really all about until 20 years later. Not a month goes by, no matter what city I'm in, that somebody I meet for the first time doesn't say, 'Weren't you on that '66 team that played Michigan State?' It must have been watched by everybody in the country."

Emotionally drained and physically battered, the Irish limped through the next week of practice and

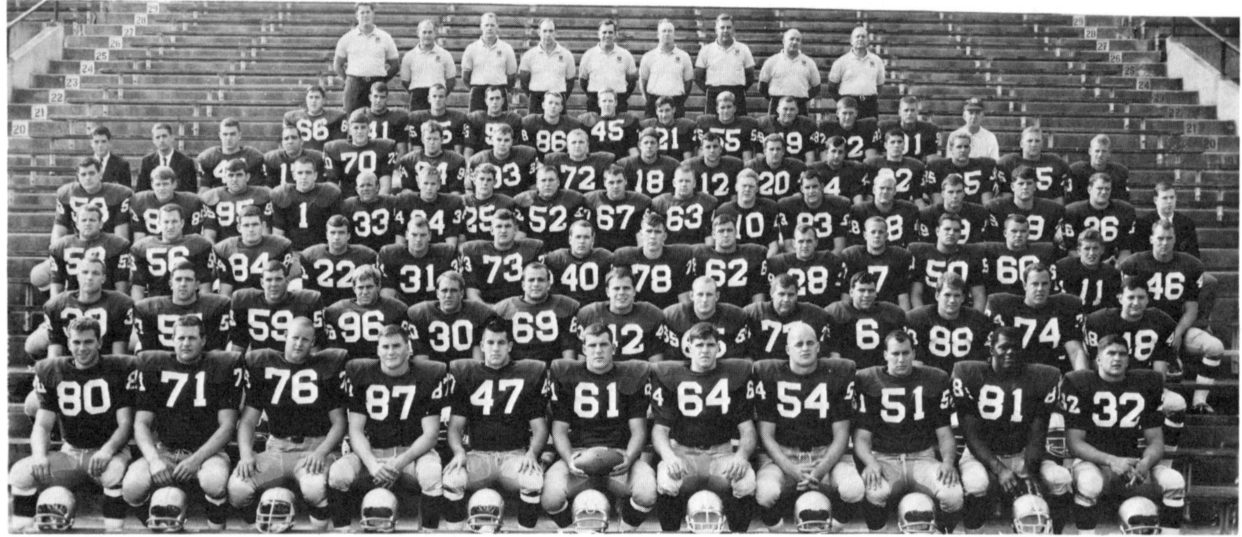

The 1966 Fighting Irish: Front row (left to right)—Don Gmitter, Paul Seiler, Tom Regner, Tom Rhoads, Nick Eddy, Jim Lynch, Pete Duranko, George Goeddeke, John Horney, Alan Page, Larry Conjar. Second row—Bob Hagerty, Tim Gorman, Dick Swatland, Leo Collins, Jim Kelly, Joe Marsico, Angelo Schiralli, Ron Jeziorski, Harry Alexander, Hugh O'Malley, Allen Sack, Kevin Hardy, Dave Zurowski. Third row—Gerald Kelly, Dave Martin, Mike Heaton, Dave Haley, Paul May, Rudy Konieczny, Tom O'Leary, Mike Kuzmicz, Steve Quinn, Rocky Bleier, Tom Schoen, John Pergine, Mike McGill, Jim Ryan, Tim Wengierski. Fourth row—John Lium, Alan VanHuffel, Lou Fournier, Kevin Rassas, Mike Burgener, Dan Harshman, Jim Smithberger, Chuck Grable, Dan Dickman, Joe Freebery, Mike Earley, Bob Zubek, Roger Fox, Tom Quinn, Mike Bars, Bill Bartholomew, manager Jack Sullivan. Fifth row—Manager Al Kramer, manager Kevin Moran, Mike Holtzapfel, Chuck Landolfi, Fred Schnurr, Bill Skoglund, Chuck Lauck, Eric Norri, Tom Slettvet, Tom Reynolds, Bob Gladieux, Mike Franger, Paul Snow, Ed Vuillemin, Bob Kuechenberg, Coley O'Brien. Sixth row—Pat Schrage, John Lavin, Jim Seymour, Terry Hanratty, Curt Heneghan, Jim Leahy, Frank Criniti, Tim Monty, Tom McKinley, George Kunz, Brian Stenger, trainer Gene Paszkiet. Seventh row—Coaches Brian Boulac, George Sefcik, Jerry Wampfler, Tom Pagna, head Coach Ara Parseghian, coaches Paul Shoults, John Ray, Joe Yonto, Wally Moore.

had little contact work. They saved their energy for Southern Cal.

"I was very much concerned about the (USC) game," Parseghian recalled. "We were coming off such an emotional game. All that buildup—I've never seen anything like it. We had to make a lot of adjustments and, personally, I was getting criticized. . . . But the one thing we had going for us was that Michigan State could do nothing about that game. Their season was over. We still had the opportunity to demonstrate that we were a helluva football team."

They didn't blow their chance. O'Brien threw three touchdown passes (two to Seymour) to lead the Irish to a 51-0 whipping of the Trojans.

"It was one of those games when everything worked and went our way," Seymour said.

A story filtered down to sports editor Doyle following that victory. The Rev. Theodore Hesburgh, then president of the university, was in Paris the day of the USC game and reportedly contacted the local news outlet to check the result. In English-accented French he asked for the score, and in French-accented English he got the answer: 51-0, Notre Dame. Certain that something must have been lost in the translation, he kept insisting it was impossible, that the man must have misunderstood his question.

The information was correct, of course, and Notre Dame had another national championship. The Irish, who had slipped to second in the UPI poll after the Michigan State tie, were a unanimous No. 1 choice in the final rankings. The Sporting News even selected Parseghian as its Coach of the Year.

The wonderful chemistry of that team still exists. Many players remain in close touch through summer golf outings and home football weekends. And when 72 players were contacted about a 20-year reunion at the 1986 Notre Dame-Penn State game, 65 attended.

"From the look on their faces when they were introduced (at halftime)," Seymour said, "they would have loved to have the chance to suit up and play there again."

They'd probably hold their own.

Notre Dame, 1966

ROAD TO GREATNESS

1966 RESULTS (9-0-1)

Opponent	Score	Opp. Record	Opp. Bowl Game
Purdue	26-14	9-2-0	Rose (W)
at Northwestern	35-7	3-6-1	
Army	35-0	8-2-0	
North Carolina	32-0	2-8-0	
at Oklahoma	38-0	6-4-0	
*Navy	31-7	4-6-0	
Pittsburgh	40-0	1-9-0	
Duke	64-0	5-5-0	
at Michigan State	10-10	9-0-1	
at Southern California	51-0	7-4-0	Rose (L)

*Philadelphia.

FACTS AND FIGURES

The Fighting Irish shut out six of their last eight opponents in 1966. . . . Notre Dame defeated all but two opponents by three or more touchdowns, and their average margin of victory was 32.4 points. . . . Against their five opponents with winning records, the Irish's average margin of victory was 27.2 points per game. . . . Notre Dame's opponents compiled an overall record of 54-46-2 (.539 winning percentage). . . . The Irish faced three teams ranked in the final Associated Press and United Press International polls. They soundly defeated the two opponents that went to bowl games (Purdue and Southern California) and tied second-ranked Michigan State. . . . The 1966 squad was Ara Parseghian's first unbeaten team. . . . The Irish led the nation's major colleges in scoring offense and finished third in total offense, second in scoring defense, fourth in total defense and ninth in rushing defense. . . . Joe Azzaro tied for ninth among the nation's major-college placekickers with 47 points. . . . Nick Eddy led the Irish in rushing in 1965 and 1966. . . . Terry Hanratty and Jim Seymour led the Irish in passing and receiving, respectively, for three consecutive years (1966-68). . . . Seymour set a Notre Dame record by averaging 6.9 receptions per game in '66. . . . Safety Tom Schoen led the team in punt-return average and interceptions in 1966 and 1967. . . . Jim Lynch, Alan Page, defensive tackle Kevin Hardy and guard Tom Regner were named to The Sporting News' 1966 All-America team. . . . Lynch and Regner also received academic All-America honors. . . . The last time an opponent blocked a Notre Dame punt and returned it for a touchdown was in 1966, when Navy's Jon Bergner blocked a punt, scooped it up and ran 25 yards for a score.

STATISTICAL LEADERS

PASSING

	Att.	Comp.	Yards	TD	Pct.	Int.
Terry Hanratty	147	78	1247	8	53.1	10
Coley O'Brien	82	42	562	4	51.2	6

RUSHING

	Att.	Yards	Avg.	TD	Long
Nick Eddy	78	553	7.1	8	77
Larry Conjar	112	521	4.7	7	30
Rocky Bleier	63	282	4.5	4	22
Coley O'Brien	40	135	3.4	2	25
Terry Hanratty	50	124	2.5	5	52

RECEIVING

	Rec.	Yards	Avg.	TD	Long
Jim Seymour	48	862	18.0	8	84
Rocky Bleier	17	209	12.3	1	45
Nick Eddy	15	123	8.2	0	16
Bob Gladieux	12	208	17.3	2	46
Brian Stenger	6	86	14.3	0	20

SCORING

	TD	FG	PAT	Points
Nick Eddy	10	0	0	60
Jim Seymour	8	0	0	48
Joe Azzaro	0	4	35	47
Larry Conjar	7	0	*1	44
Terry Hanratty	5	0	*1	32
Rocky Bleier	5	0	0	30
Bob Gladioux	5	0	0	30

*Two-point conversion.

KEY CHARACTERS

The Conductor

COACH: Ara Parseghian.

Record: 95-17-4, 11 years at Notre Dame.

Parseghian succeeded Hugh Devore at Notre Dame in 1964 and went on to join Knute Rockne and Frank Leahy as the only coaches to guide Irish teams more than seven seasons. . . . He played halfback and coached under Woody Hayes at Miami of Ohio. . . . He became Miami head coach in 1951, moved to Northwestern five years later and spent eight years there before taking the Notre Dame job. . . . He compiled a 24-year career coaching mark of 170-58-6 and earned election to the College Football Hall of Fame. . . . His 1966 Irish team was a consensus national champion, and his 1973 squad finished first in the Associated Press poll. . . . All 11 of his Notre Dame teams finished among both AP and United Press International's Top 20, and nine of those teams finished in the Top 10 of both polls. . . . His teams never had a losing season at Notre Dame. Four had no more than one loss, and his 1966 and '73 teams were unbeaten. . . . Parseghian directed his Irish teams to a 3-2 bowl record and a 14-11-3 mark against teams ranked in the Top 20. . . . Notre Dame's 1970 Cotton Bowl loss to Texas marked the first Irish bowl appearance since 1925, and Parseghian-coached teams went on to play in the Cotton Bowl (1971), Orange Bowl (1973), Sugar Bowl (1974) and Orange Bowl (1975) in four of the next five years. . . . He coached 21 consensus All-Americas, including at least one in each of his 11 seasons. . . . He also coached the 1971 Lombardi Award winner, defensive end Walt Patulski. . . . Parseghian's coaching career began after he played two seasons with the Cleveland Browns of the National Football League.

Personal Data:

Born: May 21, 1923, in Akron, O.
High School: Akron South High.
College: Akron and Miami of Ohio.

The Supporting Cast

HALFBACK: Nick Eddy.

Eddy was a consensus All-America in 1966 and finished third in that year's Heisman Trophy balloting. . . . He finished his career with 1,615 yards rushing, a 5.5-yard average and 17 touchdowns. . . . He arrived at Notre Dame with little fanfare and went on to become a key figure for the 1966 national championship team. . . . He lettered from 1964-66 and went on to an injury-shortened professional career.

Personal Data:

Born: August 23, 1944, at Dunsmuir, Calif.
High School: Tracy High in Tracy, Calif.

QUARTERBACK: Terry Hanratty.

The flamboyant Hanratty was the heart and his favorite target, split end Jim Seymour, was the soul of Notre Dame's offenses from 1966-68. . . . The gutty Hanratty seemed to have that special knack for always finding a way to win. . . . He was a consensus All-America in 1968 and finished among the top 10 in Heisman balloting three consecutive seasons, placing third in 1968. . . . He still holds Notre Dame records for average passing attempts and completions for a season and career and ranks third with 4,152 passing yards. . . . His average of 209.4 yards per game passing in 1968 is second on Notre Dame's all-time list, and his 27 career touchdown passes is fourth best. . . . He lettered from 1966-68.

Personal Data:

Born: January 19, 1948, in Butler, Pa.
High School: Area Senior High in Butler.

LINEBACKER: Jim Lynch.

Lynch, a unanimous consensus All-America selection in 1966, was the heart of Notre Dame's defense. . . . He was team captain in 1966, the year he won the 1966 Maxwell Award as the top college player in the nation. . . . He led the 1965 and '66 teams with 108 and 106 tackles, respectively. . . . He lettered from 1964-66 and went on to a distinguished pro career with the Kansas City Chiefs.

Personal Data:

Born: August 28, 1945, in Lima, O.
High School: Central Catholic High in Lima.

DEFENSIVE END: Alan Page.

Page was the leader of the Irish defensive front and a major factor in the team's six shutouts in 1966. . . . He lettered from 1964-66 and was a consensus All-America his senior season. . . . He played in the 1967 College All-Star Game and went on to become a dominating force with the Minnesota Vikings and Chicago Bears of the NFL. . . . He is a member of the Pro Football Hall of Fame.

Personal Data:

Born: August 7, 1945, in Canton, O.
High School: Central Catholic High in Canton.

FINAL 1966 WIRE SERVICE RANKINGS

ASSOCIATED PRESS

1. **NOTRE DAME**	6. Nebraska
2. **Michigan State**	7. **Purdue**
3. Alabama	8. Georgia Tech
4. Georgia	9. Miami (Fla.)
5. UCLA	10. SMU

Only Top 10 ranked.

UNITED PRESS

1. **NOTRE DAME**	11. Florida
2. **Michigan State**	12. Mississippi
3. Alabama	13. Arkansas
4. Georgia	14. Tennessee
5. UCLA	15. Wyoming
6. **Purdue**	16. Syracuse
7. Nebraska	17. Houston
8. Georgia Tech	18. **Southern Cal**
9. SMU	19. Oregon State
10. Miami (Fla.)	20. Virginia Tech

Bold face indicates Notre Dame opponent.

The Beast Of the East

Pittsburgh, 1980-81
By Phil Axelrod

Pittsburgh Coach Jackie Sherrill championed his 1980 Panther team as the best ever assembled, talentwise.

Pittsburgh Coach Jackie Sherrill was in a mischievous mood when he pitted college football's most overpowering defense against one of its most explosive offenses on that sultry September afternoon in 1980.

A sharp blast from his whistle halted practice and sent players scurrying into a huddle at midfield. Sherrill walked to the 1-yard line, put down a ball and smiled. "First-team offense, first-team defense," he barked. "Get out there."

Hugh Green, Ricky Jackson and the rest of the Panthers' defensive crew strapped on their helmets and sauntered into position. Stoically, Dan Marino, Mark May and Russ Grimm led the offense into position for battle.

"I knew it would be a war," Sherrill recalled. "There was a lot of talent on that field. A lot of pride, too."

Marino took the snap from center, spun to his right and planted the ball into the midsection of 230-pound fullback Randy McMillan. The lines collided with a thunderous crash and McMillan lunged toward the goal line, grinding his torso through a maze of tangled shoulder pads.

The offensive players shot their arms skyward to signal a touchdown. The defense stomped up and down in celebration.

"We stuffed it," remembered linebacker Sal Sunseri. "No way did they make it. They *thought* they made it."

After a brief scuffle, Sherrill's directive clarified matters. Obediently, Marino and Co. tramped off to run laps as the howling defenders sprinted to the locker room.

That was the final play of the final scrimmage of fall camp. It also was the first, and last, time Sherrill pitted his first-team offense against his starting defense. "I didn't do it again because I didn't want them to hurt each other," he said. "They really went after each other."

★ ★ ★

The names roll off the tongue, a litany of All-America and Pro Bowl talent. Hugh Green, Ricky Jackson, Dan Marino, Russ Grimm, Jimbo Covert, Carlton Williamson, Bill Maas, Bill Fralic, Mark May, Sal Sunseri.

Wearing the old gold and blue of the Panthers, they were the principals in Pitt's back-to-back 11-1 seasons in 1980 and 1981, including a consensus No. 2 finish in the 1980 final polls.

"That was the best football team ever assembled, talentwise," Sherrill said of his 1980 squad. "They get a lot better when you sit back and look at what they've done. Never, ever, has a team produced that many great players."

Nineteen players from that team, including first-round draft picks Green, McMillan and May, signed National Football League contracts straight out of college. Faced with the loss of 15 starters, including nine on defense, the 1981 Panthers nevertheless compiled the school's third straight 11-1 record and fielded the nation's No. 1-ranked defense for the second consecutive year.

"I have never seen a college defense like that," Foge Fazio, the Panthers' defensive coordinator, said of those Pitt squads. "It was an attacking defense. They shut people down and took the ball away from them."

Green and Jackson, the defensive ends in 1980, were quiet assassins. Linemates Greg Meisner, Bill Neill and Jerry Boyarsky howled like wild animals as they lined up over the ball. The middle three linemen in '81—Dave (The Freak) Puzzuoli, J.C. Pelusi and Maas—were known as the "Pac-Men."

"You know, like the video game with those little dots, except our guys eat defensive backs," Sunseri explained at the time.

"They were hunters," Fazio recalled. "They had a lot of fun out there. They had a great time. It didn't matter what the score was."

Planted in the middle of the craziness was the captain, Sunseri, a live wire whom Fazio likened to "another coach on the field."

"The huddles were wild," Sunseri said. "We knew what we had. We knew we had the Number 1 defense in the country. What I had to do was clog up the middle and bounce people outside to the All-Pros. We dominated teams."

In effect, they destroyed them, particularly in 1980. Other than Florida State, whose 36-22 victory deflated Pitt's national championship hopes, no one made even the slightest dent in the Panthers' iron curtain.

"Everybody they played that year took a pounding," Sherrill said. "They hurt people. That's the

Defensive end Hugh Green was a quiet, deadly and durable assassin who never ceased to amaze apprehensive Pittsburgh opponents with his devastating talent.

The presence of Hugh Green and Ricky Jackson (above) at opposite ends of Pittsburgh's defensive line discouraged opposing offenses from running wide.

kind of team I like. They had speed, they had quickness, they had size, they had all the physical tools and they had all the intangibles. They were flat out physically tough.

"If you put those guys in a room, they were going to come out. They intimidated people. They had all the ingredients it took. It was amazing to watch them play the game."

Green was nothing short of amazing and, arguably, the most devastating defensive end in collegiate history. He started all but one game in his four seasons at Pitt, missing only the first play of the 1977 opener against Notre Dame because Sherrill frowned on starting freshmen. He took the field on the second play, however, and racked up 11 tackles, a blocked punt and two sacks against the eventual national champions before the game ended.

As a senior in 1980, Green received the Lombardi Award as the outstanding college lineman, the Maxwell Award as the nation's top player and The Sporting News' College Player of the Year award. He finished second in the Heisman Trophy balloting behind South Carolina running back George Rogers, the highest finish ever for a one-way defensive player.

"I think I opened people's eyes to let them see that a defensive player can be put alongside an offensive player," Green said. "I wasn't disappointed that I didn't win the Heisman because I had not gotten involved in trying to win it."

Green reflected for a moment. "I didn't get credit for winning the Heisman, but maybe someday I'll get credit for setting it up for a defensive player to win it."

His mere presence could control an entire game, which wasn't lost on pro scouts. Said Tampa Bay Buccaneers scouting director Ken Herock: "He was used like the MX missile, rotating from standup defensive end to all four linebacking positions, waiting for the proper time to explode. They disguised him so he could make plays, they moved him around a lot so that when the other team came up to the line of scrimmage, they'd say, 'Where's Green?' "

He played with a reckless abandon and enthusiasm that was contagious, especially to Sunseri.

"People were petrified of Green," Sunseri said. "But they couldn't run away from him because we had Ricky Jackson on the other side of the line. Hugh beat you with quickness. He'd tackle you and walk away. Ricky was a mean player. He'd cut your throat."

That mean streak cut through the entire Pitt defense. "See, on defense, all we want to do is hit, get up, and then hit harder the next time," Green said in 1980. "If you're gonna play at Pitt, you're gonna hit. Offense is more finesse, the witty and brainy types. Offensive players can't stand being physical. Me, if I don't crush someone on a play, I'm disappointed. Let's be truthful. Fans like the sport because of the violence."

Sunseri chuckled. "Teams were intimidated just by our talent," he said. "You look back, it's amazing to think that everybody played on that team together."

So deep was the talent that the coaching staff faced an unusual challenge.

"It was a challenge to come up with a great game plan each week," Fazio said. "We could have lined up and played it straight every week, but that

Offenses that tested the middle of the Panthers' defense in 1981 ran into the likes of 'Pac-Man' Bill Maas.

wouldn't have been fair to the players we had. They could do so much it was fun trying to figure out different things to do with them."

Besides Florida State, only Louisville and West Virginia scored more than one touchdown against the 1980 Panthers. Kansas, which accumulated four rushing yards on 32 carries, and Army, which rolled up 58 yards on 46 rushes, were notable casualties.

"We were always going for a shutout, that was the big thing," Fazio said. "We went after people. Every guy had at least one sack that year. We sent in the corners, we sent in the free safeties. We were always putting in new wrinkles."

Nothing, however, slowed down Bobby Bowden's slick Florida State squad on a hot, muggy night in Tallahassee. The Seminoles outfoxed the aggressive Panthers, keeping them off balance with sprint draws and delays, and capitalized on a sparkling kicking game and seven Pitt turnovers to drop the Panthers to 4-1.

"That game," said Sherrill, the pain seeping through his words, "cost us the national championship."

It was the only time Pitt was rendered defenseless. The Panthers had been picked by many to capture college football's national championship, principally because of that defense.

"We see nobody directly beating us," Green had said before the season. "We think about our talent and we fall out laughing. Nobody is better in the country than our front five. Then we have Marino, and there isn't anybody else like Big Mac (McMillan). We know we got it. We're a better team than the Pitt team that won it all in 1976. All they had was Tony Dorsett."

Sherrill understood that the 1980 Panthers were veterans, that most had played and partied together since they were freshmen in 1977, his first year at the Pitt helm. "Those kids had known just success here," said Alex Kramer, Sherrill's administrative assistant, noting Pitt's records of 9-2-1 in 1977, 8-4 in 1978 and 11-1 in 1979. "They didn't question whether they'd win. The only question was how they were going to win."

Which was Sherrill's area of expertise. Although a tough taskmaster, Sherrill said he was less demanding of the 1980 team than of any other because it already was well-schooled.

"The practice habits of that team were there," he said. "I didn't have to instill them. Mark May set the example. He ran to the line of scrimmage. He ran back to the huddle. Whenever it was time to play, they played. Whenever it was time to work, they worked."

Sherrill talked softly and carried a big message: His way was the only way.

"Everybody was afraid of Jackie, but everybody respected Jackie," Sunseri said. "He had a lot of different personalities out there, and he had them under control."

"When I talked to them, I talked to them as a

group," Sherrill said. "It was all positive reinforcement. You don't reach goals with negative reinforcement."

To that end, the hungry Panthers gave their all for Sherrill, hustling and hitting with ferocity—just so Marino wasn't their target. One of Sherrill's practice rules prohibited anyone from hitting Marino, which was difficult for the defense to accept at times. Near the end of a particularly grueling session, Marino pranced into the end zone and spiked the football, the accepted ritual after scoring a touchdown.

Sunseri started screaming, stomping around in circles and flailing his arms. "I lost it," he said. "It just didn't seem right to me that we couldn't touch him and he showed us up. I started screaming that it wasn't a touchdown."

Marino's safety was ensured in games, too, even without the no-contact code. "There were games when my uniform never got dirty," Marino said. "There were games when I never hit the ground. That's incredible."

His guardians in 1980 were Covert and May, a pair of mammoth tackles, guards Emil Boures, Rob Fada, Ron Sams and Paul Dunn and the center, Grimm. Man for man, they were larger than the trenchmen of the 1980 Super Bowl champion Pittsburgh Steelers.

"I don't know if anybody's ever had a line like that," said Joe Moore, the gravel-voiced coach who developed a stable of outstanding linemen at Pitt. "They were mean. They were tough. They beat people up. Grimm was the leader. He was all business when he put on his helmet. He was a total football player."

Grimm grew to 250 pounds after arriving at Pitt as a 200-pound quarterback from Southmoreland High School, about 20 miles east of Pittsburgh. "I ate my way onto the offensive line," he said. "It wasn't something I planned."

May managed to stand out from the pack, and not simply because of his size. At 6-foot-6, 282 pounds, he was likened to an aircraft carrier in Pitt's 1980 media guide. That season, he became the only Panther ever to win the Outland Trophy as the nation's outstanding interior lineman.

Although Moore was hired to keep watch on the linemen, he never suffered from tunnel vision. "I didn't want to miss the experience," he said. "I savored every moment. Out of the corner of my eye I watched Marino. There never will be another Marino. . . ."

The dropback quarterback who grew up in the shadow of Pitt Stadium was a local hero even before he played his first down for Sherrill. He was one of the most sought-after high school athletes in the country, not only for his brilliant passing at Central Catholic High School, but for his baseball skills that prompted the Kansas City Royals to select him in the June 1979 draft. By the time he was selected by the Miami Dolphins in the first round of the 1983 NFL draft, Marino had become the Panthers' all-time passing leader with 8,597 yards and 79 touchdown passes.

"There was an air about him, a kind of maturity that you don't see often in a young player," Kramer said. "He was a superb leader. He was confident and outgoing, but I don't remember him being cocky. He and Jackie had a special relationship."

The arrival of freshman tackle Bill Fralic in 1981 filled the void created by the losses of offensive linemen Mark May and Russ Grimm.

As a freshman in 1979, Marino led the Panthers to a Fiesta Bowl victory over Arizona after replacing the injured Rick Trocano in the seventh game of the season. In an abbreviated starting role, Marino set a school record for freshmen with 1,680 yards passing and headed into 1980 as the new starting quarterback.

"Right now he's probably the best at his age," Sherrill said, "but he has to improve each year."

The 19-year-old sophomore was one of the leading passers in the nation until he was felled by a knee injury against West Virginia, one week after the loss to Florida State. Marino missed the next three games but finished the regular season with 1,513 yards and 14 touchdown passes.

"At the time, I felt like I knew what I was doing," said Marino, who was intercepted 14 times. "Now I'm not sure I did."

Trocano, who had been moved to safety to make room for Marino, easily made the transition back to quarterback and led the Panthers to lopsided victories over West Virginia, Tennessee, Syracuse and Louisville. After Marino came off the bench to pass for 292 yards against Army, Trocano ran for one touchdown and passed for another in a 14-9 victory over fifth-ranked Penn State in the season finale. The victory left the third-ranked Panthers in position to become national champions, but their Gator Bowl victory over South Carolina elevated them only to No. 2 in the final polls. Undefeated Georgia, a 17-10 winner over Notre Dame in the Sugar Bowl, remained No. 1 and claimed the school's first-ever national championship.

"We were fortunate to have somebody like Rick to bring in," Sherrill said of Trocano, who departed as the Panthers' all-time leading passer with 4,219 yards. Against South Carolina, he passed for one touchdown, ran for another and directed a ball-control offense that kept George Rogers from running as much as the Gamecocks would have liked. The Heisman winner gained 113 yards (59 short of his season average) and fumbled twice, the first on the opening play from scrimmage which led to Pitt's first touchdown.

Pitt's offense had remained in high gear, thanks to Trocano and the work of the line. The Panthers finished with the nation's No. 5 passing offense and No. 8 scoring offense. Ironically, they didn't excel as a running team despite the wealth of talent up front and McMillan in the backfield.

"We never tried to run the ball," Moore said. "We never gave Randy the ball. He could have gained 1,500 yards."

A bruising runner, the "Big Mac Attack" led the team in rushing with 692 yards and struck for a team-high 11 touchdowns (including bowl game totals), one more than greyhound freshman flanker Dwight Collins, who topped the team with 827 yards receiving overall. Tight end Benjie Pryor, an outstanding blocker, led the Panthers in receptions for the second straight year with 43 during the regular season.

Though sidelined for much of the second half,

The strong arm and cool demeanor of quarterback Dan Marino kept Pitt's offense rolling through the 1980 and '81 seasons.

Marino had turned Pitt, traditionally a running team, into a team that struck quickly and often through the air. Granted, the '80 Panthers were built on defense, and that's how they won. In 1981, they relied on a winning attitude and a favorable schedule as much as Marino's strong arm and their upstart No. 1 defense.

"Last year we did it on talent," noted Sunseri after an emotional payback victory over Florida State. "This season we're doing it on feeling, on love for each other."

Sunseri was the lone returning full-time starter on defense, but fellow linebacker Rich Kraynak, the Pac-Men and defensive ends Chris Doleman and Michael Woods (a product of Natchez, Miss., like Green) upheld the tradition of their forerunners by swarming offenses with a vengeance.

"Pitt plays pressure defense—aggressive, swarming, blitzing, forcing you into mistakes," Bowden said. "Whatever you're doing, you better do it fast or else you'll be looking at second-and-15."

Reflected West Virginia Coach Don Nehlen, whose Mountaineers were shut out, 17-0: "Their secondary never gets tested. A quarterback has to rush and throw before he gets buried."

Marino, once again, had time enough to dig a bunker, thanks to a rock-solid offensive line. The loss of May and Grimm was eased considerably by the presence of freshman Bill Fralic, a young behemoth of a tackle.

"I laughed the first time I saw him," Moore said. "He was that good."

Good isn't flattering enough for the way Marino performed. He was at the peak of his game, throwing for 2,876 yards and 37 touchdowns, both single-season Pitt records (including bowl game totals). "Statistically, that was my best year," he said. "We took a lot of people by surprise. We had so many guys leave, but we had so many quality people back."

His dazzling passing indirectly bolstered the defense, which felt it had something to prove in the face of questions about its inexperience. "Just knowing we had Marino on our side helped the defense," Sunseri said. "We became a lot more reckless because we knew that he could get us points back in a hurry."

Marino became the school's all-time leading passer in the ninth game, a 48-0 victory over Army which saw split end Julius Dawkins tie his single-game Pitt record with four touchdown receptions. Dawkins would finish the regular season with a school-record 15 touchdown grabs to lead the nation. Halfback Bryan Thomas, a junior, became only the third Pitt back to rush for more than 1,000 yards, finishing the season with 1,003.

Not even Marino, however, could prevent the Penn State avalanche in the season finale. After rid-

Pittsburgh split end Julius Dawkins, who caught 15 touchdown passes to lead the nation in 1981, pulls in a pass against West Virginia.

ing atop the national polls for weeks, the undefeated Panthers' Cinderella season crumbled under a 48-14 loss.

"I have never been in a more disconsolate locker room," Kramer said. "It was very depressing. Some of the players were crying. It was very unsettling."

What made it more heartbreaking was the fact that Pitt had led, 14-0, and was marching toward another touchdown when Marino was intercepted in the Penn State end zone on the first play of the second quarter. That play swung the momentum to the visiting Nittany Lions, who tied the score before halftime, then struck for two touchdowns to start the third quarter on 42- and 45-yard pass plays from Todd Blackledge to Kenny Jackson. The Panthers never recovered and finished the game with seven turnovers.

"That was the first time that team faced adversity," said Sunseri, whose Panthers had won 17 straight games. "I think we got a little undisciplined and out of character. That loss was the worst feeling I ever felt in my life."

Said Sherrill: "We were letting Danny try to win it the easy way. We weren't being physical. When it started turning around, we felt we could still let it rip. But we lost our composure. After the game, I was upset. We, as coaches, should prevent those things from happening."

What does Marino, who threw four interceptions, remember about that game? "I know we were disappointed," he said. "But you can't let something like that bring you down."

Which was exactly what he said as Pitt prepared to meet Georgia in the Sugar Bowl. The Panthers, who had slipped to eighth in the United Press International rankings and 10th in the Associated Press

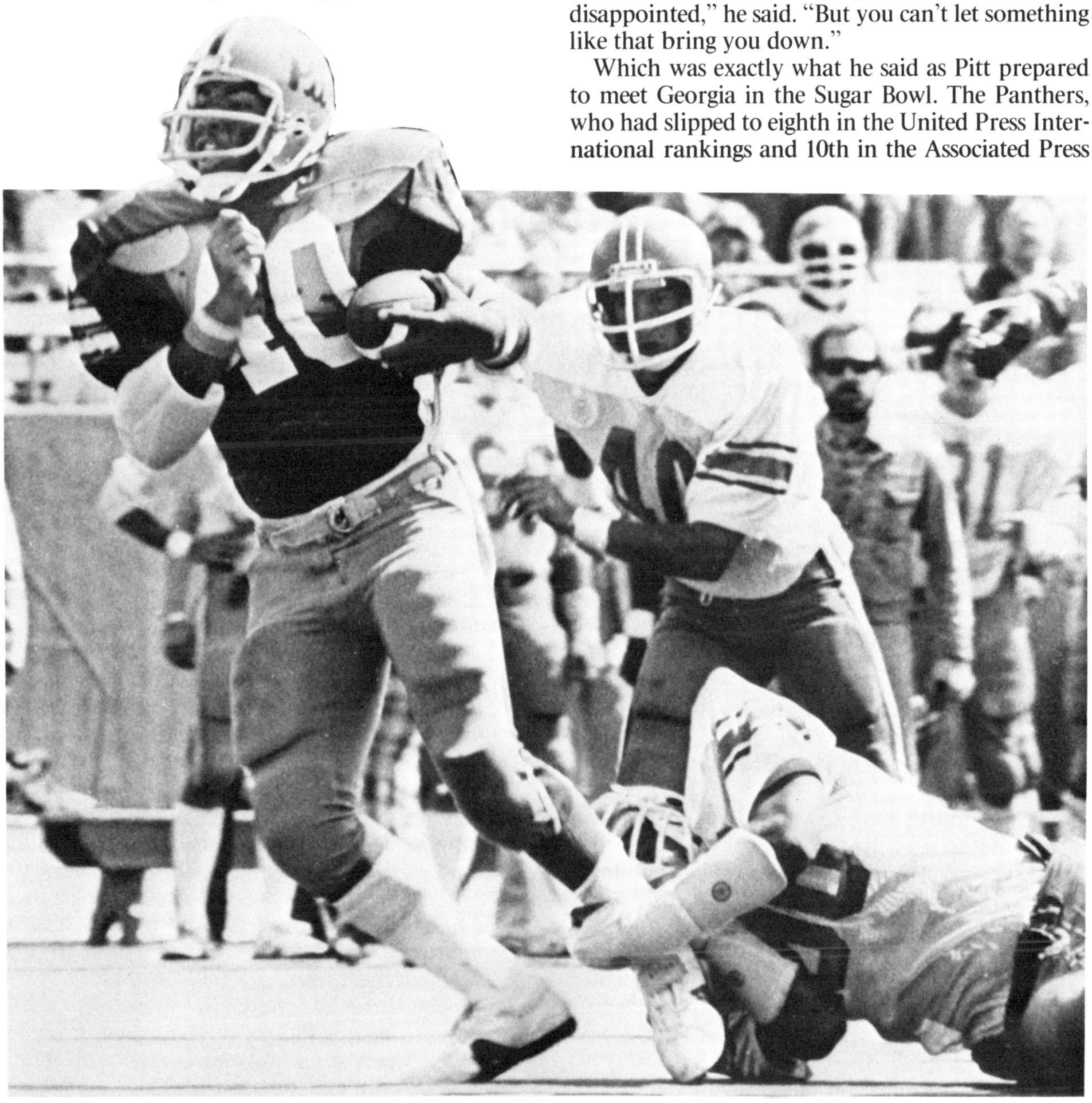

Randy McMillan, a bruising 230-pound fullback, was available when Marino & Co. needed those tough yards.

The 1980 Panthers: Front row (left to right) —Lynn Thomas, Joe McCall, Keith Williams, Bryan Thomas, Willie Collier, Hugh Green, Don Smith, Fran Washington, Troy Hill, Ray Jones, Terry White, Larry Sims, Artrell Hawkins, Rick Ryan, Pappy Thomas. Second row—Barry Cavagnaro, Barry Compton, Anthony Gourdine, Pat Sweeny, Mort Williamson, Terry Dillon, Fred Biearman, C. Ketchen, Dexter Hardy, Charlie Brown, Chris Warman, M. Thomas, Curtis Royal, Mike Vidunas, J. Sparrow. Third row—Dave Trout, E. Harris, Paul Scruppi, Wayne DiBartola, Mike Christ, Michael Woods, Dave Hepler, Todd Maragas, Rick Asberry, Rick Dukovich, Tim Lewis, B. Woodland, Hank Royal, Stan Boyarsky, Thomas Flynn, Marc Bailey. Fourth row—Clarence Norwood, Mike Chobany, Jay Pelusi, Charles Iorio, B. Albercci, Gary Tammaro, Dan Cavanaugh, Ricky Jackson, Dan Marino, Bill Beach, Mark Wohler, Greg Ganzer, Michael Martin, Sal Sunseri, Randy McMillan, Paul Vidunas. Fifth row—Gary Zingler, Rick Trocano, Mark Reichard, Butch Baieri, Carlton Williamson, Rich Kraynak, Dwight Collins, Greg Meisner, Mike Dombrowski, John Brown, Dan Short, Ed Moore, Tony Campbell, Chuck Palla, Pat McQuaide, Robert Steinbeck. Sixth row—Charles Jones, Ray Lao, Thad Jenkins, Sam Pilato, Bert Bertagna, Dennis Ballard, Al Wenglikowski, Phil Puzzuoli, Bill Legg, Emil Boures, Lou Lamanna, Julius Dawkins, Benjie Pryor, Bryan Watkins, Tony Aloia. Seventh row—Darryl Boots, Tim Quense, Tony Magnelli, Juan Polanco, Ron Killen, Jeff Casper, Terry Quirin, Jerry Boyarsky, Dan Daniels, Dave Bucklew, Steve Fedell, Robert Fada, Dexter Edmonds, Bill Wallace, James Shriver. Eighth row—Russ Grimm, Paul Dunn, Greg Christy, Roosevelt Reede, Don Gildea, Bill Neill, Bill Maas, John Hendrick, Mike Gazda, Mark May, Chuck Blucher, Ron Sams, Thomas Johnson, James Sweeney, Jimbo Covert, Skip Sylvester.

poll, redeemed themselves with a 24-20 victory over Herschel Walker and the Bulldogs on Marino's 33-yard touchdown pass to John Brown in the waning seconds.

"It was fourth-and-5," Marino recalled. "I was just trying to get a first down. Georgia decided to blitz, and Brown beat them down the middle. If they had played smart, we wouldn't have scored on that play."

The touchdown strike, with 35 seconds left, was Marino's third of the game and second to Brown. His touchdown pass to Dawkins got Pitt in front for the first time on the opening drive of the second half.

"There are a lot of quarterbacks in the country who could throw like we did if they had the time we did," said Marino, whose 34 touchdown passes during the regular season led the nation.

Sherrill concurred. "The offensive line did the best job it's done all year and did the job on the blitz on that pass by Danny," he said.

The defense did a job on one of the nation's top running backs for the second straight year, holding Walker to 84 yards rushing, his lowest total of the season.

Although the Panthers climbed only as high as second in the final UPI poll and fourth in AP, the victory put the finishing touch on what was the winningest three-year stretch in Pitt history.

"I don't know if Pitt, or anybody else, will ever have that many great athletes at the same time," Sherrill said. "We had a great player at every position on the field, offense and defense. We didn't have a weakness those years."

Pittsburgh, 1980-81

ROAD TO GREATNESS

1980 RESULTS (11-1)

Opponent	Score	Opp. Record	Opp. Bowl Game
Boston College	14-6	7-4-0	
at Kansas	18-3	4-5-2	
Temple	36-2	4-7-0	
Maryland	38-9	8-4-0	Tangerine (L)
at Florida State	22-36	10-2-0	Orange (L)
West Virginia	42-14	6-6-0	
at Tennessee	30-6	5-6-0	
at Syracuse	43-6	5-6-0	
Louisville	41-23	5-6-0	
at Army	45-7	3-7-1	
at Penn State	14-9	10-2-0	Fiesta (W)
GATOR BOWL			
South Carolina	**37-9**	**8-4-0**	

1981 RESULTS (11-1)

Opponent	Score	Opp. Record	Opp. Bowl Game
Illinois	26-6	7-4-0	
Cincinnati	38-7	6-5-0	
at South Carolina	42-28	6-6-0	
at West Virginia	17-0	9-3-0	Peach (W)
Florida State	42-14	6-5-0	
Syracuse	23-10	4-6-1	
at Boston College	29-24	5-6-0	
at Rutgers	47-3	5-6-0	
Army	48-0	3-7-1	
at Temple	35-0	5-5-0	
Penn State	14-48	10-2-0	Fiesta (W)
SUGAR BOWL			
Georgia	**24-20**	**10-2-0**	

FACTS AND FIGURES

Defensive end Hugh Green was named The Sporting News' 1980 College Player of the Year. . . . Offensive tackle Mark May joined Green on The Sporting News' 1980 All-America squad, while quarterback Dan Marino received TSN honors in 1981. . . . Tutored by defensive coordinator Foge Fazio, the Panthers led the nation in total defense in both 1980 and 1981. . . . Pitt was especially tough against the run, ranking first in rushing defense both seasons. . . . Pitt opponents averaged only 11 points per game in 1980 as the Panthers ranked seventh nationally in scoring defense. . . . Offensively, Pittsburgh ranked among the top scoring teams in both 1980 and 1981. . . . The Panthers had solid slates both seasons: In 1980, their opponents' combined record was 75-59-3, a .558 winning percentage; in 1981, Pitt's foes were 76-57-2, a .570 winning percentage. . . . The Panthers won 13 of their 24 games over both seasons by 20 points or more.

STATISTICAL LEADERS

PASSING

	Att.	Comp.	Yards	TD	Pct.	Int.
Dan Marino (1981)	339	200	2615	34	59.0	21
Dan Marino (1980)	211	109	1513	14	51.7	14
Rick Trocano (1980)	144	78	1246	10	54.2	11

RUSHING

	Att.	Yards	Avg.	TD	Long
Bryan Thomas (1981)	204	1003	4.9	7	64
Wayne DiBartola (1981)	145	648	4.5	3	47
Randy McMillan (1980)	134	633	4.7	9	45
Joe McCall (1980)	105	453	4.3	4	19

RECEIVING

	Rec.	Yards	Avg.	TD	Long
Benjie Pryor (1980)	43	538	12.5	4	28
Julius Dawkins (1981)	40	690	17.3	15	65
Bryan Thomas (1981)	40	393	9.8	0	26
John Brown (1981)	37	468	12.6	6	33

SCORING

	TD	FG	PAT	Points
Julius Dawkins (1981)	15	0	0	90
Dave Trout (1980)	0	12	35	71
Dwight Collins (1980)	10	0	0	60
Snuffy Everett (1981)	0	4	43	55
Randy McMillan (1980)	9	0	0	54

KEY CHARACTERS

The Conductor

COACH: Jackie Sherrill.

Record: 50-9-1, 5 years at Pittsburgh.

Sherrill succeeded Johnny Majors as Pittsburgh coach in December 1976 after posting a 3-8 mark in his only season as coach at Washington State. . . . He was a high school All-America in Biloxi, Miss., before becoming a versatile performer at Alabama under Bear Bryant. . . . He played on the Crimson Tide teams that won a consensus national championship in 1964 and finished first in the Associated Press poll in '65. . . . He served as a graduate assistant at Alabama and assistant at Arkansas, Iowa State and Pittsburgh before taking the Washington State job in 1976. . . . His teams won 11 games in three of his five seasons at the Pittsburgh helm and played in five consecutive bowl games, a first for Pitt teams. They lost only in the 1978 Tangerine Bowl to North Carolina State. . . . The 1980 and '81 Panther squads finished second in the United Press International Top 20 polls, and four of his five teams finished in the Top 10 in both wire-service rankings. . . . He posted a 2-3 record against archrival Penn State. . . . Sherrill, who ranks fourth on Pittsburgh's all-time coaching victory list, produced six consensus All-Americas in his five seasons. . . . In 1982, he was appointed head coach and athletic director at Texas A&M, where he compiled a 45-23-1 mark in his first six seasons while leading the Aggies to three consecutive Cotton Bowls, an A&M first. . . . His career coaching record through the 1987 season is 98-40-2 in 12 years.

Personal Data:

Born: November 28, 1943, in Duncan, Okla.
High School: Biloxi High in Biloxi, Miss.
College: Alabama.

The Supporting Cast

DEFENSIVE END: Hugh Green.

Green was one of college football's most outstanding defensive players ever. . . . From the time he donned the Panther jersey in 1977, he destroyed opponents and dominated games. . . . He finished second in the 1980 Heisman Trophy balloting and was named to The Sporting News' All-Time All-America Team selected in 1983. . . . He was a consensus All-America in 1978 and a unanimous consensus selection in both 1979 and '80. . . . He won the 1980 Lombardi Award and lettered from 1977-80.

Personal Data:

Born: July 27, 1959, in Natchez, Miss.
High School: Natchez North High.

QUARTERBACK: Dan Marino.

Marino finished fourth in the 1981 Heisman balloting and ninth in 1982. . . . Although considered one of the best quarterbacks of the decade, Marino never was a consensus All-America. . . . He was the classic dropback passer and often compared by Sherrill with former Alabama and professional greats Joe Namath and Ken Stabler. . . . He ranks as Pittsburgh's all-time leader in passing (8,597 yards, including bowl games) and total offense (8,290 yards) and holds numerous other Pitt passing records. . . . Marino, who lettered from 1979-82, was named to the AFC Pro Bowl team in each of his first five professional seasons with the Miami Dolphins. . . . An outstanding prep baseball player, he was selected by the Kansas City Royals in the fourth round of the 1979 draft.

Personal Data:

Born: September 15, 1961, in Pittsburgh.
High School: Central Catholic High in Pittsburgh.

FINAL 1980 WIRE SERVICE RANKINGS

ASSOCIATED PRESS		UNITED PRESS	
1. Georgia	11. Southern Cal	1. Georgia	11. Brigham Young
2. PITTSBURGH	12. Brigham Young	**2. PITTSBURGH**	12. Southern Cal
3. Oklahoma	13. UCLA	3. Oklahoma	13. Baylor
4. Michigan	14. Baylor	4. Michigan	14. UCLA
5. Florida State	15. Ohio State	**5. Florida State**	15. Ohio State
6. Alabama	16. Washington	6. Alabama	16. Purdue
7. Nebraska	17. Purdue	7. Nebraska	17. Washington
8. Penn State	18. Miami (Fla.)	**8. Penn State**	18. North Carolina
9. Notre Dame	19. Mississippi State	9. North Carolina	19. Florida
10. North Carolina	20. SMU	10. Notre Dame	20. SMU

FINAL 1981 WIRE SERVICE RANKINGS

ASSOCIATED PRESS		UNITED PRESS	
1. Clemson	11. Nebraska	1. Clemson	11. Brigham Young
2. Texas	12. Michigan	**2. PITTSBURGH**	12. Ohio State
3. Penn State	13. Brigham Young	**3. Penn State**	13. Southern Cal
4. PITTSBURGH	14. Southern Cal	4. Texas	14. Oklahoma
5. SMU	15. Ohio State	**5. Georgia**	15. Iowa
6. Georgia	16. Arizona State	6. Alabama	16. Arkansas
7. Alabama	**17. West Virginia**	7. Washington	17. Mississippi State
8. Miami (Fla.)	18. Iowa	8. North Carolina	**18. West Virginia**
9. North Carolina	19. Missouri	9. Nebraska	19. Southern Mississippi
10. Washington	20. Oklahoma	10. Michigan	20. Missouri

Bold face indicates Pittsburgh opponent.

Duff's Toughs Deliver Knockout

Michigan State, 1965-66
By Jack Ebling

"Duff's Toughs" had gotten a little roughed up during a disappointing 1964 season at Michigan State. Admittedly, the Spartans "felt they got pushed around by the other boys in the league a little too much," Coach Duffy Daugherty said. That they packed on several pounds of muscle over the subsequent summer didn't exactly pump up the coaching staff.

"Every day in September when I'd see that schedule on the back of the scoreboard at home," defensive line coach Hank Bullough said in 1965, "I'd break out in a cold sweat. Penn State, Michigan, Ohio State. . . . 'Just no way,' I'd say to myself. 'No way.' "

Bullough stopped short of beating his head against the wall. After all, lineman Pat Gallinagh made teammates cringe by practicing that self-psyching routine against the lockers. But it was symbolic of the contagious aggression that boiled over during the Spartans' 1965 and 1966 seasons. Once busted, Michigan State took to busting heads and punishing opponents with a fervor that bordered on downright madness.

"A certain amount of pride was taken in knockouts," said Don Japinga, cornerback and captain of the defense in 1965. "We were playing for the play

Michigan State Coach Duffy Daugherty was an amiable, fun-loving Irishman who could rule with an iron fist when the need arose.

after, like a lot of great defenses. We'd take one or two piling-ons without batting an eye."

Or batter a teammate in practice to settle a score. "One time, Ron Goovert and Robert Viney really got into it," Japinga said. "The fight lasted almost two hours before they both dropped from exhaustion."

Collectively, the 1965-66 Spartans dropped 19 opponents and claimed back-to-back Big Ten Conference championships with a 19-0-1 record in regular-season play. They lost only to UCLA, 14-12, in the 1966 Rose Bowl, and tied Notre Dame, 10-10, the following November in one of the most discussed games in college football history. Both decisions ultimately kept Michigan State out of the No. 1 slot in the final Associated Press rankings. Otherwise, the Spartans were spotless, silencing teams as they'd never been silenced before.

In 1965, they held Michigan to minus 51 yards rushing, Ohio State to minus 22 yards and Notre Dame to minus 12 yards with the nation's No. 1 defense against the run. They led in scoring defense, too, surrendering an average of only 6.2 points per game.

"The '65 team had clearly the better defense of the two," said defensive end Charles (Bubba) Smith. "It never stepped on the field thinking there was any possible way it could lose. If we'd had an offense to match our defense, there's no question we'd have been the all-time greatest team. Instead, we were one of the greatest."

The National Football League apparently agreed. Smith, halfback Clint Jones, roverback George Webster and split end Gene Washington were among the first eight draft selections following the 1966 season. Both Smith and Webster were two-time consensus All-Americas and the most celebrated members of the Spartan defense.

So imposing was the defense that nearly all opponents were forced to the air—whether they had a passing quarterback or not. Teams that tried to run to the right ran into Smith. If they went left, they were leveled by wild man Bob Viney, only 6-foot and 214 pounds—and all of it dynamite. If they explored the middle, they were met by linebackers Ron Goovert, Charlie (Mad Dog) Thornhill and Webster, who combined a linebacker's hitting power, a lineman's strength and a halfback's speed as the Spartans' rover.

"George Webster was the greatest player I ever played with or against," Japinga said. "He had an incredible instinct for the football, and he literally punished every ballcarrier.

"Webster was a much better player than Bubba. Actually, Robert Viney at the other end was better than Bubba. But the 'Kill, Bubba, Kill' thing had its own mystique, and at 6-7, 300 pounds, he was something of a freak."

The 'Kill, Bubba, Kill!' chant filled Spartan Stadium on Saturdays and became part of defensive end Bubba Smith's Michigan State legacy.

Smith had a persona that exceeded even his considerable ability, and fans saluted their man-eating defensive monster with "Kill, Bubba, Kill!" chants at Spartan Stadium. Without question, he was the big man on campus, a party waiting to happen—and a good portion of Michigan State's female population had open invitations.

"You see, as a sophomore, when we were 4-5, it wasn't a whole lot of fun," Smith said. "The next two years, it was a party. I know I had a real good time."

Fast times, indeed. Smith moved at a similar gait on the field, thundering across the turf with startling speed and agility. "The only thing that keeps him from being on the track team is the fact that he's too big to run in one lane," said track Coach Fran Dittrich, only half-joking. Smith moved in the fast lane on the highway, too, in a new Buick Riviera with "Bubba" emblazoned on the side. An investigation by the Big Ten found the car had been purchased legally by his father in Beaumont, Tex.

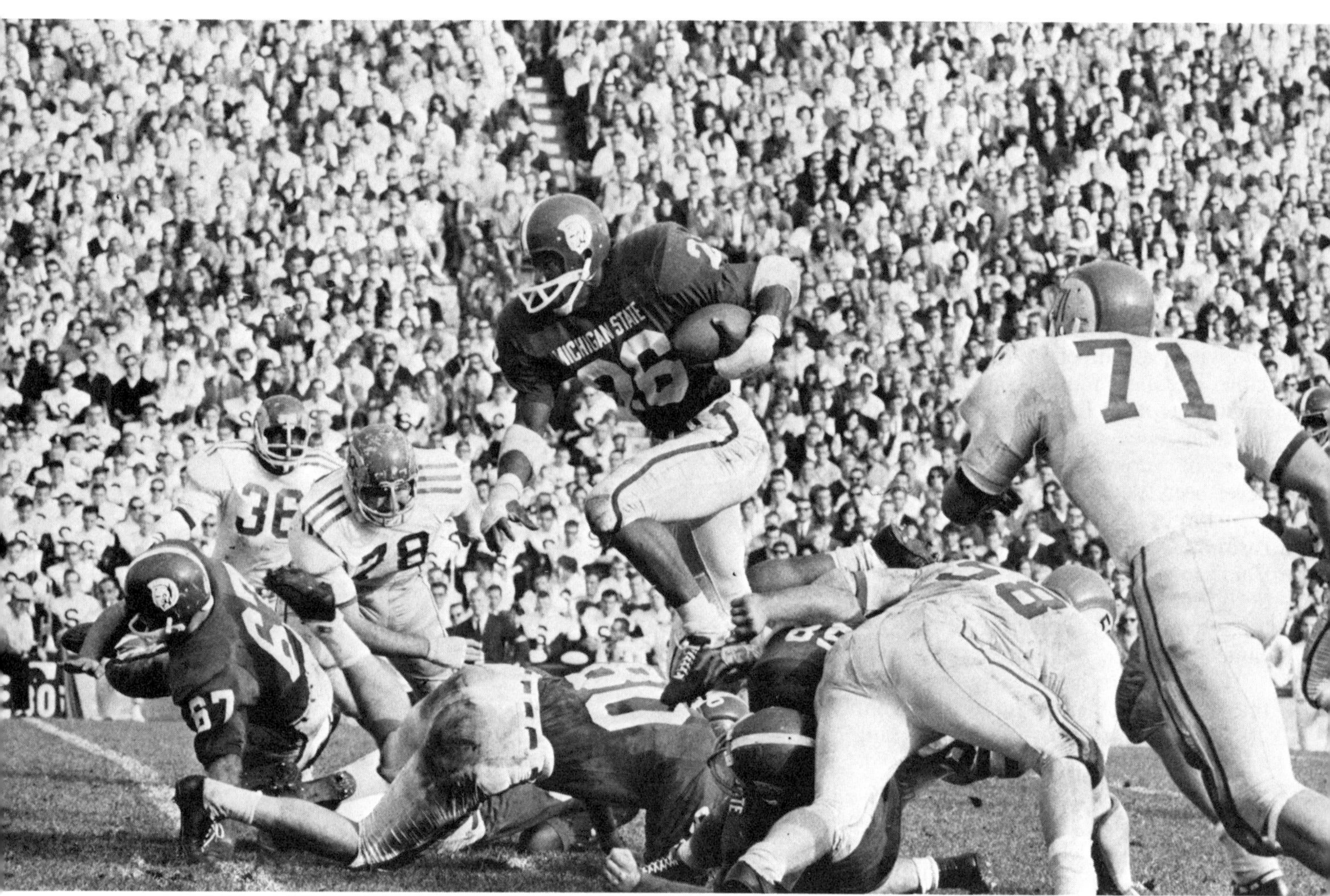

High-stepping halfback Clint Jones was an important figure in Coach Duffy Daugherty's ball-control offense.

Other Michigan State standouts had similar faraway addresses. Webster and defensive halfback Jim Summers hailed from South Carolina. Jimmy Raye, the quarterback in 1966, migrated from North Carolina. Washington was from La Porte, Tex. Fullback Bob Apisa and barefoot kicker Dick Kenney both were recruited from Hawaii. "First they had to swim to California, then we did the rest," quipped Daugherty.

With many Southern schools still segregated, Daugherty was able to mine a mother lode of exceptional black talent, to everyone's benefit. "College was probably the greatest time and the greatest learning experience of my life," Smith said. "I was learning about a whole new world. I'd never really talked to a white person before I got to Michigan State."

He talked to plenty once he arrived, including several at the Selective Service office. "I remember going before the draft board after I'd already stood them up four times," Smith said. "They said I was only 6-foot-4. No matter what I did, they said I passed."

The incident passed without Smith being drafted.

Michigan State's offense passed more than it ever had. Washington and either Raye or Steve Juday, the quarterback and team's most valuable player in 1965, formed potent combinations, even if the Spartans seldom threw before third down. Juday, an all-around intellectual and stern boss ("He's not the type of player you give a hotfoot to, know what I mean?" said one player), set records in 1964 and 1965 for most passes attempted.

"Duffy really preferred a ball-control offense and that's just what we had," Washington said. "My best games came when we were behind and had to play catch-up." In 1965, when Michigan State came from behind in six of its 10 victories, Washington set a single-season school record with 40 receptions.

"You have to remember the era," Juday said. "When I walked out of there, I had almost every passing record and some of them were embarrassments."

Much like the scores were to the opposition: 32-7

over Ohio State in 1965, 49-7 over Northwestern in '65, 42-8 over Penn State in 1966 and then 56-7 over Iowa. But the biggest embarrassment might have come in an odd-ending 24-7 victory over archrival Michigan in 1965.

"There were only a few seconds left, and I went back on the field to grab the game ball," Juday said. "Suddenly, Bob Apisa calls a timeout and the official says I have to stay in the game. I said, 'OK, guys, let's run one play into the line, and no cheap shots!' Well, Apisa goes about 35 yards, runs over about half the Michigan team and fires the ball into row 60.

"Our offense could have done a lot more, but we were a team that took advantage of its strengths. We knew we didn't have to score 40 points to win, so we stayed away from high-risk plays and turnovers."

The offense also stayed away from the defense whenever it could. Confrontations in practice left little doubt about which was the stronger unit.

"Even Duffy would just get livid when the offense would struggle in practice," Japinga said. "We'd say, 'OK, the old man's getting mad. Let them catch the ball.' "

If the offense caught too many, the defense caught hell, usually from Bullough, who'd routinely challenge Smith one-on-one without pads.

"Hank didn't want us to give up a yard, not even one," Smith said. "I remember one day the rock squad gained a yard against us, and we wound up running 165 40s!"

The Sgt. Rock drill routine must have helped because the Spartans held 16 of their 21 opponents in 1965 and 1966 to 10 points or less. Players were forever visiting Bullough's office to discuss combat strategy "and when they leave they always want to take a movie of one of the games back home to study," the coach said.

"It started in the Penn State game in '65," Smith said. "Hank told (290-pound guard) Harold Lucas, 'Their center is up for All-American and I want you to show him who you are. I'll give you five plays to put him out.'

"On the third play of the game, they carried the guy off on a stretcher."

Still, some doubted Michigan State's toughness. In the fifth game of the 1965 season, Ohio State Coach Woody Hayes decided to run into the teeth of the Spartans' defense—and specifically, at No. 95, Smith. The Buckeyes failed to run for a first down all day.

"Woody told my dad the day before the game, 'We're going right at your son,' " Smith said. "That's what they did the first series, and they lost about 15 yards."

The next week, Purdue tried a different approach, with quarterback Bob Griese passing, running and

Roverback George Webster, a two-time consensus All-America, was a defensive force who literally punished opposing ballcarriers.

kicking his club to a 10-0 halftime lead.

"Hank told me, 'You take the quarterback on the option and make him pay every time he runs it,' " Smith remembered. "By the end of the second quarter, there were no more options. And in the second half, his passing wasn't the same."

Griese completed only two passes after the intermission. Purdue never advanced beyond its 42-yard line in the third quarter or its 25 in the fourth. Meanwhile, Apisa and Jones pounded away at the Boilermakers' defense, rallying the Spartans to two fourth-quarter touchdowns and a 14-10 victory.

Michigan State's intensity reached its peak in the final game of the 1965 season against fourth-ranked Notre Dame, which had trounced the Spartans 34-7 in 1964. It was only the second time the Irish had beaten a Daugherty-coached Michigan State team in

Fullback Bob Apisa made the long 'swim' from Hawaii to become a member of Michigan State's football powerhouse.

10 tries.

"When we practiced there on Friday, their band played 'Old McDonald Had a Farm,' " Japinga said, "and they had at least 10,000 fans there to watch practice.

"The next day, Thornhill knocks the steel door to our dressing room off its hinges. Smith and Viney get in a fight over who's using the ankle wrap machine first. And when Juday and I are leading them out the tunnel, a fight breaks out. Viney has (Irish halfback) Nick Eddy pinned against a wall, and everyone else has squared off."

Viney was only slightly in control during the game, transferring his hostility to anyone wearing blue and gold.

"Viney tackled Nick Eddy on the Notre Dame sideline, and he gets up and starts after (Coach) Ara Parseghian, calling him some incredible names," Japinga said. "I tell you, the guy was absolutely nuts."

Things hardly were under control during Michigan State's extended Rose Bowl holiday in California. The undefeated Spartans already had been voted No. 1 in the final United Press International poll, and Rose Bowl opponent UCLA, a two-touchdown underdog, had been easy prey in a 13-3 season opener.

"When we beat Notre Dame, 12-3, we thought we'd already won the national championship," Smith said. "No one was fired up to play UCLA again."

Bruins quarterback Gary Beban, however, had matured rapidly since the opener (1,336 yards passing and 576 rushing), and Mel Farr was a powerful, explosive halfback. Still, the Spartans' offense had the aerial threat of Juday-to-Washington and the grinding ground attack of Apisa and Jones, a slashing runner who had scored a school-record 12 touchdowns. And regardless, this game was supposed to be dominated by the Michigan State defense.

"The Rose Bowl was just the most huge disappointment you could imagine," Japinga said. "Duffy told us all to enjoy it, and no one was thinking about football. Finally, we went to a monastery, but that was a desperation move."

The Spartans had been sun worshiping and sightseeing since mid-December and Daugherty wanted a change of scenery. Few understood the visitors' state of mind. Jim Murray wrote in the Los Angeles Times that the "Jolly Green Giants" should have been favored by 40 points and playing the Rams instead of UCLA.

"It was the classic setup," Juday said. "We walked around with that 'Green Machine' attitude, with our chests all pumped out. And UCLA kind of slinked around behind us."

Only minutes before game time, Japinga realized the magnitude of the problem. "Everyone was won-

Most of Michigan State's pass-catching responsibilities rested in the sure hands of split end Gene Washington.

dering if their girlfriends made it out and where their parents were sitting," he said. "No one was thinking about football. Finally, in the locker room, I said to Juday, 'Steve, we've got trouble here! We're just not ready!' "

The Bruins were prepared after watching Michigan State game films from the last five seasons. "We're gonna try and swarm 'em," drawled UCLA Coach Tommy Prothro, who stationed eight or nine men near the line in all but third-and-long situations.

"It was an interesting year from a play selection standpoint," Juday recollected. "Duffy and I were close, but I could begin to see his collar tighten on the sideline. Each of the last four games, there were more plays sent in."

UCLA gained a 14-0 halftime advantage by employing such plays as the onside kick, tackle-eligible pass and the "shadow set," in which receivers Kurt Altenburg and Dick Witcher lined up directly behind one another. "We decided that it was no use trying to get at Michigan State with anything but unorthodox tools," Prothro said.

The Bruins were outgained, 314-212, but they capitalized on two lapses by Michigan State's special teams. Japinga, subbing for regular-season punt returner Drake Garrett, fumbled a punt away at his own 6-yard line. Beban rolled to the left for five yards, then ran right for the final yard and his first of two touchdowns.

"Duffy got the kickoff return team together after their score and said, 'Now, watch for the onside kick!' " Japinga said. "A few seconds later, all five of our front guys just turned and sprinted downfield and no one was close to the kick."

UCLA recovered at the Michigan State 42. In five plays, including a 27-yard pass to Altenburg from the shadow set, Beban put the Bruins ahead 14-0 with a one-yard sneak.

Juday, meanwhile, was having little success. He would complete only six passes all afternoon—most in the final minutes—and throw three interceptions. By the fourth quarter, Daugherty had begun shuttling quarterbacks to shake up the attack.

"You see, the Rose Bowl was a showcase game, and Juday hadn't been drafted," Smith said. "Now, Juday was a helluva Spartan, but that just wasn't his day. Jimmy came in and it was bop, bop, score. If he'd have been in earlier, we would have won."

Juday actually scored the Spartans' final touchdown on a one-yard sneak with 31 seconds left, and his 42-yard strike to Washington set up Apisa's 38-yard scoring run midway through the fourth quarter. It was Raye, however, who pitched out to Apisa for a last-gasp two-point conversion try that could have tied the game in the final half-minute. UCLA's Bob Stiles, the game's most valuable player, stopped Apisa short of the goal line with a brutal hit that knocked the defensive back out cold.

"To this day, I think if I'd have stayed in we'd have made it," Juday said. "I'd run that play a lot more than Jimmy had. But it was a game that never should have come down to a single play.

"And had we not lost that last game, we'd have commanded a lot more respect. We could have gone down as one of the greatest teams in history."

They had entered the game rated No. 1 in both polls but, as an experiment, the AP delayed its final rankings until the bowl games had been completed. In a startling shakeup, Alabama leapfrogged Michigan State, Arkansas and Nebraska when the three top-ranked teams suffered their first losses of the season (Nebraska to Alabama in the Orange Bowl). The Spartans slipped to No. 2 behind the Crimson Tide.

"We might not have won the national championship in every poll, but we were by far the most dominant team in the country," Japinga said. "Our defense was an offensive weapon."

"I'd characterize the '65 team as having strong senior leadership and strong junior talent," said offensive captain Juday. "The real horsepower was in the underclassmen."

In 1966, those horses filled the leadership roles admirably. "My senior year, Duffy really wanted me to play in the spring game," remembered Washington, an NCAA and Big Ten hurdles champion. "Ohio State was on campus that day for a dual meet, and I was supposed to run the 100, the hurdles and the 400 relay. They started the meet at 11 a.m. so I could still get over to football."

Washington was only one of a legion of Daugherty admirers.

"If you look at the numbers, I think he was right with Woody in terms of national championships, coach of the year awards and everything else," Washington said. "If you look at the players he prepared for the pros, he'd compare very favorably with anyone."

Unlike the hard-boiled Hayes, Daugherty was a good egg, an amiable yet astute coaching legend who made football fun with his sparkling personality and easy-flowing wit. Daugherty called the 1965 squad his most thrilling and explained its success with typical humor: "The secret of this team is that our good sophomores and juniors haven't had the full benefit of my coaching experience."

Those players helped the Spartans outscore their opponents 103-7 in the final quarter, bringing Daugherty acclaim as the best fourth-quarter coach in the country. "Maybe so," he acknowledged. "I'm not very quick-witted and it takes me awhile to find out what's going on."

Before the 1966 season, Daugherty admitted the Spartans faced an added obstacle because they were ineligible to return to the Rose Bowl under Big Ten rules. "We'll try to make our squad realize that the conference championship is incentive enough to play just as hard as we did last season."

And with Juday gone, Raye was viewed as the key to the Spartans' success. "He's probably the best running quarterback we've ever had and we hope he'll pass better than people think he will," Daugherty said. "As to his leadership abilities, only game action can prove that."

Raye proved to be an inspiration, throwing 10 touchdown passes (second-most in school history) while gaining 557 yards as the Spartans' No. 2 rusher behind Jones, a consensus All-America pick. Apisa, who in 1965 had gained more yardage (666) than any other fullback in Michigan State history, scored a team-leading nine touchdowns despite missing two games with a knee injury.

Michigan State wound up undefeated and became the first Big Ten team to win successive conference championships since the 1954-55 Ohio State Buckeyes. After winning their first nine games, the Spartans played to a 10-10 tie in their season finale against top-ranked Notre Dame, which sealed a national championship by running out the clock

The 1966 Spartans: Front row (left to right)—Dick Kenney, Bob Brawley, Larry Lukasik, John Mullen, Chuck Lowther, Clint Jones, head Coach Duffy Daugherty, George Webster, Charlie Thornhill, Phil Hoag, Jeff Richardson, Jerry West, Gene Washington. Second row—Wade Payne, Sterling Armstrong, Dwight Lee, Drake Garrett, John Kettunen, Jerry Jones, Pat Gallinagh, Bubba Smith, Tom Skidmore, Dick Reahm, Jim Summers, Ron Ranieri, Larry Smith, Maurice Haynes. Third row—Jess Phillips, Eddy McLoud, Jim Juday, Nick Jordan, Tony Conti, Joe Przybycki, Dave Techlin, George Chatlos, Bob Lange, Mike Bradley, Mitch Pruiett, Clint Meadows, Bob Apisa, Ken Heft, Jimmy Raye. Fourth row—Jack Zindel, Clint Harris, Don Baird, Roger Ruminski, Gary McGaughey, Regis Cavender, Bill Ware, Al Brenner, Neal Peterson, Mike Mahady, Charles Bailey, Duane McIver, Charles Wedemeyer, Jim Ruschak, Bill Feraco, Frank Waters. Fifth row—Equipment managers Martin Daly, Ken Earley; coaches Henry Bullough, Dan Boisture, Vince Carillot, Al Dorow; Dwight Romagnoli, Ted Bohn, Bob Super, Mike Young, Mike Garofalo, Don Warnke, Dick Berlinski, Paul Lawson; coaches Cal Stoll, Ed Rutherford, Gordon Serr; trainers Gayle Robinson, Clyde Stretch, Clint Thompson; manager Jim Orr.

against the Spartans then shellacking Southern Cal, 51-0, in their final game.

"Twice we made a tackle, called timeout and said some awful nasty things about their parents," Smith remembered. "But they knew if they tied, they'd end up winning."

Webster was equally frustrated after the game. "We started asking them if they wanted a tie," he said. "They said nothing back to us. They wouldn't even look us in the eye. How I wish we could have played them another half."

The Michigan State defense sent an early calling card, knocking out Irish quarterback Terry Hanratty and center George Goeddeke in the first quarter. The Spartans took a 10-0 lead in the second quarter on substitute fullback Reggie Cavender's four-yard run and Kenney's 47-yard field goal, but the Irish battled back with a 34-yard scoring pass from backup Coley O'Brien late in the quarter and a 28-yard field goal on the first play of the final quarter.

With a first-and-10 on their 30 and 1:24 to play, however, the Fighting Irish opted for four running plays to pick up a first down. After O'Brien was dropped for a seven-yard loss on the next play, he scrambled to the Notre Dame 39 as time expired.

Parseghian drew considerable criticism but adamantly defended his play-it-safe strategy. "It had to do with Kenney's ability as a field-goal kicker," he explained. "If it was early in the fourth quarter it would have been different, but we weren't going to give up the ball deep in our own territory and take a risk on losing the game after battling like we did."

After holding a commanding lead in the polls, the Irish slipped to second behind Michigan State in the UPI rankings but regained the top spot—and a national championship—after routing Southern Cal.

"I don't see how any team could be rated over our team," Daugherty said after the Notre Dame contest. "There's no way. Here's a team that's gone 20 games in regular-season play without a defeat. If a coach asked for anything more than that, he'd just be selfish. . ."

If Daugherty had, it's hard to believe that these Spartans wouldn't have given it to him.

Michigan State, 1965-66

ROAD TO GREATNESS

1965 RESULTS (10-1)

Opponent	Score	Opp. Record	Opp. Bowl Game
UCLA	13-3	8-2-1	Rose (W)
at Penn State	23-0	5-5-0	
Illinois	22-12	6-4-0	
at Michigan	24-7	4-6-0	
Ohio State	32-7	7-2-0	
at Purdue	14-10	7-2-1	
Northwestern	49-7	4-6-0	
at Iowa	35-0	1-9-0	
Indiana	27-13	2-8-0	
at Notre Dame	12-3	7-2-1	
ROSE BOWL			
UCLA	**12-14**	**8-2-1**	

1966 RESULTS (9-0-1)

Opponent	Score	Opp. Record	Opp. Bowl Game
North Carolina State	28-10	5-5-0	
Penn State	42-8	5-5-0	
at Illinois	26-10	4-6-0	
Michigan	20-7	6-4-0	
at Ohio State	11-8	4-5-0	
Purdue	41-20	9-2-0	Rose (W)
at Northwestern	22-0	3-6-1	
Iowa	56-7	2-8-0	
at Indiana	37-19	1-8-1	
Notre Dame	10-10	9-0-1	

FACTS AND FIGURES

Coach Duffy Daugherty was named The Sporting News' 1965 Coach of the Year. . . . Four Spartans were named to The Sporting News' 1966 All-America team: split end Gene Washington, halfback Clint Jones, defensive end Bubba Smith and roverback George Webster. . . . All four were voted to the all-time Spartan team in 1969 by Michigan State fans, who selected Webster as the school's greatest player ever. . . . The Spartans ranked second nationally in total defense in 1965 and eighth in 1966. . . . They surrendered 6.2 points per game in 1965, best in the nation. . . . The Michigan State rushing attack was ranked among the nation's best in both 1965 (sixth) and 1966 (eighth). . . . Only four of the Spartans' 21 opponents over both seasons scored more than 10 points. . . . Just nine of the Spartans' opponents finished with winning records. . . . The combined record of the opposition in 1965 was 59-48-4, a .550 winning percentage; in 1966, 48-49-3, a .495 winning percentage. . . . In each season, the Spartans posted victories over the eventual Rose Bowl champion: In 1965, they defeated UCLA (which then won the rematch in Pasadena) and in 1966, Purdue. . . . The Spartans posted a 5-1-1 record against teams that finished in the final Top 20 rankings.

STATISTICAL LEADERS

PASSING

	Att.	Comp.	Yards	TD	Pct.	Int.
Steve Juday (1965)	168	89	1173	7	53.0	7
Jimmy Raye (1966)	123	62	1110	10	50.4	8

RUSHING

	Att.	Yards	Avg.	TD	Long
Clint Jones (1965)	165	787	4.8	10	80
Clint Jones (1966)	159	784	4.9	6	79
Bob Apisa (1965)	122	666	5.5	9	39
Bob Apisa (1966)	86	445	5.0	8	49
Jimmy Raye (1966)	122	436	3.5	5	30

RECEIVING

	Rec.	Yards	Avg.	TD	Long
Gene Washington (1965)	40	638	16.0	4	44
Gene Washington (1966)	27	677	25.0	7	64
Clint Jones (1965)	26	308	11.8	2	34

SCORING

	TD	FG	PAT	Points
Clint Jones (1965)	12	0	*1	74
Bob Apisa (1965)	9	0	*1	56
Bob Apisa (1966)	9	0	0	54
Dick Kenney (1965)	0	11	20	53

*Two-point conversion.

KEY CHARACTERS

The Conductor

COACH: Hugh (Duffy) Daugherty.

Record: 109-69-5, 19 years at Michigan State.

Daugherty succeeded Clarence (Biggie) Munn in 1954. . . . He had played at Syracuse when Munn was an assistant coach and was hand-picked by Munn as his replacement at Michigan State. . . . He is a member of the College Football Hall of Fame. . . . His 1955 and 1966 teams were ranked second in the final Associated Press and United Press International polls, and his 1965 squad was rated first by UPI and second by AP. . . . Seven of Daugherty's teams finished in the Top 10 of both polls. . . . A number of his assistants went on to head their own programs, including Bob Devaney, Dan Devine, Bill Yeoman, Lou Agase, Denny Stolz, Cal Stoll and current Spartan Coach George Perles. . . . He died in 1987 at the age of 72.

Personal Data:

Born: September 8, 1915, in Emeigh, Pa.
High School: North Cambria High in Barnesboro, Pa.
College: Syracuse.

The Supporting Cast

HALFBACK: Clint Jones.

Jones was a consensus All-America in 1966. . . . He scored four touchdowns and ran for 268 yards to set Big Ten records in a 1965 game against Iowa. . . . He finished his career as the Spartans' No. 2 all-time rusher with 1,921 yards. . . . He lettered from 1964-66 and finished sixth in the 1966 Heisman Trophy voting.

Personal Data:

Born: May 24, 1945, in Cleveland.
High School: Cathedral Latin in Cleveland.

DEFENSIVE END: Charles (Bubba) Smith.

Smith, one of the all-time great college linemen, combined size, speed and strength to dominate opposing offenses. . . . He was a consensus All-America in 1965 and a unanimous pick in 1966. . . . Smith was a three-year letterman (1964-66) and is a member of the College Football Hall of Fame.

Personal Data:

Born: February 28, 1945, in Beaumont, Tex.
High School: Pollard High in Beaumont.

SPLIT END: Gene Washington.

Washington is generally regarded as the best receiver to don a Spartan uniform. . . . He set school receiving records for most 100-yard games (six), receptions and yardage in one game (nine and 150), touchdowns in one game (three in 1965) and receptions in a season (35 in 1964 and 40 in '65). . . . His average of 25 yards per catch in 1966 remains a Michigan State record. . . . Washington caught 102 career passes for 1,857 yards and 16 touchdowns. . . . He lettered from 1964-66.

Personal Data:

Born: January 25, 1944, in LaPorte, Tex.
High School: Baytown Carver High in LaPorte.

ROVERBACK: George Webster.

Webster was a quick, hard-hitting defender who earned unanimous consensus All-America honors in both 1965 and '66. . . . He is a member of the College Football Hall of Fame and was named to The Sporting News' All-Time All-America Team selected in 1983. . . . He lettered from 1964-66.

Personal Data:

Born: November 25, 1945, in Anderson, S.C.
High School: Westside High in Anderson.

FINAL 1965 WIRE SERVICE RANKINGS

ASSOCIATED PRESS

1. Alabama	6. Missouri
2. MICHIGAN STATE	7. Tennessee
3. Arkansas	8. Louisiana State
4. UCLA	**9. Notre Dame**
5. Nebraska	10. Southern Cal

Only Top 10 ranked.

UNITED PRESS

1. MICHIGAN STATE	**11. Ohio State**
2. Arkansas	12. Florida
3. Nebraska	**13. Purdue**
4. Alabama	14. Louisiana State
5. UCLA	15. Georgia
6. Missouri	16. Tulsa
7. Tennessee	17. Mississippi
8. Notre Dame	18. Kentucky
9. Southern Cal	19. Syracuse
10. Texas Tech	20. Colorado

FINAL 1966 WIRE SERVICE RANKINGS

ASSOCIATED PRESS

1. Notre Dame	6. Nebraska
2. MICHIGAN STATE	**7. Purdue**
3. Alabama	8. Georgia Tech
4. Georgia	9. Miami (Fla.)
5. UCLA	10. SMU

Only Top 10 ranked.

UNITED PRESS

1. Notre Dame	11. Florida
2. MICHIGAN STATE	12. Mississippi
3. Alabama	13. Arkansas
4. Georgia	14. Tennessee
5. UCLA	15. Wyoming
6. Purdue	16. Syracuse
7. Nebraska	17. Houston
8. Georgia Tech	18. Southern Cal
9. SMU	19. Oregon State
10. Miami (Fla.)	20. Virginia Tech

Bold face indicates Michigan State opponent.

The Mad Magicians Of Ann Arbor

Michigan, 1947
By Steve Kornacki

The University of Michigan football team toured Paramount Studios in Hollywood prior to capping an undefeated season with a smashing victory in the 1948 Rose Bowl. Bob Chappuis, a Time magazine coverboy, and Bump Elliott posed with film stars such as Marlene Dietrich, Bob Hope and Bing Crosby. The team was given the red-carpet treatment and rubbed elbows with the movie industry's big names.

Little did Tinsel Town's stars, producers and directors realize what a real-life drama they had before them.

These Wolverines were proof that fact often is superior to fiction. They conquered adversity with a rare blend of teamwork and flair.

Michigan's offensive backfield was nicknamed the "Mad Magicians" because its members possessed slick ballhandling skills. The backs were a basketball team in pads. And playing the game was the easy part for the 1947 Wolverines, many of whom had traveled an extremely bumpy road en route to their places on the roster. World War II detoured their youth, and experiences worthy of a full-length feature resulted.

John Wayne would have been a natural to play Alvin Wistert, the rugged, out-of-my-way defensive tackle. He arrived in Ann Arbor as a 31-year-old attending the university on the GI Bill. An elbow injury had short-circuited his professional baseball ambitions and a Marine officer angered him into pursuing football after the war.

The German army nearly claimed backfield standout Chappuis. The Heisman Trophy runner-

Fritz Crisler, a coaching perfectionist who demanded a lot from his players, molded Michigan into a postwar football power.

Michigan's 1947 backfield included such talent as (left to right) wingback Bump Elliott, quarterback Howard Yerges, fullback Jack Weisenburger and tailback Bob Chappuis.

up of 1947 had been shot down over Italy during the war and listed as missing in action for three months. Audie Murphy would have been perfect to portray him.

Then there was Chalmers (Bump) Elliott, the guy everyone liked. He was "the red-topped galloper" who made the biggest plays in the biggest games. Why not Van Johnson in this role?

Bruce Hilkene, the captain on a team with so many leaders, was a Gregory Peck type. It was Hilkene who called for a players-only meeting prior to Michigan's midseason game against Minnesota in '47. The session became a weekly ritual, serving to air gripes and help the squad focus on its stretch drive.

The Wolverines beat Minnesota, 13-6, after Wistert vowed to avenge three consecutive losses that brother Albert, a former Michigan star, had endured to the Golden Gophers in the early 1940s. The next week, the Wolverines traveled to Illinois and notched a seven-point victory over the Fighting Illini.

Everybody else on Michigan's '47 schedule lost to the Wolverines by three or more touchdowns. The Wolverines finished the regular season with a perfect record, but they wound up second to mighty Notre Dame in the final official poll of the season, conducted by the Associated Press in early December.

The Wolverines, obviously not content with a runner-up role, won the national championship in 1948 and pushed their winning streak—initiated in 1946—to 25 games before finally losing three games into the 1949 season. But Herbert Orin (Fritz) Crisler wasn't on the sidelines after 1947. The legendary coach handed the team to assistant Bennie Oosterbaan and concentrated on his role as athletic director.

"After the Rose Bowl, Fritz resigned," Wistert said. "Later, he told us he did it because this (the '47 unit) was the greatest team he ever coached. He said that he would forever set us as the standard, and added that that would be unfair."

Crisler had been wooed by the University of California and the All-America Football Conference after the 1946 season. The new professional league offered him \$50,000 to become its commissioner, but Crisler despised the pros and refused. Cal guaranteed him \$20,000 for a \$2,000 raise. The coach interviewed for the Berkeley post, but he turned down the attractive offer.

"I wondered if the Michigan of the future would be like the Michigan of the past," he said. "I wanted to be sure our kids would have an equal chance in competition with kids from other schools."

Crisler wanted stability and got it. Remaining as athletic director until 1968, he hired only one other coach besides Oosterbaan—Bump Elliott, who took over the job in 1959.

"Fritz was the key to the whole thing," Chappuis said of the man who had enjoyed enormous coaching success at Princeton before taking the Ann Arbor job in 1938. "He required that you do what was asked, and made you believe that if you did as

Michigan's biggest offensive weapon was Chappuis, who is pictured (above) in 1946 carrying a would-be Army tackler toward the end zone.

he said, you would win."

Said Wistert: "Fritz demanded a pro performance from rank amateurs."

Coaching a postwar team required a special touch. The Michigan players varied in age from 18 to 31. Many returned from the service only to find others at their positions. Crisler, discovering a loophole of sorts in the substitution rules, devised a system of two-platoon football. It doubled his number of starters, smoothed over egos and gave Michigan a fresher team.

Crisler's scheme to infuse fresh talent into his lineup first attracted major attention in Michigan's 1945 game against powerful Army.

"The substitution rule was changed in 1941," Crisler explained in the book "The Wolverines," a history of Michigan football. "Until that time, players could not re-enter a game in the same quarter they had left. The restriction was removed, and all that remained was the provision allowing a player to enter the game at any time the clock is stopped.

"Three little words, 'at any time,' gave me the opportunity of using separate teams for offense and defense." The contest against Earl (Red) Blaik's Army juggernaut proved an opportune time for Crisler to put his theory into practice.

"I knew our boys could not stay with that great Army team for 60 minutes," said Crisler, reflecting on the Cadets' manpower advantage in Michigan's fifth game of the '45 season. "Our only hope was to play our best tacklers on defense and our best runners and blockers on offense. We tried to keep as many fresh players in the game as possible. I don't think anyone had used the four-man front before, and this helped. Only our halfbacks and safetyman were left in the game to play offense." Army won, but "only" by a 28-7 score in what turned out to be the Cadets' second closest game of the season.

After finishing the 1945 season with a 7-3 record, the Wolverines then compiled a 6-2-1 mark in 1946. Hilkene viewed Crisler's substitution plan as crucial to the team's success.

"Our postwar mix was not really working," Hilkene explained. "Some of the guys didn't seem like Michigan players and it was difficult for Fritz to blend us. We had kids just out of high school, guys back from the service and oldies such as Wisty and J.T. White (listed as 27 years old in the 1947 Michigan media guide).

"We had three or four former first-stringers at

A 1947 program for the Michigan-Stanford game at Ann Arbor featured Wolverine captain Bruce Hilkene, the strong, silent leader of the team.

some positions. Platooning solved the problems that had developed and gave us a really tough team. Bump was the only one to go both ways at halfback."

The Wolverines had closed the '46 season with four straight victories after going winless for three consecutive games. The most demoralizing loss came by a touchdown to two-time defending national champion Army.

"That's when Fritz decided to make it fun," Hilkene said. "We had just lost to the Army group that had Glenn Davis and Doc Blanchard. Late calls went against us and Fritz wasn't one to use sour grapes. He told us to never talk about it and we never did.

"Fritz cut those plays out of the game films. He didn't want us to see it again and feel morbid about a game we deserved to tie or win. Eventually, he burned all the film from that game.

"Fritz told us that we should have fun and we began having that. And we started winning. Our strong finish in '46 gave us the impetus for '47. We had such strong camaraderie."

And such talent.

Chappuis won consensus All-America honors in 1947, while Elliott, quarterback Howard Yerges and end Bob Mann joined Chappuis on the all-league team. Wistert and receiver Richard Rifenburg, prominent players on the '47 Michigan team, would earn consensus All-America status in 1948.

"We were loaded," Hilkene said. "One time I visited some injured veterans with Bennie Oosterbaan and Chappy. Everybody was telling Chappy what a great player he was. He shook his head and said, 'I don't know how I can be credited with being a good football player when the guy behind me is a better runner.' He was talking about (Gene) Derricotte. That's the way we felt about each other.

"What a great group of people to be around. It was one of the finest experiences of my life and I have a very fond feeling for all of them. Every five years, we have a reunion. And of the 44 guys we took to the Rose Bowl, 90 percent or more show up every time. Guys come from Hawaii, California, all over."

Said Chappuis: "Everyone liked one another and that carries over to today."

Said Wistert: "Even though we belonged to different fraternities, we partied together."

Chappuis credited the personality mesh to "the coaching genius" of Crisler. And while Crisler's two-platoon innovation was critical to Michigan's success, the team also benefited from—and possessed a spirit representative of—the postwar mood. It was great to be at peace, in college and playing football. Nobody realized this quite as much as Chappuis, who parachuted from a B-25 over enemy territory in Italy and ran for his life in the foothills of the Alps.

"I was part of a six-man crew based on (the island of) Corsica and a substitute that day," Chappuis said. "It was my 21st mission and I was the radio operator and gunner. We got shot down, bailed out and came down in an olive orchard. An Italian partisan scout saw us parachute and approached us on a bicycle. We didn't know who he was at first, but he took us to a farm house.

"One was taken prisoner and five of us were taken in by the partisans. We moved around a lot so as not to keep a fresh trail and were in a little town, roughly halfway between Milan and Verona. The German headquarters were practically next door. They fed us, kept us warm and saved our lives. I still hear from those people, and we've visited both ways."

Three months passed and the war ended.

"We went back to our regional outfit and found out we had been reported missing in action," Chappuis said. "My parents did not know if I was alive or well. When I got out, there was no question I was going back to Michigan, where I had played as a sophomore in 1942."

Crisler was excited to get Chappuis back—but

concerned, too.

"I had heard reports that returning football players weren't the same as they were before going away to war," the coach said. "You can imagine my feeling when I saw Chap out there in practice, the same uncomplaining, hard-working kid he was before the war. Then I went ahead and built our attack around him. You know the result."

While Chappuis had played for Michigan before World War II, Bump Elliott and Wistert became first-time Wolverines after the war, when their hitches in the Marines ended. Both were influenced by their brothers, but for entirely different reasons.

"Pete (Elliott) had been sent to Michigan during the war as part of the Navy V-12 program and I was sent to Purdue for the V-12 Marine Corps program," Bump said. "When I was discharged, I saw no reason to go back to Purdue. And the only reason I went to Michigan was because my brother was there."

Wistert returned to Ann Arbor in an attempt to accomplish what he'd set out to do a dozen years earlier.

"I'd left Chicago to attend Ann Arbor High my senior year," Wistert said. "I could not play athletics as a transfer but wanted to go there in order to get a principal's recommendation to Michigan. I worked out with the Michigan baseball team that spring. My brother, Whitey, played both sports (football and baseball) at Michigan, and that's how I knew the baseball coach, Ray Fisher.

"Whitey signed with the Cincinnati Reds. Fisher told me: 'I can't wait for you. You're better than your brother right now.' I loved baseball and wanted to be a major league pitcher. I said, 'To hell with school.' I played in an industrial league in Jackson (Mich.) that year and signed with Cincinnati in 1936. I jammed my elbow that winter and at spring training in '37, I found out it was bone chips. My career was over and I went to work for Procter and Gamble until 1942, when I went in the service."

Francis (Whitey) Wistert, a Wolverine footballer in 1931, 1932 and 1933, and another brother, Albert Wistert, a Michigan gridder in 1940, 1941 and 1942, had been named All-America players in their final collegiate seasons. Accordingly, the Wistert name was familiar to many people Alvin encountered.

"An officer came up," Alvin recalled, "and asked: 'Could this be the erstwhile All-America and Philadelphia Eagle, Al Wistert? I saw you play against the Giants last year. Great game!' Being Alvin and Albert, it was easy for us to get confused.

"He was wringing my hand with a handshake, but I told him that I was Alvin and not Albert. The guy all but wiped his hand off. He was so affronted. Now, I was mighty proud of what my brothers did. But I was so damned sick of saying, 'No, he's my brother.' I decided that when I got back, I was going to Michigan.

Michigan 'Conductor' Fritz Crisler looks out the window as Richard Rifenburg (above) and Bruce Hilkene climb aboard a train before a 1947 road game.

"Whitey had worn number 11 as a tackle because he played in the days before TV games, when numbers were given out indiscriminately. Albert came along and wore it, too. They asked if I wanted it. I said, 'It's a helluva load, but I'll take it.' And so now you have a helluva oddity: Three brothers who all played tackle, wore the same number (which the school retired) and made All-America at the same university. And then became the only three brothers ever to make the College Football Hall of Fame. I guess I lived down the stigma of my brothers."

He also settled a score for Albert while inciting Michigan to victory in the first key game of the 1947 season. In Albert's three varsity seasons, the Wolverines lost three times to Minnesota by a total of 10 points.

Said Wistert: "I got up in front of the team and vowed, 'Over my dead body will those bastards beat us!' "

Another quarterback for the Wolverines was Pete Elliott, a good athlete who also performed on the basketball court.

The Gophers, heavy underdogs despite boasting a 3-1 season record, took a 6-0 second-quarter lead against an unbeaten Michigan team that had leveled Michigan State, Stanford, Pittsburgh and Northwestern by a combined score of 222-34. But Bump Elliott caught a 40-yard touchdown pass from Chappuis later in the period and Jim Brieske tacked on the conversion kick for a 7-6 Michigan advantage.

Said Chappuis: "Howard Yerges, who shared the quarterbacking with Pete Elliott, called the play and said, 'We haven't been behind in any game at the half and I don't want to go in behind in this one.'

"Howard walked away and I talked to Bump because I would be throwing from left halfback. I said, 'Bump, I'm not getting an awful lot of time. (Leo) Nomellini and (Clayton) Tonnemaker are putting on a good rush.' Bump told me he'd be down in the corner of the end zone. I threw just as those two knocked me to the ground. I had to wait until the film session on Monday to actually see it completed."

The battle for the Little Brown Jug remained in doubt halfway through the fourth quarter of the game at Michigan Stadium. The Wolverines' Jack Weisenburger then intercepted a pass and returned it to the Gophers' 21-yard line. Derricotte scored on the next play, bolting through a gigantic hole on the left side. Final score: Michigan 13, Minnesota 6.

"We beat 'em in every one of my three seasons," Wistert recalled, chuckling.

Up next was Illinois in Champaign. Bump Elliott, from nearby Bloomington, made it quite a homecoming. He returned a punt 74 yards for a touchdown in the first quarter. Blocks by Mann, Rifenburg and Derricotte left him untouched.

"I caught the ball back with Derricotte," Elliott said. "I took two steps straight ahead and then veered outside. It was enough to take them all inside and nobody came close to me. The blockers set up a perfect wall, and all I had to do to score was not fall down."

The Fighting Illini tied the game in the second quarter before Chappuis and Bump Elliott teamed on a 52-yard pass play to set up what proved to be the game-winning touchdown. Hank Fonde's nine-yard run notched the TD and Brieske followed with his second point-after kick as Michigan slipped ahead, 14-7. There would be no more scoring in the first half, as Elliott made a key interception at the Michigan 8 late in the second period. Indeed, no additional points would go up on the scoreboard for the remainder of the game.

The Michigan defense hit its stride in this contest, with end Leonard Ford standing out with his afternoon-long incursions into the Fighting Illini's backfield.

After their triumph over Illinois, the Wolverines allowed just six points in their final three regular-season games. They shut out Indiana, 35-0, and blasted Wisconsin, 40-6, before spilling archrival Ohio State, 21-0. Besides the continued outstanding play of Ford, Michigan received top-caliber defensive performances from guards Joe Soboleski and Quent Sickels, tackles Wistert and Ralph Kohl and linebackers Dan Dworsky and Dick Kempthorn, among others.

In compiling a 9-0 record, Michigan had led the nation in total offense with 412.7 yards per game and in passing with 173.9 yards per contest.

"We were red-hot in every way," Bump Elliott said.

The New York World-Telegram wrote: "The success of the team can be attributed to several things. (1) precision ballhandling; (2) excellent execution of the fundamentals; (3) a great forward-passing game with Bob Chappuis throwing to a number of fine receivers; (4) fullback Jack Weisenburger, greatest spinner since Bob Westfall; (5) Bump Elliott, the little fellow who made reverses go for nine touchdowns; (6) the free-substitution rule which permitted Crisler wide latitude."

The "Mad Magicians" were a one-of-a-kind offense. They ran out of the single wing with Chappuis at tailback (the equivalent of left halfback, or the primary passing position in this alignment), Bump Elliott at wingback (right halfback), Weisenburger at fullback and Yerges or Pete Elliott at quarterback.

"All four of the backs were able to pass and run,"

With pictures of her three All-America sons in prominent display, Josephine Wistert listens to a 1947 Michigan broadcast. The pictures (left to right) are of Francis, Albert and Alvin.

Bump Elliott said. "That's because we'd all been quarterbacks or left halfbacks at some time."

"A big play was the buck lateral," Chappuis said. "In the single wing, the quarterback shifted to blocking back. The fullback would take the snap from center to 'buck' the line and spin to hand off. We had a lot of deception and worked hard on honing it in practice. We were always on the same page."

Amos Alonzo Stagg, Crisler's coach at the University of Chicago, said, "The way they pass the ball around is beautiful to behold."

The Wolverines met Stagg, then 85, twice that season. Crisler took the team to meet him on a road trip.

"We stopped at Stagg Field in Chicago on the way to Northwestern," Wistert said. "Before I go further, you should know two things. First, Rifenburg was the only guy on the team who could get away with pulling anything on Fritz. He was a clown and a guy everyone liked. And second, Crisler's favorite two words for a guy who messed up in practice were jackass and double-jackass. OK?

"Well, we're on Stagg Field and Rifenburg said: 'I can see it all now. I can see you at practice, Coach, with Stagg watching over there. And Stagg shouts, 'Fritz! Fritz! You jackass, you!' Everyone laughed, even Fritz."

Crisler invited Stagg to address the team prior to the Rose Bowl, and the old coach said, "Score the first touchdown and keep scoring."

The Wolverines took the message to heart, beating the Trojans, 49-0. In the next day's headlines, they were the "Michigan 49ers." The Wolverines scored 21 first-half points and deflated Southern Cal with a 21-point fourth-quarter onslaught.

"Our depth had a lot to do with their frustration," Wistert said. "They had an All-America end named Paul Cleary, and at the end of the game he walked by and said: 'All-America, hell. No way. I'm not even going to play pro ball after this.' We rather humbled them that day." (Cleary's bruised ego eventually healed enough for the Trojans' star to spend two seasons in the pros, with AAFC teams.)

Weisenburger scored three touchdowns in the Rose Bowl on short bursts. Michigan's four other

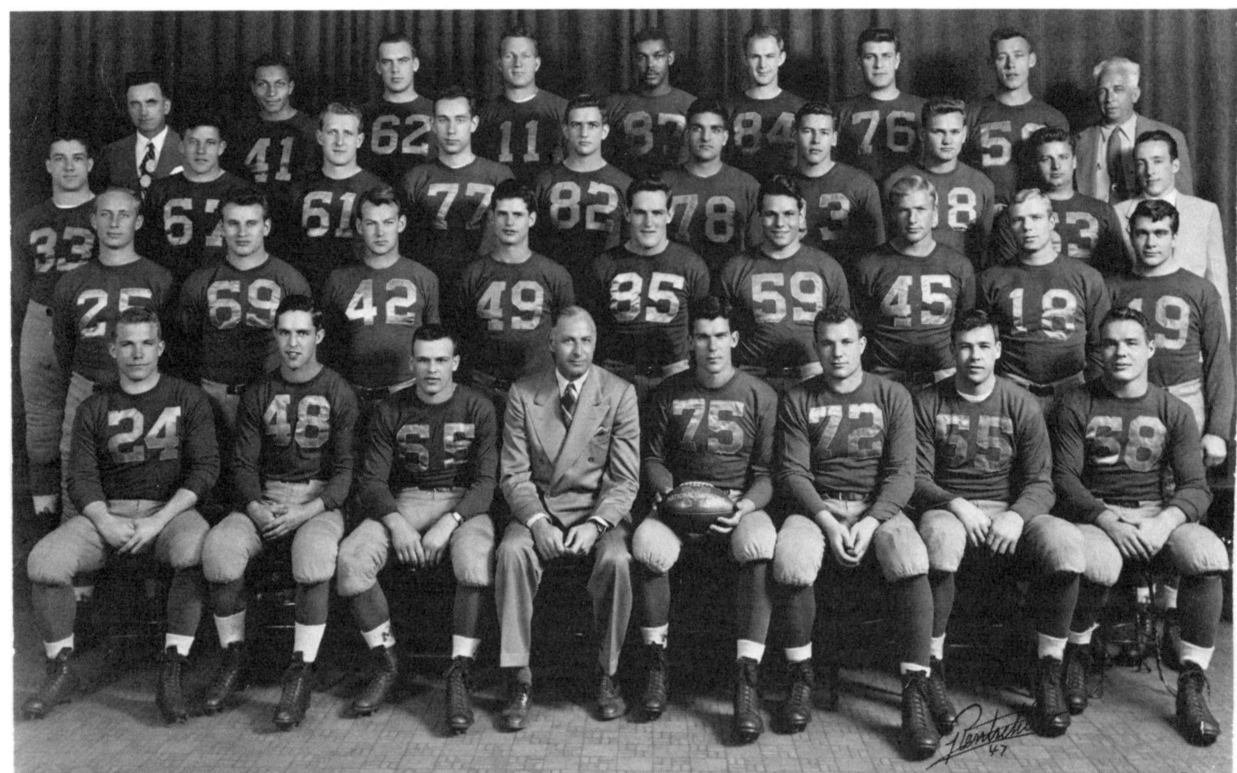

The 1947 Wolverines: Front row (left to right) —Howard Yerges, Jack Weisenburger, Dominic Tomasi, Head Coach Fritz Crisler, Bruce Hilkene, Bill Pritula, J.T. White, Stuart Wilkins. Second row—George Kiesel, Joe Soboleski, Walter Teninga, Bob Chappuis, Ed McNeill, Dan Dworsky, Pete Elliott, Bump Elliott, Hank Fonde. Third row—Tom Peterson, Don McClelland, Lloyd Heneveld, George Johnson, Bob Hollway, Pete Dendrinos, Donovan Hershberger, Dick Kempthorn, Kurt Kampe, manager E. Kirk McKinney Jr. Fourth row—Trainer Jim Hunt, Gene Derricotte, Quent Sickels, Alvin Wistert, Leonard Ford, Irvin Wisniewski, Ralph Kohl, Jim Brieske, equipment manager Henry Hatch.

TDs came on pass plays, with Chappuis throwing to Bump Elliott and Yerges, Fonde connecting with Derricotte and Yerges teaming with Rifenburg.

Chappuis had severely injured a hamstring muscle days before the game but never thought of sitting out the New Year's Day battle.

"I didn't come out until we were far ahead," he said. "I was all taped up and couldn't have hurt worse. On this team, everyone felt like we were letting the rest down if we did not do the job.

"The warmth we had for each other was always there. It was something how we came together and held each other up. It really sounded like something out of a Hollywood script."

The script even had a surprise ending, in the form of a special post-bowls poll taken by the Associated Press.

AP, of course, already had declared Notre Dame the national champion based on the results of its final regularly scheduled poll, conducted three weeks before the bowl games. The Fighting Irish, not receptive to bowl invitations in those days, also had posted a 9-0 record and topped the AP rankings seven times in the poll's 10-week run. When the Irish weren't No. 1, the Wolverines were. In fact, Notre Dame and Michigan were the nation's top two teams throughout 1947.

Despite Notre Dame's upper hand for most of the season—in the last official poll, the Irish had 107 first-place votes compared with the Wolverines' 25—there was a public clamor for a rethinking of the best-in-the-land issue after Michigan's demolishing of Southern Cal in the Rose Bowl. AP responded to the hue and cry by announcing, as reported in a New York Times story, that it would be "polling member newspapers throughout the country. Each paper is to ballot on which team it likes—as of now—Michigan or Notre Dame ... The new poll may show any switch in sentiment on the basis of Michigan's strong Rose Bowl showing ... but, of course, will not supersede the regular-season poll."

By a nearly 2-to-1 margin, the voters rated Michigan No. 1. The tally was 226 for the Wolverines and 119 for the Fighting Irish (with 12 calling it a draw).

While this poll was non-binding and thus little more than a beauty contest, it offered yet another subplot worthy of consideration by the Hollywood moguls.

Michigan, 1947

ROAD TO GREATNESS

1947 RESULTS (10-0)

Opponent	Score	Opp. Record	Opp. Bowl Game
Michigan State	55-0	7-2-0	
Stanford	49-13	0-9-0	
Pittsburgh	69-0	1-8-0	
at Northwestern	49-21	3-6-0	
Minnesota	13-6	6-3-0	
at Illinois	14-7	5-3-1	
Indiana	35-0	5-3-1	
at Wisconsin	40-6	5-3-1	
Ohio State	21-0	2-6-1	
ROSE BOWL			
Southern Cal	**49-0**	**7-2-1**	

FACTS AND FIGURES

Michigan's offense came out smokin' in 1947, as Michigan State, Stanford, Pittsburgh and Northwestern would attest. Those teams, the Wolverines' first four opponents of the season, yielded an average of 55.5 points to Coach Fritz Crisler's team. . . . Michigan wound up leading the nation in total offense, passing offense and scoring offense. . . . No one on the Wolverines' regular-season schedule finished among the Associated Press' final Top 20 teams. It was left, then, to Rose Bowl foe Southern California to furnish top-caliber competition. Supposedly, that is. The Trojans, ranked No. 8 in AP's last poll of the season, turned out to be no match for No. 2 Michigan and fell victim to a 49-0 blowout. . . . The Pasadena appearance on January 1, 1948, was only the second bowl game in the Wolverines' history. Forty-six years earlier, Michigan had played in its first postseason contest. And that, too, was in Pasadena. The score of the 1902 Rose Bowl game: a familiar-sounding 49-0, with the Wolverines pounding Stanford that time around. . . . While the '47 Wolverines generally had an easy time of it, winning seven of their games (including the Rose Bowl) by four or more touchdowns, Crisler's athletes encountered tough hurdles on consecutive weekends at midseason. First, Minnesota battled gamely before bowing by a 13-6 score; then Illinois gave Michigan a 14-7 scare. . . . When the Wolverines' high-powered attack was slowed down to some degree after its first-month onslaught, the defense proceeded to assert itself. Starting with the Minnesota contest and running through the Rose Bowl game, Michigan allowed only 19 points in six games. . . . Six opponents put together winning records, but Michigan's opposition managed only a 41-45-5 record overall. That's a winning percentage of .478.

STATISTICAL LEADERS

PASSING

	Att.	Comp.	Yards	TD	Pct.	Int.
Bob Chappuis	86	48	976	11	55.8	5
Wally Teninga	25	11	283	0	44.0	6
Pete Elliott	8	5	70	1	62.5	1

RUSHING

	Att.	Yards	Avg.	TD
Jack Weisenburger	101	682	6.7	7
Bump Elliott	68	438	6.4	7
Bob Chappuis	113	419	3.7	5
Gene Derricotte	28	169	6.0	5
Bob Mann	15	129	8.6	1

RECEIVING

	Rec.	Yards	Avg.	TD
Bump Elliott	16	318	19.9	2
Bob Mann	12	302	25.2	3
Howard Yerges	11	117	10.6	1
Dick Rifenburg	6	156	26.0	0

SCORING

	TD	FG	PAT	Points
Bump Elliott	9	0	0	54
Jack Weisenburger	7	0	0	42
Bob Chappuis	5	0	0	30
Gene Derricotte	5	0	0	30
Bob Mann	4	0	0	24

KEY CHARACTERS

The Conductor

COACH: Herbert (Fritz) Crisler.

Record: 71-16-3, 10 years at Michigan.

Crisler succeeded Harry Kipke as Michigan coach in 1938. . . . He is the only coach to appear with two different teams on The Sporting News' list of 25 greatest teams. Crisler also coached the 1933 Princeton team that went undefeated and was ranked 25th by The Sporting News poll. . . . He began his college coaching career at Minnesota in 1930, moved to Princeton in 1932 and took over the Michigan reins in '38. . . . He added the responsibilities of athletic director in 1941, a post he held until his retirement in 1968. . . . He compiled an overall coaching record of 116-32-9 and is a member of the College Football Hall of Fame. . . . He is credited with founding the two-platoon system used in football today and he created the distinctive winged-helmet still worn by Michigan's Wolverines. . . . He died in 1982 at the age of 83.

Personal Data:

Born: January 12, 1899, in Earlville, Ill.
High School: Earlville High and Mendota High in Mendota, Ill.
College: Chicago.

The Supporting Cast

HALFBACK: Bob Chappuis.

Chappuis was second to Notre Dame's John Lujack in the 1947 Heisman Trophy balloting. . . . He was the team's 1946 most valuable player and a unanimous consensus All-America in 1947. . . . He was a hard-driving runner with amazing power for his 185-pound frame. . . . He lettered in 1942 and then served in World War II before returning to letter in '46 and '47. . . . He made his way back to U.S. lines after being shot down over Italy in the war.

Personal Data:

Born: February 24, 1923, in Toledo, O.
High School: DeVilbiss High in Toledo.

HALFBACK: Chalmers (Bump) Elliott.

Elliott was the team's most valuable player in Michigan's 1947 championship season. . . . He was a speedy back with shifty moves and was a perfect complement to counterpart Bob Chappuis, a triple-threat star on the other side of Michigan's backfield. . . . He led the '47 Wolverines in scoring (54 points) and receiving (16 catches) and finished second with 438 yards rushing. . . . He began his career at Purdue, transferring to Michigan after serving with the Marines in World War II. . . . He was the brother and teammate of Pete Elliott, a quarterback and future college coach. . . . He returned to Ann Arbor in 1959 as head coach and directed the Wolverines to a 51-42-2 record before turning over the reins in 1969 to current Coach Bo Schembechler. . . . He led the Wolverines to a 9-1 mark in 1964, which included a 34-7 victory over Oregon State in the 1965 Rose Bowl. . . . That Michigan team finished fourth in the national polls.

Personal Data:

Born: January 30, 1925, in Detroit.
High School: Bloomington High in Bloomington, Ill.

FULLBACK: Jack Weisenburger.

Weisenburger was small for a fullback, but his ballhandling magic often is credited for making Michigan's 1947 offense go. . . . He was Michigan's 1947 leading rusher with 682 yards and a 6.7-yard average. . . . He was a triple-threat halfback until Crisler switched him to fullback in his junior season. . . . He served as the Wolverines' punter and averaged 37.5 yards per kick in '47. . . . He lettered from 1944-47.

Personal Data:

Born: Muskegon Heights, Mich.

TACKLE: Alvin Wistert.

Wistert was a consensus All-America in 1948 and '49. . . . He is a member of the College Football Hall of Fame and the Michigan Hall of Honor. . . . He lettered from 1947-49 and was 33 years old in his senior season. . . . He transferred to Michigan from Boston University. . . . His brothers, Albert and Francis, were consensus All-Americas at Michigan in 1942 and 1933, respectively. . . . The three brothers all wore No. 11. . . . Alvin's Michigan career did not begin until after he had served in World War II.

Personal Data:

Born: June 26, 1916, in Chicago.
High School: Carl Schurz High in Chicago.

FINAL 1947 WIRE SERVICE RANKINGS

ASSOCIATED PRESS

1. Notre Dame	6. Alabama	11. Army	16. Oklahoma
2. MICHIGAN	7. Pennsylvania	12. Kansas	17. N.C. State
3. SMU	**8. Southern Cal**	13. Mississippi	18. Rice
4. Penn State	9. North Carolina	14. William & Mary	19. Duke
5. Texas	10. Georgia Tech	15. California	20. Columbia

Bold face indicates Michigan opponent.

Unbeaten, Untied And Unrewarded

Penn State, 1968-69
By Ronnie Christ

Joe Paterno's 1968 and '69 teams were first in the hearts of Penn State fans, but second in the national polls.

They had won every game in both the 1968 and 1969 seasons to preserve one of the longest unbeaten streaks in college football history. Their defense was praised as one of the greatest units ever, yet they would never enjoy the satisfaction of being ranked No. 1. For posterity, Penn State's Nittany Lions would know the feeling of being slighted by the President of the United States.

Even before the bowl games were played following the 1969 season, President Richard M. Nixon presented a national championship plaque to the Texas Longhorns to commemorate the 100th anniversary of college football. To placate Penn State, Nixon said he would award the Lions a plaque to honor their 29-game unbeaten streak.

Coach Joe Paterno politely told the President what he could do with his trophy.

"I always wondered how Nixon could know so much about college football in 1969 and so little about Watergate in 1973," Paterno once remarked.

Two decades later, the Penn State coach reflected on "what I believe were our greatest teams," with a fondness for what they accomplished and a sadness that they never received due recognition.

"It is still hard for me to believe that one of those teams wasn't Number 1," Paterno said. "It's still kind of sad. Either one was good enough to be national champion.

"People still identified Eastern football with the Ivy League. I tried to tell people how good Eastern football was, but no one would listen."

For almost three years, the Nittany Lions didn't lose a game. Beginning with a 50-28 victory over Boston College on October 14, 1967, they were undefeated in 31 straight games before losing to Colorado, 27-3, on September 27, 1970.

The Lions were loaded with individual talent. Led

by defensive tackle Mike Reid, they had eight players who would be named to various first-team All-America squads during their college careers.

Reid, the maestro who conducted Penn State's unfinished symphony, was remembered by defensive coach Jim O'Hora for his "Jekyll-Hyde personality." Off the field, he was a quiet music major who often sat at the piano to lead teammates in song. On the gridiron, he was a dynamo who struck fear in the hearts of opponents. "I can remember in high school and college the specific sensation of running into people," Reid recalled years later. "I remember enjoying that."

The 6-foot-3, 240-pound destroyer's dedication, however, carried as much impact as his bone-shattering tackles.

"I was a sophomore on the '68 team and I looked in awe at the great players all around me," recalled Fran Ganter, now Penn State's offensive coordinator. "Reid was my favorite. I learned from him what leadership means to a team.

"If Mike said we were going to run through a wall, the other players would have followed him. If you had to go to war, he was the guy you wanted to lead you. He had great strength and quickness, but most of all, he had heart. He wanted to beat the hell out of the other guys on every play. He aspired to be great and it was contagious."

Reid, who first aspired to be a concert pianist, became the only Penn State player ever to receive the Outland Trophy as the outstanding lineman in college football in 1969. And after being named to The Sporting News' AFC All-Star team three times in a five-year pro career with the Cincinnati Bengals, Reid returned to the piano to become a Grammy Award winner and songwriter of the year in country music.

Tight end Ted Kwalick became the first Penn State player to receive All-America recognition in two seasons (1967 and 1968) and the Lion who received perhaps the highest compliment. "He is better at his position than anyone I've seen play at any position," UCLA Coach Tommy Prothro said in 1968. "I've seen halfbacks closer to O.J. Simpson than other tight ends closer to Kwalick."

Kwalick had hands large enough to grab notoriety ("I could never find a pair of gloves large enough") and speed enough (4.6 seconds for 40 yards) to break a big play. "With Kwalick, it's not so much the catch that's important," Paterno said at the time. "It's the run after the catch.

"Just his presence in the lineup sets up situations we ordinarily wouldn't see. Kwalick stablilizes the defense. We can almost predict the kind of defense we are going to see."

The Penn State lineup also boasted first-team All-America talent in:

The on-field persona of defensive tackle Mike Reid stood in stark contrast to the music man's quiet off-field demeanor.

- Linebacker Dennis Onkotz, a quarterback in high school who became the first Nittany Lion to be a two-time consensus All-America.
- Safety Neal Smith, who came to University Park as a walk-on and left with a school-record 19 career interceptions and All-America honors on three teams as a senior.
- Halfback Charlie Pittman, who scored a school-record 32 touchdowns in a career that culminated in 1969 with All-America recognition by the Football Coaches poll.
- Linebacker Jack Ham, a 1988 enshrinee in the

Linebacker Dennis Onkotz, pictured above after a 1968 interception, was Penn State's first two-time consensus All-America.

pro football Hall of Fame, who wasn't an All-America pick until 1970—when he was a consensus selection.

• Lydell Mitchell, the Lions' No. 3 rusher in 1969, and Dave Joyner, an alternate at offensive tackle that season, who would receive honors in 1971 (Joyner as a consensus pick).

Any all-time Penn State football team would have to include most of these players, many of whom still believe they were unjustly denied a national title. Others believe they were victims of circumstance.

When the 1969 team accepted an Orange Bowl invitation in mid-November, Penn State was ranked third by United Press International and fourth by the Associated Press. Second-ranked Texas was scheduled against Arkansas (third in AP, fourth in UPI) in a December 6 season finale. Unbeaten Ohio State, a solid No. 1, was prevented from returning to the Rose Bowl—or going to any other bowl—under Big 10 rules, but the Buckeyes were considered a cinch to defeat Michigan on November 22 and be voted national champions in the polls.

"Writers were proclaiming Ohio State as the team of the century," Pittman remembered. "The feeling of the players at that time was that if we had no chance of being No. 1, why go (to the Cotton Bowl) and play Texas on its home field? We had gone to the Orange Bowl the previous year. The players enjoyed the trip and liked the idea of going back to Miami."

After Ohio State-Michigan, one had to wonder. The Wolverines upset Ohio State, 24-12, and Texas shot to first in the polls. "And we're committed to go to Miami," Reid said. "It was a real mess."

But he didn't feel cheated. "You live by the poll and you die by it," he said.

The irony of all this is that Cotton Bowl representative Field Scovell kept cautioning Paterno that Big Eight Conference champion Missouri, their eventual Orange Bowl opponent, was stronger than people realized. "That was part of the problem," Paterno said. "No one knew how good the Big Eight was. Field saw a lot of teams. We should have taken his advice. We should have gone to the Cotton Bowl."

Instead of settling the No. 1 issue in a head-to-head confrontation with Texas, the Nittany Lions finished second in the final polls—and in the eyes of Nixon, who proclaimed the Longhorns national champions after they edged Arkansas, 15-14, on December 6.

"There is no doubt about it," Pittman says today. "A lot of us felt cheated out of the chance to be Number 1. . . .

"I know there wasn't a better defensive unit in the country. We didn't throw much, but we could run with anybody. When you had backs like we had, why bother to throw?

"The words we all hated to hear Joe say in practice were, 'Blue against blue.' That meant our first offense was going against our first defense. The one thing I always wanted to know when I had the football was where Reid was. I had one eye on him all the time. I figured everyone else I could handle."

Oddly, Reid wasn't around when the most successful era in Penn State history was launched in the second week of the 1967 season. He had suffered a season-ending knee injury in the opener, a 23-22 loss to Navy that left Paterno worried about his suspect defense composed mostly of holdover seniors. With potent Miami (Fla.) next on the schedule, the second-year coach decided it was time to make changes, that his promising sophomores were ready to play.

Jim Kates, Pete Johnson and Onkotz took over at linebacker. Steve Smear was at defensive tackle, while Smith took over at defensive halfback. Miami was held scoreless until the final 40 seconds and Penn State prevailed, 17-8. The next week, UCLA escaped with a 17-15 victory. It would be the last game this group of Nittany Lions would lose. They capped an 8-2 season with a 17-17 tie against Florida State in the Gator Bowl.

"I look at the way Miami is playing defense (in the 1980s) and they're doing some of the things we did then," Paterno said. "The reason we could do them is because we had players with strength, quickness, poise, intelligence, pride and great leadership."

The Penn State defense captured the hearts of fans with its aggressive, create-havoc style. In 1968, the defense set up or scored 145 of the Lions' 339 points, intercepting 25 passes and recovering 17 fumbles. In the season opener against Navy, the Nittany Lions intercepted five passes and recovered four fumbles in a 31-6 rout. The offense exploded in the final three games, racking up 57 points against Maryland, 65 against Pitt and 30 against Syracuse, which had gone into the game with the nation's No. 2 defense.

The one team that gave Penn State a scare was Army, which arrived at Beaver Stadium with a slick quarterback-tight end combination of Steve Lindell and Gary Steele. "Lindell was just fantastic that day," said Paterno, recalling the quarterback's 258 yards passing and two touchdowns passes in a 28-24 loss.

Army had closed to 22-17 after Lindell's 58-yard pass to Steele set up Charlie Jarvis' one-yard plunge with 2:29 remaining. When the Cadets attempted an onside kick on the ensuing kickoff, the ball squirted from a pileup and into Kwalick's hands. He grabbed it on the run and galloped 53 yards into the end zone. Lindell hit Steele with an eight-yard touchdown pass on the next series, but Army couldn't recover a second onside kick and Penn State held on for its sixth win.

What impressed Jarvis about Penn State?

"The fact that most of the defensive unit is made up of juniors and sophomores. They hit like seniors."

The next week, the fourth-ranked Nittany Lions turned Reid and Smear loose on Miami. They sacked quarterback Dave Olivo for 31 yards in losses, forced him to fumble twice and pressured him into throwing two interceptions. Ham pitched in with a fumble recovery and blocked punt (his third of the season), helping the defense hold Miami to 17 yards rushing and three yards passing in the second half.

"They deserve their rating right up among the best teams," Miami Coach Charlie Tate said after the game. "Reid and Smear are the best pair of defensive tackles we have ever faced. Penn State has some great folks and those two are at the top."

No one ever felt safe running in Smear's direction, but the hard-hitting tackle actually practiced restraint if given the opportunity to dish out an excessively violent hit. When Penn State faced Ohio in 1969, Bobcats quarterback Cleve Bryant entered the game with a bad knee. "Mike and I told him," Smear said, "that we would see to it that his knee wasn't injured anymore, if possible.... Nobody was going to go after his knee to put him out of the game because he was such a good quarterback. When we told him that, he kind of looked surprised, but he said thanks."

For the '68 season, Reid and Smear combined for 108 tackles, four fumble recoveries and two blocked kicks for the first Penn State team ever to win 10

Linebacker Jack Ham, who went on to earn a spot in the pro football Hall of Fame, was murder on opposing quarterbacks.

Tight end Ted Kwalick was a big man with big hands and the speed and ability to break the big play.

games and only the third to go untied and undefeated. They were perhaps the top defensive tackle tandem in college football, yet they deflected praise to the "Rover Boys" at linebacker—Onkotz, Kates and Ham.

The offense had its heroes, too, as it set school records with 2,739 rushing yards and 4,025 yards in total offense.

In the finale against Syracuse, Pittman ran 27 yards for his 14th touchdown of the season, a school record, while running mate Bobby Campbell piled up 239 yards, 11 shy of a school mark. His 87-yard touchdown run was the longest from scrimmage for Penn State since 1894 and helped ease the senior's disappointment over missing three early-season games with a shoulder separation.

Both Campbell and Pittman rushed for more than 100 yards in four games.

"I don't care what you say," Syracuse assistant Joe Zombathy said, "you won't find a better set of halfbacks than Pittman and Campbell in the country. Sure, Southern Cal has O.J. Simpson, but they don't have another running back to match the tandem Penn State has."

That running attack was the key as the Nittany Lions prepared to face sixth-ranked Kansas in the 1969 Orange Bowl, the game that would produce the most dramatic ending in Penn State history. First-year Lion quarterback Chuck Burkhart, never rated among the better passers, had thrown mostly in the direction of Kwalick, who led the team with 403 yards receiving. Burkhart's strength was poise, however, and he seldom committed mistakes with the potent backfield behind him.

"For the first time that season, we just stumbled around offensively," Paterno recalled. "I don't know why, but we couldn't get untracked. I think someone forgot to tell us how good Kansas was defensively.

"We needed some great plays by our defense, especially by Reid. He sacked the Kansas quarterback when we really needed it (twice) and then we blocked their punt."

Kansas, the Big Eight co-champion, had the nation's No. 3 scoring offense, averaging 38 points per game behind the left arm of quarterback Bobby Douglass and the powerful running of fullback John Riggins. It was Kansas' defense, however, that made the big plays early in the Orange Bowl, intercepting two passes and recovering a fumble on Penn State's first three possessions. The second interception set up a first-quarter drive that put the Jayhawks ahead, 7-0. Penn State didn't score until late in the second quarter, when Pittman romped 13 yards untouched into the end zone.

With only 2:04 left in the game, Kansas had the ball and a 14-7 lead. The Jayhawks' Donnie Shanklin already had been voted the game's most valuable player after returning a punt 40 yards to set up Riggins' touchdown plunge early in the final quarter. But on this, Kansas' final possession, Douglass would be sacked by Reid on successive plays, setting up a fourth-down punting situation at the Kansas 25. When Smith burst in to partially block the kick, Penn State had a life and the ball at midfield with 1:16 remaining.

Penn State's ground attack centered around Charlie Pittman, who scored a school-record 32 career touchdowns, and Lydell Mitchell, another solid breakaway threat.

On the sideline, Paterno set the Penn State strategy. He ordered Campbell to run a deep post on the first play while Burkhart merely heaved the ball as far as he could. "I don't expect to complete it," Paterno said, "I just want to loosen up their defense so we can get the ball to Kwalick. Just don't throw an interception."

In the huddle, Campbell turned to Burkhart. "I'll run the post," he said. "You get the ball to me and I'll catch it."

With Paterno expecting the incompletion, Campbell hauled in Burkhart's perfect pass and carried it to the Kansas 3-yard line. After two plunges into the line, Paterno called an inside reverse to Pittman.

"I went into the line and realized I didn't have the football," Pittman remembered. "I thought I fumbled it. I thought I was going to be the goat of the game. Then all of a sudden I see Chuck standing in the corner of the end zone with the ball."

On a daring, improvised bootleg, Burkhart had scampered into the end zone for his first career touchdown with 15 seconds left. Now, Penn State had a chance to win on a two-point conversion attempt.

Kansas wasn't fooled on this pass play to Campbell. The toss was knocked away and the Jayhawks had won, 14-13. Or had they? While Kansas celebrated, officials waved off the play. Illegal procedure, Kansas—for 12 men on the field. And game films showed they had been there *for the last four plays!*

"That answered a lot of questions we had," Pittman said. "On those plays at the goal line, we kept asking in the huddle who was missing a block. Everybody kept saying they got their man. One of our guys said it seemed like Kansas had an extra linebacker that was always making the tackle."

Given a second chance, Campbell took a handoff and powered 1½ yards into the end zone for the two points that gave Paterno his first bowl victory. Two days later, the Nittany Lions were ranked second in the final AP poll, their highest finish ever,

Though the picture's a little fuzzy, it clearly shows that Kansas (white jerseys) was using 12 players in the closing moments of the 1969 Orange Bowl.

behind unbeaten Ohio State.

"Was this a great team, should it have been ranked Number 1?" Paterno mused after the season. "Well, it had great talent, great attitude, great leaders and all the other things a great team must have. I know this: It would have taken a great team to beat us."

Pittman still relishes Campbell's brilliant swan song. "Campbell got us there so he deserved the chance to win it," Pittman said. "When Joe sent a play in with Campbell, you had no idea of what it would be when he got to the huddle. You could be sure it involved him. Bobby was a money player. He and Franco (Harris) were a lot alike. They drove Joe crazy because they did it their way."

Campbell wasn't around in 1969, so Reid and Smear did it their way. They inspired a defense that not only set a single-season school record for fewest points allowed (87) but actually scored more points than all of their opponents (107). The running game was something to behold, too, as Pittman, Mitchell and newcomer Franco Harris led the Lions to 2,412 rushing yards, third-most in school history.

"They were a group of players with character and quality," Paterno said. "I think that's why we were able to go 11-0 again."

And that character was put to its biggest test in the Nittany Lions' fifth game, against big rival Syracuse.

"It was a game Syracuse should have won," Paterno said. "They had a chance to kick a field goal near the end of the half and they passed it up. They went for the touchdown and didn't get it."

Indeed, the Nittany Lions had held on a fourth-and-one play at their 2-yard line, but Syracuse still enjoyed a 14-0 lead at halftime. There were two talks in the Penn State locker room. First, Paterno called for pride and poise. He said there was no disgrace in losing when a team did its best, something he didn't think the Lions had done.

Then Reid asked the coaches to leave.

"He really let us have it," remembered Pittman. "This was Mike Reid at his emotional best."

Yet even after recovering a third-quarter fumble on the Syracuse 11, Penn State failed to score. Just when it looked as if the unbeaten streak would end at 23 games, the Lions scored twice in the fourth quarter for their 16th straight victory. And once again, it was the defense that created the comeback opportunity.

Ham ignited the rally by recovering a fumble at the Syracuse 32. After a key pass interference call and Mitchell's four-yard touchdown run, the Lions recreated their 1969 Orange Bowl dramatics, failing on an initial two-point conversion attempt, then succeeding after Syracuse was called for holding.

Time was running out, but there was no sense of desperation or panic. "The guys on offense all felt that somehow the defense would go back out and come up with yet another big play," Ganter recalled.

It did. The defense held Syracuse and forced a punt, but John Ebersole got a hand on the kick and Penn State had the football on the Syracuse 39. On the second play, Harris dashed 36 yards for the touchdown and Mike Reitz kicked the winning extra point.

"I just wish somebody would say how great our team is," Paterno said after the game. "The sign of a great football team is when you beat a good football team and don't play well."

There also was the added pressure of maintaining the nation's longest undefeated streak and the recurring criticism about the schedule, which Reid merely shrugged off. "When we tried to tell everyone we had a tough schedule . . . when Joe said everybody would play us 100 percent, that everybody would be sky-high for us, nobody wanted to believe it.

"If anything remains to be proven, I don't know what it would be. If nobody else wants to buy us, then that's how it'll have to be."

The rest of the season was a breeze. The Lions defeated Ohio (42-3), Boston College (38-16), Maryland (48-0), Pitt (27-7) and North Carolina State (33-8). In the finale, a national TV audience watched the Lions hold the Wolfpack to just 21 yards in total offense.

The defense was even better in a 10-3 victory over Missouri in the Orange Bowl. The Tigers had been rated three-point favorites, principally because they had played a "tougher schedule" and had explosive scoring potential with quarterback Terry McMil-

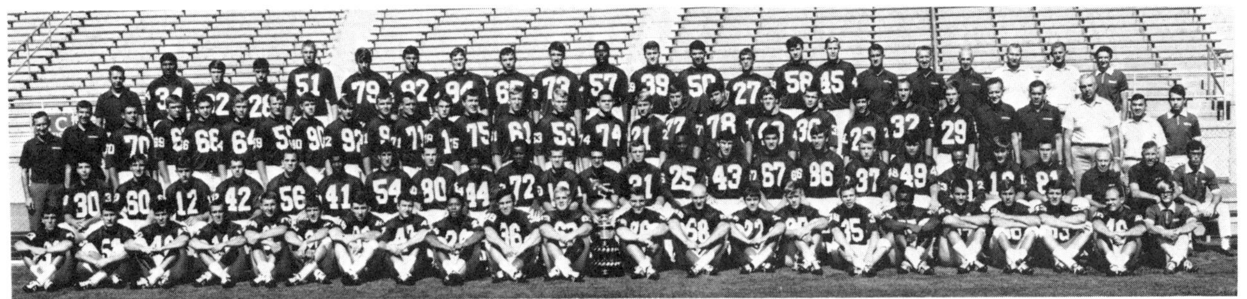

The 1969 Nittany Lions: Front row (left to right) —Chip Carroll, Dave Radakovich, Pete Johnson, Wally Cirafesi, George Kulka, Neal Smith, John Ebersole, Paul Johnson, Charlie Pittman, Don Abbey, Tom Jackson, Steve Smear, Mike Reid, Chuck Burkhart, Dave Rakiecki, Dennis Onkotz, Jim Kates, Ed Stofko, Greg Edmonds, Jack Ham, Joel Ramich, manager Steve Kauffman. Second row—Gary Gray, Charlie Zapiec, Terry Stump, Fran Ganter, Warren Koegel, Charlie Wilson, Steve Prue, Gary Hull, Charlie Adams, Doug McArthur, Mike Smith, Head Coach Joe Paterno, George Landis, Mike Cooper, Gary Deuel, Bob Holuba, Jim McCord, Bob Garthwaite, Jerry Bulvin, Lydell Mitchell, Bob Parsons, Craig Lyle, coach Earle Bruce, coach J.T. White, manager Ken Campbell. Third row—Coach George Welsh, coach Gerald Sandusky, Dave Joyner, Bob Spirnak, George San Fillipo, Jim Fickes, Mike Botts, Jim Sample, Tom Templeton, Marshall Wagner, Bob Knechtel, Eric Bass, Gary Carter, Bill Ericsson, Ron Pavlechko, Mark Bauer, Ron Haverstock, Dan Mercinko, Vic Surma, Glen Cole, Greg Ducatte, Charlie Mesko, Ed Plachecki, Tom Bryant, coach Dan Radakovich, coach Jim Weaver, trainer Chuck Medlar, trainer Ed Sulkowski, manager Steve Manbeck. Fourth row—Manager Clarence Thompson, Franco Harris, Mike Reitz, Stan Baran, Pat Lukasavich, Frank Ahrenhold, Wayne Munson, Tom Brown, Gary Klossner, Fred Speers, John Booth, Steve Brezna, Paul Hrabovsky, Greg Pfennig, Jim Bauman, John Aumiller, coaches Bob Phillips, Frank Patrick, Jim O'Hora; trainers Jim Hochberg, Gerald Slagle; manager Russell Albert.

lan, wide receiver Mel Gray and running back Joe Moore, the nation's No. 3 rusher.

The Nittany Lions swarmed Missouri, however, intercepting seven passes, an Orange Bowl record, and recovering two fumbles to push their unbeaten string to 30 games. Moore's first-quarter fumble, forced by Reid, set up the only touchdown of the game, a 28-yard pass play from Burkhart to Mitchell just 21 seconds after the Lions' had kicked a field goal.

"We couldn't block Reid and Smear," Missouri Coach Dan Devine said. "They got in there and got it done."

Asked how long the Lions could have contained Missouri, Onkotz was to the point: "Forever."

Paterno still regards Onkotz as one of State's all-time great linebackers. "If Reid had not been there," Paterno said, "Onkotz would have taken over the leadership of those teams."

Onkotz picked off two Missouri passes, as did Smith and defensive back George Landis, while end Gary Hull had one interception. "I remember how worried our defensive coaches were about the speed of Missouri's receivers, especially Mel Gray," Pittman said. "I don't think he caught a pass against us."

Correct, Charlie. Meanwhile, Burkhart was basking in the spotlight. The quarterback who supposedly couldn't throw passed for 187 yards and his second touchdown of the season, enough to earn MVP honors against a Tiger defense that proved to be almost as impressive as Penn State's.

"We didn't go into the game planning to throw," Paterno remembered. "Missouri stacked against our running game. They put eight men on the line. We had to throw. Chuck got a bum rap. For two years, he made the big plays for us when we most needed them."

Missouri Coach Dan Devine said he didn't see how any team could be better than Penn State. "Texas may be No. 1, but they never would have scored against Penn State," he said. "If I had a vote, I might vote a tie.... I can guarantee you that I wouldn't vote Penn State No. 2 under any circumstances."

Nevertheless, Texas, which defeated Notre Dame in the Cotton Bowl, 21-17, finished atop both the AP and UPI polls with Penn State No. 2.

Paterno, who rejected a chance to coach the Pittsburgh Steelers for his old friend Dan Rooney after the 1968 season, will always have a special feeling for his "Grand Experiment." That's what he called his attempt to make Penn State a football power without breaking NCAA rules and while players learned "about all the other things college has to offer."

"Those players set a standard for all who followed," Paterno said. "They secured my career for me. They were great players on great teams who should have been recognized as national champions. As far as we at Penn State are concerned, they are champions."

Penn State, 1968-69

ROAD TO GREATNESS

1968 RESULTS (11-0)

Opponent	Score	Opp. Record	Opp. Bowl Game
Navy	31-6	2-8	
Kansas State	25-9	4-6	
at West Virginia	31-20	7-3	
at UCLA	21-6	3-7	
at Boston College	29-0	6-3	
Army	28-24	7-3	
Miami (Fla.)	22-7	5-5	
at Maryland	57-13	2-8	
at Pittsburgh	65-9	1-9	
Syracuse	30-12	6-4	
ORANGE BOWL			
Kansas	**15-14**	**9-2**	

1969 RESULTS (11-0)

Opponent	Score	Opp. Record	Opp. Bowl Game
at Navy	45-22	1-9-0	
Colorado	27-3	8-3-0	Liberty (W)
at Kansas State	17-14	5-5-0	
West Virginia	20-0	10-1-0	Peach (W)
at Syracuse	15-14	5-5-0	
Ohio University	42-3	5-4-1	
Boston College	38-16	5-4-0	
Maryland	48-0	3-7-0	
at Pittsburgh	27-7	4-6-0	
at North Carolina State	33-8	3-6-1	
ORANGE BOWL			
Missouri	**10-3**	**9-2-0**	

FACTS AND FIGURES

The Nittany Lions fielded a bone-crushing defense, ranking second nationally in scoring defense in 1969 (8.7 points per game) and sixth in 1968 (10.6). . . . Penn State rated No. 3 in the nation in total defense in 1969. . . . The Nittany Lions' opponents in 1968 had a combined record of 52-58, a .473 winning percentage. . . . In 1969, they compiled a 58-52-2 mark, a .527 winning percentage. . . . Penn State's average margin of victory over both seasons was just over 21 points. . . . Tight end Ted Kwalick was named to The Sporting News' 1968 All-America team and defensive tackle Mike Reid to the '69 TSN squad. . . . Kwalick, Reid, linebacker Dennis Onkotz, defensive tackle Steve Smear and halfback Charlie Pittman were named to the Associated Press' 1968 All-East team. . . . Reid, Onkotz, Smear, Pittman, safety Neal Smith, offensive guard Charlie Zapiec and linebackers Jim Kates and Jack Ham were selected to the 1969 AP All-East squad.

STATISTICAL LEADERS

PASSING

	Att.	Comp.	Yards	TD	Pct.	Int.
Chuck Burkhart (1968)	177	87	1170	6	49.2	7
Chuck Burkhart (1969)	114	59	805	1	51.8	9

RUSHING

	Att.	Yards	Avg.	TD	Long
Charlie Pittman (1968)	186	950	5.1	14	57
Bob Campbell (1968)	127	751	5.9	7	87
Charlie Pittman (1969)	149	706	4.7	10	24
Franco Harris (1969)	115	643	5.6	10	44
Lydell Mitchell (1969)	113	616	5.5	6	71

RECEIVING

	Rec.	Yards	Avg.	TD	Long
Ted Kwalick (1968)	31	403	13.0	2	63
Greg Edmonds (1969)	20	246	12.3	0	28
Leon Angevine (1968)	17	226	13.3	2	26
Charlie Pittman (1968)	14	196	14.0	0	38
Lydell Mitchell (1969)	13	206	15.8	0	66

SCORING

	TD	FG	PAT	Points
Charlie Pittman (1968)	14	0	0	84
Charlie Pittman (1969)	11	0	0	66
Franco Harris (1969)	10	0	*2	64
Mike Reitz (1969)	0	7	33	54
Bob Campbell (1968)	7	0	*1	44

*Two-point conversion.

KEY CHARACTERS

The Conductor

COACH: Joe Paterno.

***Record:** 207-48-2, 22 years at Penn State.

Paterno succeeded Rip Engle as Penn State coach in 1966. . . . He played quarterback for Engle at Brown University and served as his assistant at Penn State for 16 years before taking over. . . . Under Paterno, Penn State has dominated East Coast football for two decades and developed one of the most successful programs in the country. . . . Paterno ranks behind only Oklahoma's Barry Switzer among active coaches with an .809 winning percentage. . . . Paterno has never had a losing season and 13 of his teams have won 10 games or more. . . . His teams captured consensus national championships in 1982 and 1986 and have finished 15 times among the Associated Press' Top 10 and 13 times among United Press International's Top 10. . . . Paterno has led the Nittany Lions to 18 bowl games, compiling a 12-5-1 record. . . . He has made four appearances in the Orange Bowl, four in the Sugar Bowl and two in the Cotton Bowl, winning six of the 10 contests. . . . His teams have enjoyed four unbeaten seasons—1968, 1969, 1973 and 1986. . . . Five other teams have lost only one game. . . . In 1987, he became only the ninth coach in collegiate history to post 200 or more career victories on the Division I level. . . . He has produced 18 consensus All-Americas and has sent more than 100 players to the National Football League.

Personal Data:

Born: December 21, 1926, in Brooklyn, N.Y.
High School: Brooklyn Prep.
College: Brown.

*Indicates totals through 1987 season.

The Supporting Cast

TIGHT END: Ted Kwalick.

Kwalick became Penn State's first-ever unanimous consensus All-America in 1968. . . . A devastating blocker with superb hands, he is considered the best tight end ever to play at Penn State. . . . Kwalick lettered from 1966-68 and finished fourth in the '68 Heisman Trophy balloting.

Personal Data:

Born: April 15, 1947, in McKees Rocks, Pa.
High School: McKees Rocks Montour High.

LINEBACKER: Dennis Onkotz.

Onkotz was the first of many Nittany Lion linebackers to earn All-America status under Paterno and help give Penn State the reputation as Linebacker U. . . . He became the first Nittany Lion to earn consensus All-America status in two consecutive seasons, 1968 and 1969. . . . He lettered from 1967-69.

Personal Data:

Born: February 6, 1948, in Northampton, Pa.
High School: Northampton Area High.

DEFENSIVE TACKLE: Mike Reid.

Reid was a dominant figure who intimidated enemy ballcarriers with his strength and speed and refused to allow yardage through the middle of the Nittany Lion defense. . . . He won the Outland Trophy in 1969 and is a member of the College Football Hall of Fame. . . . He finished fifth in the 1969 Heisman Trophy balloting and was a unanimous consensus All-America the same year. . . . He followed his successful college career by becoming an All-Pro tackle with the Cincinnati Bengals and, most recently, a Grammy-winning songwriter and producer. . . . He was considered by many to be Paterno's most talented lineman. . . . He lettered in 1966 and from 1968-69.

Personal Data:

Born: May 24, 1947, in Altoona, Pa.
High School: Altoona High.

FINAL 1968 WIRE SERVICE RANKINGS

ASSOCIATED PRESS		UNITED PRESS	
1. Ohio State	11. Oklahoma	1. Ohio State	12. Alabama
2. PENN STATE	12. Michigan	2. Southern Cal	13. Oregon State
3. Texas	13. Tennessee	**3. PENN STATE**	14. Florida State
4. Southern Cal	14. SMU	4. Georgia	15. Michigan
5. Notre Dame	15. Oregon State	5. Texas	16. SMU
6. Arkansas	16. Auburn	**6. Kansas**	17. Missouri
7. Kansas	17. Alabama	7. Tennessee	18. Ohio University
8. Georgia	18. Houston	8. Notre Dame	Minnesota
9. Missouri	19. Louisiana State	9. Arkansas	20. Houston
10. Purdue	20. Ohio University	10. Oklahoma	Stanford
		11. Purdue	

FINAL 1969 WIRE SERVICE RANKINGS

ASSOCIATED PRESS		UNITED PRESS	
1. Texas	11. Nebraska	1. Texas	11. Tennessee
2. PENN STATE	12. Houston	**2. PENN STATE**	12. Nebraska
3. Southern Cal	13. UCLA	3. Arkansas	13. Mississippi
4. Ohio State	14. Florida	4. Southern Cal	14. Stanford
5. Notre Dame	15. Tennessee	5. Ohio State	15. Auburn
6. Missouri	**16. Colorado**	**6. Missouri**	16. Houston
7. Arkansas	**17. West Virginia**	7. Louisiana State	17. Florida
8. Mississippi	18. Purdue	8. Michigan	18. Purdue
9. Michigan	19. Stanford	9. Notre Dame	San Diego State
10. Louisiana State	20. Auburn	10. UCLA	**West Virginia**

Bold face indicates Penn State opponent.

Hurricane Miami Sweeps the Nation

Miami, 1986-87
By Jim Martz

Miami Coach Jimmy Johnson (left) and his Hurricanes came out on the short end of their 1987 Fiesta Bowl meeting with Penn State and Coach Joe Paterno.

The trigger man and top gun in Miami's 1986 offense was Heisman Trophy-winning quarterback Vinny Testaverde.

Tears of frustration and pain swelled the eyes of wide receiver Michael Irvin in the closing seconds of the University of Miami's agonizing 14-10 loss to Penn State in the 1987 Fiesta Bowl.

One year later, with three minutes remaining in Miami's Orange Bowl showdown with Oklahoma, Irvin again lost his composure. Tears of joy this time.

"I just couldn't stop crying," he said.

And for good reason. After falling frustratingly short in two consecutive bowl games, Miami's Hurricanes finally had welcomed a new year with cheers. National championship cheers.

"We've finally gotten our national title—two years late," Irvin said after the Hurricanes' 20-14 victory over Oklahoma on the first night of 1988. "The monkey is finally off our backs."

Retribution. Vindication. Satisfaction. Relief. Destiny. Those were some of the words being thrown around by Miami Coach Jimmy Johnson and his players in the wake of their title-clinching victory.

After having won 32 consecutive regular-season games, the eighth-longest streak in NCAA history, the Hurricanes were proud owners of their second national championship in five years.

"People didn't think there was any way we could do anything in 1987," said Irvin. "We had just lost shots at two national titles. We could have lost our intensity. But we had the character to keep fighting till we won one. We had to go out and prove the world wrong."

Flash back to the din of the 1986 Sugar Bowl in New Orleans' noisy Superdome. The 10-1 Hurricanes, in a position to claim a national championship because of other New Year's Day upsets, were stunned, 35-7, by a supposedly overmatched Tennessee team. National honors went to Oklahoma, a team the Hurricanes had defeated, 27-14, in a mid-season game in Norman, Okla.

Most of that Miami team returned for the 1986 season, and the Hurricanes steamrolled to an 11-0 regular-season record, including a 28-16 triumph over Oklahoma at Miami. But in the battle for No. 1, pitting top-ranked Miami against second-ranked and 11-0 Penn State in the January 2 Fiesta Bowl, the Hurricanes turned the ball over seven times. Heisman Trophy winner Vinny Testaverde, who had missed a month of bowl practice because of a motor scooter accident, threw five interceptions.

In the National Football League draft four months later, Testaverde, running back Alonzo Highsmith and defensive tackle Jerome Brown were the first, third and ninth picks overall. Center Gregg Rakoczy and linebacker Winston Moss were selected in the second round, offensive lineman Paul O'Connor in the fifth and running back Darryl Oliver in the 11th. Then, two days before the start of the 1987 season, dominant defensive tackle Dan Sileo lost an NCAA eligibility ruling. He subsequently went to the Tampa Bay Bucs in the NFL supplemental draft and started for most of the season.

Contending for the national title again seemed unlikely. Most preseason polls ranked the Hurricanes 10th or lower. Undaunted, they went out and

With Testaverde's departure, Steve Walsh took over at quarterback and directed the 1987 Hurricanes to a national championship.

achieved what their 1986 brethren couldn't—a 12-0 record.

"In the 23 years I have coached college football, I think the 1986 team, week in and week out, was the best I have ever seen," said Johnson, who took the Miami job in 1984 after five seasons at Oklahoma State. "But the '87 team ended up being even better.

"They did everything asked of them. They beat the No. 2 team in the country (Florida State), the No. 3 team (Oklahoma) and a total of six bowl teams (the others being Florida, Arkansas, Notre Dame and South Carolina), three of which played New Year's Day."

Asked why Miami went 12-0, the talkative Irvin said, "I think it was just destiny. The 1986 team was better. In '86, we out-played Penn State. We had a much better team, we just weren't due to win the game.

"It was just like in 1987 when Florida State out-played us but we won the game, 26-25. It had to be destiny. God felt sorry for us. He said, 'These guys have been working hard for a few years. Let's give them a championship.' "

Hard work, indeed. One factor that made both the 1986 and '87 squads click was the wealth of talent that led to fierce competition for starting positions.

"If you weren't performing, you were going to move down," said offensive guard Scott Provin, a part-time starter in '86 and a regular in '87. "The second and third teams always were pushing the first team and would get total performance out of us in practice.

"And in both years, we definitely were the most conditioned team in college football. We were in better shape than anybody in the third quarter and outscored teams by a big margin in that quarter (135-21 in 1986, 104-20 in 1987)."

Running back Melvin Bratton, whose hobby was acting and had played some bit parts on television and in movies, said embarrassment was a factor, too. Embarrassment?

"On both teams, we had this thing where we established embarrassment. We'd criticize each other," he said. "If someone made a mistake, we would say, 'You can't come back and do that again.' We didn't want to look bad against each other, even in practice."

But the Hurricanes didn't take each other too seriously.

"There were a lot of gags," said Provin. "We realized we were out there for fun. During the championship game against Oklahoma, Melvin would be talking in the huddle and the offensive line would tell him to get a breath mint."

Once, during a Tuesday practice before a big game, Bratton caught a pass, collapsed and clutched his knee. Hurricane players and coaches stared in shock. Trainer Kevin O'Neill, 300 yards away, sprinted to the fallen hero.

As O'Neill bent down to assist, a grinning, obviously faking Bratton looked up and said, "Relax, relax. I just want to see what coach Brodsky will do."

Running backs coach Joe Brodsky, along with fellow assistants Gary Stevens (offensive coordinator and quarterbacks) and Hubbard Alexander (receivers), were the firm hands that molded and remolded a Hurricane offense that annually took a beating in the NFL draft but never skipped a beat on the field.

Johnson used the same offense that was designed by his predecessor, Howard Schnellenberger. It was a pro-style attack patterned after the one used by the Miami Dolphins. The Hurricane defense was a standard 4-3, watched over and refined by defensive coordinator and linebackers coach Dave Wannstedt.

Though both the 1986 and '87 teams employed the same swarming, bone-crushing defensive style and pro-style offense, they developed different personalities. In '86, it was a "domineering, boisterous attitude, a cockiness that '87 did not have," said Johnson. "In 1987, the dominant players had a businesslike approach and confidence that may have allowed them to go 12-0 instead of 11-1.

"The '86 team almost challenged anybody to even come close to them. The closest other than Penn State was Florida, a 23-15 loser. But 1987 was a businesslike group that took care of work.

"In '86, the team took on the personality of Jerome Brown, Highsmith and Testaverde, a domineering style of play because of its physical ability. And '87 took on a personality of safety Bennie Blades, running back Warren Williams and sophomore quarterback Steve Walsh—quiet leaders who performed well. At times, Melvin Bratton would jump in there, but he wasn't boisterous like Brown. Michael Irvin was more flamboyant, but not necessarily boisterous."

Irvin was the 14th of 16 children, and his father, a Baptist minister, had died before he saw his son play for Miami. The most prolific touchdown catcher in Hurricane history, his nickname was "Playmaker."

Irvin's flamboyance was punctuated by a diamond stud in his left earlobe, two thick gold chains, a frequent wide grin and a constant barrage of rat-a-tat comments.

Irvin on Irvin:

- On his love of football: "I'm just like the businessman who works hard all week and gets drunk on Friday night. Football is my alcohol."
- On what he tells a defensive back after catching a touchdown pass: "Hey, don't worry about getting beat. I beat everybody."
- On Miami's confidence: "We feel we can beat anybody. If the San Francisco 49ers showed up here, we'd think we actually had a shot. Until it was 38-0 at halftime."

Defensive tackle Jerome Brown dominated opponents and helped instill cockiness into the 1986 Hurricane game plan.

Walsh, the man under the spotlight before the 1987 season began, had huge shoes to fill, never mind his size-12 feet. He didn't have Testaverde's arm, but he had the touch. An honors student in high school, he was unflappable and a leader who didn't need to shout.

In the first two games of 1987 against Florida and Arkansas, he completed 37 of 55 passes for 449 yards and two touchdowns. And he was intercepted just once. Testaverde was not forgotten, but he had been replaced. The Hurricane quarterback tradition started by Jim Kelly and Bernie Kosar in the early 1980s continued.

Walsh reminded most observers of Kosar, the mastermind of the '83 championship team. He was cool under pressure and had a knack for calling audibles. His coolness was demonstrated in the 1988 Orange Bowl when he justified Johnson's third-quarter decision to go for a first down rather than a field goal on a fourth-and-four play at Oklahoma's 29-yard line. The Hurricanes were leading at the time, 10-7.

He tossed a six-yard out-pattern pass to Bratton while being nailed by the Sooner defense. And three plays later, Walsh fired the game-sealing pass to Irvin.

Testaverde, the starter in 1985 and '86, had been a quarterback's quarterback—a coach's dream and a defense's worst nightmare. He was big (6-foot-5, 218 pounds) and strong (bench pressing more than 325 pounds) and possessed quick feet and an ability to throw on the run.

He had come to Miami in the fall of 1982 in a freshman class that included Kosar. Under the tutelage of quarterback coach Earl Morrall, the former Baltimore Colts and Miami Dolphins standout, he played a backup role to Kelly.

In a close battle for the starting job in '83, he lost out to Kosar and was redshirted. And in '84 he was relegated to mopup duty behind Kosar. Testaverde considered transferring, but he stuck it out and his patience was rewarded.

When Kosar decided to pass up his final two years of eligibility and was selected by the Cleveland Browns in the 1985 NFL supplemental draft, Testaverde went on to shatter school records Kosar had just established. And in 1986, Testaverde went Kosar one better, becoming Miami's first-ever Heisman Trophy winner.

Testaverde established himself as the Heisman front-runner in the fourth game of the season, the nationally televised showdown in the Orange Bowl between No. 1 Oklahoma and No. 2 Miami. He completed 14 consecutive passes en route to a 21-of-28, 261-yard, four-touchdown performance in the Hurricanes' impressive victory.

That game also provided the impetus for Miami's reputation as a headstrong, cocky, boisterous team. Criticism got so bad that many wondered if Miami players were wearing black hats under their white helmets.

There were charges of taunting and unsportsmanlike behavior. There were brushes with the law. And the media played up the bad guy-versus-good guy angle at the Fiesta Bowl when several Hurricanes arrived in Phoenix wearing combat fatigues.

"A lot of people cut down Miami, but it didn't bother us," Brown said.

Every little incident was magnified. Even the 1987 team, which went so far as to wear coats and ties on trips, never could completely shake the image. A week before the 1988 Orange Bowl battle against Oklahoma, linebacker George Mira Jr. and offensive tackle John O'Neill were suspended when NCAA pre-bowl drug tests determined they had taken a diuretic drug banned because it is commonly used to mask steroids.

Provin, a member of both the 1986 and '87 teams, felt the bad-guy image wasn't fair and pointed out players' involvement with community service projects.

"There were things the media didn't see," he said, "like the blood drive for South Florida every year, the involvement with the Special Olympics and several guys speaking against drugs."

About two-thirds of the players and coaches attended pregame church services conducted by the team's chaplain, Father Leo Armbrust. At the service before the 1988 Orange Bowl, players talked about the headlines ("Class Beats Crass") the year before.

"These teams overcame distractions," said Johnson. "I know a lot of teams have closeness and unity. It's on all championship teams. This was the closest group I've been around, for the simple reason they did have some adversity going all the way back to the end of 1984."

Johnson was referring to a season-ending trio of defensive fiascos involving a 42-40 loss to Maryland when the Hurricanes blew a 31-0 halftime lead, a 47-45 loss to Boston College on the famed Hail Flutie pass by quarterback Doug Flutie, and a 39-37 Fiesta Bowl setback to UCLA.

"The adversity solidified them," said Johnson. "I know it sounds a little trite, but there really was a strong bond on this team."

Though the 1987 Hurricanes lacked the marquee names of '86, the NFL recognized the talent. In the draft, the third player taken in the first round was Blades, leader of the "Bennie and the Jets" secondary which operated by the motto, "A headache for every reception." Irvin was the 11th pick. Both had grown up in the same Fort Lauderdale neighborhood as another first-round draft choice, Michigan State running back Lorenzo White.

Wide receiver Michael Irvin was colorful and flamboyant, but backed up his words with excellent, big-play numbers.

Wide receivers Brian Blades, Bennie's brother, and Brett Perriman went in the second round, as did defensive end Daniel Stubbs. Offensive tackle Matt Patchan was selected in the third and strong safety Darrell Fullington in the fifth.

Bratton, whose draft stock dropped when he suffered a knee injury late in the Oklahoma game, and Williams were picked in the sixth round. Tight end Alfredo Roberts went in the eighth, defensive tackle

When the 1987 national-champion Hurricanes wanted to establish a ground game, they turned to speedy running back Melvin Bratton.

Derwin Jones in the 10th and Mira Jr., son of former Miami All-America quarterback George Mira, in the 12th.

That's 20 players drafted in two years, 10 in the first two rounds.

"Both teams were talented, and both were extremely confident they were as good as any team in the country," said Johnson, whose 93-player championship team included 65 Floridians, 43 from South Florida. "Both from day one set sights on winning the national championship. It was not a matter of slipping up on No. 1 or sneaking in the back door.

"The '85 team had a chance to win it. With one senior starting, they fell into that situation. No one expected us to do a whole lot. Then they won 10 straight and got in a position to win it all.

"That set the stage for the '86 team. And even though we lost a lot off the '86 team, the disappointing loss to Penn State pretty much set the stage for '87, which might not have been as talented. Attitude-wise it put them up there in a position to challenge for the title."

Johnson blamed himself for the Sugar Bowl loss to Tennessee in '85. "I didn't prepare the team as well as I should have, and we were overconfident," he said.

He played the Fiesta Bowl loss to Penn State over and over in his mind and watched it on film until his bloodshot eyes resembled road maps.

"For the most part, our team was as prepared for that game as you can expect any team to be," said Johnson. "The defense held them to eight first downs, one in the second half, and 162 yards total offense.

"Our offense gained 445 yards against an outstanding defense, the only flaw being the receivers dropping some balls. But that was through not working with Vinny for a time. His pass has some velocity on it. In throwing five interceptions and fumbling twice after receptions, we still had a chance to win it up to the last play.

"You really can't fault anything except Vinny having the fall on the motor scooter and missing a month of work before the biggest game of his life. He missed the last regular-season game and he had only 10 practices before the bowl game because of awards and rehabilitation. He still had scabs and wasn't 100 percent when we arrived in Phoenix.

"The rustiness of the quarterback, the focal point of our offense, cost us. I don't blame Vinny. It was a freak accident. Looking back, the backup quarterback (Geoff Torretta) might have given us a chance to win the national championship because he had been at practice. We had been so dominating, the only way we would lose it was to beat ourselves."

And that's just what the 1987 team didn't do. It didn't beat itself. It committed only 16 turnovers (seven fumbles, nine interceptions) all season, including just one in the Orange Bowl against Oklahoma.

"In 1986, we were a big-play club with a bomb or a mad scramble," said Provin. "In '87, we had a more concentrated offense. We moved the sticks, though, and I think we were just as explosive.

"In 1987, we were definitely hungry. We saw the preseason rankings of 15, 12 and 10. Everybody on

The glue in Miami's 1986 and '87 defenses was safety Bennie Blades, pictured (above) making a tackle in the Hurricanes' 1986 victory over Oklahoma.

the team knew we were good. The coaches would tell us we had the ability to win it all because the talent was here. We realized after the Florida State game it could become a reality again."

The 1987 Hurricanes came of age in their third game, against what many believe was the Seminoles' finest team ever.

Florida State, playing in front of its home fans in Tallahassee, dominated the first three quarters, taking a commanding 19-3 lead. But Walsh struck for touchdown passes of 49 yards to Bratton and 26 to Irvin and capped both scores with two-point conversions to forge a tie. When Bennie Blades recovered a late fumble at his 11-yard line, Miami converted the turnover into a 73-yard Walsh-to-Irvin touchdown strike.

The Seminoles scored in the closing moments, but Miami reserve defensive back Bubba McDowell knocked down a two-point conversion pass to save the 26-25 victory. Florida State won its remaining games and finished second in the final rankings, marking the first time in college football history that teams from the same state had finished 1-2 in the polls.

As No. 2 Miami approached its Orange Bowl game against top-ranked Oklahoma, however, it looked like the Hurricanes might be bridesmaids for the third year in a row. As three-point underdogs on their home field, they faced a defense that had allowed the fewest points in the nation for the second straight season, and they were operating with a patchwork offensive line and their leading tackler on the bench. Tackle Patchan had suffered a knee injury in workouts, and Mira and O'Neill were under suspension. Yet they were barely missed.

Mira's replacement, sophomore Bernard (Tiger) Clark, called defensive signals and made 14 tackles, broke up a pass and recovered a fumble to earn Most Valuable Player honors in the game. Miami's line protected Walsh as he completed 18 of 30 passes for 209 yards and two touchdowns. And the special

End Daniel Stubbs (above, 96) and linebacker George Mira Jr. (below) were key members of the 1987 Hurricanes' punishing defense.

teams contributed.

"Our 1987 team was more balanced than '86," Johnson said. "The '86 team was devastating on defense and offense, but was just adequate in the kicking game.

"The '87 team was proficient in all three areas. In the Orange Bowl against Oklahoma, Greg Cox kicked a 56-yard field goal with the wind and 48 yards against the wind. Jeff Feagles hit a 68-yard punt into the wind to get us out of a hole.

"Randal Hill had good kickoff returns for field position all year. And Cox all year hit field goals when we needed them, which was the winning difference in the Florida State game."

But holding onto the ball and protecting the quarterback were Miami's real keys to success.

"The '87 team also didn't allow the sacks and turnovers," Johnson said. "We had only 10 sacks the first eight games under Walsh and 13 overall. In '86, we had 32. That was a key in beating Oklahoma. They couldn't get to Walsh.

"Also, in the big games we didn't turn it over and the opponents did. Against Florida State, the pass interception by Stubbs and Blades' fumble recovery as the Seminoles were going in to score in the fourth quarter were keys in that game."

In winning the 1987 national championship, the Hurricanes improved their five-year record to 52-9,

The 1986 Hurricanes: Front row (left to right)—Winston Moss, Willis Peguese, Daniel Stubbs, Ed Davis, Vinny Testaverde, Gregg Rakoczy, Greg Cox, Bill Hawkins, Bill Schaefer, David Guest, Scott Provin, Chris Bell, Mike Pigza, Jimmie Jones, Brian Smith, Derwin Jones. Second row—Assistant equipment manager Mike Short, trainer Kevin O'Neill, coaches Ron Meeks, John Fontes, Tom Tuberville, Chuck Pagano, Carlos Mainord, Butch Davis, Dave Wannstedt; Head Coach Jimmy Johnson; coaches Gary Stevens, Don Soldinger, Stu Rodgers, Hubbard Alexander, Joe Brodsky, Gary Ghormley, Art Kehoe, Tony Wise, Bill Foran, Pat Jacobs. Third row—Assistant trainer Al Bellamy, Bernard Clark, Bud Nemeth, Bret Velde, Mark Seelig, Jeff Feagles, Alan Karras, Warren Williams, Bobby Harden, Edgar Benes, J.C. Penny, Steve Staffier, Robert Thomas, Brian Blades, Brett Perriman, equipment manager Marty Daly. Fourth row—Selwyn Brown, Eric Ham, Alonzo Highsmith, Tim Sims, Tracy Waiters, Fred Highsmith, Randy Shannon, Vic Morris, Steve Rosinski, Darren Handy, David Kintigh, Russell Maryland, Kevin McCutcheon, Darryl Oliver, Bennie Blades, John O'Neill, Don Ellis. Fifth row—Dan Mariscal, Rod Carter, Rod Holder, Sandy Jack, Melvin Bratton, Michael Irvin, Rodney Hill, Greg Jones, Michael Johnson, Barry Panfil, Kirk Sandifer, Bubba McDowell, Doug McFadden, George Mira Jr., Cleveland Gary. Sixth row—Kenny Berry, Earnest Parish, Darrell Fullington, Percy Wilson, Geoff Torretta, Gary Mahon, Dennis Kelleher, Rob Canei, Luis Cristobal, Steve Kazdin, Nick Kondiakis, Steve Walsh, Jerome Brown, Tolbert Bain, Jason Hicks, Dan Sileo. Seventh row—Rob Chudzinski, Kevin Harris, Paul O'Connor, Basil Proctor, Matt Patchan, Andre Brown, Bill Turkowski, Alfredo Roberts, Charles Henry, Maurice Maddox, Greg Mark, Dave Alekna, Mike Sullivan, Marcus Kinlaw, John Hunt, Bobby Garcia.

a winning percentage of .852. That was the best in the nation. Oklahoma was second with 50-9-1 for an .842 winning percentage, followed by Nebraska (51-10, .836), Brigham Young (52-13, .800) and Auburn (47-12-2, .787).

Johnson, noted for his well-coiffed hairstyle that never seems to rustle in Miami's ocean breezes, took control of the Hurricanes when Schnellenberger resigned after spring practice in 1984. Johnson's teams went on to compile a 41-8 record through 1987, with five of the losses coming in 1984. He was 15-8 against teams ranked in the Top 20 and 12-2 against Oklahoma, Notre Dame, Florida State and Florida. The Sooners lost only three games from 1985 through '87, all to Miami.

Playing a national schedule and not belonging to a conference, the Hurricanes naturally are consumed by the passion to be No. 1 every year.

"By design, we allowed the players to continually remind each other what our goal was," said Johnson. "In 1986, before each game and after I had made my talk to the team, we cleared out the dressing room of all personnel other than players. We let the more vocal players remind them of our goals and to not come up short after we had come so far.

"I'd wait in the doorway and within hearing of what the players were saying so I could steer it in the right direction. By the players saying this, it was a heck of a lot better than me standing up and saying it. It was almost an attitude that could build."

Perhaps the best game of the 1986 and '87 seasons would have been the '86 Hurricanes against the '87 Hurricanes. The cocky 'Canes against the businesslike 'Canes. Which would win?

"Definitely 1986," said Irvin. "That was a squad and a half."

Provin: "Hopefully it would be a tie."

Bratton: "I'll call it dead even."

And Johnson: "There would be too many ifs. If the '86 team didn't make mistakes, it would win. But that's what made the '87 team win the national championship. It didn't make mistakes."

Miami, 1986-87

ROAD TO GREATNESS

1986 RESULTS (11-1)

Opponent	Score	Opp. Record	Opp. Bowl Game
at South Carolina	34-14	3-6-2	
at Florida	23-15	6-5-0	
Texas Tech	61-11	7-5-0	Independence (L)
Oklahoma	28-16	11-1-0	Orange (W)
Northern Illinois	34-0	2-9-0	
at West Virginia	58-14	4-7-0	
at Cincinnati	45-13	5-6-0	
Florida State	41-23	7-4-1	All-American (W)
at Pittsburgh	37-10	5-5-1	
Tulsa	23-10	7-4-0	
East Carolina	36-10	2-9-0	
FIESTA BOWL			
Penn State	**10-14**	**12-0-0**	

1987 RESULTS (12-0)

Opponent	Score	Opp. Record	Opp. Bowl Game
Florida	31-4	6-6-0	Aloha (L)
*Arkansas	51-7	9-4-0	Liberty (L)
at Florida State	26-25	11-1-0	Fiesta (W)
Maryland	46-16	4-7-0	
at Cincinnati	48-10	4-7-0	
at East Carolina	41-3	5-6-0	
Miami of Ohio	54-3	5-6-0	
Virginia Tech	27-13	2-9-0	
Toledo	24-14	3-7-1	
Notre Dame	24-0	8-4-0	Cotton (L)
South Carolina	20-16	8-4-0	Gator (L)
ORANGE BOWL			
Oklahoma	**20-14**	**11-1-0**	

*Little Rock

FACTS AND FIGURES

The Hurricanes proved themselves by defeating the best. Miami posted a 5-1 record against teams that ranked among the Top 20 in the 1986 and 1987 final wire-service polls. The Hurricanes also defeated nine of 10 opponents that played in bowl games during the same span by an average of 18.2 points per game. . . . Miami's opponents posted a combined record of 71-61-4 (.537 winning percentage) in 1986 and 76-62-1 (.550) in '87. . . . Defensive end Daniel Stubbs joined Bennie Blades on the 1987 consensus All-America team. . . . With the likes of Testaverde, wide receiver Michael Irvin and fullback Alonzo Highsmith, the Hurricane offense received most of the notice. But the defense was Miami's key to success, ranking among the national leaders in several categories, including total defense (fifth in '86 and sixth in '87), scoring defense (fourth in '86 and third in '87), rushing defense and passing defense. . . . The Hurricanes also ranked second in 1986 and fifth in 1987 in scoring. . . . Stubbs led the Hurricanes in sacks with 26½, and linebacker George Mira Jr. led in tackles with 269 during the 1986 and 1987 campaigns combined.

STATISTICAL LEADERS

PASSING

	Att.	Comp.	Yards	TD	Pct.	Int.
Vinny Testaverde (1986)	276	175	2557	26	63.4	9
Steve Walsh (1987)	298	176	2249	19	59.1	7

RUSHING

	Att.	Yards	Avg.	TD	Long
Warren Williams (1987)	135	673	5.0	5	49
Melvin Bratton (1987)	119	473	4.0	9	21
Alonzo Highsmith (1986)	105	442	4.2	4	22

RECEIVING

	Rec.	Yards	Avg.	TD	Long
Michael Irvin (1986)	53	868	16.4	11	50
Michael Irvin (1987)	44	715	16.3	6	73
Brett Perriman (1986)	34	647	19.0	4	50

SCORING

	TD	FG	PAT	Points
Greg Cox (1987)	0	17	43	94
Melvin Bratton (1987)	11	0	0	66
Michael Irvin (1986)	11	0	0	66

KEY CHARACTERS

The Conductor

COACH: Jimmy Johnson.

***Record:** 41-8, 4 years at Miami.

Johnson succeeded Howard Schnellenberger on June 5, 1984. . . . Following an 8-5 initial campaign, the Hurricanes proceeded to contend for national championships the next three seasons. . . . The national crown eluded Johnson and the Hurricanes in 1985 and 1986 because of losses to Tennessee and Penn State in the Sugar and Fiesta bowls, respectively. . . . The Hurricanes compiled a 23-1 mark in 1986 and 1987, which included consecutive undefeated regular seasons. . . . Before accepting the reins at Miami, Johnson compiled a 30-25-2 record at Oklahoma State during a five-year tenure. . . . During his collegiate career at Arkansas, Johnson lettered three times as an offensive guard, serving as captain for the 1964 undefeated national championship Razorback squad. He later was named to the Razorbacks' All-Decade Team (1960s).

Personal Data:

Born: July 16, 1943, in Port Arthur, Tex.
High School: Jefferson High in Port Arthur.
College: Arkansas.

*Indicates totals through 1987 season.

The Supporting Cast

SAFETY: Bennie Blades

Blades was the glue that kept the Hurricanes' defensive unit together during the 1986 and 1987 campaigns. . . . He had a penchant for the big play and played with tremendous emotion. . . . He possessed outstanding speed and was invited to the 1984 Olympic Trials. . . . He set the Miami career interceptions record with 19 and led the nation in interceptions with 10 in 1986. . . . Blades finished with 15 interceptions in his last 22 regular-season games. . . . He was co-winner of the 1987 Jim Thorpe Award and a consensus All-America in 1986 and 1987.

Personal Data:

Born: September 3, 1966, in Fort Lauderdale, Fla.
High School: Piper High in Sunrise, Fla.

DEFENSIVE TACKLE: Jerome Brown.

Brown was a dominant force as the anchor of the Hurricane defensive line. . . . He was a superior pass rusher who was effective against the run when necessary. . . . Brown single-handedly slowed powerful Oklahoma in a pivotal 1986 victory, registering 11 tackles while nullifying a potent Sooner rushing attack. . . . Brown earned consensus All-America honors in 1986 and was a finalist for both the Outland Trophy and Lombardi Award.

Personal Data:

Born: February 2, 1965, in Brooksville, Fla.
High School: Hernando High in Brooksville.

QUARTERBACK: Vinny Testaverde.

Testaverde led the Hurricanes to a 21-3 record as the starter during the 1985 and 1986 campaigns. . . . He won the Heisman Trophy in 1986 while also garnering All-America honors. . . . Testaverde, who followed in the footsteps of former Miami quarterback greats Jim Kelly and Bernie Kosar, used superior size and strength to avoid oncoming opponents. Those skills were illustrated during a 10-yard scramble for a 1986 first down against Oklahoma when Testaverde went sideline-to-sideline, seemingly avoiding the entire Sooner defense. That play was considered among the most memorable of the decade. . . . Testaverde later was selected as the first choice in the 1987 National Football League draft.

Personal Data:

Born: November 13, 1963, in Brooklyn, N.Y.
High School: Sewanhaka High in Floral Park, N.Y.
Prep School: Fork Union Military Academy in Fork Union, Va.

FINAL 1986 WIRE SERVICE RANKINGS

ASSOCIATED PRESS		UNITED PRESS	
1. Penn State	11. Arizona	**1. Penn State**	11. Louisiana State
2. MIAMI (Fla.)	12. Baylor	**2. MIAMI (Fla.)**	12. Texas A&M
3. Oklahoma	13. Texas A&M	3. Oklahoma	13. Baylor
4. Arizona State	14. UCLA	4. Nebraska	14. UCLA
5. Nebraska	15. Arkansas	5. Arizona State	15. Iowa
6. Auburn	16. Iowa	6. Ohio State	16. Arkansas
7. Ohio State	17. Clemson	7. Michigan	17. Washington
8. Michigan	18. Washington	8. Auburn	18. Boston College
9. Alabama	19. Boston College	9. Alabama	19. Clemson
10. Louisiana State	20. Virginia Tech	10. Arizona	**20. Florida State**

FINAL 1987 WIRE SERVICE RANKINGS

ASSOCIATED PRESS		UNITED PRESS	
1. MIAMI (Fla.)	11. Oklahoma State	**1. MIAMI (Fla.)**	11. UCLA
2. Florida State	12. Clemson	**2. Florida State**	12. Oklahoma State
3. Oklahoma	13. Georgia	**3. Oklahoma**	13. Tennessee
4. Syracuse	14. Tennessee	4. Syracuse	14. Georgia
5. Louisiana State	**15. South Carolina**	5. Louisiana State	**15. S. Carolina (tie)**
6. Nebraska	16. Iowa	6. Nebraska	15. Iowa (tie)
7. Auburn	**17. Notre Dame**	7. Auburn	17. Southern Cal
8. Michigan State	18. Southern Cal	8. Michigan State	18. Michigan
9. UCLA	19. Michigan	9. Texas A&M	19. Texas
10. Texas A&M	20. Arizona State	10. Clemson	20. Indiana

Bold face indicates Miami (Fla.) opponent.

Touchdown Tony's Salvation Show

Pittsburgh, 1976
By Scott Pitoniak

August 18, 1973. Johnny Majors, the new Pittsburgh football coach, is in Hershey, Pa., for his first look at his prize recruit.

Tony Dorsett, a 150-pound running back, makes a quick impression.

Dorsett is running wild in the Big 33 high school all-star game that pits the best from Pennsylvania against the best from Ohio. He grabs a pitchout and sweeps to his right, but the entire defense appears to be waiting at the line of scrimmage. He slams on the brakes, reverses his field and accelerates past three startled defenders as he turns the corner. He eludes another would-be tackler with a head fake, and yet another with a spin move. Finally, he is dragged down while trying to bull over a much larger player.

Majors shakes his head in disbelief but reins in his emotions until he reaches the privacy of his hotel room. He closes the door.

"Whoooeee," he screams. "We've got ourselves a running back."

Actually, the Pitt Panthers had themselves much more. They had a ticket to a national championship.

★ ★ ★

When Anthony Drew Dorsett announced in April 1973 that he would attend the University of Pittsburgh, friends suggested he have his head examined.

The Panthers hadn't won a national title since

Tony Dorsett, Pittsburgh's little bundle of dynamite, rushed for 6,082 career yards and helped lift the Panther program back into national prominence.

Tony Dorsett's speed and elusiveness left would-be tacklers in his wake and opposing teams in the dust of Pittsburgh's 1976 championship run.

1937 and hadn't been ranked in the final polls since 1963. Coming off a dreadful 1-10 campaign in 1972, the school's worst record ever, the accomplishments of Pop Warner and Jock Sutherland seemed like ancient history. Under the two legendary coaches, eight Pitt teams were accorded national championship recognition between 1915 and 1937. Now, attendance had slipped to 21,050 fans per game. There were Saturdays when the major high schools in western Pennsylvania drew almost as well as the Panthers.

Compounding matters, there had been whispers that if newly appointed Coach Johnny Majors didn't produce a winner, Pitt might de-emphasize football and replace the Notre Dames on its schedule with the Carnegie-Mellons. Some joked that Dorsett was going from Hopewell High in Aliquippa, Pa., to Hopeless U.

But the son of a steelworker had his reasons for saying yes to Pitt and no to Penn State, Notre Dame, Alabama and scores of other schools that were courting him.

"I had always been an introverted kid and I figured it might be good to go to a college close to home," Dorsett said. "I figured if I got homesick, I'd only be a half-hour drive away from Mom and Dad."

The Panthers had won only 16 of their previous 72 games, but Dorsett didn't envision a dismal future.

"You aren't going to believe this," he said "but a bunch of us guys got together during our freshman year and said we were going to win the national championship by the time we were done at Pitt. Of course, we didn't tell anybody else about it because they would have laughed us out of town.

"I had attended some of Pitt's games while I was in high school and they were competitive. They'd usually lose, but it didn't seem like they were missing that much. They just needed some speed and direction."

Dorsett figured he could provide the speed and Majors the direction.

As a Tennessee tailback in the mid-1950s, Majors led the Volunteers in rushing, passing and punting, played safety, was a unanimous All-America and second to Paul Hornung in the 1956 Heisman Trophy balloting. In his first collegiate coaching assignment, he took over an Iowa State program that had been a combined 4-14-2 in the two seasons before he arrived in 1968 and led the Cyclones to two bowl games—their first ever—in five years. In 1971, he was named Big Eight Coach of the Year.

One of Majors' priorities upon arriving at Pitt was to halt Penn State's invasion of football-rich western Pennsylvania. He began by assigning Jackie Sherrill, his defensive coordinator and right-hand man, to recruit Dorsett.

"Recruit is not the word," Dorsett recalled, laughing. "Jackie just about moved in with us. My mom loved the guy. By the time I committed to Pitt, he was one of the family."

Dorsett had plenty of company when he reported for training camp in August 1973. Those were the days before scholarship limitations, and Majors handed out more than 80 full rides that year.

"Football is a numbers game and Pitt had fallen way behind many of the schools on its schedule,"

Majors explained. "Pitt was giving out 25 scholarships a year, while most of its opponents were giving out twice as many. I told the Pitt people during the interview process that if you are truly interested in upgrading your program, you have to increase the number of football scholarships dramatically. There is strength in numbers."

And fear as well.

Al Romano, a consensus All-America at middle guard in 1976, was from Solvay, N.Y., a tiny suburb of Syracuse. He was one of several recruits who found that first camp frightening.

"There must have been about 120 guys there," Romano said. "I figured there was no way I was going to make this team. They had six or seven other scholarship players at my position alone. After a couple of practices, I called my dad to come down after me. I wanted to leave. He told me to hold on awhile longer and if I still felt the same way, he would come and get me."

The revival of Pittsburgh football can be traced directly to Coach Johnny Majors, who played the recruiting numbers game and won.

Romano stuck it out with several others who would form the nucleus of Pitt's undefeated national champions four seasons later. But the central figure of that 1976 team, the man who at times seemed to carry the entire Pitt football program on his not-so-wide shoulder pads, was Dorsett.

"He's the sort of runner who comes along once in a lifetime," center John Pelusi said. "And I'm so glad he came here in my lifetime."

Majors already was convinced of Dorsett's greatness after watching that spectacular run in the Big 33 game. But several Pitt assistant coaches and most of Dorsett's peers weren't converted until the Panthers' first intrasquad scrimmage in the 1973 fall camp.

On the opening play, the 5-foot-10, 155-pound Dorsett sprinted 80 yards for a touchdown. Before the scrimmage ended, he broke free for several more long runs. The Pitt defensive coaches were distraught, but Majors consoled them.

"There's nothing wrong with our defense," he said. "We can't stop Dorsett, but nobody else is going to be able to stop him, either."

His words proved prophetic.

In four years, Dorsett rushed for an NCAA-record 6,082 yards, won the Heisman Trophy as a senior and had his No. 33 jersey retired before his playing days were through. More impressive, he helped the Panthers make one of the most rapid turnarounds in football history.

In 1973, Dorsett rushed for 1,586 yards (most ever by a college freshman and the first 1,000-yard season in Pitt history) as the Panthers went 6-4-1 and earned an invitation to the Fiesta Bowl. It was the Panthers' first winning season since 1963 and their first bowl appearance since 1956.

The next season, Dorsett's rushing yardage slipped to 1,004, but Pitt climbed another notch, to 7-4. In only his 15th career game, Dorsett broke Marshall Goldberg's all-time Pitt rushing record of 1,957 yards.

In 1975, Dorsett rebounded with 1,544 yards as the Panthers again finished 7-4. They earned a bid to the Sun Bowl, where they defeated Kansas, 33-19, as Dorsett, quarterback Robert Haygood and fullback Elliott Walker each rushed for more than 100 yards.

"That Sun Bowl game was a springboard," Romano said. "We figured everything was in place for us to take the final step. We entered training camp in 1976 believing we were legitimate contenders for the national title."

The national media gave the Panthers glowing

notice as well. Pitt was ranked ninth by both the Associated Press and United Press International in the preseason rankings. "I think it's realistic to put us in the top 10," Majors concurred. "We have the overall talent to have a very explosive offense."

Certainly, the Panthers could strike quickly with racehorses Gordon Jones at split end, Willie Taylor at flanker and Walker at fullback. Then there were the two old reliables, tight end Jim Corbett and place-kicker Carson Long, who would set an NCAA career record for points scored by a kicker.

Dorsett had the perfect venue to begin his assault on Archie Griffin's major-college career rushing mark with a tough road test against Notre Dame first on the schedule. "I haven't told this before," Dorsett said at the time, "but four years ago I was being recruited by Notre Dame and I heard that one of their coaches called me a skinny, little kid who was too small for big-time football. That has always been incentive enough for me."

As a 19-year-old freshman, Touchdown Tony rushed for 209 yards to become the first player to crack the 200-yard barrier against Notre Dame. Although limited to 61 yards in 1974, Dorsett redeemed himself the following year with 303 yards rushing against the Irish, a single-game Pitt record.

Notre Dame and its passionate followers were determined not to be subjected to more humiliation. On the bus ride to the stadium, Dorsett noticed several dummies of himself hanging from trees. "One of the dorms had a huge tombstone with my number 33 on it," he recalled. "The inscription read, 'Here lies Tony Dorsett, buried under a sea of Notre Dame tacklers.' "

Even the Notre Dame grounds crew got in on the act. "The grass must have been a foot high," Dorsett said, chuckling. "They figured they could slow us down because they knew our team speed was far superior."

The strategy failed. Dorsett ran for 61 yards on the Panthers' first play from scrimmage and finished with 181 yards rushing as Pitt romped, 31-10.

"If we had had any doubts about just how good we were, that got rid of them," Romano said.

The following week, Pitt destroyed Georgia Tech but lost Haygood, the No. 1 quarterback, for the rest of the season with a knee injury. Junior Matt Cavanaugh bounced off the bench in the second quarter to pass for two touchdowns and run for another in the Panthers' 42-14 victory.

"We had gone into the season believing either one was capable of leading us," Majors recalled. "I knew Matt could carry the load."

He unloaded a school-record five touchdown passes two weeks later to burn a stubborn Duke defense that tried to gang up on Dorsett. The Blue Devils did, indeed, "limit" Dorsett to 129 yards by stacking the line, but Cavanaugh connected on 14 of 17 passes for 339 yards in the 44-31 victory.

When starting quarterback Robert Haygood was injured early in 1976, Matt Cavanaugh (above) stepped in to guide the bowl-bound Panthers.

The message was clear: These were the Pitt Panthers, not the Pitt Dorsetts.

"I was by no means a one-man show," Dorsett said. "We had so many different poisons for you to take. If you wanted to make me a marked man and put your cornerbacks on the line of scrimmage then, fine, Matt would just beat your butt with passes to Gordon Jones and Jim Corbett. And our defense wasn't exactly chopped liver, either. Those guys were so underrated. People still don't realize what a great defense that was. I was so happy they were on my side and not trying to put a hurt on me. We were a talented football team."

And a colorful one, too.

"Everybody had a nickname," said Romano, who was known as Omar Sharif for his resemblance to the handsome actor. "The best nicknames belonged to the offensive linemen. My favorite was the one Pelusi gave offensive tackle John Hanhauser. John was an enormous human being. He had to turn sideways just to get through the doorway. One day, Pelusi started calling Big John, the USS Hanhauser. It stuck."

And with Matt "Beef" Carroll stationed alongside at guard, the left side of the Pitt line was one mound of pounds. The "Bozo" at right guard, Tom Brzoza, was definitely no clown but a crack blocker who

Hard-charging middle guard Al Romano was one of the prime movers on Pittsburgh's championship-caliber defense.

excelled downfield.

After butting heads everyday with Pelusi, Hanhauser and Co. in practice, the defense had to endure the line's tactics at mealtime.

"We called them the hogs and pigs, and if you ever saw them eat, you'd understand why," he said. "They'd eat steak after steak after steak. And when the meat was gone, they would start gnawing on their plates and the table cloths."

The Pitt defense wasn't without its characters. The line, featuring Romano in the middle and Randy Holloway and Don Parrish at right and left tackle, respectively, was known as the Oreo Cookie. "I was white and they were black," Romano explained.

One of the starting linebackers was Arnie Weatherington, a nasty player who rarely smiled. "He had one mood—miserable," recalled Romano, laughing. "Arnie was the type of guy who would make a great tackle but would come back to the huddle, shaking his head and swearing at himself because he hadn't torn the guy's helmet off.

"It was fun playing with that type of player. In fact, it was fun playing with most of those guys. We were a close-knit, fun-loving bunch. We busted each other's chops, but we respected each other."

It took only the first few games for the Panthers' defense to earn the respect of its peers. Although it remained somewhat overshadowed by Dorsett's fireworks, the defense wound up ranked fourth in the nation against the run, sixth in total defense and first in lowest completion percentage allowed. Safety Bob Jury and monster back Jeff Delaney combined for 16 interceptions to rank among the NCAA leaders.

"You could say it bothers us when the offense gets all the credit," remarked Holloway, who recorded a team-leading 16 sacks. "It gets us cranky sometimes but we know without them, we can't win."

The offense received its worst blow of the season when Cavanaugh suffered a fractured ankle during the second quarter of a 27-6 victory over Louisville in week five. The Panthers had to call on Tom Yewcic, a walk-on quarterback who once had ranked ninth on the team depth chart.

Yewcic's relief job was a near disaster. One day after throwing two touchdowns for the junior varsity, Yewcic lost two fumbles, threw an interception and completed only one pass for four yards.

"I thought our national championship dreams were dead," Romano admitted. "Hell, just the week before I was kicking the crap out of Yewcic in practice. Now, all of a sudden, our scout team quarterback was going to be our starting quarterback."

The team quickly recovered from the shock of Cavanaugh's injury. At the Monday practice after the Louisville game, the Panthers began treating Yewcic, the nephew of former Michigan State quarterback Tom Yewcic, as if he had been the starter since training camp.

"It was a tremendously difficult situation for a kid who had never taken a varsity snap before to be thrown into," Romano said. "It was uncomfortable enough for him. Imagine what a wreck he would have been if we hadn't rallied around him and given him our wholehearted support?"

Later that week, Majors pulled Yewcic aside and gave him a full scholarship. "I wanted to let him know, sink or swim, he was our quarterback until Matt came back," Majors said.

Yewcic completed only two of seven passes in his first start against Miami (Fla.) on October 16, but it mattered little. Dorsett turned one of the completions into a 40-yard touchdown and piled up 227 yards rushing and two more scores as the Panthers crushed Miami, 36-19, to improve to 6-0.

"It was a gutty performance by Tommy, considering the circumstances," Majors said. "It also was a great performance by Dorsett. Miami knew we would have to rely on Tony even more because of the quarterback situation and they still couldn't stop him."

The next week, Dorsett supplanted Griffin as the all-time major college rushing leader as Pitt annihilated Navy, 45-0. His 32-yard touchdown sweep around left end on his final carry of the afternoon boosted his career rushing total to 5,206 yards, 29 ahead of the former Ohio State star.

"I'm hoping I can push that record up so far that no one can ever dream of besting it," Dorsett said afterward. "Maybe they can hope for Number 2, but I want that record to be mine as long as I'm on this earth."

The stage was set for Pitt's biggest scare of the season—and the defense's biggest two plays.

Syracuse came to the Steel City on October 30 featuring a 3-4 record and a scrambling quarterback named Bill Hurley. Few expected much of a game. The oddsmakers figured Dorsett would run wild and the Pitt defense would put the clamps on the elusive Hurley.

They were half right.

Dorsett, overcoming a bruised leg, jammed elbow and a poked eye, gained 241 yards, but Hurley was the dominant player this day, passing for 203 yards and rushing for 112 more.

"I was from near Syracuse," Romano recalled, "and there was no way I was going to lose to those guys because I would never hear the end of it when I returned home. I told (defensive end) Cecil Johnson I would pay him $100 if he knocked Hurley out of the game. He knocked him out all right, but only for a couple of plays, so I didn't feel obligated to pay up."

Late in the fourth quarter, it appeared Hurley would deliver the knockout punch. Pitt was leading, 20-13, but the Orangemen had the ball on the Panthers' 11, where they faced a third-and-one.

"I was tired and scared to death," Romano said. "We had tried everything against Hurley and nothing was working. He was killing us running the ball and killing us passing it. I was praying to myself, 'Please, Lord, just let us hold them one more time. Just one more time.' "

Somebody up there must have been listening.

On third down, Hurley handed off to Jim Sessler. The burly fullback bulled into the left side of the line for an apparent first down, but the officials' spot indicated otherwise. "To be honest with you, they made the first down," Romano admitted. "Of course, I wasn't about to tell the officials that they had goofed."

On fourth down, Hurley called an audible that was recognized by Romano and Joe Stone, an offensive lineman who played defense in short-yardage situations. They quickly notified their teammates. When the ball was snapped, Romano knifed through and wrapped an arm around Sessler's ankle. A millisecond later, Parrish, Weatherington and several other defenders swarmed in to bury Sessler. Pitt had stopped the Orangemen.

"Those may have been the two biggest plays of the season," Romano said. "We don't stop them, we don't win the national championship."

Following the stand, Dorsett ripped off gains of 28 and 33 yards, setting up Long's 29-yard field goal to ice a 23-13 win.

The next week, with Cavanaugh back and the Panthers rolling over Army, 37-7, an announcement over the Pitt Stadium public-address system trumpeted that No. 1 Michigan had lost to Purdue, 16-14. The Panther crowd of 45,753 began chanting, "We're Number 1." Two days later, the pollsters agreed. For the first time that season, Pitt was atop the AP and UPI rankings.

"I've always said that besides being good, you have to catch some breaks to win a national championship," Majors said.

By this time it was a foregone conclusion that Dorsett would win the Heisman Trophy. He had easily distanced himself from the main competition, Southern Cal running back Ricky Bell and Michigan running back Rob Lytle. He also was far from being the shy kid who had arrived on the Pitt campus in 1973.

"I think my success forced me to come out of my shell and deal with people," he said. "After my freshman year, I was on the banquet circuit a lot. There was even one banquet where I sat at the same table as the President of the United States. After that experience, I enrolled in some communications courses. I knew if I continued to be successful, I would be in even more demand with the media. There would be no place for me to hide."

Gradually, Dorsett became comfortable with his celebrity status. By his senior year, he appeared to revel in the postgame interview sessions with hordes of reporters from around the country.

"It was amazing to watch the transformation in his personality," said Bill Hillgrove, Pitt's longtime play-by-play announcer. "His freshman year he was so timid, almost frightened by interviews. His senior year, it was as if he was holding court. He'd always wait until the very last question in the press conference had been answered. There were times when there would be a lull in the proceedings and Tony would liven things up by saying something outlandish. The media loved him."

Despite all of the attention, he never behaved as if he were better than his teammates.

"I think the thing we respected most about him was that he wasn't a prima donna," Romano said. "I can honestly say there wasn't any jealousy toward him by anybody because we all knew how great he was and we all knew that he was the main piece of the puzzle. We also respected the fact that he would play hurt. A lot of great players take time off if they get a hangnail. Tony wasn't that big, but he kept playing with nagging injuries. That's pretty impressive when you consider he was a marked man. Every team wanted to be the one to knock

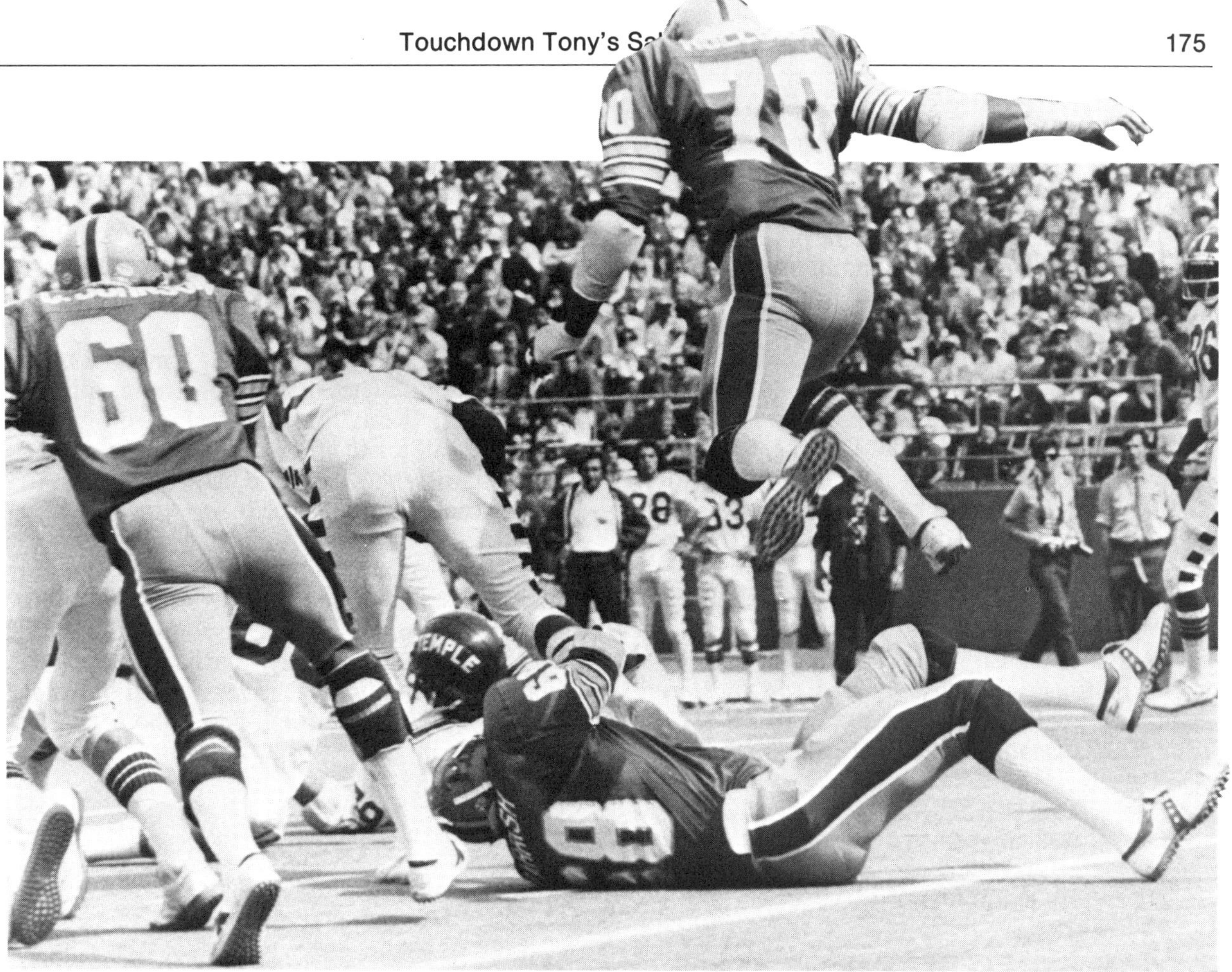

Defensive tackle Randy Holloway (70) leaps over a fallen teammate as he hunts down the ballcarrier during Pitt's 1976 game against Temple.

Tony Dorsett out for good."

During halftime of a tougher-than-expected 24-16 victory against West Virginia on November 13, Pitt retired Dorsett's No. 33. "I was so honored," he recalled. "But I kind of wished they had waited until after the season because we had some unfinished business. I didn't want anything to detract from our preparations for Penn State."

The Panthers hadn't beaten Penn State since 1965 but finally ended the Nittany Lions' mastery with a 24-7 spanking at Three Rivers Stadium. Dorsett romped for 224 yards to crack the career 6,000-yard barrier and establish an NCAA single-season rushing record of 1,948 yards.

The Panthers' 11-0 record topped their previous best of 10-0 in 1904, but their joy was tempered by the news that Majors would leave after the season to become coach at Tennessee.

"We had mixed emotions about it, but everyone, including the underclassmen, seemed to understand," Dorsett said. "Coach Majors had resurrected Pitt football. He had done everything he could, and it was understandable that he wanted to return home. The important thing was that he wasn't leaving a sinking ship. He had left (new coach) Jackie Sherrill with a full cupboard."

The Panthers had voted to go to the Sugar Bowl to play once-beaten Georgia, the No. 4 team in UPI, No. 5 in AP. Bulldogs Coach Vince Dooley had been among the challengers to the Panthers' right to the top spot in the polls.

"There was still this feeling that Eastern football wasn't on par with the rest of the country," Romano said. "Despite all we had accomplished, people still tried to downgrade us, saying we hadn't played anybody. I know that's the way the people in Georgia felt."

To the amazement of many, Majors did not place many restrictions on his players when the team arrived in New Orleans the week before the Sugar Bowl.

"I didn't want to bog them down with unrealistic curfews," the coach said. "I didn't want to tell them that they weren't allowed to have a beer or two. To me, a bowl game is a reward for a good season. I didn't want them to slack off in practice and I didn't want them getting into trouble, but I did want them to have a good time."

That they did, taking in all the sights and sounds of the French Quarter. They sampled the striptease joints, the jazz bars and the discos. There were times when Pitt players would roll into the hotel just in time to catch the bus to practice. That was in stark contrast to the behavior of the Bulldogs, who had to be in their rooms by 9 p.m.

"We felt sorry for those guys," Romano said. "We'd be sitting in a bar with some of them, and all of a sudden they would be scrambling out of there so fast you'd think someone had dropped a bomb."

While patrolling Bourbon Street in their letterman jackets, the Pitt players often encountered rowdy Georgia fans.

"They were the most arrogant, obnoxious people I've ever met," Dorsett said. "They kept telling us how we were no good and how I was going to be dog food for their Bulldogs. As it turned out, that was probably our easiest game of the year. It was so one-sided, it was boring."

If there was any doubt about Pitt deserving its No. 1 ranking, it was laid to rest on the Superdome carpet that New Year's Day. The Panthers bolted to a 21-0 halftime lead on a six-yard run by Cavanaugh, a 59-yard pass to Jones and Dorsett's 11-yard scamper. Cavanaugh, voted the game's most valuable player, wound up passing for 192 yards while Dorsett rushed for 202, a Sugar Bowl record.

This game, however, belonged to the Panther defense, which intercepted four passes, recovered two fumbles and limited three Georgia quarterbacks to three completions in 22 attempts.

Dooley said he had never seen a more complete football team. "They have everything you look for," he said. "I can't see any weaknesses on either side of the ball for them, only strengths."

The Panthers, 27-3 victors, had become the first Eastern team since Syracuse in 1959 to win the national title.

"We had accomplished our mission," said Dorsett, the first major-college back to compile four 1,000-yard seasons. "I think back to those college days often, and I can't help but smile. I've never had more fun in my life. We were a part of history. We helped save Pitt football and nobody can take that away from us."

The 1976 Panthers: First row (left to right)—Carson Long, Ralph Still, Bob Haygood, Tom Yewcic, Matt Cavanaugh, Mark Schubert, Bentley, Jeff Delaney, George O'Korn, Mark O'Toole, Kornick, Wayne Adams, Woody Jackson, Dave Migliore, Jo Jo Heath, Randy Reutershan, Joel Anderson, Mike Prokopovich, James Wilson, Steve Harris, Fred Jacobs, Don Spiranac, Mike DeLisio, Gordon Jones, Marc Torquato, Ray Kemp, Mike Balzer, Gary Arcuri, Larry Felton. Second row—Willie Taylor, Bob Hightower, Bob Jury, Leverga Walker, Tony Dorsett, Elliott Walker, Dave DiCiccio, Willie Marsh, Bob Rechichar, Willie Collier, LeRoy Felder, Blazek, Paul Janov, Bob Harshman, Jim Chapin, Chuck Bonasorte, Larry Swider, Scott McKeel, Ron Medley, Tom Rechichar, Bob Hutton, Ed Brosky, Bernardo Paez, Thom Sindewald, Ken Dapp, John Falvo, John Pelusi, Jeff Pelusi, Mike Lenosky, Mike Linn. Third row—Dan Noble, Steve Clemons, Kurt Kovach, Al Chesley, John Takacs, Desmond Robinson, Jim Hissom, Gary Tyra, James Cramer, Weatherington, Cecil Johnson, Art Bortnick, Jerry Dempsey, Rich Lucente, Milt Schuler, Jeff Matthews, John Hanhauser, Dave Treiber, George Link, Tom Brzoza, Don Parrish, Brad Schmidt, Randy Holloway, Al Papay, Dan Zelahy, Jim Triscila, Joe Stone, Head Coach Johnny Majors. Fourth row—Willie Tolbert, Walt Brown, Ed Gallagher, George Messich, Matt Carroll, David Logan, Jim Buoy, Ed Wilamowski, Jim Corbett, Steve Gaustad, Art Brown, Randy Johnson, Kunkel, David Bucklew, Bill Vitalie, Stepanovich, Rich Cooper, Tom Connors, Scott Hartman, Steve Pritchard, Al Romano, Tim Madison, Ron Boone, Kurt Brechbill, Jim Morsillo, Joe Tutela. Fifth row—Coaches Bob Matey, Joe Avezzano, Larry Holton, Jim Dyar; Steve Fedell, Rocky DeStefano, Allan Barboza, Bob Gruber, Coyle, Coaches Bobby Roper, Harry Jones, Bill Cox, Joe Madden.

Pittsburgh, 1976

ROAD TO GREATNESS

1976 RESULTS (12-0)

Opponent	Score	Opp. Record	Opp. Bowl Game
at Notre Dame	31-10	9-3-0	Gator (W)
at Georgia Tech	42-14	4-6-1	
Temple	21-7	4-6-0	
at Duke	44-31	5-5-1	
Louisville	27-6	4-7-0	
Miami (Fla.)	36-19	3-8-0	
at Navy	45-0	4-7-0	
Syracuse	23-13	3-8-0	
Army	37-7	5-6-0	
West Virginia	24-16	5-6-0	
Penn State	24-7	7-5-0	Gator (L)
SUGAR BOWL			
Georgia	**27-3**	**10-2-0**	

FACTS AND FIGURES

The Panthers charged to their first perfect season in 58 years behind the splendid coaching of Johnny Majors, The Sporting News' 1976 Coach of the Year, and the stunning running of halfback Tony Dorsett, The Sporting News' Player of the Year. . . . Pitt triumphed with an ideal blend of offense and defense, ranking among the nation's top teams in several categories. . . . The Panther offense rated sixth in scoring, seventh in rushing and 12th in total offense. . . . Defensively, Pitt ranked fourth against the run, sixth in total defense and 13th in points allowed. . . . Dorsett led the nation in scoring, all-purpose yardage, rushing yardage and rushing yards per game. . . . Larry Swider ranked fifth in the nation with a 44.8-yard punting average. . . . The Panthers drew some criticism for a regular-season schedule that offered an average menu of opponents, only two of which managed winning records. . . . Pitt's 12 opponents overall had a combined record of 63-69-2, a .478 winning percentage. . . . The Panthers won their four road games by an average margin of 26.8 points and scored more than 30 points in half of their 12 contests. . . . Eight members of the 1976 squad were named to the All-Time Pitt team (1910-86): Split end Gordon Jones, defensive tackle Randy Holloway, quarterback Matt Cavanaugh, fullback Elliott Walker, defensive backs Bob Jury and Jeff Delaney, placekicker Carson Long and Dorsett. . . . Ten players were named to either the 1976 AP or UPI first-team All-East squads: Middle guard Al Romano, offensive guard Tom Brzoza, tight end Jim Corbett, tackle John Hanhauser, defensive end Cecil Johnson, center John Pelusi, Dorsett, Holloway, Jury and Long

STATISTICAL LEADERS

PASSING

	Att.	Comp.	Yards	TD	Pct.	Int.
Matt Cavanaugh	92	55	854	8	59.8	3
Tom Yewcic	34	14	218	2	41.2	2

RUSHING

	Att.	Yards	Avg.	TD	Long
Tony Dorsett	338	1948	5.8	21	61
Elliott Walker	74	354	4.8	3	69
Matt Cavanaugh	86	351	4.1	4	29

RECEIVING

	Rec.	Yards	Avg.	TD	Long
Jim Corbett	33	528	16.0	2	41
Gordon Jones	18	306	17.0	4	51
Willie Taylor	14	248	17.7	3	66

SCORING

	TD	FG	PAT	Points
Tony Dorsett	22	0	*1	134
Carson Long	0	16	42	90
Gordon Jones	4	0	0	24
Matt Cavanaugh	4	0	0	24
Willie Taylor	4	0	0	24

*Two-point conversion.

KEY CHARACTERS

The Conductor

COACH: Johnny Majors.

Record: 33-13-1, 4 years at Pittsburgh.

Majors succeeded Carl DePasqua at Pittsburgh in 1973 and revived a program that hadn't had a winning season since 1963. . . . Coming off a 1-10 1972 campaign, Pitt's worst ever, Majors' first two teams went 6-5-1 in 1973 and 7-4 in '74. . . . The Panthers broke into the national rankings in 1975, finishing 8-4 as the No. 15 team in the final Associated Press poll and No. 13 in United Press International. . . . Majors' '76 Panthers were undefeated and the consensus choice as national champion. . . . Pitt attended bowl games in three of Majors' four seasons—the school's first postseason appearances since 1956—and posted a 2-1 record. . . . Though Majors coached just four seasons at Pittsburgh, only four other Panther coaches have won more games. . . . Majors, a member of the College Football Hall of Fame, was a unanimous consensus All-America tailback at Tennessee in 1956, when he finished second to Paul Hornung in the Heisman Trophy balloting. . . . He was an assistant coach at Tennessee, Mississippi State and Arkansas before accepting his first head coaching job at Iowa State in 1968. . . . He coached the Cyclones to a 24-30-1 record in five seasons, including visits to the 1971 Sun Bowl and 1972 Liberty Bowl. . . . After his four-year stay at Pitt, Majors returned to coach his alma mater in 1977. . . . He has a 77-47-6 record in 11 seasons at Tennessee. . . . Under Majors, the Volunteers have had three nine-victory seasons. . . . He has coached Tennessee to five victories in eight bowl appearances, including a 35-7 win over once-beaten Miami (Fla.) in the Sugar Bowl following the 1985 season. . . . He has coached six consensus All-Americas—two at Pittsburgh and four at Tennessee. . . . In 20 years, Majors has a 134-90-8 coaching record.

Personal Data:

Born: May 21, 1935, in Lynchburg, Tenn.
High School: Huntland High in Huntland, Tenn.
College: Tennessee.

The Supporting Cast

QUARTERBACK: Matt Cavanaugh.

Cavanaugh was the strong-armed leader who played in the shadow of Tony Dorsett. . . . His 3,378 career passing yards rank fifth on Pittsburgh's all-time list. . . . He lettered from 1975-77 and finished seventh in the 1977 Heisman Trophy balloting.

Personal Data:

Born: October 27, 1956, at Youngstown, O.
High School: Chaney High in Youngstown.

HALFBACK: Tony Dorsett.

Dorsett won the 1976 Heisman Trophy after placing 11th in the 1973 balloting, 13th in 1974 and fourth in 1975. He is the only player in history to receive votes in four seasons. . . . Dorsett is the NCAA's all-time leading rusher with 6,082 yards. . . . He ranks fourth on the all-time career rushing charts with a 141.4-yard per game average. . . . Dorsett was the nation's leading rusher in 1976, averaging 177.1 yards per game. . . . He was a unanimous consensus All-America in 1976 and an honorable mention selection on The Sporting News' All-Time All-America team selected in 1983. . . . Dorsett set an NCAA record by gaining 100 yards or more 33 times in his career. . . . He rushed for 200 yards or more in 10 games, including a high of 303 yards against Notre Dame in 1975. . . . Dorsett was the first of only two players in NCAA Division I history to rush for more than 1,000 yards in four consecutive seasons. . . . He also ranks as the Division I-A career scoring leader among non-kickers with 356 points. . . . He lettered from 1973-76.

Personal Data:

Born: April 7, 1954, at Rochester, Pa.
High School: Hopewell High in Aliquippa, Pa.

MIDDLE GUARD: Al Romano.

Romano was a consensus All-America in 1976 and the team's defensive leader. . . . He was runner-up in the 1976 Outland Trophy balloting and ranks among the finest defensive linemen ever to play at Pitt. . . . Romano lettered from 1973-76.

Personal Data:

Born: April 4, 1954, at Solvay, N.Y.
High School: Solvay High School.

FINAL 1976 WIRE SERVICE RANKINGS

ASSOCIATED PRESS		UNITED PRESS	
1. **PITTSBURGH**	11. Alabama	1. **PITTSBURGH**	11. Maryland
2. Southern Cal	12. **Notre Dame**	2. Southern Cal	12. **Notre Dame**
3. Michigan	13. Texas Tech	3. Michigan	13. Texas Tech
4. Houston	14. Oklahoma State	4. Houston	14. Oklahoma State
5. Oklahoma	15. UCLA	5. Ohio State	15. UCLA
6. Ohio State	16. Colorado	6. Oklahoma	16. Colorado
7. Texas A&M	17. Rutgers	7. Nebraska	17. Rutgers
8. Maryland	18. Kentucky	8. Texas A&M	18. Iowa State
9. Nebraska	19. Iowa State	9. Alabama	19. Baylor
10. **Georgia**	20. Mississippi State	10. **Georgia**	Kentucky

Bold face indicates Pittsburgh opponent.

When You Wish Upon a Wishbone

Oklahoma, 1974-75
By Bill Connors

The 1974 Oklahoma Sooners were being feted in Oklahoma City while Lamar Hunt waited for Coach Barry Switzer's decision. Hunt, the Kansas City Chiefs' owner, had offered Switzer the coaching job with his National Football League club.

Just before the banquet festivities got under way that evening, Switzer decided to remain at Oklahoma. Why?

"Because," he said, "we have more Number 1 draft picks than the Chiefs."

Switzer, indeed, had inherited "what coaches would kill for." In 1970, four years after coming to Oklahoma as an assistant, he had installed a wishbone offense that would become legendary as it was played out by explosive backfields that high-stepped to greatness. Three years later, when Chuck Fairbanks departed to coach the New England Patriots, he was guiding the Sooners to their first unbeaten season since 1956 and the 1973 Big Eight Conference title.

In Switzer's words, "Walt Disney couldn't have written a better script" for what followed the next two seasons.

In 1974, the Sooners were 11-0 and, despite being on NCAA probation and banned from postseason bowls, voted national champions by the Associated Press. The following year, they survived a November loss to Kansas that ended their 37-game unbeaten streak and rebounded to claim a unanimous national championship by toppling Michigan in the Orange Bowl.

The cast was essentially the same each year. It featured a breathtaking halfback who soared in silver shoes; two brother giants who made a fortress of the defensive line; a quarterback who was a licensed Baptist minister; two split ends who scored often on rare receptions and a selfless supporting cast that upheld the heritage of Sooner football.

Switzer laughed with them, cried with them, encouraged them, scolded them and explained his success with a favorite line: "You gotta be lucky."

It didn't hurt having consensus All-America talent in offensive guard John Roush, defensive end Jimbo Elrod, linebacker Rod Shoate, running back Joe Washington and the brothers Selmon, defensive tackle Lee Roy and middle guard Dewey.

"I think Little Joe and Lee Roy and the other great players made better players out of those of us who had only average talent," quarterback Steve Davis said. "We had great people and it was a lot of fun to play for Switzer."

But perhaps no one made Saturday afternoons more of a picnic than Washington, a dazzling runner, crack blocker, good receiver and sensational quick-kicker. "Little Joe was the best player and best person I was ever around," fullback Jim Littrell said 13 years after lining up with Washington in the same backfield.

The feet inside Washington's silver shoes made moves that opponents could scarcely believe or describe, much less cope with. He ran much like a tornado bouncing through a mountain range—spinning sideways, hurtling blockers, bolting through holes and leaving behind piles of bodies. The Sporting News reported that, "Every time Washington gets the ball, there's an anticipation that something you have never seen previously is going to happen." Texas Coach Darrell Royal noted that Washington "might go through a keyhole."

Lee Roy Selmon simply ran through people with unbridled fury. "Lee Roy was the quickest and strongest person of his size (6-foot-2, 260 pounds) I've ever seen," defensive coordinator Larry Lacewell said. "It is lucky that he did not have a mean bone in his body and never got mad at anybody, or we would have been going to a lot of funerals."

Brother Dewey did have a mean streak, though he admitted he "would like to be known as a nice guy." He'll be remembered as one of the most devastating forces on a defense that blanketed opponents while the Sooner offense rolled up the score.

"I felt blessed to be on such a great team," Washington remembered. "I go around bragging to everybody about how many great players we had on those teams. But I think we might have been better in '73."

The Sooners had finished 10-0-1 that season, won the Big Eight title and wound up ranked No. 2 in the nation by United Press International, No. 3 by AP. Heading into 1974, Switzer, The Sporting News' Coach of the Year in '73, didn't expect as much.

"Our 1974 team cannot possibly be as good as last year's Big Eight champions because of the experienced starters we lost from the best defensive team in the country," he said.

"Seven defensive starters graduated. Almost our entire secondary, with the exception of Randy Hughes, is gone. All of our ends except Jim Elrod won't be back. And, of course, our Number 1 loss was Lucious Selmon, one of the best down linemen to ever play here."

The Sooners were, however, bringing back the same elusive backfield and two talented split ends, juniors Tinker Owens and Billy Brooks. Perhaps most important, they lost only one starter off their massive offensive line.

"We had such a great defense and so many great backs that I don't think our offensive linemen got the credit they deserved," Washington said. "They did not have great talent but those suckers blocked. They would hustle downfield. (Tackle) Jerry Arnold was the best at this I ever played with. Every time I had a long run I would see Number 74 down there taking somebody out."

With Arnold and Co. as his earthly protectors, Davis certainly feared no evil. "Our success in '73

Oklahoma Coach Barry Switzer (right) and Nebraska Coach Tom Osborne get together for a brief chat prior to the 1974 battle in Lincoln.

gave us great confidence in '74," said the quarterback who would compile a 32-1-1 record as a starter. "It was not arrogance, but we never considered the possibility of losing. We did not have many close games in '74."

The opener with Baylor was closer than anyone expected and cost the Sooners in the AP rankings (UPI did not rank teams on probation in 1974). The Bears, who would shock the Southwest Conference by winning their first league title since 1924, were decisively outgained but remained in contention until the fourth quarter, when the Sooners' 21-point outburst pushed them to victory, 28-11.

"Oklahoma was ranked Number 1 in the preseason for the first time (since 1957) and the next week they dropped us," Roush said. "We didn't get back to Number 1 until the Missouri game (in Week 8)."

The Sooners' only other scare through the first nine weeks came against archrival Texas, who had been humiliated, 52-13, by Oklahoma in 1973. Royal had the Longhorns primed for a fanatical effort and they led, 13-7, in the fourth quarter when Brooks brought the Sooners back on a 40-yard reverse that Switzer did not want to use.

"When I heard Galen (offensive coordinator Galen Hall) call the reverse, I didn't think it was the right spot and I started to tell him to call another play," Switzer said. "For some reason, I didn't say anything. The next thing I knew, Billy Brooks was in the open field and we won, 16-13. Sometimes, even when you have the best players, you gotta be lucky."

Lady Luck was elsewhere when the Sooners' missed the extra point after Brooks' score and Texas subsequently moved the ball to midfield. On fourth-and-one, Earl Campbell plunged for an apparent first down, but Elrod blindsided the star back, forcing a fumble that set up a game-winning 37-yard field goal by Tony DiRienzo.

A week later, Washington rushed for a career-high 211 yards against Colorado, which made the 49-14 laugher especially fulfilling.

"The only game besides Kansas we lost in my four years at Oklahoma was at Colorado when I was a freshman (in 1972)," Washington said. "That was the first time I wore the silver shoes. In '74, the Colorado coach (Bill Mallory) said Oklahoma was undisciplined and he could not imagine a coach letting one of his players wear silver shoes.

"Barry walked up to me that morning after reading that comment in the paper and said, 'Little Joe, you get me in more trouble.' So it was gratifying to me personally to have a good game against Colorado."

Each week, Washington applied a fresh coat of silver paint to the shoes and trimmed them in red. "Maybe I'm superstitious," he said, "but I always thought good shoes helped you perform better."

With the Sooners serving the final year of their two-year probation due to altering a player's transcript, the Nebraska game at Lincoln was "our bowl game," Switzer said.

Cornhuskers Coach Tom Osborne dug into his playbook of tricks and used an 11-yard throwback

The class of Oklahoma's blazing backfield in 1974 and '75 was fleet Joe Washington, the man with the silver shoes.

pass to quarterback David Humm for a touchdown that gave Nebraska a 14-7 lead early in the third quarter. When freshman Elvis Peacock fumbled the ensuing kickoff and the Huskers recovered inside Oklahoma's 20-yard line, Hughes said, "they were awful close to having us on the ropes."

But the Sooners held, Nebraska missed a field goal and Davis directed three long, clinical touchdown drives to spark a 28-14 victory.

"I don't know if we ever executed the wishbone any better than we did on those three drives," Switzer said. "Steve Davis was great."

Davis did not complete a pass but rushed for two touchdowns and 112 of the Sooners' 482 yards. He considered it "one of my better games. I remember on one of those drives we had third-and-16 and I rolled out to pass and had to run. I think I made 19 yards. It was maybe the best run I ever made."

Interestingly, Davis, whose best performances occurred in high-stakes games, selected a pregame incident at Iowa State as one of his most memorable moments. When the captains went to midfield for the coin toss, Davis said, "Several girls were out there and one of them pinched me in my private parts. She was beautiful, too."

The Nebraska game was a showcase for Hughes as well. At 6-4, 205 pounds, he dished out jarring tackles and was widely regarded as the best to ever play strong safety at Oklahoma. In three seasons, the speedy Hughes would intercept 14 passes, one shy of Darrell Royal's three-year school record, but he felt "very frustrated" as 1974 unfolded.

"Teams would not pass against us," he said. "When they tried, Lee Roy and Dewey mauled them. We didn't even have to blitz. I felt left out."

Nebraska's Humm, however, challenged Hughes and the big senior safety picked off two fourth-quarter passes to kill the Huskers' comeback hopes. "That," said Hughes, "was the highlight of my career."

In the season finale the next week, Hughes played an unfamiliar role, that of emotional catalyst, when Oklahoma State carried a 13-10 lead late into the third quarter. The Cowboys, bound for the Fiesta Bowl, had shut down the Sooner offense, which was in anticlimactic form.

Hughes rarely ever raised his voice but suddenly erupted at Roush and Arnold: "You guys better get off your ass and start playing!"

Davis looked up, thinking Hughes was dressing down the entire offense. "We deserved it," he said. "We were flat. Every other time we needed an emotional shot, it was Switzer who provided it. But Randy did it that day. It was so unlike him. But he got our attention and I credit him with getting us going."

It wasn't so much the one game that triggered Hughes' outburst, but frustration stemming from the previous three seasons. "Each of the first three years I was at OU, we had a chance to win the national championship and didn't. Nebraska won the big game in '71; Colorado upset us in '72 and we tied Southern Cal in '73.

"Now, after working so hard and getting to the last game of the season, it looked like Oklahoma State was going to knock us out of another championship. I guess it did shake everybody up. I remember Switzer looking at me like he couldn't believe I'd said it."

The Sooners responded by scoring 34 unanswered points to win, 44-13. After running back Grant Burget's four-yard run and Davis' one-yard sneak gave Oklahoma a 23-13 lead, Washington demoralized the Cowboys with an unbelievable 57-yard punt return for a touchdown. Eight tacklers had Washington trapped near the sideline at midfield, completely blocking him from view. Suddenly, he burst out of the maze of bodies and into the clear for a touchdown. "It was an unbelievable play, even for Little Joe," Littrell said.

Explained Lacewell: "Oklahoma State didn't have any experience in trying to tackle a ghost."

Following the bowl games, UPI crowned once-beaten, once-tied Southern Cal as its national champion while AP selected the 11-0 Sooners. At the Hula Bowl, Roush said, Trojans Coach John McKay, Switzer and their respective senior all-stars were discussing the split championship.

"McKay said USC was not going to give rings because everybody knew Oklahoma was the true national champion," Roush said. "I looked at him and thought, 'You don't believe that.' But, boy, I believed it."

Ironically, a bitter recruiting experience indirectly helped the Sooners win a share of the national championship. Ike Forte, a gifted junior-college halfback, had pledged to attend Oklahoma but wound up at Arkansas, Switzer's alma mater. Switzer was furious. But in the Razorbacks' 1974 opener, Forte scored a touchdown that helped defeat USC, 22-7. Had Forte attended Oklahoma, the Trojans may have flirted with a perfect season and claimed AP's top spot, as well.

"You gotta be lucky," Switzer said.

The rankings were of little concern to linebacker Gary Gibbs, a senior starting for the first time. "I was so awed by Rod and the Selmons and Randy that all I could think about was not to embarrass myself," said Gibbs, who became the Sooners' defensive coordinator in 1981.

Oklahoma ranked sixth in the nation in total defense and fifth in scoring defense, helping the Sooners outscore their opponents by a 43-8 average. Shoate received consensus All-America honors for the second consecutive year and led the team in tackles, most of which were audible far across the field. "We ain't had anybody who busts 'em like he does," Lacewell said.

The Sooners claimed almost half the spots on the all-conference defensive team with Shoate, Hughes, Elrod and both Selmons receiving recognition. Six players also received offensive honors: All-Americas Roush and Washington (who finished third in the Heisman voting), tight end Wayne Hoffman, guard Terry Webb, Arnold and Owens.

Davis showed he was the ideal wishbone quarterback—fast, strong and flexible—by passing for 11 touchdowns (on only 26 completions) and rushing for 659 yards. Overall, Oklahoma's receiving corps—Owens, Brooks, Hoffman and Washington—recorded 13 touchdowns on 33 receptions. Switzer had described Davis as "not a great athlete but ideal for this team. He's got fullback legs, halfback speed and quarterback mentality."

Indeed, he was the unfaltering leader of an offense that topped the country in rushing, scoring and total offense. Led by Washington's career-high 1,321 yards rushing, the Sooners rolled up just under 439 yards rushing per game, second in NCAA history only to the '71 Sooners' 472-yard average. Littrell, who became a starter when Waymon Clark (a 1,000-yard rusher in '73) was dismissed for disciplinary reasons, piled up 837 yards behind Washington.

The off-season that followed was a heady one for Oklahoma. The players were honored and toasted as if astronauts home from the moon. No one was more in demand than Davis.

The handsome, charismatic quarterback/minister was eyed by both political parties as a future governor or senator. Others regarded him as the next Billy Graham. That summer, Davis leased an airplane to fly to preaching engagements around the country. "I just see the good that results in it for all of the young people," he said.

When practices began, Davis and Washington were excused from most contact drills and scrimmages. They don't believe they got soft, but when the Sooners opened defense of their championship (ranked No. 1 by AP and UPI), the two seniors were symbolic of a ragged, erratic team that played to its potential only when it sensed a challenge.

Washington's rushing yardage fell by almost 500 yards. Davis passed for only one touchdown and rushed for a career-low 512 yards, looking as though he spent all of his preparation time in the pulpit. Not so, he maintained.

"I never worked harder for a season than I did before my senior year," he said. "I wanted to have my best year. We were not complacent. We were off probation and the chance to go to the Orange Bowl was almost as big an incentive as winning the national championship again.

"But I put a lot of pressure on myself and made some terrible mistakes and had a humiliating season. I sensed from the coaches that they really wanted to get Joe the ball so he could win the Heisman. I did, too. We all wanted Joe to win it.

"In my effort to get him the ball, I made mistakes in judgment. I forced things, which is not the wishbone style, and I fumbled a lot. I knew I was not playing well and the longer it went, the worse I felt. I got to where I was scared to go out there. But I assure you, it was not from getting soft or complacent."

Washington agreed. "I practiced the same way before the '75 season that I practiced before '74," he said. "I never did take much contact. I think it helped me.

"But I did get frustrated. I had some little injuries and didn't play much in some of those early blowouts. I realized by then I could win the Heisman and it bothered me that I wasn't getting the yards, even in the close games—and we had some."

Once again, Switzer had sounded a cautious note. "We should have a good football team but we won't be as good as we were last season," he said.

"Rod Shoate is gone at linebacker and Hughes graduated, too. You just don't go out and replace two super players like that. We may never replace

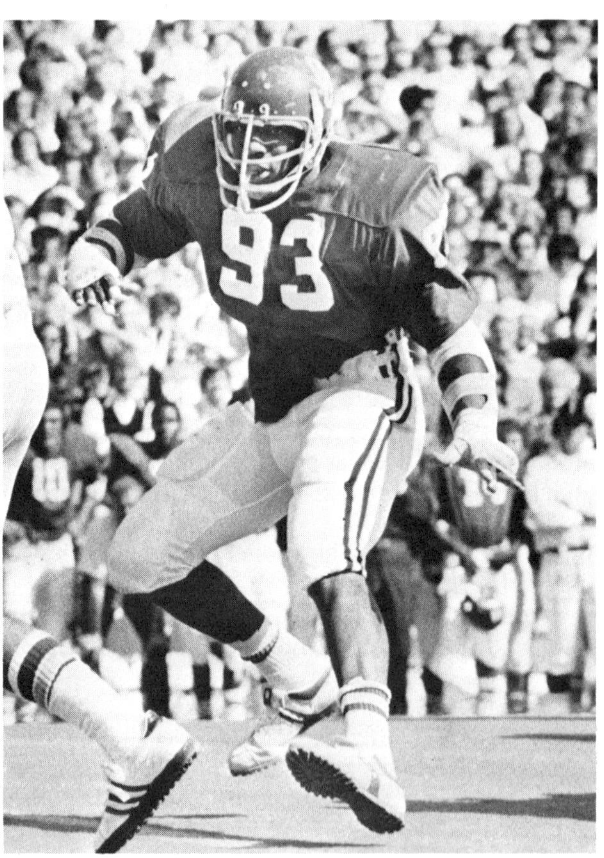

Any team that dared test the inside of Oklahoma's defense had to deal with the massive and powerful Lee Roy Selmon.

them."

Switzer also was worried about losing cornerback Tony Peters, defensive end Ron Waters, Gibbs, Hoffman and the left side of his offensive line.

"Every team on our schedule scares me," he said. "We had to come from behind to beat Texas, Nebraska and Oklahoma State last year and we had some close games with some other folks. . . ."

In 1975, the Sooners barely held off unsuspecting Miami (Fla.), 20-17, when the defense set up two touchdowns in a 20-point second quarter then held off a furious Hurricane rally in the fourth period. They escaped with a 21-20 victory in the Big Eight opener against Colorado when the Buffaloes' kicker missed an extra-point attempt with 1:23 remaining. When the Sooners ran out the clock, they were booed.

"But we played great in the big games," Davis said.

In the second game, Washington outgained Tony Dorsett, 166 yards to 17, in a 46-10 rout of Pittsburgh. Strong safety Scott Hill leaped over a Pitt blocker and knocked Dorsett out of the game with a tackle that Sooners assistant Warren Harper said "turned Dorsett to rubber." The tackle is legendary at Oklahoma, and Dorsett once asked a former coach, "Whatever happened to that guy who came out of the sky to tackle me?"

As if Lee Roy wasn't enough, brother Dewey handled Oklahoma's middle-guard duties and made life miserable for opposing ballcarriers.

After the game, Dorsett said, "Joe Washington gets my vote for the Heisman and Oklahoma is the greatest team I ever saw."

Besides a 24-17 victory over Texas, the six weeks following the Pitt massacre were unimpressive. Fullback Horace Ivory ran 33 yards for a tie-breaking touchdown against the Longhorns late in the fourth quarter, and Washington bailed the Sooners out of a final hole with a 76-yard quick-kick. Texas had entered the game leading the nation in rushing, total offense and scoring but was held to 212 yards rushing, 183 below its average.

Otherwise, the raggedness continued. Against Iowa State, the Sooners set a school record with 13 fumbles, which wasn't exactly out of character considering their 58 fumbles for the season, another mark. The telltale signs were there.

Finally, on November 8, Kansas shocked the Sooners, 23-3, at Norman, to snap their winning streak at 28 games and unbeaten string at 37. It was Switzer's first loss after 29 wins and a tie. "It ain't much fun," he remarked.

The Sooners had opened the scoring on a 52-yard field goal by DeRienzo, who then missed opportunities on the next two possessions, one of which was blocked. Thereafter, the Sooners committed turnovers on eight consecutive possessions and were booed for most of the second half.

"Once in the huddle," Davis recalled, "somebody asked, 'Who are they booing?' and Terry Webb said, 'It's sure not Kansas.' They really booed us when the game ended. I felt devastated. I was involved in seven turnovers and I felt the booing was directed at me."

Curiously, Davis thought the loss "was the best thing that could have happened to us. If we had beaten Kansas, I think we would have lost to both Missouri and Nebraska. The Kansas loss eliminated the pressure. Suddenly, the things that bothered me were gone.

"I learned more about myself after that game than I did in all the victories. I also saw a more caring side by the coaches than I had ever seen before. When the game was over, Joe and I were crying and Coach Switzer had an arm around each one of us. He said, 'You guys are helluva players and I am proud of you.' "

With the Sooners written off as potential national champions—by the media, that is—Davis played "the best half of my life" the next week at Missouri, rushing for 97 yards as he led Oklahoma to a 20-0 halftime lead.

Now, however, it was the defense that would show it wasn't infallible. It had carried Oklahoma all season, overcoming the offense's many fumbles to hold time and again. Elrod, an ex-wrestler who roared about the field like an uncaged animal, emerged as one of three consensus All-Americas on the front line, along with the Selmons. The backfield had been outstanding with Zac Henderson, an all-conference pick, and Jerry Anderson, a junior-college transfer who earned a reputation as a knockout hitter.

But on a day when there were no fumbles to overcome, the defense could not stop Missouri in the second half. Quarterback Steve Pisarkiewicz guided the Tigers to four unanswered touchdowns and a 27-20 lead. And with just over four minutes remaining, the Sooners faced a fourth-and-one predicament at their own 29-yard line.

Missouri, expecting Davis to sneak or give to the fullback for an inside play, replaced standout safety Kenny Downing with a lineman. Davis, however, pitched to Washington, who cut around Missouri's left flank and burst into a secondary whose fastest operative was now on the sideline, helplessly watching the 71-yard touchdown run. Washington ran to the same side on the two-point conversion, barely diving over the goal line for a 28-27 lead. With 1:02 remaining, Missouri missed a field goal and the Sooners were set for a showdown with unbeaten Nebraska the next Saturday.

Asked why the Sooners ran a high-risk play on fourth down, Switzer said, "It's not high-risk when you give the football to the best back in America."

"That was the most gratifying play of my career," Washington said. "By then, the Heisman and everything were gone. It was great to make a play like that in such a critical situation."

Against Nebraska, the defense righted itself by causing six turnovers and the Sooners erupted for 21 points in the fourth quarter to win a share of the Big Eight title and a trip to the Orange Bowl to play fifth-ranked Michigan.

Defensive end Jimbo Elrod roamed the football field like a predator on the hunt.

"Before the game," Davis remembered, "when the seniors were being introduced for our last home game and our first time on the field since the Kansas loss and the booing, I thought, 'We are going to win this one for ourselves.'

"It was a very satisfying game for me. I just wish we had played all year like we played after the Kansas loss. We stopped trying to force things and did whatever the defense gave us. If we had done that all year, I think Joe would have won the Heisman."

The Sooners moved up to third in the final regular-season polls as they prepared for Michigan, one of the nation's top rushing teams with Rob Lytle and Gordon Bell, both 1,000-yard runners.

"I don't remember anybody saying anything about us still having a shot at the national championship until that night," Davis said. "We just looked at the Orange Bowl as a reward that was overdue. It was the first bowl for most of us. We were ready for the beach."

What they got was more like Parris Island as Switzer broke character and became a taskmaster. He dismissed Ivory, the second-leading rusher, before the team left Norman because of a dormitory incident. He tongue-lashed the players upon their arrival in Miami for their conduct on the plane. He stunned his aides by ordering a scrimmage on the first day of practice.

"The German was mad and it was just what we needed," Davis said. "But it was scary. It was the first time the Number 1 offense had ever gone against the Number 1 defense. No one was excused. I had to run at Jimbo Elrod and Little Joe was tackled by Lee Roy on the first play. Now that's scary."

Switzer, though, was open as usual with the press. Michigan writers were surprised when they were permitted to watch the Sooners practice. Explaining his policy, Switzer said, "Nobody knows more about the Selmons than we do and we can't block them, either." Lee Roy had capped a remarkable senior year by winning the Lombardi Award as the outstanding college lineman and the Outland Trophy as the outstanding interior lineman.

As Oklahoma went through its pregame warm-ups, news arrived that UCLA had upset top-ranked Ohio State in the Rose Bowl.

"I gave the pregame prayer in the Orange Bowl," Davis said, "and the public address announcer, who could not hear me, announced Ohio State had lost. The crowd went wild. I am praying and everybody is yelling. When I went back to the dressing room, Galen Hall said, 'Steve, this game just got a lot more important.' "

Michigan's defense realized that, too. "They

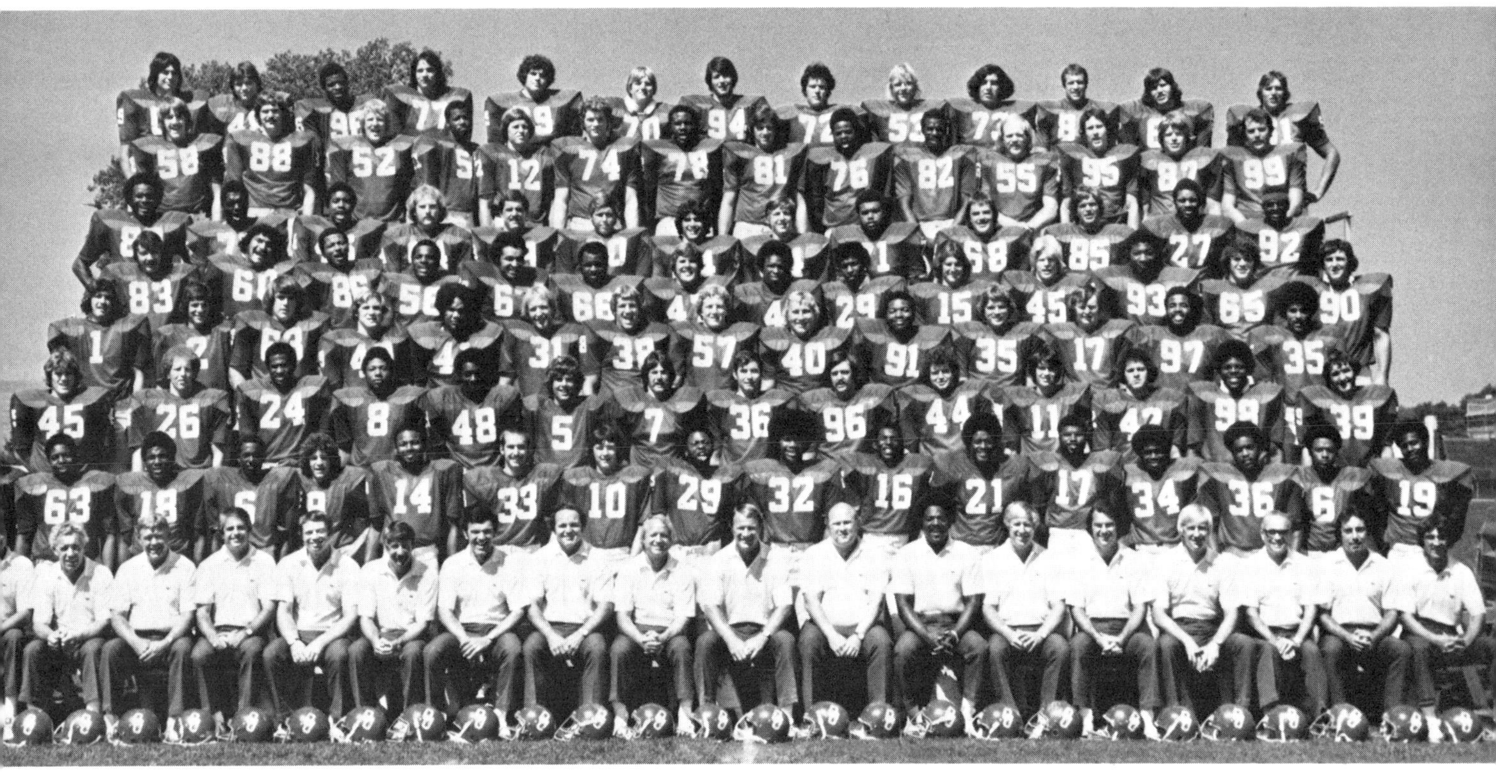

The 1975 Sooners: Front row (left to right)—Coaches Bill Shimek, Bob Proctor, Jack Baer, Don Jimerson, Steve Barrett, Warren Harper, Jerry Pettibone, Rex Norris, Larry Lacewell; Head Coach Barry Switzer; Coaches Galen Hall, Wendell Mosley, Don Duncan, Jim Helms, Gene Hochevar, Ken Rawlinson, Gerald O'Dell, Mike Shanahan. Second row—Larry Briggs, Tyrone Armstrong, Ed Williams, Terry Williams, Lee Hover, Kerry Jackson, Jerry Shirk, Jimbo Owens, Richard McCampbell, Horace Ivory, Terry Peters, Sidney Brown, Jerry Anderson, Jimmy Rogers, Jeff Brown, Louis Patmon, Vickey Ray Anderson. Third row—Steve Kunkle, Frank Rohr, Joe Washington, Myron Shoate, Tyrrell Jackson, Steve Davis, Scott Hill, Jerry Foster, Mike Mitchell, Ted Phillips, Tinker Owens, Jim Littrell, George Walrond, Steve Larghe. Fourth row—Zac Henderson, Dean Blevins, Jay Holman, Danny McCullough, Jim Culbreath, Eric Van Camp, Jamie Thomas, Obie Moore, Bill Dalke, Dewey Selmon, Roger Owens, Ken Crosswhite, Ken Franklin, John Bunch. Fifth row—Linc Thomas, Jaime Melendez, Reggie Mathis, Glen Comeaux, Don Morton, Terry Webb, George Davis, Elvis Peacock, Mike Pleasant, Mike Birks, Doug Simcik, Lee Roy Selmon, Larry Duke, Jody Farthing. Sixth row—Mike Phillips, Chez Evans, Calvin Harris, Gary Bishop, Marty Brecht, Lonnie Wright, Jimbo Elrod, Reed Coody, Anthony Bryant, Phil Applegate, Gary Potters, Jerry Reese, Victor Brown. Seventh row—Jeff Bodin, Duane Baccus, Todd Dutton, Mike Spencer, Joe McReynolds, Brett Cargill, Leo Martin, Keith Thomas, Richard Murray, Billy Brooks, Dennis Buchanan, Marshall Cantrell, John Randolph, David Bentley. Eighth row—Ralph Kulbeth, Russ Williamson, Terry Sherman, David Hudgens, Mike Vaughan, Phil Roland, Joel Estes, Jim Dodds, Rusty Griffis, Sam Claphan, Craig Lund, Karl Baldischwiler, Jeff Ward.

knocked Joe's helmet off on the first play and gave me a headache on the second play," Davis said.

Davis recovered, however, to put the Sooners ahead with two long plays that broke a scoreless tie in the second quarter. First, Owens made a spectacular catch of a pass for a 40-yard gain to the Michigan 39. "He might drop one pass a year," Hall would say, "and that will be in practice. And I'm not sure he's dropped one every year."

On the next play, Davis handed off to Brooks on a reverse and the fleet receiver streaked into the end zone for a touchdown. Davis ran 10 yards for a second score in the fourth quarter for all the points Oklahoma would need to win, 14-6. "Oklahoma is a great, great team with the best manpower we've ever played against," Michigan Coach Bo Schembechler said. "I will vote them Number 1."

The next day, the Sooners were atop the AP and UPI polls to claim the school's second pair of back-to-back national championships, having won under Bud Wilkinson in 1955 and 1956.

"Only a school with the tradition of Oklahoma could lose a game in November the way we did and still be national champion," Switzer said. He savored the moment and added:

"You gotta be lucky."

Oklahoma, 1974-75

ROAD TO GREATNESS

1974 RESULTS (11-0)

Opponent	Score	Opp. Record	Opp. Bowl Game
Baylor	28-11	8-4-0	Cotton (L)
Utah State	72-3	8-3-0	
Wake Forest	63-0	1-10-0	
*Texas	16-13	8-4-0	Gator (L)
at Colorado	49-14	5-6-0	
Kansas State	63-0	4-7-0	
at Iowa State	28-10	4-7-0	
Missouri	37-0	7-4-0	
at Kansas	45-14	4-7-0	
at Nebraska	28-14	9-3-0	Sugar (W)
Oklahoma State	44-13	7-5-0	Fiesta (W)

*Dallas.

1975 RESULTS (11-1)

Opponent	Score	Opp. Record	Opp. Bowl Game
Oregon	62-7	3-8-0	
Pittsburgh	46-10	8-4-0	Sun (W)
at Miami (Fla.)	20-17	2-8-0	
Colorado	21-20	9-3-0	Bluebonnet (L)
*Texas	24-17	10-2-0	Bluebonnet (W)
at Kansas State	25-3	3-8-0	
Iowa State	39-7	4-7-0	
at Oklahoma State	27-7	7-4-0	
Kansas	3-23	7-5-0	Sun (L)
at Missouri	28-27	6-5-0	
Nebraska	35-10	10-2-0	Fiesta (L)
ORANGE BOWL			
Michigan	**14-6**	**8-2-2**	

*Dallas.

FACTS AND FIGURES

The Sooners faced stiff competition in 1974 and '75, with 14 of their 23 opponents posting winning records.... In 1974, Oklahoma's opponents had a combined record of 65-60, a .520 winning percentage; in '75, they were 77-58-2, a .570 winning percentage.... The Sooners were 8-1 against regular-season opponents who played in bowl games.... Oklahoma scored more than 40 points eight times over both seasons and won 16 times by at least two touchdowns.... The Sooner offense was overwhelming in 1974, leading the nation in scoring (43 points per game), total offense (507.7 yards per game) and rushing (438.8 yards —second only to the '71 Sooners' 472.4-yard average, an NCAA record).... Defensively, the Sooners ranked sixth in total defense and fifth in scoring defense in 1974.

STATISTICAL LEADERS

PASSING

	Att.	Comp.	Yards	TD	Pct.	Int.
Steve Davis (1974)	63	26	601	11	41.3	4
Steve Davis (1975)	56	19	438	1	33.9	7

RUSHING

	Att.	Yards	Avg.	TD	Long
Joe Washington (1974)	194	1321	6.8	12	65
Joe Washington (1975)	171	871	5.1	11	71
Jim Littrell (1974)	124	837	6.8	1	45
Steve Davis (1974)	165	659	4.0	9	33
Horace Ivory (1975)	102	649	6.4	5	35
Steve Davis (1975)	171	512	3.0	6	33
Clyde Russell (1974)	53	480	9.1	3	70

RECEIVING

	Rec.	Yards	Avg.	TD	Long
Tinker Owens (1975)	9	241	26.8	1	43
Tinker Owens (1974)	18	413	22.9	5	43
Billy Brooks (1974)	7	176	25.1	3	72
Billy Brooks (1975)	5	114	22.8	0	54
Wayne Hoffman (1974)	6	98	16.3	4	30

SCORING

	TD	FG	PAT	Points
Joe Washington (1974)	14	0	0	84
Joe Washington (1975)	12	0	*1	74
Tony DiRienzo (1975)	0	13	33	72
Tony DiRienzo (1974)	0	6	39	57
Steve Davis (1974)	9	0	0	54

*Two-point conversion.

KEY CHARACTERS

The Conductor

COACH: Barry Switzer.

***Record:** 148-26-4, 15 years at Oklahoma.

Switzer has successfully followed in the footsteps of Oklahoma coaching greats Bud Wilkinson and Chuck Fairbanks.... His teams have won three Associated Press national championships, including back-to-back titles in 1974 and '75, and United Press International crowns in 1975 and '85.... Switzer coached the Sooners to 29 victories and one tie before suffering his first coaching loss.... The Sooners were 32-1-1 during Switzer's first three seasons, losing only to Kansas, 23-3, in 1975.... In 1973, his first campaign, Switzer was chosen The Sporting News' Coach of the Year.... The Sooners have dominated under Switzer, winning 10 or more games 10 times and eight of 12 bowl contests.... Only once has a Switzer-coached Oklahoma team won fewer than eight games (7-4-1 in 1981).... Switzer ranks as the winningest active Division 1-A coach with an .843 winning percentage.... He is a superb recruiter and surrounds himself with an excellent coaching staff.... He has coached at least one consensus All-America in each of his 15 campaigns.... Switzer was a center and linebacker at Arkansas and captain of the Razorbacks' 1959 Southwest Conference champion.... He served as an assistant at Arkansas and Oklahoma for 11 years.

Personal Data:

Born: October 5, 1937, in Crossett, Ark.
High School: Crossett High.
College: Arkansas.

*Indicates totals through 1987 season.

The Supporting Cast

QUARTERBACK: Steve Davis.

Davis tasted defeat at Oklahoma only once, finishing his Sooner career with a 32-1-1 mark.... He was a master of the wishbone offense and spiced his statistics with 21 career touchdown passes.... His 1,821 yards total offense in 1973 rank second in the Sooner record book, and he ranks fourth on the Sooners' all-time passing and total offense charts.... Davis lettered from 1973-75 and fancied a 6-0 record against archrivals Nebraska and Texas.

Personal Data:

High School: Sallisaw, Okla.

DEFENSIVE TACKLE: Lee Roy Selmon.

Selmon is one of seven players to win the Outland Trophy and Lombardi Award in the same season (1975).... He finished ninth in the 1975 Heisman Trophy balloting and was a unanimous consensus All-America in '75.... He teamed with brother Dewey on Oklahoma's defensive line and is considered one of the best ever to play his position.

Personal Data:

Born: October 20, 1954, at Eufaula, Okla.
High School: Eufaula High.

HALFBACK: Joe Washington.

Washington is one of the most exciting players in Oklahoma history and the school's all-time leading rusher with 3,995 yards.... A 1974 unanimous consensus All-America, Washington finished third and fifth, respectively, in the 1974 and '75 Heisman Trophy balloting.... He ranks third in career total offense at Oklahoma with 4,035 yards.... A dynamic kick returner, Washington also holds the single-season record for punting average (50.2 yards on 10 kicks in 1975).... He lettered from 1973-75.

Personal Data:

Born: September 24, 1953, at Crockett, Tex.
High School: Lincoln High in Port Arthur, Tex.

FINAL 1974 WIRE SERVICE RANKINGS

ASSOCIATED PRESS		UNITED PRESS	
1. **OKLAHOMA**	11. N.C. State	1. Southern Cal	11. Houston
2. Southern Cal	12. Michigan State	2. Alabama	12. Florida
3. Michigan	13. Maryland	3. Ohio State	13. Maryland
4. Ohio State	14. **Baylor**	4. Notre Dame	14. **Baylor**
5. Alabama	15. Florida	5. Michigan	15. Texas A&M Tennessee
6. Notre Dame	16. Texas A&M	6. Auburn	
7. Penn State	17. Mississippi State **Texas**	7. Penn State	17. Mississippi State
8. Auburn		8. **Nebraska**	18. Michigan State
9. **Nebraska**	19. Houston	9. N.C. State	19. Tulsa
10. Miami (Ohio)	20. Tennessee	10. Miami (Ohio)	

NOTE: Oklahoma omitted because of NCAA probation.

FINAL 1975 WIRE SERVICE RANKINGS

ASSOCIATED PRESS		UNITED PRESS	
1. **OKLAHOMA**	11. Texas A&M	1. **OKLAHOMA**	11. Maryland
2. Arizona State	12. Miami (Ohio)	2. Arizona State	12. Texas A&M
3. Alabama	13. Maryland	3. Alabama	13. Arizona **Pittsburgh**
4. Ohio State	14. California	4. Ohio State	
5. UCLA	15. **Pittsburgh**	5. UCLA	15. California
6. **Texas**	16. **Colorado**	6. Arkansas	16. Miami (Ohio)
7. Arkansas	17. Southern Cal	7. **Texas**	17. Notre Dame West Virginia
8. **Michigan**	18. Arizona	8. **Michigan**	
9. **Nebraska**	19. Georgia	9. **Nebraska**	19. Georgia Southern Cal
10. Penn State	20. West Virginia	10. Penn State	

Bold face indicates Oklahoma opponent.

Biggie Munn's Little Big Men

Michigan State, 1952
By Jack Ebling

It wasn't their size but their technique and toughness that ultimately mattered. True, "Biggie" was boss, and it was his little big men at Michigan State who dominated college football in the early 1950s.

From 1950 through 1953, the small-but-stubborn Spartans won 28 consecutive games, capping the school's most successful era with an 8-1 1953 season and a Rose Bowl victory over UCLA in their first official year of Big Ten Conference play. It was in 1952, however, that Clarence (Biggie) Munn's undefeated forces skyrocketed to national prominence by claiming their first-ever national championship.

"One of the top 25 teams? An excellent choice!" said halfback Don McAuliffe, captain of the 1952 Spartans. "The only thing we lacked was ability."

What the '52 Spartans didn't have were eight offensive and three defensive starters from the 1951 squad that was undefeated and ranked second nationally in the final polls. Gone were quarterback Al Dorow, top receiver Bob Carey and tackle Don Coleman, who all received All-America recognition. No problem.

"The greatest thing we had going for us wasn't our talent," insisted Frank Kush, the mayhem-minded middle guard on defense. "It was togetherness and poise. We never pushed the panic button."

Aside from a few gifted athletes—Kush, McAuliffe and linebacker Dick Tamburo were All-America selections on numerous teams—Munn's Spartans were basically a blue-collar bunch with unmatched tactics and toughness.

On offense, Michigan State baffled opponents with probably the most complex system in football, a multiple offense that boasted innumerable variations of the wing- and T-formations. The state-of-the-art attack was Munn's brainchild, but he still remained committed to the fundamentals.

"After 30 years of football as a player and coach," he said in 1952, "I've learned it is a simple game. There are only two things to it: blocking and tackling. . . ."

But he wasn't averse to psychological motivation.

"Biggie always had a gimmick," Tamburo said. "Before one game, he pulled a lit torch out from behind his back and screamed, 'Men, you've got to catch fire!'

"Another time, he gave us all little pocket mirrors and said, 'You can fool me and you can fool Duffy (Daugherty, his assistant). But remember, you can't fool the man in the mirror.' "

An All-America guard at Minnesota in 1931, Munn had developed great lines as an assistant at Michigan prior to taking over as coach at Michigan State in 1947. He was a disciplinarian who lived by a motto that was displayed prominently in his office: "The difference between good and great is just a little extra effort."

"By '52, we'd already heard Biggie for three years," said middle linebacker and team humorist Doug Weaver. "There was kind of a love-hate relationship, but we all respected him. We were always superbly prepared."

"As a technical coach, Biggie was really superior," Kush said. "His multiple offense was as diversified and sophisticated as you'd ever find."

The defense was a simple-but-devastating 5-3-3 alignment, one that worked because its players always did. "Teams couldn't make the length of their noses against us," Weaver said. "The big thing to me was that everyone really liked each other. That, and our overall toughness."

No one was tougher than Kush and Tamburo, though ends Ed Luke, Don Dohoney and Bill Quinlan were hardly timid.

Clarence (Biggie) Munn, a disciplinarian, motivator and superior tactician, lifted Michigan State's football program into the national spotlight.

"We had some damn tough guys, I'll tell you that," Kush said. "Don Dahoney was a tough SOB. And Quinlan would just kick the hell out of you."

Indeed, they were Kush's kind of guys. "Kush would knock your ass off," Weaver said of the 180-pound whirlwind. "I think he had a fight every practice. Me, I just wanted to jump off the pile with my back to the press box."

Weaver, appointed Michigan State's athletic director in 1980, did considerably more than that. He'd line up right behind Kush and finish the wreckage. He finished off Purdue in 1952 with a fourth-quarter interception to save a 14-7 victory—and some say he's still paying teammate Morley Murphy for jumping offside to nullify an interception by teammate John Wilson.

"Dale Samuels had driven Purdue to our 25," recalled Wilson, a cornerback and Rhodes scholar. "Finally, he throws one over the middle and I intercept it. I'm practically off the field when I see the flag on Morley.

"Now, (two plays later) darned if Doug doesn't intercept on a tackle-eligible. The headline was 'Hoosier Beats Boilermakers,' after Samuels had hit him right in the chest."

The Indiana native didn't dispute that. "Yeah, I intercepted at the 8, and I must have run to the 8½," said Weaver, who actually snared the pass at the 4-yard line and returned it to the 18. "But, hey, Tamburo recovered three fumbles against Notre Dame and I say I caused all three."

The Spartans defeated the Fighting Irish, 21-3, in the eighth game of the season to virtually lock up the No. 1 spot in the United Press and Associated Press polls. That wouldn't have been possible if they hadn't escaped with two victories to open the season—a 27-13 come-from-behind win at Michigan and a 17-14 last-second decision at Oregon State.

McAuliffe came to the rescue in the opener, galloping 70 yards for a touchdown to touch off a 27-point rally that snuffed out Michigan's 13-0 lead.

"I know I'll never forget it," Kush said. "Both guards pulled and turned upfield, and Don made one of the greatest runs I've ever seen. It was probably the key play of the season."

"I ran mostly from fear," McAuliffe said. "It was about a three-mile run. But with the blocks I had from Gordie Serr and Doug Bobo, I could have scored if I'd had acute arthritis."

The Oregon State game was memorable for one of Munn's best halftime performances and Michigan State's only field goal of the season, a second-chance chip shot by Gene Lekenta following an off-side call against the Beavers. After the game, a photographer asked Munn if he'd pose, kissing Lekenta's foot. His reaction endures as one of loudest sounds ever heard in Portland.

"We almost got our butts beat," Kush remembered. "We'd snuck out and had a pretty good party. Bill Quinlan got in a tussle and I can still see Henry Bullough, smoking his cigars. Anyway, we were losing and we should have been kicking the hell out of them. Biggie said, 'Here, read your damn press clippings,' and threw them all on the floor. Finally, one guy did and was Biggie furious."

Halfback Don McAuliffe was captain of the 1952 Spartans and a major reason for the team's successful championship run.

McAuliffe relishes the memory. "Everyone was terrified of Biggie, but Ray Vogt picked up the clippings and started reading," he explained. "He was kind of a loose goose and he said, 'Hey, they spelled

Michigan State defensive standouts Doug Weaver (left) and Frank Kush went on to big things, Weaver as Spartan athletic director and Kush as a successful coach at both the collegiate and professional levels.

my name right.' "

They spelled McAuliffe's name right, too, in reports that he was linked with hoods after being robbed at gunpoint of his teammates' Notre Dame tickets.

"Don said we had a chance to make $50 a ticket," Kush remembered. "In those days, we got two tickets for each year (of academic standing), so I figured my eight tickets (he was a senior) were worth $400. But when he got back, he said, 'Polack, they put a gun on me!' I said, 'Don't give me that shit! Just give me the money!'

"I still think he got half of it back somehow as a kickback."

"Ahh, Frank's mind is crumbling!" McAuliffe said. "They were offering $100 a ticket, and Kush said he'd cover for me with Biggie. I missed a meeting and Kush told him I had an exam.

"Anyway, it was a misty, rainy night and the guy said I had to come downtown to get the money. As soon as we hit the doorstep, he whips out a .32 stub on me. My father had been a Chicago cop in the Capone era, and I knew what that was.

"There I am, with $6 in my pocket and no more tickets. The hard part was telling Biggie. He just said not to say anything to anyone."

Munn seldom said anything to McAuliffe or any other player for conversation's sake. "We hardly spoke for a year and a half," said McAuliffe, a former Notre Dame and Navy man who came to Michigan State on the GI Bill. "I was a passer and I'd been taught how to release a ball by (Irish Coach) Frank Leahy. Biggie didn't like the way I did it and made me a halfback."

Said Tamburo: "I played in the (1953) East-West Shrine Game and Biggie was the head coach. Until then, on the flight out to California, I didn't think he knew I even had a first name."

Assistant coaches Daugherty, Earle Edwards, Steve Sebo, John Kobs, Don Mason and Dan Devine related to the players a bit better.

"I loved Duffy," said Tamburo, who would become athletic director at Texas Tech and Arizona State. "He recruited me, and I ate a lot of spaghetti dinners at his home. He really cared for you and made you relax."

"Duffy was like a father figure," Kush said. "Biggie was more of an overseer, but Duffy and Earle Edwards really blended us together."

McAuliffe concurred. "Cohesiveness was one of our keys," said the Spartans' captain. "I've always said it's the perfect mix—a couple of Polacks, a few

Michigan State quarterback Tom Yewcic (right) poses with teammate Evan Slonac, who gained 382 yards for the 1952 Spartans.

blacks, a Welshman or two and an Irishman to lead them!"

At times, McAuliffe's teammates weren't sure where they'd been led.

"He was a little older (he turned 25 during the season) and more mature than the rest of us," said Kush, a transfer from Washington & Lee. "Of course, he had a little less hair, too. At the end of one term he says, 'Let's have a party! It's on me!' Later, we found out he'd sold our books and we were really paying for it."

Michigan State paid dearly in 1952 for its fledg-

Quarterback Tom Yewcic, also a talented baseball player, was a member of the Detroit Tigers' organization for 10 years after leaving Michigan State. Billy Wells (right) was the '52 Spartans' leading rusher.

ling Big Ten status. Although a member of the conference since 1949, the Spartans had not yet played a full league schedule and were ineligible for Rose Bowl consideration. In 1950, they had been turned down by conference members for participation in any other bowl game.

"The other Big Ten teams weren't about to help the country bumpkins in any way," McAuliffe said.

That they already realized that may have eased the disappointment in 1952. "We'd beaten Penn State and Notre Dame, but I don't remember any gnashing of teeth that we couldn't go to a bowl game," Wilson said. "I think there was more frustration being undefeated our junior year and not winning the national championship."

"We'd lost a lot of great players," Weaver said. "We practically had to build a whole new offensive team, and that was one hell of a job."

But in the final year before a brief return to one-platoon football, the 1952 Spartans accomplished all the schedule allowed. Their third straight victory over both Michigan and Notre Dame (the first time anyone had beaten Leahy's Irish three times running) erased part of the school's "hayseed" image and left little doubt about its football ability. Texas A&M, Syracuse, Penn State, Indiana and Marquette were flattened and outscored, 233-47.

For the season, Michigan State outscored its opponents, 312-84, and never surrendered more than 14 points in a game. The Spartans ranked third nationally in total offense and had the No. 1 defense against the run, testament to Munn's teaching the blocking and tackling fundamentals.

Another trademark was depth. Billy Wells, star of the "Pony Backfield" in 1953, led the team with 585 yards rushing, followed by McAuliffe (531), LeRoy Bolden (414) and Evan Slonac (382). Only McAuliffe weighed more than 175 pounds.

Quarterback Tom Yewcic, property of the Detroit Tigers' organization from 1954 through 1963 (and a veteran of one major league at-bat, in 1957) passed for 941 yards and 10 touchdowns. His wonderfully named backup, Willie Thrower (who was credited with being the first black quarterback in National Football League history for his October 18, 1953, appearance with the Chicago Bears), totaled 400 yards and five touchdowns. And they did it behind a reconstructed line whose biggest man,

The 1952 Spartans: Front row (left to right)—Frank Kush, Ed Timmerman, Doug Bobo, Ray Vogt, Ed Luke, John Wilson, Doug Weaver, Head Coach Biggie Munn, Don McAuliffe, Wayne Benson, Paul Dekker, Leo Boyd, Joe Klein, Dick Panin, Jack Morgan. Second row—Bill Postula, Ferris Hallmark, Bert Zagers, Jim Ellis, Tom Saidock, Bob Edmiston, Don Schiesswohl, Howard Adams, Willie Thrower, Gordon Serr, Dick Tamburo, Vince Pisano, Chuck Frank, Don Dohoney, Larry Fowler. Third row—Al Fracassa, John Matsock, Phil Keller, Dale Knight, Ellis Duckett, John Paior, Gerald Luzader, Morley Murphy, LaVerne Kline, Ted Kepple, Jim Neal, Gene Lekenta, Fred Rody, Tom Yewcic, Bob Breniff, Dan Carroll, Dale Foltz, Charles Fairbanks, Don Cutler. Fourth row—Charles Gelal, Henry Bullough, LeRoy Bolden, Tom Baer, Bill Ross, Warren Spragg, Roland Dotsch, Gerald Musetti, Donald Kauth, Jack Edwards, Gene Molak, Randy Schrecengost, Evan Slonac, Billy Wells, Bernie Raterink, Alex Bleahu, Rex Corless, Harry Tamburo, Jim Jebb, Vic Postula. Fifth row—Coaches John Kobs, Earle Edwards, Steve Sebo.

center Jim Neal, weighed 215 pounds.

"We weren't large physically but our team's speed made up for it," said Munn, voted Coach of the Year by his fellow coaches. "Modern football is becoming more and more a game of mobility and so our speed stood us in good stead."

Years later, he still contended the '52 Spartans were "undoubtedly the strongest, deepest club we'd yet had at Michigan State."

It's tough to tell who led the Spartans in spunk, although Weaver, a transfer from Yale, might have been the banty rooster of the bunch. In Michigan State's 41-14 victory over Indiana, 10 players were ejected for fighting. Predictably, some would say, Weaver was one of two Spartans banished.

"Knowing Weaver, he was probably the damn instigator," Kush said.

"Actually," said the accused, "I stepped between two guys as peacemaker and really caught a good one. Of course, my macho instincts demanded that I answer. I got thrown out—and I think the other guy was still standing."

For every big play from Kush or McAuliffe, the Spartans received steady contributions from players such as safety Jim Ellis or linebacker Ed Timmerman. It was a different group in a different era, but just what Munn and his staff needed to mold a championship team.

"To be successful, you have to have talent, coaching and a favorable schedule," Weaver said. "We had all three, some luck with injuries and a hell of a program."

It was a program of comparative moderation, like the others of its time. College football in the early 1950s wasn't the full-time job it is today.

"Today, the three R's in football are recruiting, revenue and recognition," said Kush, who would coach in the college and professional ranks. "It wasn't that way back then. We didn't have daily meetings and all that crap."

"It was much saner then," said Wilson, who would become president of Washington & Lee. "We were all students. There wasn't nearly the pressure to bring in athletes with zero preparation in secondary education.

"Overall, our priorities were far better then. We had three-sport athletes, something you seldom see today. Bob Carey won nine letters and my brother, Pat, won six."

Virtually all the Spartans left with the most important letters: BA or BS. Many earned graduate degrees as well.

"I'm just very pleased the way so many of our players have contributed to society," Wilson said. "We've had a lot of guys become successful in sports and in business. The quality of our people has been proven out."

The quality of Michigan State's football team had been verified long before that, but only shortly after it had been perceived as an athletic pretender.

"We didn't have much exposure and I don't think we were really aware of just how good we were," Kush said. "But you know, we always had some pretty damn good times."

Michigan State, 1952

ROAD TO GREATNESS

1952 RESULTS (9-0)

Opponent	Score	Opp. Record	Opp. Bowl Game
at Michigan	27-13	5-4-0	
at Oregon State	17-14	2-7-0	
Texas A&M	48-6	3-6-1	
Syracuse	48-7	7-3-0	Orange Bowl (L)
Penn State	34-7	7-2-1	
at Purdue	14-7	4-3-2	
at Indiana	41-14	2-7-0	
Notre Dame	21-3	7-2-1	
Marquette	62-13	3-5-1	

FACTS AND FIGURES

Although not yet eligible for the Big Ten Conference title —and, in turn, a trip to Pasadena to play in the Rose Bowl—Michigan State rolled to the 1952 national championship behind a complex multiple offense that powered its way to more than 40 points four times and a savage defense that dished out mayhem. . . . Biggie Munn, voted Coach of the Year by his peers, led the Spartans to their second consecutive unbeaten season against a 1952 slate that featured three opponents that finished in the wire services' Top 20 rankings. . . . Five of Michigan State's nine foes posted winning records but fell to the Spartans by an average of 21.4 points. . . . The opposition posted a combined record of 40-39-6, a .506 winning percentage. . . . Michigan State pushed its victory string to 24 games. . . . The Spartans' defense was unyielding against the run, surrendering only 83.9 yards per game, tops in the nation. . . . Offensively, Michigan State attacked with a baffling array of formations, ranking second in the nation in scoring offense (34.7 points per game), third in total offense (428.7 yards) and fifth in rushing offense (272.4 yards). . . . Though they made their mark as a deep, powerful unit, the Spartans were shut out in the consensus All-America honor roll. . . . Several players, however, received first-team All-America honors on various squads: defensive guard Frank Kush, halfback Don McAuliffe, linebacker Dick Tamburo, split end Ellis Duckett, quarterback Tom Yewcic and halfback James Ellis. . . . End Paul Dekker, Kush and Tamburo were first-team selections on the 1952 United Press All-Midwest team, while McAuliffe and tackle Gordon Serr were second-team picks. . . . McAuliffe would finish eighth in the Heisman Trophy balloting behind winner Billy Vessels, the Oklahoma Sooners' halfback.

STATISTICAL LEADERS

PASSING

	Att.	Comp.	Yards	TD	Pct.	Int.
Tom Yewcic	95	41	941	10	43.2	5
Willie Thrower	49	29	400	5	59.2	3

RUSHING

	Att.	Yards	Avg.	TD	Long
Billy Wells	118	585	5.0	6	20
Don McAuliffe	98	531	5.4	7	70
LeRoy Bolden	53	414	7.8	7	43
Evan Slonac	75	382	5.1	3	26

RECEIVING

	Rec.	Yards	Avg.	TD	Long
Paul Dekker	13	171	13.2	1	39
Ellis Duckett	10	323	32.3	5	80
Doug Bobo	8	231	28.9	2	49
Don McAuliffe	8	194	24.3	2	61

SCORING

	TD	FG	PAT	Points
Evan Slonac	4	0	37	61
LeRoy Bolden	9	0	0	54
Don McAuliffe	9	0	0	54
Billy Wells	6	0	0	36
Ellis Duckett	5	0	0	30

KEY CHARACTERS

The Conductor

COACH: Clarence (Biggie) Munn.

Record: 54-9-2, 7 years at Michigan State.

Munn was a consensus All-America guard at Minnesota in 1931. . . . He served as an assistant at Minnesota, Syracuse and Michigan and as coach at Albright and Syracuse before taking over the Spartans' helm in 1947. . . . Munn lost his first game at Michigan State, 55-0, to archrival Michigan but closed his career in style, winning 36 of his final 38 games. . . . After losing his first three encounters with Michigan, Munn swept the final four contests. . . . He guided the Spartans to undefeated seasons in 1951 and 1952 and a school-record 28-game winning streak that stretched from the fourth game of the 1950 season through the fourth game of 1953. . . . Munn's Spartans finished among the top-three ranked teams from 1951 through 1953. . . . He practiced a motto displayed on the walls of his office: "The difference between good and great is just a little extra effort.". . . Among those who tutored under Munn were Forest Evashevski, Duffy Daugherty, Dan Devine and Bob Devaney. . . . Munn was active as Michigan State's athletic director from 1954 through 1971. . . . He is a member of the College Football Hall of Fame. . . . He died in 1975 at the age of 66.

Personal Data:

Born: September 9, 1908, in Minneapolis.
High School: North High in Minneapolis.
College: Minnesota.

The Supporting Cast

DEFENSIVE GUARD: Frank Kush.

Kush was Lombardi-tough as both a player and coach, offering no sympathy and expecting perfection. . . . He was a first-team All-America selection on six squads in 1952. . . . Kush coached at Arizona State from 1958-79, compiling a 176-54-1 record. . . . He led the Sun Devils to a 6-1 record in bowl games, including a 17-14 victory over Nebraska in the 1975 Fiesta Bowl that capped a 12-0 season. . . . Kush compiled an 11-28-1 record as coach of the Baltimore/Indianapolis Colts from 1982-84. . . . He also coached in the Canadian and United States football leagues. . . . Kush lettered from 1950-52.

Personal Data:

Born: January 20, 1929, in Windber, Pa.
High School: Windber High.

HALFBACK: Don McAuliffe.

McAuliffe received the 1952 Walter Camp Trophy as College Back of the Year. . . . He earned first-team All-America honors on five teams. . . . McAuliffe finished his career tied for the Spartans' lead in touchdowns with 20. . . He lettered from 1950-52.

Personal Data:

Born: October 13, 1927, in Chicago.
High School: Leo High in Chicago.

LINEBACKER: Dick Tamburo.

Tamburo was named the Spartans' most valuable player in 1952. . . . He received first-team All-America recognition on eight teams. . . . Duffy Daugherty said of Tamburo: "Tamburo is one of the roughest and smartest linebackers I've ever seen. But his most important asset is heart. Hence, the bigger and tougher the opposition, the bigger and tougher Tamburo is.". . . Tamburo served as associate athletic director at Fresno State, Kent State, Illinois and Missouri and as athletic director at Texas Tech and Arizona State. . . . Tamburo lettered from 1950-52.

Personal Data:

Born: February 6, 1930, in New Kensington, Pa.
High School: New Kensington High.

QUARTERBACK: Tom Yewcic.

Yewcic passed for more than 150 yards three times during the 1952 season, including a 202-yard effort against Texas A&M. . . . His career rushing-passing average of 6.6 yards per attempt ranks second only to Earl Morrall's 7.4-yard average in Michigan State history. . . . Yewcic's 18 career touchdown passes rank seventh in the Spartan record book. . . . Yewcic, also a star on the Spartans' baseball team, lettered from 1951-53.

Personal Data:

Born: May 9, 1932, in Conemaugh, Pa.
High School: Conemaugh High.

FINAL 1952 WIRE SERVICE RANKINGS

ASSOCIATED PRESS

1. **MICHIGAN STATE**	11. Wisconsin
2. Georgia Tech	12. Tulsa
3. **Notre Dame**	13. Maryland
4. Oklahoma	14. **Syracuse**
5. Southern Cal	15. Florida
6. UCLA	16. Duke
7. Mississippi	17. Ohio State
8. Tennessee	18. **Purdue**
9. Alabama	19. Princeton
10. Texas	20. Kentucky

UNITED PRESS

1. **MICHIGAN STATE**	11. Texas
2. Georgia Tech	12. **Purdue**
3. **Notre Dame**	13. Maryland
4. Oklahoma	14. Princeton
Southern Cal	15. Ohio State
6. UCLA	Pittsburgh
7. Mississippi	17. Navy
8. Tennessee	18. Duke
9. Alabama	19. Houston
10. Wisconsin	Kentucky

Bold face indicates Michigan State opponent.

Team UCLA Keeps the Faith

UCLA, 1954
By Tracy Dodds

UCLA Coach Red Sanders (second from right) and assistant Tommy Prothro (right) watch closely as their Bruins do battle in a 1954 game.

Ask Terry Debay, quarterback of the UCLA football team that finished the 1954 season atop the United Press poll, what made that group of Bruins so successful, so special, and Debay will quote neither a coach nor a teammate. Instead, he will refer the questioner to a passage in the gospel according to Matthew (21:22), wherein Jesus says: "And whatever you ask in prayer, you will receive, if you have faith."

The Bruins, Debay explains, had faith.

Eight of UCLA's 11 starters were active in the Campus Crusade for Christ. No one associated with the 1954 Bruins, UCLA's only national championship football team, fails to acknowledge the impact of the religious fervor.

And everyone on the team had faith in Coach Henry R. (Red) Sanders and the "outdated" single-wing offense he had installed when he took the UCLA job in 1949.

The Bruins also had faith in each other. Indeed, there was a feeling among the senior starters that this was to be their year.

"None of us on the team ever had a big, macho, 'We're No. 1!' kind of attitude," Debay said. "It was more like a feeling that we were a part of something good. That we were lucky to be where we were, doing what we were doing, being a part of it. It was Camelot, and one day it started unfolding."

Primo Villanueva, the tailback and, many would say, the standout player among those national champions, recalls: "It was a wonderful, special time in my life not because of the success on the gridiron, but because of the comradeship the players shared. We were such a close-knit group.

"It sounds like a cliche, but really, truly, we were a *team.* That was our strength. UCLA had had a star the year before in Paul Cameron. He was a big, strong back who could straight-arm a guy or do the side-stepping like a Red Grange. Not me. I was a little 160-pound kid who was running behind the real stars, our linemen. We really respected our linemen. They were held in very high esteem—and that started with Red.

"When we would break down the film, they were just pretty to watch. When two guards would pull out, shoulder to shoulder, in step like soldiers marching, it was a thing of beauty. Anybody could hold the ball and run with it behind those guys.

"One thing Red Sanders couldn't stand was a team with one star standing out. With our team, every play was a team play. . . .

"There's a picture that hangs in the athletic department that shows the two guards pulling, the quarterback, the fullback and myself on a sweep, and we're all in step," he said. "All of us have our right foot on the ground at the same time. It's an illustration of power and teamwork.

"I think that tells it all. When you break it down and look at it, we had some guys go on to play pro ball, but there were no superstars. Our success came because of the type of guys that we had and the way we played as a team."

It was a squad that in the course of the '54 season included eight black players overall, a truly integrated team in those days. Kenny Washington and Jackie Robinson had played at UCLA earlier, but it was still noteworthy when a university recruited beyond the black superstar. In the South, black players—and in many cases, black students—were not even considered at major universities.

Villanueva was of Mexican descent. He came from the tiny California border town of Calexico. Growing up in Calexico, Villanueva says, you learned to make ethnic and racial distinctions.

That it was Sanders, whose Southern roots were exposed every time he spoke, who made the major breakthrough in integrating the UCLA football team was not lost on Villanueva.

"We used to joke among ourselves that he sounded like the slave owners that you read about in books that used to whip their slaves," Villanueva said. "We usually thought about that during practice. Sometimes we'd laugh and sometimes we'd get mad. He was an extremely tough taskmaster. But he treated everyone the same. I always got the feeling that to him, we were all bodies in football uniforms.

"I don't know whether that was really how he felt or not. He wasn't the kind to walk up and put an arm around you and tell you what he was thinking. He was pretty distant. But we all had a tremendous respect for him and for what he made of us."

In the book "Touchdown UCLA," it is noted: "Southerner Sanders was asked the inevitable question of the times regarding his attitude toward blacks. 'I'm prejudiced in favor of any boy who can play football, and intolerant of any player who won't block and tackle.' "

Villanueva's wife gave birth to their second child while Villanueva was playing for UCLA and they named the baby George Henry—for assistant coach George Dickerson and for Henry (Red) Sanders.

Dickerson was one of only two members of the 1948 Bruins' staff retained by Sanders when the coach moved to UCLA after six seasons as the head man at Vanderbilt. Dickerson later had a brief stint as UCLA's head coach. Also on Sanders' staff were Tommy Prothro, Jim Myers and Bill Barnes. Prothro later was a head coach at Oregon State and UCLA and also in the National Football League. Myers went on to the top job at Iowa State and Texas A&M and later became an assistant with the NFL's Dallas Cowboys. And Barnes, too, eventually was head coach at UCLA.

Sanders had brought together, in 1954, not only a group of talented players, but also a team of tal-

UCLA's brightest star in '54 was Primo Villanueva, the talented tailback who is shown (above) on a ground-gaining excursion against Southern Cal.

ented coaches. And Sanders taught them, too.

John Peterson, who was captain of the 1954 Bruins, makes this observation: "I used to have some friends on the basketball team, and from time to time I'd drop in at their practices. I was always struck by the similarities between Coach (John) Wooden and Coach Sanders. Of course, we didn't know, then, that Coach Wooden was going to win all those national championships (a record 10). That hadn't started yet.

"We just knew that Coach Wooden was a good coach. He taught the same kind of concentration and discipline in practice that Coach Sanders taught. With both of them, every minute of practice was exactly planned. The whistle would blow, you do this and this. The whistle would blow again, you do this and this. Every minute was important."

Sanders and Wooden both believed that games were won or lost in practice. Take care of business in practices and the matter of winning and losing takes care of itself.

The UCLA football team won its first game in 1954 by the score of 67-0. But that was no great shock, considering that the men from Westwood had finished among the top five in both final wire-service polls of 1953. The Bruins had almost everyone back from the team that had gone 8-1 in the '53 regular season before losing in the Rose Bowl. The '54 opener, against the Naval Training Center of San Diego, was treated as a practice game, with Sanders playing everyone on the bench before the second quarter was out and trying every play and every combination.

As far as Sanders was concerned, that blowout was good for pointing out all of his team's imperfections. As one of his players put it, "No matter what the score was on Saturday, we were always dirt on Monday."

The second game, at Kansas, was more of a test, but the Bruins won that one by 32-7. The Bruins started impressively with 18 first-period points but struggled through an unproductive second quarter. That worked out for the best, though, because it prompted an adjustment for the all-important Maryland game that was up next.

In the single-wing offense, the quarterback was, as Debay himself explains, "a glorified blocking back." The key player was the tailback, who would get the ball on the snap and have the option to run, pass or hand off. The way Sanders liked to run the single wing, the tailback also was the signal-caller.

That changed at Kansas. Debay recalls: "In the

second quarter of the Kansas game, coach Prothro called me to the sideline and told me that I was going to start calling the signals. Primo wasn't getting it done. You know why? Primo was such a humble and sweet guy, that he wouldn't call plays for himself—and we needed him running the ball and passing the ball. Primo was a real talent.

"I was a blocking-back grunt. I knew my role. But I had always understood the game. I had always known that the Lord had given me that, and I always thought, 'If only I could call the plays. . . .' So when coach Prothro told me, 'You've got it,' I said, 'Praise the Lord.'

"For the rest of the season, it always seemed to me that the Lord was telling me the play to call. It would just be in my head. There were times when my calls would go against what the 'rules' would call for in that situation, but somehow it would work out."

So, the Bruins were 2-0 going into a much-ballyhooed game against Maryland, the defending national champion. A crowd of 73,376 gathered at the Los Angeles Memorial Coliseum on a Friday night to see one of the toughest, hardest-hitting, most intense football games played in many, many years.

Sanders didn't have to lay down the law to get his athletes to play at an optimum level for a big game. After all, his "Ten Commandments of Football," posted on the wall in the Bruins' locker room, were to be adhered to at all times. They started with "1. The team that makes the fewest mistakes wins. 2. Press the kicking game, for it is here the breaks are made. 3. Play for and make the breaks; when one comes your way, score. . . ."

The importance of Sanders' commandments was borne out against Maryland. Sanders and Maryland Coach Jim Tatum, longtime friends, had even chatted before the game about the importance of the kicking game, with Tatum acknowledging that Sanders certainly knew how to coach that facet of the game.

UCLA scored first, recovering a dropped snap on a punt on the Maryland 11 in the first quarter and scoring on one of fullback Bob Davenport's famous "pogo" jumps over the line. The extra-point kick went wide.

The Bruins and Terrapins hammered away, holding each other off with careful, conservative football until late in the third quarter when Maryland launched a 63-yard drive that culminated in a touchdown on the second play of the fourth period.

All-league talent Sam Boghosian was a big part of UCLA's strong offensive line in the Bruins' championship 1954 season.

The TD and ensuing conversion kick thrust the Terrapins into a 7-6 lead.

But Maryland soon shanked a punt, giving UCLA the ball 15 yards from the goal line. Villanueva positioned the Bruins for Davenport's second pogo jump over the top with a great run around the left end on a third-and-six play.

Debay's call on the play that set up Davenport's over-the-top, game-winning score was a case of trusting in the man upstairs to give him the right instincts. "Davenport had already carried the ball about 30 times," Debay recalled. "They were giving us the middle. But on that play, Davenport takes the ball, spins and hands it to the tailback. The tailback has to beat the end to the outside. I have to get there first, to block the end.

"When it worked, we all said, 'Oh, Lord, You are so good.' " UCLA won, 12-7.

Up next was the Bruins' Pacific Coast Conference opener against the Washington Huskies at Seattle. Knowing that the Rose Bowl's no-repeat rule meant UCLA couldn't play in the Pasadena classic even if the Bruins did win the conference championship, Sanders' players were starting to think about their place in the national rankings.

The UCLA team, described in the newspapers as "a quiet, confident crew," retreated to the Lake Wilderness Resort in Maple Valley, an hour from Seattle, to get some rest, do some praying and tend to some studying. Whatever preparations the Bruins made, they were barely enough.

Injuries took their toll in what turned out to be a close call against Washington. After leading 21-0, the Bruins withstood a furious Husky rally and won only because the Huskies missed the conversion kick after their second touchdown.

Considering the injuries and the score of the Washington game, there were those who considered the 13½-point spread favoring UCLA over Stanford the next week to be a little too generous. After all, Stanford did have a 3-1 record and John Brodie at quarterback.

So?

Answering a local radio announcer who had called the Bruins' single-wing offense an antiquated "horse-and-buggy" alignment and at the same time avenging a one-point loss suffered at the hands of the Stanford team in 1953, UCLA stunned a Coliseum throng of 70,555 with a 72-0 cakewalk.

In explaining why he had stayed with the single wing over the years, Sanders always would go beyond the "X's" and "O's" to add that other teams

UCLA fullback Bob Davenport was a bruising runner famous for his 'pogo' jumps over opponents' lines in short-yardage situations.

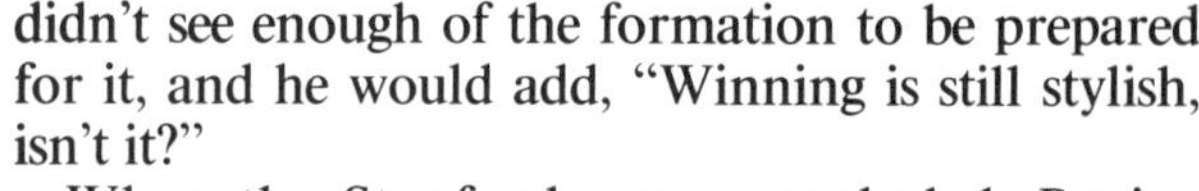

didn't see enough of the formation to be prepared for it, and he would add, "Winning is still stylish, isn't it?"

When the Stanford game concluded, Bruins guard Sam Boghosian (later an assistant coach in the pro ranks) shouted, "So we got a horse-and-buggy offense, huh? Some horses, though!"

The Bruins' defense wasn't too shabby, either. Against Brodie and company, UCLA intercepted eight passes.

Yellowed newspaper clippings of the game, carefully pasted and saved in the archives at UCLA, report: "Stanford was all but blotted off the good, green earth. . . . The Calexico Kid stopped Stanford's opening drive attempt by grabbing off John Brodie's pass and engineering a 46-yard march to the first Bruin touchdown. . . ."

Reporters asked Sanders whether he was trying to pour it on for the sake of the national rankings, as the score would indicate, or whether he was trying to show compassion, as his substitution pattern would indicate. The coach responded: "Neither one. We used everybody on the bench, but everybody was hot. I don't believe in deliberately trying not to gain. That wouldn't be fair to the players or the fans. You naturally rest and save your regulars in a game like this."

Well rested, the Bruins, ranked No. 3 in both wire-service polls, traveled to Corvallis, Ore., the next week and beat up on Oregon State. The poor Beavers knew what they were in for. The Bruins went in favored by more than four touchdowns and Sanders, saying he was "taking no chances," got his line back at full strength with the return of Peterson, who had injured a knee in the second game of the season.

Although the Bruins were not a real big team overall, they were talented across the front line with All-America Jack Ellena at left tackle and all-league players Boghosian and Jim Salsbury at the guard slots. Bob Long was another standout player, earning All-PCC honors at end.

Entering the game against the overmatched Oregon State team, Sanders warned the Bruins of the danger of an upset. Apparently forgetting he had rested his starters in the blowout of Stanford and that his team was listed behind only Oklahoma and Wisconsin in the national rankings, Sanders said

Jim Decker was a halfback whose biggest contribution to UCLA's 1954 championship run was an interception that short-circuited a desperation Southern Cal rally.

Jim Salsbury (above), an all-league offensive guard, joined guard Sam Boghosian and All-America tackle Jack Ellena on UCLA's superior offensive line.

the Bruins had just completed their worst week of practice and were "dead on their feet, careless and have their minds on other matters."

Quite a kidder, that Red. Final score: UCLA 61, Oregon State 0.

There really *was* some cause for concern the next Saturday when the Bruins, elevated to No. 1 by United Press but still rated No. 3 by the Associated Press, played Pappy Waldorf's California Golden Bears before 64,000 in Strawberry Canyon. UCLA was matched against one of Cal's all-time great passers in Paul Larson. But while Larson was his usual brilliant self that day, completing 25 of 38 passes for 280 yards, he wasn't getting into the end zone. And Villanueva was rolling up some offense of his own, averaging 9.7 yards a play. UCLA prevailed, 27-6, and won over AP's pollsters in the process. In the next wire-service rankings, Sanders' team headed both polls.

Sanders expressed dissatisfaction with his team's offensive effort in a 41-0 victory over Oregon in the next-to-last game of the regular season. But he had no complaints with the way the Bruins shut down Oregon quarterback George Shaw, the nation's leader in total offense. The Bruins held Shaw to just 29 yards rushing and passing.

In the closing minutes of the game, Prothro told the Bruins they were within reach of the school season scoring record. It was Sam Brown who scored the touchdown that broke the mark of 327 points that had been set by the 1946 team in 11 games, including the Rose Bowl. The 1954 team had 333 points after the Oregon contest, its eighth game of the year, and 367 at season's end.

The nation's coaches were smitten with UCLA and they left the Bruins No. 1 in the UP poll. Not even a "bye" on November 13—coupled with No. 2 Ohio State's decisive victory over a good Purdue team—swayed the coaches. But the sportswriters—and there were a lot more of them in the Midwest than on the Pacific Coast—replaced the Bruins with the Buckeyes atop the AP poll after Woody Hayes' team had downed the Boilermakers, 28-6.

The buildup for the 1954 UCLA-Southern California game, scheduled November 20, was something special—befitting the situation. It was UCLA, No. 1 in one poll, against a USC team that was Rose Bowl-bound with an 8-1 record (and also ranked among the Top Ten nationally).

Jack Tobin wrote in the Los Angeles Mirror: "At every corner today the game is the paramount subject with a large number of frantic fans looking in vain for seats—any seat at any price.

"The tempo for Saturday's 2 p.m. kickoff, 48 hours away, is more characteristic of such football-mad cities as Madison, Wis., and Columbus, O., rather than blasé Los Angeles, which is seldom bothered by anything short of smog or earthquake.

"Bruin athletic officials declared today that they have never been sold out so early for a Trojan game as they were for this one." A crowd of 102,000-plus was assured for UCLA's season finale.

As game day neared, Sanders climbed up into his 20-foot coaching tower to take an overview of the Bruins' final practice and proclaimed his team ready for its archrival.

UCLA scored quickly in the big game, exploiting a play that Sanders had added just for the Trojans.

Debay remembers it this way: "We were at about the 47 or 48 of USC when I decided it was time to call the pass play to the end, and when I looked to see who the end would be that Primo would throw to and I saw that it was Heydenfeldt, a guy I had played with since our days at Canoga Park High School, I was so excited.

"The play is designed to make the defensive halfback think it's a run. Then Primo would have to throw it behind the safety, who was Jon Arnett. Now, we know that Primo can't throw the ball more than about 30 yards, but Primo jumps up in the air and throws it about 50 yards. The adrenaline is pumping, the Lord is blessing us and he throws for a touchdown."

The game then turned into a defensive blockbuster, with the UCLA line exerting tremendous pressure on Trojans quarterback Jim Contratto and the Bruins stopping the Southern Cal rushing game dead in its tracks. By game's end, USC had a total of five yards on the ground.

The Trojans' biggest chance to score came in the third period when an interception by Marv Goux gave the Trojans the ball at the UCLA 45. USC marched to the 8, but UCLA's Jim Decker snuffed out the threat with an interception (on which he made a dazzling return to the Trojans' end zone, only to have the play short-circuited because of a clipping penalty).

As the Trojans got more and more desperate for points, UCLA took advantage of their gambles. The Bruins proceeded to score 27 fourth-quarter points and finished with a 34-0 victory.

USC Coach Jess Hill said, "The Bruins richly deserve their No. 1 rating in the nation. After they defeated Maryland, the country's No. 1 team a year ago, I said UCLA deserved to be ranked No. 1, and I've never changed my mind. Their line is very, very powerful, better defensively than offensively. They didn't really march on us, but defensively, they certainly had us."

After the Southern Cal game and the ensuing celebration, there was nothing for the Bruins to do in this era of pre-bowl final polls except wait and watch and hope to win the national title. They wound up with half-a-loaf, with United Press sticking with UCLA as the top team in the land and the Associated Press opting for Ohio State (a 20-7 victor

The 1954 Bruins: Top row (left, moving clockwise) —Hardiman Cureton, Jim Salsbury, John Peterson, Rommie Loudd, Primo Villanueva, Russ Hampton, Preston Dills, John Farhood, Bruce Ballard, John Hermann, Bob Heydenfeldt, Jim Decker, Terry Debay, Sam Boghosian, Jack Ellena, Roger White, Gerry McDougall, Gerry Okuneff, Doug Bradley, Clarence Norris, Don Shinnick, Tom Thaxter, Bob Long, Bob Bergdahl, Sam Brown, Bob Davenport, Steve Palmer, Doug Peters, Jim Brown, Warner Benjamin, manager Morgan, Jack McKay, Mike Riskas, Dick Braunbeck, Joe Ray, Gil Moreno. Center (left to right) —Coaches Tommy Prothro, Bill Barnes, Jim Myers; Head Coach Red Sanders; coaches Deke Brackett, George Dickerson, John Johnson.

over USC a month later in the Rose Bowl).

Debay reflected on the Bruins' year-that-was.

"Bob Heydenfeldt and I used to work in the cafeteria at (UCLA's) Kirkhoff Hall," said Debay, voted the 1954 team's most valuable player, "and one Monday morning, after our days of playing football were over, in walked Coach Sanders. I just stopped and said, 'Bob, look who's here.' He was just so intimidating. There was such a mystique and a genius about him. We felt like little kids when he was around. He grabbed a cup of coffee and said. 'Terry, Bob get a cup of coffee and sit down here.' Heck, we didn't even know that he knew our first names.

"We sat down and he said, 'I just want you to know that you are two of the finest young men I have ever known, and if there is ever anything I can do for you, any time, any place, you just let me know.'

"He left us both sitting there with tears in our eyes.

"When Bob and I get together, even now, we talk about that day, and we talk about what a miracle the entire season, our entire career was. It was incredible. The whole four years went flying by. But when we look back on it, it was as if God assembled the players, the coaches, everybody and made a glorious thing happen."

UCLA, 1954

ROAD TO GREATNESS

1954 RESULTS (9-0)

Opponent	Score	Opp. Record	Opp. Bowl Game
San Diego NTC	67-0		
at Kansas	32-7	0-10-0	
Maryland	12-7	7-2-1	
at Washington	21-20	2-8-0	
Stanford	72-0	4-6-0	
at Oregon State	61-0	1-8-0	
at California	27-6	5-5-0	
Oregon	41-0	6-4-0	
Southern California	34-0	8-4-0	Rose (L)

FACTS AND FIGURES

UCLA's Bruins were dynamite on both sides of the ball in 1954, topping the nation in scoring offense and scoring defense. Coach Red Sanders' crew averaged 40.8 points per game and limited opponents to a mere 4.4 per outing. . . . For Stanford, Oregon State, Oregon, Southern California and the San Diego Naval Training Center (a non-collegiate entry), playing the Bruins was a Bad Day at Black Rock. Those five teams fell to UCLA by—believe it or not—a combined score of 275-0. . . . Besides their prowess in manufacturing and denying points, the Bruins also stood out on the rushing-defense chart. Their yield of only 73.2 ground yards per game ranked No. 1 in the country. . . . The '54 Bruins were fifth nationally in rushing offense, eighth in total defense and 10th in total offense. . . . The strength of the opposition hardly had the Uclans quaking in their cleats. UCLA's eight collegiate opponents combined for 33 victories, 47 losses and one tie, or a .414 winning percentage. . . . Washington, winner of just two of 10 games in '54, managed to give the unbeaten Bruins some uneasy moments, though. The Huskies went down reluctantly, 21-20, collecting half of the points scored against UCLA all year. That season total of 40 points allowed remains an all-time Uclan low. . . . Sam Brown averaged 26.2 yards per punt return in 1954, the best performance in Bruins' history for a player with 10 or more returns. Brown also holds the school career record for punt-return average (19.5 yards) and the single-game UCLA mark for punt-return yards (132, against Stanford in '54). . . . While Bob Davenport and Primo Villanueva were UCLA's big-name ground-gainers, thanks in large measure to their touchdown totals of 11 and nine, respectively, it was Jim Decker who paced the squad in rushing yardage and average gain. Decker carried the ball only 47 times, but netted 508 yards. That figures out to 10.8 yards per crack.

STATISTICAL LEADERS

PASSING

	Att.	Comp.	Yards	TD	Pct.	Int.
Primo Villanueva	49	23	400	5	46.9	7
Doug Bradley	31	20	229	2	64.5	2

RUSHING

	Att.	Yards	Avg.	TD
Jim Decker	47	508	10.8	4
Primo Villanueva	87	486	5.6	9
Bob Davenport	105	479	4.6	11
Gerry McDougall	43	226	5.3	4
Don Shinnick	28	210	7.5	1
Doug Peters	42	181	4.3	2
John Hermann	23	155	6.7	4
Sam Brown	23	135	5.9	3

RECEIVING

	Rec.	Yards	Avg.	TD
Rommie Loudd	13	157	12.1	4
Bob Long	11	157	14.3	0
Bob Heydenfeldt	6	110	18.3	1
John Hermann	5	73	14.6	2

SCORING

	TD	FG	PAT	Points
Bob Davenport	11	0	0	66
Primo Villanueva	9	0	0	54
Sam Brown	6	0	9	45
Rommie Loudd	5	0	0	30
John Hermann	2	0	17	29
Doug Bradley	3	0	9	27

KEY CHARACTERS

The Conductor

COACH: Henry (Red) Sanders.

Record: 66-19-1, 9 years at UCLA.

Sanders succeeded Bert LaBrucherie at UCLA in 1949. . . . He was known as a practical joker who related well to his players and did not use a drill-sergeant approach. He was a calm figure on the sideline and had the reputation as a top-notch game-day coach. . . . He perfected the single-wing offense, which his teams executed with precision . . . . He based his offense on the formation employed by Bob Neyland, former Tennessee coach,though he took the quarterback out from under the center and added a few running plays and passes. . . . His teams were ranked in the final Top 10 of both the Associated Press and United Press polls from 1952-55 and he took two UCLA teams to the Rose Bowl, losing to Michigan State both times—28-20 after the 1953 season and 17-14 after the '55 campaign. . . . His unbeaten 1954 team won UPI's national championship and was ranked second in AP's final poll. . . . The 1954 and '55 teams won 10 consecutive games, still a UCLA record. . . . He coached five consensus All-Americas at UCLA and is a member of the school's Athletic Hall of Fame. . . . Sanders played his collegiate football at Vanderbilt, where he lettered from 1924-26, and also played basketball and baseball as well. . . . He served as an assistant coach at Louisiana State before taking over at Vanderbilt. He coached the Commodores from 1940 through 1942 and returned in 1946 after serving in the Navy during World War II. . . . He compiled a 36-22-2 record in six years at Vanderbilt and remains the Commodores' third winningest coach. . . . Sanders compiled a 102-41-3 overall record in 15 years.

Personal Data:

Born: March 5, 1905, in Asheville, N.C.
College: Vanderbilt University.

The Supporting Cast

FULLBACK: Bob Davenport.

Davenport gained the tough inside yards and also was a tough, hard-hitting defensive back. . . . He was among the finest overall players on the squad and was voted most valuable Bruin in 1955. . . . He was voted UCLA's offensive rookie of the year in 1953 as a sophomore and led the team in scoring in '54 with 66 points. . . . He was a three-year letterman (1953-55) and is a member of the UCLA Athletic Hall of Fame.

Personal Data:

Born: April 30, 1933, at Long Beach, Calif.
High School: Jordan High in Los Angeles.

QUARTERBACK: Terry Debay.

Debay's importance to the 1954 team was deceiving from a statistical point of view, yet he was the team's most valuable player. . . . He played with reckless abandon as a defensive back and excelled offensively as a blocker in Coach Red Sanders' single-wing offensive scheme. . . . He lettered from 1951-54.

Personal Data:

Born: August 4, 1933, at Canoga Park, Calif.
High School: Canoga Park High.

TACKLE: Jack Ellena.

Ellena ranks among the best linemen to strap on football gear in Westwood. . . . He teamed with guard Jim Salsbury on offense to open gaping holes. . . . He was a consensus All-America in 1954 and finished seventh in Heisman Trophy balloting that year. . . . The three-year letterman (1952-54) is a member of the UCLA Athletic Hall of Fame.

Personal Data:

Born: October 27, 1931, at Susanville, Calif.
High School: Lassen High in Susanville.

HALFBACK: Primo Villanueva.

Nicknamed the "Calexico Kid," Villanueva was a triple-threat star who successfully replaced UCLA legend Paul Cameron. . . . He led the 1954 Bruins in passing (23 completions in 49 attempts for 400 yards and five touchdowns) and finished second in rushing (486 yards) and scoring (54 points). . . . He also was a talented defensive back who lettered in 1953 and '54.

Personal Data:

Born: December 2, 1931, in Calexico, Calif.
High School: Calexico High.

FINAL 1954 WIRE SERVICE RANKINGS

ASSOCIATED PRESS		UNITED PRESS	
1. Ohio State	11. Miami (Fla.)	**1. UCLA**	**11. Southern Cal**
2. UCLA	12. West Virginia	2. Ohio State	**Maryland**
3. Oklahoma	13. Auburn	3. Oklahoma	Georgia Tech
4. Notre Dame	14. Duke	4. Notre Dame	14. Duke
5. Navy	15. Michigan	5. Navy	15. Michigan
6. Mississippi	16. Virginia Tech	6. Mississippi	16. Penn State
7. Army	**17. Southern Cal**	7. Army	17. SMU
8. Maryland	18. Baylor	8. Arkansas	18. Denver
9. Wisconsin	19. Rice	9. Miami (Fla.)	19. Rice
10. Arkansas	20. Penn State	10. Wisconsin	20. Minnesota

Bold face indicates UCLA opponent.

Chinese Bandits Of the Bayou

Louisiana State, 1958
By George Morris

The Chinese Bandits of 1959 featured six of the group's 1958 charter members: Mel Branch (75), Duane Leopard (71), Gus Kinchen (81), Andy Bourgeois (80), Darryl Jenkins (10), John Langan (53) and Hart Bourque (32).

Their names, carrying such a distinct Louisiana flavor—Andy Bourgeois, Emile Fournet, Hart Bourque, Merle Schexnaildre—remain household words in the Bayou State three decades after their collegiate football careers ended.

"I never did get to the spotlight," Schexnaildre said, "but every week I run into people in Louisiana who, when I say who I am—and I don't flaunt it—say, 'The Schexnaildre who played for LSU?' Would you believe that? Every week!"

Still, outside their home state, these football players of yesteryear remain mostly anonymous. John Langan. Tommy Lott. Duane Leopard. Gaynell (Gus) Kinchen. Darryl Jenkins. Henry Lee Roberts. Of the 11-man unit, only Mel Branch went on to play professional football.

That, however, is looking at these players' talents on an individual basis. The athletes won their fame on a collective basis when, in 1958, they burst on the nation's sports consciousness as the most famous group of football substitutes ever to play the game.

The "Chinese Bandits."

They certainly weren't the best athletes on Louisiana State's national championship team. Halfbacks Billy Cannon, who would win the Heisman Trophy a year later, and Johnny Robinson, who would go on to Super Bowl stardom for the Kansas City Chiefs, were the Tigers' full-fledged stars. Tommy Davis would become a standout National Football League kicker, and two other regulars, quarterback Warren Rabb and fullback J.W. (Red) Brodnax, would experience brief pro careers.

Yet, the "Chinese Bandits" and their less-famous contemporaries, Louisiana State's "Go" team, were what transformed LSU from the mediocrity of its first three seasons under Coach Paul Dietzel to the national-powerhouse status enjoyed in the fall of 1958.

"We were average ball players," said Bourque, a certified Bandit, "playing in an above-average situation."

A season before, the Tigers had many of the same players, plus fullback Jimmy Taylor, an eventual Pro Football Hall of Famer. That team hit the halfway point of the '57 season with a 4-1 record, but lost four games in a row before beating intrastate rival Tulane to salvage a break-even record and, quite possibly, Dietzel's job. Dietzel had compiled an 11-17-2 mark during his initial three years in Baton Rouge.

The Bayou Bengals' coach didn't need anyone to tell him what his biggest problem was. The shortcoming had become painfully evident in the middle of the 1956 season, in a game against archrival Mississippi. Dietzel's first unit was talented enough to play with the best of teams—as evidenced by the Tigers' 17-14 halftime lead over the powerful Rebels—but in this era of one-platoon, limited-substitution football, 11 skilled players could carry a team only so far.

"I looked at the team that had been playing all the football," Dietzel recalled. "I almost had to squeegee them off the floor. They were absolutely whipped. Ole Miss had played three teams against them. That game proved we couldn't play people like Ole Miss with one football team." The Rebels proceeded to go on a 32-point scoring binge in the second half en route to a 46-17 smashing of the Tigers.

Team depth became Dietzel's No. 1 priority when—with only three seniors and 15 lettermen—he opened spring practice in 1958, the first year that the coach had a squad made up entirely of his own recruits. And what a group of recruits it was.

Cannon, a 6-foot-1, 204-pounder, lived up to his surname. Speed? He ran a 9.5-second 100-yard dash. Strength? One would-be Mississippi State tackler was sent to the hospital with a broken collarbone after running into a Cannon forearm. Zeal? In the ninth grade, to his parents' dismay, he intentionally flunked to ensure he'd grow big enough to play high school football.

Unite Cannon with fellow juniors Robinson, Rabb and center Max Fugler, and LSU had the heart of Dietzel's first *full* recruiting class, which had gone undefeated as freshmen two years before.

All were excellent players both on offense and defense. But, when Dietzel looked around the practice field that spring, he saw plenty of athletes with strong offensive or defensive skills but only a few players other than his top 11 who were good enough to play both ways. At this time, substitution rules permitted an athlete who started a quarter to be removed from the period only once. If, after his return, he was removed again, he had to stay out until the quarter ended.

Only 30 years old when LSU hired him in 1955 off Earl (Red) Blaik's Army staff, Dietzel already had shown himself willing to break with custom. He outfitted his players in flashy uniforms and, after a play was called, the Tigers sprinted to the line of scrimmage and virtually leaped into their stances.

"People would leave the stadium saying, 'Well, we got beat again, but I'll tell you one thing: They sure looked good coming out of the huddle,' " Dietzel cracked.

Making this team better after the ball was snapped was another story, but the young coach brought innovation and enthusiasm to the task. For backup players, he reasoned, why not form one team of offensive specialists and another of defensive stalwarts and try to rotate them as much as possible?

Dietzel's concept was hailed as revolutionary, although his name for the defensive specialists was less than original.

Nine years earlier, while a defensive coach under Sid Gillman at the University of Cincinnati, Dietzel sought some inspiration for his troops. One day, one of the characters in the "Terry and the Pirates" comic strip gave the young coach a motivational idea.

According to Dietzel, the character said "these Chinese bandits are the most vicious people in the world." Not a bad name for a defensive unit.

"I cut out that comic strip and put it on our bulletin board," Dietzel remembered. "I said, 'Instead of being known as the defensive team, we're going to be known as the 'Chinese Bandits.'

"Very frankly, the name did not sweep the nation."

It would in 1958.

The Big Three of LSU's 1958 offense, posing with Coach Paul Dietzel: Billy Cannon (20), Johnny Robinson (34) and Warren Rabb (12).

After choosing his first unit, made up of the squad's top 11 all-around players and called the "White" team because LSU always wore white jerseys in those days, Dietzel selected his offensive squad and named it the "Gold" team because of the color of its practice jerseys (later, "Gold" was shortened to "Go"). Then he put together a unit that, in effect, was his third team. And its members knew it.

"With maybe one or two exceptions, I don't think there were too many of us who could have played college ball (as major contributors)," Bourque said of this band of reserves. "I think . . . he (Dietzel) made us believe we were actually better than what we were."

To help the players believe in themselves, Dietzel resurrected the upbeat Bandits nickname and bestowed it upon this feisty group.

Dietzel wasn't content to tinker with only part of his team. Since his troops were small—Cannon weighed more than anyone on the first-team line except left guard Larry Kahlden—the LSU coach was determined to take advantage of what appeared to be the Tigers' No. 1 asset, speed. Accordingly, Dietzel invited Delaware Coach Dave Nelson, the acclaimed architect of the winged-T formation, to Baton Rouge that spring to show the Bayou Bengals the nuances of his offense.

With its counters, reverses and men in motion, the winged-T allowed the offense to take advantage of opponents' pursuit and to use running backs to double-team opponents at the point of attack. Three of LSU's backfield starters—Cannon, Robinson and Rabb—were from Baton Rouge, so they spent the summer working together on the offense.

Nobody knew exactly what to expect from the changes being made at Louisiana State, but no one seemed to expect much. Neither wire-service poll included the Tigers in its earliest rankings.

"There was no pressure on us," Rabb said. "We weren't supposed to win anything."

That began to change almost from the start. The Tigers opened the season on a rainy night in Houston with a 26-6 victory over Jess Neely's Rice Owls, who had beaten LSU the previous two seasons. The weather seemed to have no effect on the Tigers' offense, a fact that was not lost on Alabama Coach Bear Bryant, who was there to scout the game.

"Does the winged-T help LSU?" a reporter asked.

The center of Paul Dietzel's powerful offensive line was manned by experienced junior Max Fugler.

Speedy halfback Billy Cannon, a future Heisman Trophy winner, was the top gun in Louisiana State's 1958 offensive arsenal.

"I think LSU helps the winged-T," Bryant growled.

So solidly had LSU performed against Rice that no particular notice was made of the reserve forces. A week later, that would be different.

The opposition in the second week of the season would be Alabama. The game, marking Bryant's debut as Crimson Tide coach, matched teacher against student. Bryant had coached at Texas A&M the previous four years and he had spent the eight seasons prior to that at Kentucky, where one of his assistants was a young man named Paul Dietzel. The coaching pairing itself made for a noteworthy night.

A collapse of end-zone bleachers made it a memorable evening, too. During the first quarter, dozens of spectators were injured—luckily, no one was killed—when the bleachers gave way.

As for what transpired on the field, the defenses dominated as neither team scored in the first quarter. Then, in the second period, a Cannon fumble was picked off in the air by Alabama's Duff Morrison, who rambled to the Louisiana State 4 before being caught by Scotty McClain.

Dietzel waved the Bandits onto the field.

"It was a shock to me and everyone else," Bourque recalled.

"I figured they're going to score anyway," Dietzel said, "and our 'White' team is tired, so there's no sense in getting their daubers down right there. So I put the Bandits into the game."

Bryant sent Bobby Jackson to the left. No gain. Mack Wise tried behind right guard. Two yards. Jackson went left again. One yard. The Crimson Tide was still a yard away. Bryant opted for a field goal.

A legend was born.

"That really was the first time we figured out the Bandits could get the job done," said Dietzel, whose team wound up a 13-3 winner in the game played at Mobile.

The Bandits' reputation was spreading, although LSU fans still weren't sure about their team as a whole. The Tigers had broken into the rankings of both polls, but only 45,000 fans—22,500 below capacity—ventured to Tiger Stadium to watch a lackluster 20-6 victory over Hardin-Simmons. It was figured that a stiffer test—and a chance to get a real line on the team—would come the following week in the Orange Bowl against independent Miami.

The game was no contest. LSU walloped the Hurricanes, 41-0, demonstrating its depth by pouring on 20 points in the final quarter.

"I think the Miami game was when it really dawned on us that we might have a pretty good football team," Dietzel said.

Another realization was taking place: The Bandits were going to have to learn to play some offense, all because they were getting too efficient for their own good. A swarming bunch, the Bandits were stopping offenses so quickly, either on downs or with turnovers, that it was getting impossible to substitute for them. One such instance took place against Miami as Schexnaildre, who was returning to action after badly gashing a calf muscle in the season opener, recalled vividly.

Fullback J.W. (Red) Brodnax was proficient at clearing away defensive players for LSU's talented group of running backs.

"There was no way of getting a punter on the field," said Schexnaildre, who played with his right leg heavily taped. "Apparently, whoever was in charge of the Bandits defensively didn't know what to do when we took the ball away and then ran on offense and they left us in to kick back to Miami. Since I was in the fullback position, who do you think kicked the ball? I think I kneed it over the line of scrimmage about 20 yards (15, actually). But we were playing so well."

Indeed. That victory not only won over many of the nation's sportswriters and coaches, who moved LSU into the Top 10 in both polls (at No. 9), but attracted a record crowd of 65,000 to Tiger Stadium for a game against Kentucky. Those fans were rewarded with a 32-7 beating of the Wildcats. The 5-0 start was the school's best since 1929, and when the Associated Press moved the Tigers to No. 3 as a result, it was their loftiest ranking since finishing No. 2 in 1936.

Naturally, the Tigers were now Louisiana heroes, and none more so than the Bandits. A Memphis disc jockey produced a song in their honor that was all the rage. A Baton Rouge merchant promised free coolie hats to the first 2,000 LSU students who visited his store—and was so inundated he had to order 2,000 more.

Dietzel, never one to let a motivational opportunity pass, arranged for the LSU band to play a Bandits theme when the unit first entered the Tigers' next game, against Florida. Like most things that season, it worked like a charm. The Bandits made a fumble recovery on the first play.

"They didn't run off the field, they floated," Dietzel said. "They were the wildest bunch you ever saw."

Florida, however, turned out not to be awed by the Bandits or the Tigers' ranking. Although Cannon ran over Vel Heckman, the Gators' All-Southeastern Conference tackle, for a touchdown that gave Louisiana State a 7-0 first-half lead, Florida was bigger and deeper than the teams the Tigers had faced previously. The Gators tied the score early in the fourth quarter, and for the first time in the season, LSU was not in command as the end neared.

Thinking it would take a field goal to win the game, Dietzel instructed Davis to warm up his kicking leg. Minutes passed, and the Tigers couldn't advance into field-goal range. The perfect season was in jeopardy.

Finally, the break came: A short Florida punt gave LSU the ball at the Gators' 43 with just minutes left, at which point assistant coach Charlie McClendon rushed over to Davis to ask if his leg was sufficiently warmed up.

"If I warm it any more," Davis replied, "it'll fall off."

Thanks to Cannon, there was little time for that to happen. The bruising halfback carved out runs of eight, four and seven yards, pacing an eight-play drive that reached the Gators' 7. It cost Louisiana State a delay-of-game penalty to get Davis onto the field, but his kick was good from 19 yards out with 2 minutes, 56 seconds remaining and LSU held on to survive a major scare.

"If you're going to go undefeated, you've got to win the close ones," Dietzel said. "You've got to be good, but you've got to be lucky, too."

The following week, Louisiana State became the Associated Press' No. 1 team—United Press International, unconvinced, listed the Tigers fifth—and the Tigers celebrated their move atop AP's poll by scoring a 14-0 triumph over Mississippi. Reflecting on that contest against the Rebels, Dietzel said the game films "showed something I've never seen before anywhere, and I'm sure I won't see again. The first time the Bandits were in the game there were six straight defensive plays where you could count nine of them putting leather to the Ole Miss ballcarrier. That's an honest count; nine men hit him before he could get to the ground."

Dietzel's pride in his special unit was evident years after the "Chinese Bandits" had inflicted their particular brand of mayhem on the opposition.

"It was an incredible thing," he said. "A middle guard named Tommy Lott was promoted from the Bandits to the first team and he refused to go. I reminded him that 'Chinese Bandits' was really a nice term for last-string players. He begged to stay.

"I gave the Bandits socks with a red stripe on the top. It was a matter of real pride. They became brilliant at gang-tackling . . . They allowed less than one yard per carry all that year."

After a 50-18 crushing of Duke in the eighth game of LSU's season—a contest in which Schexnaildre scored his lone touchdown of the year with a one-yard thrust that broke a 6-6 tie—the wire services were finally in agreement: Paul Dietzel's Bayou Bengals were No. 1 in the land. All that stood in the way of a perfect season and a national championship were Mississippi State and Tulane.

And, it seemed, the Almighty.

The heavens opened up the two days prior to the

Tommy Davis was capable of running with the ball, but his special talent was kicking, a skill that later earned him acclaim in the National Football League.

Mississippi State game, scheduled November 15 in Jackson, turning the field into a quagmire. The slippery turf neutralized Louisiana State's speed advantage, and the Maroons did the rest by diagnosing the winged-T fakes and keeping Cannon and Robinson in check. The Tigers ran just seven first-quarter plays. LSU lost three fumbles, and Mississippi State turned one of them into a second-quarter touchdown and a 6-0 halftime lead.

The Tigers were ripe to be upset until the "White" team recovered a third-quarter fumble at the Mississippi State 34. LSU was able to knot the score on a Rabb-to-Billy Hendrix pass on a fourth-and-goal play from the 5, and Davis' extra-point kick provided the margin of victory.

"How in the world we beat them, I'll never know," Bourque said. "The good Lord just said we were going to win that game and He gave it to us."

As if that bit of providence was not enough, LSU received additional help that day. As the Tulane team returned to New Orleans after losing at Vanderbilt, Green Wave captain Claude Mason offered the opinion that "we'll beat LSU because they'll choke"—and he made the remark within earshot of a reporter.

A record Louisiana sports crowd of 83,221 made its way to Tulane Stadium the following Saturday to see if Mason knew of what he spoke. Coming from a member of a team that had struggled to a 3-6 record, the "choke" claim was pretty audacious stuff.

However, for 30 minutes on the floor of the stadium that annually played host to the Sugar Bowl, Mason's prediction seemed within the realm of possibility. Tulane played LSU on even terms until late in the first half when Dietzel's troops finally broke through. Cannon accounted for the first score of the game, bolting into the end zone on a five-yard run that capped an 11-play, 75-yard drive. The point-after try failed, though, and the Bayou Bengals' 6-0 lead held up as the halftime score.

It wasn't 6-0 for very long. And, sure enough, cries of "Choke! Choke!" soon were heard throughout the stadium. The taunts wound up being directed at the Tulane players, though, as the Green Wave was buried under a 21-0 third-quarter avalanche and a 35-0 final-period assault. Cannon scored two second-half touchdowns and Robinson amassed four TDs.

The touchdowns against Tulane brought Cannon's season total to a team-leading 11. The fleet and powerful runner also topped the Tigers in rushing with 686 yards and an average gain of 5.9 yards per carry, was second in reception yardage and shared the Tigers' interception lead with Jenkins, a member of the Bandits. It was the kind of performance that earned Cannon the No. 3 spot in the Heisman Trophy balloting, behind winner Pete

Happy LSU players give Coach Paul Dietzel a victory ride after the Tigers' Sugar Bowl triumph over Clemson.

Dawkins of Army and runner-up Randy Duncan of Iowa.

"He's by far the best athlete I've ever coached," Dietzel praised. "He's as strong, as fast and as tough as anyone I've worked with. Give him a step and he's gone. If there's no room, he'll run over you—and it'll hurt.

"He's a real intelligent boy, and in some ways he is brilliant . . . Billy always gives all the credit to his teammates, his coaches and even to the fans. He takes none for himself. You can't beat a team man like that. He is a great leader, and I think that explains our success as much as anything else."

Cannon's star would shine even brighter in 1959, a year in which he would win the Heisman and make one of the most memorable plays in collegiate football history (a game-winning, 89-yard punt return against Mississippi in a battle of unbeaten teams).

After their pounding of Tulane in the 1958 regular-season finale, the LSU Tigers would return to Tulane Stadium six weeks later and stretch their overall record to 11-0 with a 7-0 Sugar Bowl tri-

The 1958 Tigers: Front row (left to right) —Johnny Robinson, J.W. Brodnax, Mickey Mangham, Charles (Bo) Strange, Ed McCreedy, Max Fugler, Larry Kahlden, Lynn LeBlanc, Billy Hendrix, Warren Rabb, Billy Cannon. Second row—Donnie Daye, Tommy Davis, Don Norwood, Jack Frayer, Manson Nelson, Mike Stupka, Bobby Greenwood, Al Dampier, Dave McCarty, Scotty McClain, Durel Matherne, Don Purvis. Third row—Head Coach Paul Dietzel, Hart Bourque, Merle Schexnaildre, Gus Kinchen, Duane Leopard, Carroll Bergeron, Tommy Lott, John Langan, Emile Fournet, Mel Branch, Andy Bourgeois, Darryl Jenkins, Henry Lee Roberts.

umph over Clemson. Cannon's halfback pass to end Mickey Mangham accounted for the game's only touchdown, a third-period scoring play set up by a fumble recovery by the Bandits' Leopard. The victory was somewhat anticlimactic: The national title had been wrapped up in the regular season because the wire-service polls concluded their voting before the bowl games were played.

Perhaps more representative of this LSU team than yet another triumph was the practice regimen preceding the Sugar Bowl game. The Tigers routinely had a third-down drill in which their various teams would play defense for a dozen consecutive plays, with the defensive unit gaining or losing points based on whether it surrendered yardage, stopped the offense for no gain or loss of yardage or caused a turnover. Shortly before the January 1, 1959, date in New Orleans, Dietzel upped the stakes. The loser had to run to the top of Tiger Stadium. The runner-up had to run laps. The winner could go home.

The "Go" team went first and did poorly—after all, those players never played defense. The "White" team followed and played respectably.

Then came the "Chinese Bandits."

"After about seven plays, they got an insurmountable score," said Dietzel, who later coached at Army and South Carolina before eventually returning to LSU as athletic director, "and they are beating the hell out of the other two teams. They're whooping and hollering and having such a good time. I stopped practice. It was too good, and I didn't want anyone to get hurt."

The Bandits won, but they didn't go inside.

"They went down and leaned against the goalpost," Dietzel continued, "and here comes the 'White' team running laps. And every time they'd go by, the Bandits would gig them a little bit: 'Hey, look, you guys, you're doing all right. Just keep trying. You'll get a lot better. It takes a lot of time. . . . '

"That 'White' team was so mad. After practice, Cannon and Robinson came up to me and said, 'Coach, we're having that drill tomorrow night, aren't we?' You know, I wasn't very smart, but I wasn't that dumb (to repeat the drill). We'd have killed off half the squad."

Such was the spirit that helped make the 1958 Louisiana State Tigers into national champions, at the same time creating a legend that endures. The change in substitution rules brought the return of two-platoon football shortly afterward, and Dietzel's "Chinese Bandits" brainchild no longer was needed. Even today, though, whenever an LSU defensive team leaves the field after a successful series of downs, the band strikes up the same tune that greeted those famous substitutes of three decades ago.

"Napoleon was right," said Dietzel, indicating his belief in a morale-over-material philosophy. "I don't know anything I've ever done that gave me as much pleasure as coaching the 'Chinese Bandits.' "

Louisiana State, 1958

ROAD TO GREATNESS

1958 RESULTS (11-0)

Opponent	Score	Opp. Record	Opp. Bowl Game
at Rice	26-6	5-5-0	
*Alabama	13-3	5-4-1	
Hardin-Simmons	20-6	6-5-0	Sun (L)
at Miami (Fla.)	41-0	2-8-0	
Kentucky	32-7	5-4-1	
Florida	10-7	6-4-1	Gator (L)
Mississippi	14-0	9-2-0	Gator (W)
Duke	50-18	5-5-0	
†Mississippi State	7-6	3-6-0	
at Tulane	62-0	3-7-0	
SUGAR BOWL			
Clemson	**7-0**	**8-3-0**	

*Mobile, Ala. †Jackson, Miss.

FACTS AND FIGURES

Louisiana State's Southeastern Conference championship in 1958 ended a long drought for the Bayou Bengals. The Tigers had last captured the SEC title in 1936. . . . LSU's unbeaten season was its first since 1933, a year in which the Tigers won seven of 10 games and played three ties. . . . The team hadn't been dazzling the opposition in the 1950s, putting together only two winning records in the first eight seasons of the decade. And, under Coach Paul Dietzel, the Tigers weren't exactly on a roll entering the '58 season. In Dietzel's three seasons at the helm, LSU had compiled an 11-17-2 record. Plus, the Tigers had dropped four of their last five games in 1957. . . . Defense, paced by the super-aggressive "Chinese Bandits," proved a big reason for the turnaround in '58. Of LSU's 11 opponents (including Sugar Bowl rival Clemson), only Duke managed more than one touchdown against the Tigers. The Blue Devils, in fact, collected 18 points against Louisiana State. The resourceful Tigers had the perfect response to such an affront: They riddled the Duke defense for 50 points. . . . Louisiana State ranked fifth nationally in total defense in '58 and 10th in rushing defense. . . . LSU opponents played at a .518 clip, winning 57 of 113 games and being involved in three ties. . . . While halfback Billy Cannon won consensus All-America honors, it was fullback J.W. Brodnax who won designation as the most valuable player on the LSU squad. . . . The second step on the way to the national championship came in a 13-3 victory over an Alabama squad that was playing its first-ever game under Coach Paul (Bear) Bryant. . . . The final two steps of the regular season were near agony and pure ecstasy for the Bayou Bengals, who were extended to the limit against Mississippi State (a 7-6 squeaker) but then regrouped to annihilate state rival Tulane (a 62-0 final). . . . Success in the January 1, 1959, Sugar Bowl against Clemson was sweet for the Tigers, who had lost in all four of their previous appearances in the New Orleans classic.

STATISTICAL LEADERS

PASSING

	Att.	Comp.	Yards	TD	Pct.	Int.
Warren Rabb	90	45	591	8	50.0	5
Durel Matherne	38	9	160	3	23.7	4

RUSHING

	Att.	Yards	Avg.	TD
Billy Cannon	115	686	5.9	10
Johnny Robinson	86	480	5.5	4
Don Purvis	60	253	4.2	2
Tommy Davis	71	243	3.4	0

RECEIVING

	Rec.	Yards	Avg.	TD
Johnny Robinson	16	235	14.6	3
Billy Cannon	9	162	18.0	1
Billy Hendrix	8	84	10.5	4
Mickey Mangham	6	98	16.3	0

SCORING

	TD	FG	PAT	Points
Billy Cannon	11	0	8	74

KEY CHARACTERS

The Conductor

COACH: Paul Dietzel.

Record: 46-24-3, 7 years at LSU.

Dietzel succeeded Gaynell Tinsley at LSU in 1955. . . . He is one of two coaches to guide Louisiana State to two Southeastern Conference championships (1958 and '61). . . . After leaving LSU, he coached at Army from 1962-65, compiling a 21-18-1 record. He left West Point after the Cadets had suffered consecutive losing seasons for the first time since 1939-40. . . . He then took over the South Carolina reins in 1966, compiling a 42-53-1 mark over nine seasons. . . . His career coaching record was 109-95-5 over 20 years. . . . He was an assistant to Red Blaik at Army, Sid Gillman at Cincinnati and Paul (Bear) Bryant at Kentucky before returning to West Point for two seasons prior to accepting the Louisiana State head coaching position. . . . After leaving South Carolina, Dietzel served as commissioner of the Ohio Valley Conference and athletic director at Indiana before returning to LSU as athletic director. . . . He is a member of the Miami of Ohio Athletic Hall of Fame.

Personal Data:

Born: September 5, 1924, in Fremont, O.
High School: Mansfield High in Mansfield, O.
College: Duke and Miami of Ohio.

The Supporting Cast

HALFBACK: Billy Cannon.

Cannon was a top-notch talent whose speed and strength allowed him to make plays others could only dream about. . . . His 89-yard punt return for a touchdown against Mississippi in 1959 is considered one of the game's classic plays. He broke seven tackles while making several dazzling moves as he scored the only touchdown in top-ranked LSU's 7-3 victory over the third-ranked Rebels. . . . During his sometimes-spectacular college career, Cannon threw touchdown passes and scored touchdowns in every conceivable manner—rushing, receiving, returning kickoffs, returning punts and running back interceptions. . . . Cannon won the 1959 Heisman Trophy and finished third in the 1958 Heisman balloting. . . . He was a unanimous consensus All-America selection in 1958 and a consensus pick in '59. . . . He earned most valuable player honors in a 7-0 victory over Clemson in the 1959 Sugar Bowl. . . . He finished his career with 1,867 yards rushing, a 5.2-yard average per gain, 965 combined return yards, seven interceptions and 154 points. . . . He lettered from 1957-59 and is a member of the LSU Athletic Hall of Fame.

Personal Data:

Born: August 2, 1937, in Philadelphia, Miss.
High School: Istrouma High in Baton Rouge, La.

CENTER: Max Fugler.

Fugler ranks among the finest centers in LSU history. . . . He started his career at running back and chose to switch to the line. . . . In addition to opening holes for Cannon and Co., he proved to be a solid defender from his linebacker slot. . . . He was an intense, physical player who called the defensive plays for the Tigers. . . . He lettered from 1957-59.

Personal Data:

Born: August 14, 1937, in Big Spring, Tex.
High School: Ferriday High in Ferriday, La.

QUARTERBACK: Warren Rabb.

Rabb was an efficient signal caller whose development and improvement during the 1958 campaign went a long way toward dictating the success enjoyed by the Tigers. . . . He was considered a superb runner and led the '58 Tigers in passing with 45 completions for 591 yards and eight touchdowns. . . . He lettered from 1957-59.

Personal Data:

Born: December 12, 1937, in Baton Rouge, La.
High School: Baton Rouge High.

HALFBACK: Johnny Robinson.

Robinson was the team's best receiver and among its finest blockers. . . . He led the 1958 Tigers with 16 receptions and was second in rushing with 480 yards. . . . He was underrated because of the large shadow cast by teammate Billy Cannon and never received his due. . . . He went on to a standout pro career as a defensive back with the Kansas City Chiefs. . . . He was a three-year letterman (1957-59) and is a member of the LSU Athletic Hall of Fame.

Personal Data:

Born: September 9, 1938, in Delhi, La.
High School: University High in Baton Rouge, La.

FINAL 1958 WIRE SERVICE RANKINGS

ASSOCIATED PRESS		UNITED PRESS	
1. LOUISIANA STATE	**11. Mississippi**	**1. LOUISIANA STATE**	10. Syracuse
2. Iowa	12. Clemson	2. Iowa	11. Purdue
3. Army	13. Purdue	3. Army	**12. Mississippi**
4. Auburn	**14. Florida**	4. Auburn	13. Clemson
5. Oklahoma	15. South Carolina	5. Oklahoma	14. Notre Dame
6. Air Force	16. California	6. Wisconsin	**15. Florida**
7. Wisconsin	17. Notre Dame	7. Ohio State	16. California
8. Ohio State	18. SMU	8. Air Force	17. Northwestern
9. Syracuse	19. Oklahoma State	9. TCU	18. SMU
10. TCU	20. Rutgers		

Bold face indicates Louisiana State opponent.

Tide's Aerial Show Dazzles Nation

Alabama, 1934
By Al Browning

There was a time when the Big Ten Conference and the Pacific-10 Conference did not own exclusive rights to the hallowed sod at the Rose Bowl. In fact, numerous historians claim that the finest team ever to play in the granddaddy of the bowl games did not come from either of those alliances.

Additional witnesses in support of that contention can be found among the survivors from a sell-out crowd of 84,474 fans who watched Alabama defeat Stanford, 29-13, on January 1, 1935. The 1934 edition of the Crimson Tide did not receive unanimous acclaim as the national champion with that victory—unbeaten and untied Minnesota graded out on top in many of the assorted rating systems in use at that time—but its decisive conquest of the Indians (as Stanford teams were called then) gave the Tide a 10-0 record and solidified thoughts of greatness in the minds of many observers.

Even before Alabama departed for the Rose Bowl, Shipwreck Kelly, co-owner of a Brooklyn professional team, watched the Crimson Tide practice and declared it the finest collegiate squad he had seen. That statement prompted an interview with Birmingham News sports editor Zipp Newman, who wrote: "If any of the Alabama seniors want to play professional football, they can get with Kelly's Brooklyn club and sign contracts immediately. He would take the Alabama squad as it is and be satisfied they could give the tough pros a big afternoon."

Perhaps that was an overstatement by a sports columnist with an abundance of regional pride. But the fact remained that Alabama had an exceptional team that featured lightning-quick end Don Hutson, passing and running halfback Millard (Dixie) Howell and determined end Paul (Bear) Bryant, plus such raw-boned power players as tackle Bill Lee, guard Charlie Marr and fullback Joe Demyanovich as well as several other talented players who, for the most part, served as a splendid supporting cast.

And there was the coach, Frank Thomas, a scholar with a whistle around his neck. Thomas, a supreme motivator, inherited a fledgling and proud Crimson Tide program in 1931 and added to its stature by posting a 115-24-7 record in 15 seasons.

When Thomas was hired by university President George Denny to replace Wallace Wade, who had given birth to 'Bama tradition with three Rose Bowl appearances, he was told what he labeled "the hardest and coldest words" a coach could hear. After the contract was signed, Dr. Denny said: "Mr. Thomas, now that you have accepted our proposition, I will give you the benefit of my views, based on many years of observation. It is my conviction that material is 90 percent, coaching ability 10 percent. I desire further to say that you will be provided with the 90 percent and that you will be held to strict accounting for delivering the remaining 10 percent."

Thomas, a former Notre Dame quarterback who had roomed with the remarkable George Gipp and played with the Four Horsemen, was stunned by the remark. He asked Atlanta sportswriter Ed Camp if he thought the president's estimates were on target. "I think the proportion was considerably off," Camp said, "but there is no doubt the good doctor means what he said."

Though he had immediate success at Alabama, posting a 9-1 record his first season, Thomas had reason to wonder about Denny's honesty when it came to material, which is why Hutson, Howell and Bryant are considered misfits of sorts.

Hutson, who hailed from Pine Bluff, Ark., ar-

rived at Alabama as a 160-pound baseball player and track star who wanted to play football. Despite not playing high school football until his senior year, Hutson captured the attention of Alabama assistant coach Harold (Red) Drew while running pass patterns as a freshman. Drew noticed Hutson's speed (9.8 seconds over 100 yards) and invited Thomas to take a closer look. "He does go shuffling along," said Thomas, who began taking extra time to develop raw talent.

Largely because of his defensive play, Hutson joined the varsity as a sophomore in 1932. He almost left the program because of a lack of playing time but decided to stay in Tuscaloosa. He became a starter midway through his junior season, a year before his pass-catching talent made big headlines. During preseason practice in 1934, Hutson discovered that the offense was being built around his flashy dash and sure hands and Howell's crafty passing, and the result was an increase from seven catches in his first two years to 19 receptions for 326 yards as a senior. The end went on to Hall of Fame status while playing with the Green Bay Packers, leading the National Football League in pass receptions eight times, touchdown pass receptions nine times and scoring five times.

Hutson, a consensus All-America in 1934, was one of the all-time great players at both the collegiate and pro levels.

"Hutson was the class of the outfit," Bryant wrote in "Bear," his autobiography. "His daddy was a railroad man, working steady, and he had twin younger brothers whom I eventually recruited for Alabama when I became an assistant coach. The Hutsons were a very close-knit family, with great personality. Don was everybody's friend, and though he didn't have to, he waited tables and took jobs like the rest of us.

". . . He used to wear his track suit under his baseball uniform so he could run the dashes between innings. At Alabama he got up to about 194 pounds, though he wound up playing for the Packers at about 175. He could eat like a horse and not gain weight. He was, in every respect, a complete football player—a good defensive end, a fine blocker and an intelligent player.

"But oh, my, could he catch passes. In all my life I have never seen a better pass receiver. He had great hands, great timing and deceptive speed. He'd come off the line looking like he was running wide open and just be cruising. Then he'd really open up. He looked like he was gliding, and he'd reach for the ball at the exact moment it got there, like it was an apple on a tree."

The class of the 1934 Alabama team was end Don Hutson, one of the brightest stars ever to grace the college and pro football ranks.

The man most responsible for discovering Hutson's hidden talent later shivered when recalling how the Alabama Antelope almost slipped through the cracks.

"He was hard to notice," Drew said as Hutson was drawing rave reviews as a pro. "Hutson played so effortlessly and with such grace, the coaches always thought he was loafing. In reality, he was a super athlete in disguise. During spring, he would run for the track team at Alabama, then hurry off to the baseball field, where he would play without taking batting practice."

Howell also had baseball on his mind when he was lured to Tuscaloosa—or kidnaped and carried there, if you prefer. He was playing a springtime game in his hometown of Hartford, Ala., and had plans of signing a pro contract within weeks. Watching him perform from a grandstand seat was Alabama assistant coach Paul Burnum, who was so impressed with Howell's athletic ability that he telephoned Thomas and told him about it. The coach instructed his assistant to persuade Howell to return to Tuscaloosa with him. That visit prompted the future consensus All-America to join the Crimson Tide.

Howell weighed 145 pounds when he arrived for classes at Alabama. He started the first game of his junior season (1933) and led the Crimson Tide to a 34-0 victory over Oglethorpe. "I think we have our replacement for John Cain," Thomas said about a grandiose fullback and team leader who had graduated. That surprise successor became a 165-pound halfback who always seemed to play his best in important games.

"Howell was a shifty runner with reasonably good speed," said Jeff Coleman, who served as business manager for the Alabama athletic department in 1934 and accompanied the team on its trip to the Rose Bowl at the end of that season. "He was a versatile player who could do a number of things—run, pass, kick, return kicks and cover his ground on defense.

"He was a flashy-type person, something like the first coming of Joe Namath on campus in a country way. He ended up making a couple or three movies, too, and it all started with a screen test on the Rose Bowl trip. But unlike Namath, Howell wasn't the least bit aware of his glitter. He was a take-it-easy type person, kind of laid-back, who had a great sense of humor.

"Howell sort of typified that Alabama team. On the one hand, he was a great player. On the other hand, he was a consistent practical joker. In 1934 we had a happy-go-lucky group of guys that put aside all mischief once it got on the field. He sort of set the pace for the others, in that regard."

Howell, who later played minor league baseball in the Detroit Tigers' organization, definitely set standards from a statistical perspective. He finished his three-year collegiate career with 343 carries for 1,839 yards, 71 completions for 997 yards, a 40.3-yard punting average and 22 touchdowns.

When Howell graduated, Thomas praised him lavishly: "Howell always had the natural qualifications of a good halfback—speed, drive and an unusual ability to follow his interference. His mental reaction is, in my mind, what made him great. . . . He was a hard, sure tackle and was uncanny at getting in position to intercept passes. To me, he had a touch of genius in his makeup."

Bryant had less overall ability than Howell and Hutson, but what he lacked in talent he made up for through pride and determination that reflected his intense love of the game. Bryant, who hailed from tiny Moro Bottom, Ark., a suburb of almost equally obscure Fordyce, was a poor plowboy who had cleats put on his only pair of shoes so he could begin playing football in the eighth grade. As a youngster he listened to radio reports of Rose Bowl games featuring Wade-coached Alabama teams, and he dreamed of playing for the Crimson Tide, which had many players from Arkansas on its roster. Alabama, in turn, was interested in a player who was large and strong, the result of many years of farm chores. Bryant even had a nickname that proved his toughness. As a teen-ager he agreed to a deal in which he would wrestle a bear at a local theater, earning a dollar for every minute he stayed in the ring. Bryant actually pinned the bear a couple of times before fleeing when the bear's muzzle came off. Bryant never got paid, but he did get a legendary nickname.

Bryant arrived in Tuscaloosa without having met entrance requirements. He lacked a foreign language credit, which he got by attending a class at Tuscaloosa High School while practicing with the Crimson Tide freshmen and living in a small room in a cramped gym on campus. He became a consistent starter during his junior season (1934), at which time he was dubbed "the other end" because of the presence of Hutson.

Thomas quickly took to Bryant and ultimately pushed him toward a coaching career. Bryant passed up the opportunity to become a pro football player and became an exalted teacher of the sport. He posted an astounding 323-85-17 coaching record in 38 seasons, including a 232-46-9 mark in 25 years at his alma mater. His Crimson Tide teams won or shared six national championships.

"Paul was a darn good player, not a great one," Coleman said about Bryant. "He was a decent pass receiver, at least on the short ones, only he couldn't cut and run like Hutson. Mostly, his acclaim came on defense. He was a good defender because he was tough and he liked to mix it up.

"I'd say Paul was a dependable country boy who

loved to play football. That's how the coaches viewed him. He was a serious student of the game, even then. That's why they had so much confidence in him."

So did at least one of his teammates. "I think he's one of the most underrated players of all time," said Riley Smith, Alabama's starting quarterback in 1934. "To tell you the truth, the way we played in those days, going both ways for 60 minutes, I would've taken Bryant over Hutson. He couldn't catch the football like Don, of course, but he was the better of the two as a blocker and a defender."

Hutson, Howell and Bryant were the charismatic figures on the 1934 Alabama team, basically because Lee (a consensus All-America and the team captain), Marr (an All-Southeastern Conference pick), guard Bob Ed Morrow, center Kay Francis and tackle James Whatley were linemen who received less attention, and Demyanovich was a nononsense fullback who blocked a lot in the Notre Dame box offensive formation. Smith, a future college Hall of Fame member, was an excellent quarterback, and Jim Angelich was solid at the halfback spot opposite Howell. Joe Riley, a dependable passer, was Howell's steady backup.

The Alabama players were as unselfish as they were talented.

"I roomed with Hutson and Bryant," Lee said, "and got real close to them. Back then, everyone on our team had a close relationship. We had a lot of talent, no doubt about that, but we had a lot of friendship, too."

As well as a lot of respect for their coach. One of Thomas' more enviable characteristics was his ability to keep his players motivated.

"Coach Tommy always knew what to say and when to say it," Bryant recalled years later. "He wasn't much for screaming and hollering, carrying on during practice, as is the case with most winning coaches, but he knew when to bend your ear and how to do it the right way.

"For instance, I'll never forget what he did on the train ride to the (1935) Rose Bowl. I was walking past him on my way to the bathroom. He was sitting with a couple of his cronies, some big-time Alabama men, when he saw me coming. That's when he said, 'And gentlemen, here's my best player.' Well, hell, I knew I wasn't anything of the sort, not with Hutson, Howell and a bunch of the others in tow, but my chest bulged just the same. He was getting me ready to play against Stanford.

"The next year, my senior season, he and (assistant coach) Hank Crisp sort of tricked me into playing against Tennessee with a broken leg. It was just a small bone, the fibula, but it hurt like hell when I put weight on it. Lo and behold, there we were in the dressing room before that game. Coach Hank was giving us a pep talk. Then he said: 'I don't know about you other fellows, but old Number 34 will get after those Volunteers all afternoon. Isn't that right, Number 34?' I looked around the room for number 34, didn't see it, and finally, looked down at my jersey. There it was, number 34 (players sometimes wore different numbers in those days), and I put down my crutches and played. That's the

Frank Thomas, who coached the 1934 Crimson Tide to an undefeated, untied season, was a scholar with a whistle around his neck.

type ploy Coach Tommy could use."

Thomas also had a tremendous aptitude for X's and O's, as his mentor at Notre Dame had realized before the quarterback ever left South Bend.

"It's amazing the amount of football sense that Thomas boy has," Rockne said. "He can't miss becoming a great coach someday. He's a coach in combat."

Rockne's kind words proved to be prophetic as Thomas went on to coach many fine Crimson Tide teams. But his 1934 edition was his best. He seemed to know it would be great after Hutson put on weight, Howell displayed an awareness of how to run the offense, Bryant became a skillful defensive player and adequate pass receiver, Lee and Marr exhibited terrorizing tendencies on both sides of the line of scrimmage, Demyanovich showed power as a runner and blocker and the rest of the cast performed almost in step with the luminaries.

"I've never been much of an optimist, as you know," Thomas wrote in a preseason newspaper column. "I'm a realist, purely so. So I must say I'm encouraged by this Alabama squad. It's a squad that could be a big-time winner provided it practices diligently and performs intelligently in games."

It seemed as if Thomas was attempting to warn opponents as well as inspire his troops. But the Tide looked less than inspired in a 24-0 season-opening victory over Howard College of Birmingham. Demyanovich scored two touchdowns in an otherwise unimpressive debut. Howell warmed up in a 35-6 victory over Sewanee (also known as the University of the South), scoring two touchdowns, one on a 61-yard run. Halfback Young Boozer, a prominent member of the supporting cast, scored on an 80-yard kickoff return and runs of 76 and eight yards as the Tide then blasted Mississippi State, 41-0.

Then came the big game—the annual battle against Tennessee and its coach, Major Bob Neyland. Thomas lost his first two games against the Volunteers, making the demanding school president fidgety, but he had bounced back to win in 1933. After Hutson's end-around TD run spelled the difference in a 13-6 Alabama victory to make it two in a row over the hated rival, Thomas was so excited that he put the lighted end of a cigar in his mouth. When he removed it, he told his laughing players: "You've beaten Tennessee. You can go all the way."

"We really took off after the victory over Tennessee," Bryant said, "started clicking, which has been the case with so many Alabama teams through the years."

Playing only the first half, Howell ran 15 times for 152 yards in a 26-6 victory over Georgia. The Howell-to-Hutson show highlighted the next three contests as Alabama defeated Kentucky, 34-14, and

Dixie Howell, pictured above wearing his Alabama letterman sweater, was a flashy halfback with a penchant for making the big play.

posted consecutive 40-0 shutouts of Clemson and Georgia Tech.

With just one game remaining on the Tide's schedule, rumors began surfacing that Rose Bowl officials were interested in Alabama. Once-tied Stanford, which had held eight opponents scoreless that fall, was a cinch to serve as home team. But with powerful Minnesota prohibited by Big Ten Conference rules from participating in any postseason games, 'Bama loomed as Stanford's opponent if it could whip a 6-2 Vanderbilt team in its season finale.

Paul (Bear) Bryant, pictured above as a high school player in Fordyce, Ark., made up for talent deficiencies with pride and determination.

The motivational situation was tailor-made for Thomas. Just before his team took the field for its Thanksgiving Day game against Vanderbilt, the coach sent his reserves onto the playing field and instructed his starters to remain in the dressing room. He told them that he had received a telegram from Stanford, which was allowed to select its opponent, indicating that Alabama would be invited to the Rose Bowl if it was impressive in Birmingham that afternoon.

"I want you to go out there and give your greatest show today," Thomas told his starters. "You have so much at stake, you can't afford to blow it. I believe we have a fine chance of getting the Rose Bowl bid and I know you fellows want it. Well, it's up to you."

Bryant remembered his reaction to that pep talk: "It sent cold chills up my spine. I was thinking about California when we went on the field to play. But we were all thinking about whipping the hell out of Vanderbilt, too. They didn't have a prayer of a chance. We had too much riding on the outcome to muff it. Again, Coach Tommy had said the right thing."

Alabama won, 34-0, as Howell offered his best performance: 162 yards rushing, 124 yards on punt returns and a 40-yard punting average.

"Dixie was a one-man wrecking crew," Bryant said with a smile. "It was as if he thought he was our ticket to California. That's how he played when he wanted to. He could literally take control of a game. It'll remain one of the great performances by an Alabama player. It was a pleasure watching Howell and Hutson that afternoon, even when I was supposed to be blocking and tackling. And it was an even greater pleasure running off the field and hearing the Alabama band playing 'California, Here I Come.' You talk about a bunch of excited country boys."

Alabama had finished its regular season undefeated, tying Tulane for the SEC title. But the Green Wave had lost to Colgate in non-conference action and was invited to host Temple in the inaugural Sugar Bowl game. A few hours after Vanderbilt had been vanquished, the coveted Rose Bowl bid was extended to the Crimson Tide.

When Thomas accepted the offer, a wild celebration erupted in Tuscaloosa. Thousands of fans met the team upon its return to campus. Police assistance was needed to protect the happy coach and players from the enchanted crowd.

Meanwhile, sportswriters who bemoaned Minnesota's inability to accept a Rose Bowl invitation belittled the Tide. That just sparked the players' competitive spirit.

"Those kids were determined to win and make their critics look bad," Thomas said years later. "At times we had to slow their pace (in practice) for fear they would grow stale before the game."

Bryant, however, remembered Thomas working the team hard. "We had a full scrimmage on December 20, went over to the stadium and had a game, first team against second team. Our fans had us full of ourselves by then, of course, and we did terrible. Coach Tommy stopped practice and we had head-on tackling drills for what seemed like an eternity. We were supposed to leave for California at about 10 the next morning, so we were surprised when Coach Tommy called a practice for 8. That was a good one, too, and it pleased him. But they still had to hold the train an hour and wait for us."

The train ride to California was eventful. The team stopped in New Orleans for dinner with some regional sportswriters; in Texas for practice and for an emergency operation that left substitute tackle Bill Young without his appendix; in Arizona for more practice, and in New Mexico to pick up former Crimson Tide star Johnny Mack Brown, who was fast becoming a movie star but had taken the time to scout Stanford for his alma mater. He boarded the train with all manner of diagrams and reports in his possession.

An article published in the San Francisco Chronicle got an equally good read from players. "On the day that Stanford played Washington," the article stated, referring to a 24-0 Indians triumph, "it could have licked any team in the United States, including Minnesota and Alabama. It was a glorious team. But the glory is all gone. Stanford has suffered a disastrous letdown. (The Indians barely beat California, 9-7, in their last game.) Ten to one that Alabama will lick the stuffin' out of Tiny Thornhill's boys."

That assessment boosted the players' confidence, and when they arrived at their hotel in Pasadena, they were met by a cheering throng. But the Tide also heard jeers from a few fans who considered Minnesota a worthier opponent for the Indians. "That's how I like to hear them talk," said Thomas, who figured the taunts would inspire his players.

"Actually, we were too wide-eyed to care what anybody said about us," said Bryant, who was realizing his professed childhood dream of going to the Rose Bowl.

The game was sold out more than a week ahead of time and scalpers began selling tickets for $25 each. About 1,000 temporary seats were constructed, which added to the hype.

"Alabama is the most impressive football squad I have ever seen come from east of the Rockies, and Alabama is going to play the best Stanford team in history, a team as great as Southern Cal in 1931," sportswriter Braven Dyer wrote in the Los Angeles Times. "If Alabama can beat Stanford, the Pacific Coast will give Alabama full credit for (being) the greatest team ever to play in the Rose Bowl."

Crimson Tide players digested such talk and continued their adventurous ways:

- There were daily dice games in hotel rooms.

Fullback Joe Demyanovich, primarily a blocker and short yardage man, was one of the leading members of Alabama's superb supporting cast.

After catching several players in the act, Hank Crisp requested and received cash in exchange for his silence. "As I remember," Coleman said, "the team was almost late arriving at the Rose Bowl on game day because a bunch of the fellows were shooting craps when the bus was scheduled to start rolling that way."

• When fans crowded the sidelines and distracted the players during an Alabama practice, Crisp announced that he would give $2 to any player who ran over somebody and scattered the observers. Howell made a long pass to Bryant, who plowed over a man, prompting the others to move back. Mission accomplished.

"You'll have to give half of that to me," Howell said to Bryant after the end had received his $2 payoff from the assistant coach.

"Why?" Bryant said. "I was the guy who ran over the man."

"Yeah," Howell replied. "But I threw the football long on purpose. And you won't touch the football in the game if you don't give me my share."

• Hutson, Bryant, Francis, backup center Joe Dildy and a couple of other players were caught breaking training by sneaking out for ice cream. When talk surfaced that Thomas was going to send all of them home, causing Dildy to panic, Bryant settled the storm with logic.

"He isn't gonna ship you (and Francis) out of here, Dildy, because he won't have a center," Bryant said. "And he isn't gonna ship me out of here because Hutson is with us and he'll have to go, too. Coach Tommy is too smart for that. He knows he can't beat Stanford without a center and Hutson."

• Alabama players mingled with fast company when they went on a tour of a movie studio. They watched the shooting of several films and met such stars as Mickey Rooney, Dick Powell and Lana Turner.

• Ty Cobb watched Alabama practice. A

Bolstering Alabama's top-notch interior line was guard Charlie Marr.

young radio reporter named Ronald Reagan was a daily visitor in the Crimson Tide camp.

• Forever flamboyant, Howell moaned and groaned over a craving he was having for hot tamales, another form of food Thomas made off limits to his players.

"I've been thinking about them so much out here that I've got to dreaming about them," the halfback told a reporter. "I dreamed about hot tamales last night. That is, I dreamed about one hot tamale. It was as big as Bill Lee. I mean, it was too big for a football player and not big enough for a hippopotamus. The coach won't let us eat tamales now, but as soon as that game is over, well, you watch."

When the game was over, Howell might have been too full of accolades to eat anything. He took a proposed toss-up encounter and turned it into a romp.

Stanford claimed a 7-0 lead in the first quarter after Demyanovich fumbled. The Indians recovered and consensus All-America fullback Bobby Grayson scored a touchdown on a short run. But Howell returned a second-quarter punt 24 yards and sparked the Tide with his passing. Completions to Hutson, Angelich and Bryant set up Howell's five-yard touchdown run, and Stanford's lead was cut to 7-6.

On the next Crimson Tide possession, Howell's passes to Hutson and Bryant set up a field goal, giving Alabama a 9-7 lead. Moments later, the halfback ran 67 yards for a touchdown. Just seconds before halftime, Smith intercepted a pass and Joe Riley then threw a 54-yard touchdown pass to Hutson. With that flurry of scoring, Alabama had a 22-7 halftime lead and was on its way to a resounding victory.

After Stanford cut the lead to 22-13 early in the third quarter, Thomas instructed his team to run the football in an effort to kill time. Nevertheless, Howell passed 59 yards to Hutson for the final touchdown. A game that was supposed to be a nail-biter had become a rout.

During the fourth quarter, with the final score of 29-13 already showing on the scoreboard, Bryant positioned himself on defense as the Stanford offense huddled. He looked down and discovered "about three dollars" in silver coins on the playing field. He hurried to fetch the money and clutched it in his right hand, intending to carry it to the Alabama sideline after the play. To his dismay, Grayson promptly swept around end with the football, right toward Bryant. "It was the only tackle I made all day," he said, fibbing a bit. "And I lost my damn

Big Bill Lee (above) manned one tackle spot and opened holes for the likes of Dixie Howell, Jim Angelich and quarterback Riley Smith.

The 1934 Crimson Tide: Front row (left to right) —Vic Rodgers, John Bludworth, Davidson, Arthur Granger, Charlie Stapp, John Taylor, manager Hugo Mark, Ben McLeod, Temple Williamson, LeRoy Goldberg, Ralph Thompson, Joe Riley, Joe Shepherd. Second row—Jim Ryba, Ralph Gandy, A.J. McDaniel, Dixie Howell, Young Boozer, Henry Cochrane, Bill Lee, Tilden Campbell, Jim Angelich, Hilmon Walker, Angela Daneluttil, Arthur White, William Peters, Red Griffin. Third row—Joe Dildy, Riley Smith, Sam Lyon, Bob Ed Morrow, Ben Baswell, Raiford Ellis, Dick Dobbins, Raphael Sneed, Ray R. White, Jim Tipton, Clarence Rhordanz, Jim Nisbet, Les Scott, Stacy. Fourth row—William Young, Jim Radford, Ronald Coffman, Paul (Bear) Bryant, Lamar Moye, Jim Walker, T.A. McGahey, James Whatley, Thomas Keller, Charlie Marr, Don Hutson, Kay Francis, J.C. Freeman, Joe Demyanovich.

money in the process."

When the final gun sounded, Alabama left no doubt that it was the dominant team that afternoon.

"No team in the history of football, anywhere, anytime has passed the ball as Alabama passed it today," wrote Ralph McGill of the Atlanta Constitution. "And no man ever passed as did Dixie Howell, the swift sword of the Crimson attack."

Wrote legendary scribe Grantland Rice: "Dixie Howell, the human howitzer from Hartford, Alabama, blasted the Rose Bowl dreams of Stanford today with one of the greatest all-around exhibitions football has ever known."

Mark Kelly, a respected West Coast sportswriter, was equally impressed: "Then like arrows from Robin Hood's trusty bow, there shot from Howell's unerring hand a stream of passes the like of which have never been seen in football on the Coast. Zing, zing, zing! They whizzed through the air and found their mark in the massive paws of Hutson and Bryant."

Howell received the loudest ovation afforded a Rose Bowl player when he left the game in the fourth quarter. He had run for 111 yards, completed nine of 12 pass attempts for 160 yards and punted for a 43.8-yard average.

Whether he thumbed his nose at the last Stanford defender he passed while running for the 67-yard touchdown remains a topic of debate. He was accused in print of doing so the day after the game. He denied it vigorously, claiming to have simply waved at the player with a quick move of his open hand in front of his chest. He admitted, however, that the camera angle used when his picture was taken made it look as if he had thumbed his nose.

More than a decade later, when a physically ailing Thomas took Alabama to the Rose Bowl for another victory, Los Angeles Times sports columnist Vincent Flaherty remembered the incident and interviewed Howell. The former halfback continued to profess his innocence.

"Just for good measure, Dixie gave me another demonstration," Flaherty told his readers. "And although I felt like saying, 'Dixie, do you mean to stand there and tell me you didn't thumb your nose?' such magnificent prevarication deserves some premium. In fact, you can nourish naught but tremendous admiration for any man who can stick to his story after almost 11 years."

But even Coleman remained unconvinced.

"I'm sorry to say it, even after all these years, but the film I saw of that play indicates Howell did thumb his nose," Coleman said in 1988. "Maybe he didn't. It'd be nice to believe that. However, I'm left to believe he did it, but not with any malice. That'd sort of be in keeping with his personality, as well as the magnetism of that great Alabama team."

Alabama, 1934

ROAD TO GREATNESS

1934 RESULTS (10-0)

Opponent	Score	Opp. Record	Opp. Bowl Game
Howard College	24-0	3-4-2	
*Sewanee	35-6	2-7-0	
Mississippi State	41-0	4-6-0	
†Tennessee	13-6	8-2-0	
†Georgia	26-6	7-3-0	
at Kentucky	34-14	5-5-0	
Clemson	40-0	5-4-0	
at Georgia Tech	40-0	1-9-0	
†Vanderbilt	34-0	6-3-0	
ROSE BOWL			
Stanford	**29-13**	**9-1-1**	

*Montgomery, Ala. †Birmingham, Ala.

FACTS AND FIGURES

Alabama tied with Tulane for the Southeastern Conference championship in 1934, giving the Crimson Tide back-to-back titles in the league's first two seasons.... Though there wasn't a so-called official poll to tab a mythical national champion in 1934, several sources selected the Tide as the nation's best team.... Several Alabama players received All-SEC mention, including first-team picks Don Hutson, Bill Lee, Millard (Dixie) Howell and guard Charlie Marr.... End Paul (Bear) Bryant and fullback Joe Demyanovich were voted to the second team, and quarterback Riley Smith was a third-team pick.... In 1935, Smith received the Jacobs Award as the league's outstanding blocker. He also was a consensus All-America that season.... Smith is enshrined in the College Football Hall of Fame along with Thomas, Hutson, Howell and Bryant.... The 1934 team contributed 10 victories to a 14-game winning streak that began in the sixth game of the 1933 season and ended in the 1935 season opener against Howard, which managed a 7-7 tie.... The Tide faced a formidable schedule in 1934 as six of 10 opponents had non-losing records. ... Alabama defeated those six teams by an average of 22.8 points per game.... The opponents combined for a 50-44-3 record (.531 winning percentage).... The Tide posted five shutouts, including three in a row before the Rose Bowl.... Just two of 10 opponents managed more than a touchdown against Alabama, which scored 30 or more points six times.... In 1934 regular-season games, Alabama scored 287 points; the opposition, a mere 32.... Including the 29 points it scored against Stanford in the Rose Bowl, Alabama's total of 316 points was topped by only three Tide teams until 1970.... The '34 squad was the first of three undefeated Crimson Tide teams under Frank Thomas.... The 1935 bowl appearance was Alabama's fourth, all in Pasadena. Under Wallace Wade, the Tide had beaten Washington in the 1926 Rose Bowl, tied Stanford in '27 and defeated Washington State in '31.... The crowd of 84,474 fans at the '35 Rose Bowl set a new attendance record for a game featuring Alabama.... Halfback Young Boozer had the longest kickoff return of Alabama's '34 season, running back a Mississippi State kick 80 yards for a touchdown.... The longest interception return was by halfback Jim Angelich, who picked off a Vanderbilt pass and went 70 yards for a score.

STATISTICAL LEADERS

PASSING

	Att.	Comp.	Yards	TD	Pct.	Int.
Dixie Howell	76	41	597	3	53.9	3

RUSHING

	Att.	Yards	Avg.	TD
Dixie Howell	135	840	6.2	9

RECEIVING

	Rec.	Yards	Avg.	TD
Don Hutson	19	326	17.2	3

SCORING

	TD	FG	PAT	Points
Dixie Howell	10	0	0	60

KEY CHARACTERS

The Conductor

COACH: Frank Thomas.

Record: 115-24-7, 15 years at Alabama.

Thomas played football at Notre Dame for Knute Rockne, lettering from 1920-22.... He earned the starting quarterback job as a senior, only to lose it early in the '22 season to Harry Stuhldreher, one of the famed Four Horsemen.... Part of the time he was in South Bend, Thomas roomed with the legendary George Gipp.... His first head coaching job was at the University of Chattanooga, where his teams went 26-9-2 in four seasons from 1925-28.... Thomas succeeded Wallace Wade at Alabama in 1931.... In his first five seasons before the Associated Press began conducting its poll of sportswriters in 1936, Thomas directed the Crimson Tide to a combined 40-6-2 record.... From 1936-46, his teams earned four Top 10 finishes in the AP polls, plus two more in the Top 20.... Three of his squads (1934, 1936 and 1945) were unbeaten, and four others suffered just one defeat.... He led Alabama to the school's 200th victory in 1932 and its 300th win in 1946.... His teams put together three 14-game winning streaks.... The Tide won or shared four Southeastern Conference championships under Thomas.... He took the Tide to six bowl games, winning four and losing two.... He was Alabama's winningest coach until Paul (Bear) Bryant, his former player and assistant, eclipsed his records.... His teams produced eight consensus All-Americas.... He is a member of the College Football Hall of Fame.... He was forced to resign after the '46 season because of poor health.... He died in 1954 at the age of 55.

Personal Data:

Born: November 15, 1898, in Muncie, Ind.
High School: Washington High in Chicago.
College: Notre Dame.

The Supporting Cast

HALFBACK: Millard (Dixie) Howell.

Howell is a member of the College Football Hall of Fame.... He was a consensus All-America in 1934 as well as the SEC's Most Valuable Player.... Howell-to-Hutson was the most famous passing combination of the 1930s.... He accumulated 1,437 yards of total offense in 1934 (840 rushing, 597 passing), setting a school record.... He also averaged 42.1 yards on 40 punts that season.... Howell holds the Alabama record for most punting yards in a season (3,216 in 1933).... His 89-yard punt against Tennessee in '33 is a Tide record.... He holds the Alabama record for longest run from scrimmage in a bowl game with a 67-yard jaunt for a touchdown against Stanford in the 1935 Rose Bowl.... His 59-yard scoring connection with Don Hutson in the Rose Bowl tied a 'Bama bowl record for longest pass play.... He was named MVP of the '35 Rose Bowl and is a member of the All-Time Rose Bowl team.... He lettered from 1932-34.... Howell played baseball at Alabama and later in the minor leagues.... He played for the Washington Redskins of the National Football League in 1937, when the Redskins won the league title.... His NFL career ended after that season, however, when he decided to resume coaching football rather than play backup to Sammy Baugh.... He was head coach at Arizona from 1938-41, compiling a record of 23-15-4, and at Idaho, where his teams went 13-20-1 from 1947-50.... Howell died of cancer in 1971 at the age of 57.... Alabama now honors the MVP of its annual spring intrasquad game with the Dixie Howell Memorial Award.

Personal Data:

Born: November 24, 1913, in Hartford, Ala.
High School: Geneva County High in Hartford.

END: Don Hutson.

Hutson was selected to the Football Writers Association of America's All-Time team (1920-1969).... He was an honorable mention selection when The Sporting News polled coaches for their All-Time All-America team in 1983.... He earned consensus All-America honors in 1934.... He went on to become a legend with the Green Bay Packers from 1935-45.... During that span he caught an NFL-record 99 touchdown passes and led the league in TD receptions nine times, receptions eight times and receiving yardage seven times.... He tied for the league lead in field goals in 1943 and in interceptions in 1940.... Hutson is a member of the college and pro football Halls of Fame.... Said former teammate Bryant: "Don had the most fluid motion you've ever seen when he was running. It looked like he was going just as fast as possible, when all of a sudden he would put on an extra burst of speed and be gone. Don had great hands and excellent moves, but the thing that made him most dangerous was his ability to run in an open field. He could really move, with an excellent change of pace." ... He was nicknamed the Alabama Antelope.... Hutson was a good defensive player, although his counterpart at the other end of the 'Bama line, Bryant, might have been better.... He lettered from 1932-34.... He was spectacular in the 1935 Rose Bowl, catching six passes for 165 yards and two touchdowns.

Personal Data:

Born: January 31, 1913, in Pine Bluff, Ark.
High School: Pine Bluff High.

TACKLE: Bill Lee.

Lee was Alabama's best lineman of the decade.... While Howell and Hutson received most of the acclaim, Lee did the dirty work in the trenches.... He was a consensus All-America in 1934.... He was captain of the 1934 squad.... He lettered from 1932-34.... Lee played professional football for the Green Bay Packers from 1937-42 and again in 1946 after serving in World War II.... He also played for the Brooklyn Dodgers of the NFL from 1935-37.

Personal Data:

Born: August 19, 1911, in Eutaw, Ala.
High School: Green County High in Eutaw.

The Destroyers Of Minneapolis

Minnesota, 1934-35
By Charley Hallman

Bernie Bierman, alias the "Gray Eagle," was the architect of Minnesota's 1934 and '35 football powerhouses.

The 1930s—Harlow, Loy and Powell, FDR. In those days, Alf was the first name of a Kansas governor who wanted to be President. Garbo was big, her hats were bigger. Nobody had any money—the country was devastated by the Great Depression. Monstrous dust storms hit the Midwest, driving many farmers to California.

In New York, Dorothy Parker was entertaining and so was Noel Coward. Hepburn was just getting started. The Gershwins were composing, and Cole Porter lyrics were beginning to have style.

The gold standard was ending, and the relief lines were never-ending. Times were tough and so were the people.

In a country that needed heroes, such figures were hard to find. Knute Rockne was dead, Babe Ruth's career was fading, Gene Tunney and Jack Dempsey had retired and Red Grange was nearing the end of the line.

The Midwest, like the rest of the country, was down on its luck. Prohibition was over, but nobody could afford a drink.

Acclaimed sportswriter Grantland Rice found some heroes for the rest of the country at the great, red "Brickhouse," a huge football stadium bounded by Washington and University avenues and Oak Street in southeast Minneapolis—just a few blocks from the other of the Twin Cities, St. Paul.

In 1934, 1935 and 1936, the University of Minnesota had fabulous teams. "My job could be much simpler in selecting the 1934 Collier's All-America team . . . by naming the entire University of Minnesota eleven, one of the greatest, if not the greatest, football teams I ever saw," Rice said. He called the Gophers "The Destroyers," and took pen in hand to write a poem about them.

Minnesota's coach was a man called the "Gray Eagle," Bernie Bierman. Bierman had been captain of the Gophers in 1915 and later was coach at Montana, Mississippi A&M and Tulane before being called to his alma mater in 1932. His Tulane team had played in the Rose Bowl on January 1 of that year, losing to a powerful team from Southern California.

Minnesota was in a crisis situation in '32. The athletic director and football coach, Fritz Crisler, was given the option of retaining one job or the other. But Crisler wanted both and when the university regents gave him an ultimatum, Crisler left for Princeton and, of course, eventually wound up at Michigan. He had tremendous success both places.

Born near Springfield, Minn., Bierman was a three-sport letterman at Minnesota (he also was a starter on the basketball team and an excellent track man). After graduating from Minnesota, he became a successful high school coach in Montana before World War I.

When the war came, Bierman entered the Marine Corps and eventually became a captain before leaving the service in 1919. "The Marine Corps taught me discipline," Bierman said. "And organization. And to love life."

After the war, it was off to Missoula, Mont., and to Starkville, Miss., for Bierman, who fielded middling teams in a total of five years at the helm of the Montana and Mississippi A&M (later Mississippi State) football squads.

Then came great success in five seasons at Tulane —the Green Wave compiled a 36-10-2 record under Bierman's guidance—followed by the move from the New Orleans campus to Minneapolis.

Installing the single-wing offense, Bierman coached his first Gopher team to a 5-3 record. The following year, 1933, Minnesota won only half of its games, yet went undefeated in a bizarre season. The Gophers won four games, lost none and, incredibly, played four ties (including two scoreless deadlocks in succession).

In the next two seasons, Minnesota won 16 times and never lost, outscoring its opposition, 464-84. Bierman's 1940 and 1941 teams also were 16-0 and nearly as overwhelming, having a scoring advantage of 340-109.

Bierman often was asked to compare the 1934 and 1935 teams with the units he assembled in '40 and '41. All four teams claimed the national championship (as awarded by various outlets), as did the once-beaten squad of 1936. "That's an impossibility," Bierman demurred. "There were great players

Pug Lund was a do-everything star for Minnesota and the best competitor that his coach, Bernie Bierman, had ever seen.

Frank (Butch) Larson was a standout end for Minnesota's championship football teams of the mid-1930s.

on both teams."

The mid-'30s Gophers possessed a particular aura of greatness, as duly noted by the All-America selectors and press-box observer Rice. The selectors made three of Bierman's players consensus All-Americas in 1934 (in an era of 11-man squads), and Rice was so impressed by Minnesota's muscle that he penned the following verse:

Hannibal took his elephants across the well-known Alps;
The Sioux and the Comanche gathered in the pale-face scalps;
But these were only pikers who could make a woman scream,
When Minnesota's Gophers fall upon some harried team.

Old Genghis Khan, the blighter, trampled down the distant loam;
You may recall the vandals and the Goths that mangled Rome;
But who are they to take a bow on wrecking sword and shield,
When Minnesota's Gophers send their thunder down the field?

Ah, yes, I know what Caesar did to poor benighted Gaul
That had the luck to live before Stan Kostka took the ball,
Before Pug Lund came roaring through, or Bevan ripped a hole,
Or Larson's cleats tore up the sod around the winning goal.

The Gophers' serenade rings out and chills the startled breast
From feet and thunder down the turf across the ravaged West—
And towns, beleaguered, call for help or send a wailing cry,
As Kostka hammers through a line or Lund goes storming by.

Let charging lines and blocking backs stand in their right of way—
Let rivals give their skill and might to break the Gopher sway—
Their answer rings across the West in each marauding smack—
"The Norseman's on the rampage now—the Viking's day is back!"

The names Lund, Kostka and Bevan probably don't mean much to modern football fans, but to those who remember the 1930s, they were the warriors and masters of the sport. Indeed, they were Saturday's heroes.

Besides Francis (Pug) Lund, Stan Kostka, Bill Bevan and Frank (Butch) Larson, there were other big names in the Minnesota cast: George Roscoe, Julius Alfonse, Glenn Seidel, Babe LeVoir, Charles (Bud) Wilkinson, George Svendsen, Bob Tenner, Phil Bengtson, Milt Bruhn, Ed Widseth and Dick Smith.

At the other end of the spectrum was the likes of Dick Potvin. A reserve guard for the Gophers, Potvin nevertheless knew what made the team tick.

"Drill, drill, drill, one, two, three, down and shift," recalled Potvin, reflecting on a Minnesota routine. "Bernie Bierman was discipline all the way. We weren't a big team—I think we had only three or four starters over 200 pounds. But almost everyone else was 190 or 195. What made our team was quickness. We were fast.

"I was always a sub. The moments I relished were a couple of key blocks, a couple of good tackles. I also remember the end of the (1934) Michigan game. I ended up on top of the Michigan center. His name was Gerald Ford.

"He had been picked on several All-America teams and was going to play in the East-West Shrine game. He said, 'Nice game. You fellows really have a great team.' Little did I know then he'd eventually be President of the United States."

The Michigan contest was Minnesota's fifth game of the '34 season; by then, Bierman's troops had gotten up a full head of steam with their line-'em-up-and-run-over-'em style of play.

In their season opener, the Gophers played North Dakota State at the "Brickhouse," otherwise known as Memorial Stadium, and walloped the Bison, 56-12, with Kostka scoring four touchdowns and Roscoe adding two.

Then the foe was Nebraska. Bevan picked off a Cornhusker pass and returned it for a touchdown, Kostka scored two more TDs and Lund rushed for 166 yards as the Gophers spilled the Huskers, 20-0.

Before the '34 season, Lund had the little finger on his left hand amputated. Years before, he had dislocated the finger during pole-vault practice. The more Lund competed in sports, particularly football, the worse the injury became. Finally, the finger stuck straight out and wouldn't bend.

"Pug figured it was getting in the way of receiving the football," said LeVoir, one of the Minnesota quarterbacks. "And he took center snaps on every play. So, with Bernie Bierman's blessing, off came the finger. Pug always said the finger was of no use to him anyhow."

Lund, in Bierman's estimation, was "just about the greatest competitor I ever saw. You see lots of football players come and go during a coaching career. Some of these are blockers and little more. They couldn't take a ball for a gain if it meant their graduation. Others are blockers and, in addition, everything required to make an all-around star. Pug was like that.

". . . As a ballcarrier, passer, kicker, blocker and tackler, he carried out every heavy assignment we gave him. He was battered and broken up. Teeth

One of Minnesota's top linemen in 1934 and '35 was a youngster named Bud Wilkinson, who went on to fame as coach of the Oklahoma Sooners.

knocked out, finger amputated, thumb broken . . . but he carried on."

Lund expected the Gophers to have a great season in 1934.

"The funny thing was, none of us probably thought at all of being national champions," he recalled. "I mean, it wasn't a dream we had—like a good team in the 1950s or '60s would have had. We were just simple people. We thought right from the start it was going to be our year, but it wasn't a dream."

Bierman had spent the previous off-season devising a new system of blocking for the Gophers. Instead of assigning his blockers to go after specific players, Bierman ordered his players to block areas—or holes.

In the opening two victories against North Dakota State and Nebraska, the Gophers showed little of that blocking pattern, or any other innovations. Next up, however, was a road game with Eastern power Pittsburgh, whose only defeat in its 26 previous regular-season games had come a year earlier against Bierman's crew.

Bierman started cautiously against the Panthers—super-cautiously, in fact. Hoping his defenders could wear down Jock Sutherland's team and thereby create turnovers, he repeatedly ordered Lund to punt on second down.

"At the beginning, they blocked us like knives," said Bruhn, a Gopher guard who went on to considerable coaching success at Wisconsin. "But as physical attrition mounted late in the game, when we blocked them, we could hear them groaning."

Pittsburgh, despite being unable to score after recovering a Minnesota fumble at the Gophers' 6-yard line, nevertheless held a 7-0 halftime lead after a 64-yard scoring play.

Bierman, a basically quiet man who once acknowledged that he'd likely "end up laughing at myself" if he attempted to deliver an emotional locker-room talk, summed up his team's halftime situation in five words: "Two touchdowns will win it."

Even in the second half, the Gophers punted on second and third downs. Finally, the strategy paid off as Pitt misplayed a Lund kick and Larson recovered the fumble on the Panthers' 43.

The Gophers started to move and, behind Kostka's running, reached the Pitt 22. Then, as the final period began, Lund started to his right and handed off to Alfonse, who cut against the grain and scooted into the end zone. Bevan's conversion kick tied the score.

Later, with time becoming a factor in the fourth quarter and Minnesota perched on the Panthers' 18, Bierman called for a play inserted into the game plan only that week.

Kostka, the burly fullback known as the "Hammer of the North," took a direct snap from center in Bierman's buck-lateral sequence and went straight ahead. But instead of crashing into the line, he handed the ball to quarterback Seidel, who pitched to Lund running toward the right.

With the Panthers pursuing, Lund pulled up and tossed a quick pass to end Tenner, who dragged a couple of Pitt players into the end zone while scoring the game-winning touchdown. As Arthur J. Daley of the New York Times reported in his game story the next day, Minnesota had "abandoned, for just one moment, the bludgeon in favor of the rapier. . . ."

The final score was 13-7, and the game proved the only close call Minnesota had all season.

Gopher lineman Svendsen said his team's real contests in 1934 "were at practice. It was the starters against the rednecks. The competition was greater against ourselves."

Kostka remembered those scrimmages well.

"I was a member of the second team," Kostka said, "and we thought our guys were every bit as good as those on the first team. We used to have bloody wars in scrimmages and more than a few fistfights. Bernie liked that once in a while. It livened things up."

Why was the celebrated Kostka, a runner whose bull-like thrusts drew comparisons to the exploits of Gopher great Bronko Nagurski, relegated to the second team? Because of a player named Sheldon Beise. "Sheldon was one of the best blocking fullbacks who ever lived," Svendsen said. "But Kostka was like a runaway tank when he had the ball."

The two fullbacks were intense rivals, and Bierman catered to Beise because of his blocking skills. But when the chips were down, Kostka was sent into the fray.

The Gophers had another superb back in Art Clarkson, from Washington state. He made many key runs during his Minnesota tenure.

At the time, Minnesota was one of the few integrated collegiate teams. The Gophers had a promising black player in end Dwight Reed, who would gain starter status in 1935. "Minneapolis was a real melting pot," LeVoir said. "We didn't know there was a difference in color of skin, maybe because Minnesota had a tradition of playing black players."

That tradition had begun with Bobby Marshall, a Gopher star in football and baseball beginning in 1904. Marshall later became an assistant football coach at Minnesota.

Following the '34 Minnesota squad's victory at Pittsburgh, the Gophers blasted Iowa, Michigan, Indiana, Chicago and Wisconsin by a combined score of 181-19.

Sportswriters in the Twin Cities began calling the Minnesota players the "Golden Gophers." At the start of the 1933 season, Bierman outfitted the players in mustard-colored uniforms and it would be 3½ years before Minnesota lost a game wearing those yellow suits.

"It was hard for teams to pick up the ball with our players wearing those uniforms," Bierman acknowledged. "It also gave our players an identity."

Not that the players needed an identity. They had each other—and sportswriters like Rice—to sing their praises.

The players were a close-knit crew.

Another top-notch lineman and one of Minnesota's best players was Bill Bevan, a consensus All-America in 1934.

"We used to go to this little place in North St. Paul after the games on Saturday," LeVoir said. "Yes," added Kostka. "If we had 55 guys, 54 would be there. All with two bits in their pockets—the price of about five beers."

Bierman let the athletes socialize, then made them pay the price on Mondays. "He'd have us running laps all day," Svendsen said. "If they would have straightened out our jogging, we could have run to the moon and back."

Following the Golden Gophers' football fortunes helped take people's minds off the Depression.

Eric Rehnwall, a longtime St. Paul newspaper writer, was a youngster in the early 1930s.

"Gopher football was the greatest," Rehnwall said. "Every kid listened to football on Saturdays in the fall. We couldn't afford tickets—my dad worked in west-central Minnesota and never got off work until noon on Saturdays. Then, he'd head into St. Paul with a load of pheasants and farm eggs.

"When my dad got home, we'd talk about the game. Those were great players—Pug Lund, Bob Tenner, Stan Kostka, Bud Wilkinson, Dwight Reed and the others. They were idols to us kids."

"I was living with the LeVoir family," said Kostka, recalling the tenor of the times. "I paid them $7 a month. Their house had no heat, and Babe's father was dying."

LeVoir worked at a bank in Minneapolis for $50 a month to support his family. After attending class in the morning and working in the afternoon, he would hustle off to practice, "My dad died in 1935 and we struggled," LeVoir said. "But college was cheap. Our quarterly tuition was only $18."

Lund also worked for a bank. "The money I got for working, plus what could be made by selling tickets for the game, got us through," said Lund, a consensus All-America in 1934 along with Bevan and Larson.

Kostka got free meals at a restaurant because "they didn't have a cashier and I volunteered to help out."

Svendsen said team members felt proud of bringing recognition to Minnesota. "Shucks," he said, "we had the town in our hands. The enthusiasm was just tremendous—in the midst of the Depression we Minnesotans had something to brag about . . . it would have been doggone grim for people if our team hadn't brought the community together."

Each football Saturday, street cars and a procession of Fords, Buicks, Auburns and Packards made their way to Memorial Stadium. It was the place to be.

"The reception we received was tremendous," Lund said.

Just how the Gophers would be received in 1935 was the subject of considerable conjecture. After all,

Dick Smith played tackle and helped spark the talented offense that destroyed Minnesota's helpless opponents.

Minnesota star Pug Lund looks for daylight as he returns a punt during a 1933 game against Pittsburgh.

senior losses from the 1934 team included Lund, Larson, Bruhn, Tenner and tackle Bengtson (who, more than three decades later, would succeed Vince Lombardi as coach of the Green Bay Packers). Furthermore, Svendsen, Clarkson, Bevan and Kostka also were on the sidelines because—against Big Ten Conference guidelines—they had played football on the West Coast as collegiate freshmen.

"I went to the Green Bay Packers as a senior and Stan Kostka played for the old NFL Brooklyn Dodgers," Svendsen said. "We'd have preferred to stay at Minnesota."

Additionally, Minnesota lost the services of Alfonse, an academic casualty.

Despite the wave of manpower setbacks, the 1935 Gophers persevered. In fact, only Nebraska, Northwestern and Iowa gave Minnesota trouble that year. Bierman's fourth Gopher team beat the Cornhuskers, 12-7, before subduing the Wildcats, 21-13, and then the Hawkeyes, 13-6.

The other games were romps. Little Brown Jug rival Michigan, for example, was thrashed by a 40-0 score.

Reed and Ray King turned out to be tremendous replacements for ends Tenner and Larson, Widseth attained consensus All-America status at tackle and Smith stood out at that position and newcomers Rudy Gmitro, Andy Uram and Clarence (Tuffy) Thompson picked up brilliantly in the backfield for Kostka, Lund and Clarkson.

It was Roscoe, though, who saved the day in a titanic struggle against Nebraska. He returned the opening kickoff 74 yards and scored both touchdowns for the Gophers, who frustrated the Huskers with a couple of goal-line stands.

LeVoir was the team's most valuable player in 1935—Lund was so honored in '34—after filling in for Seidel at quarterback over the last five games of the season. Seidel suffered a collarbone fracture against Tulane in an early-season game, a contest in which Wilkinson, a junior guard, blocked a punt, scooped up the ball and ran for a touchdown.

In Minnesota's season finale, a 33-7 romp over Wisconsin, the Gophers scored on what might have been the ultimate football play. In those days, newspapers used to run several photos of each play. Photographers from both St. Paul and Minneapolis papers documented a Minnesota touchdown run on which all 11 Badger players were on the ground at the same time after being smacked down by Gopher blockers.

Wilkinson, a gifted athlete who as a senior in 1936 was switched from the line to quarterback and helped the Gophers win the Associated Press' first national-championship poll, was asked what made these Minnesota teams so special.

The 1934 Gophers: Front row (left to right) —Maurice Johnson, Bob Tenner, Phil Bengtson, Bill Bevan, Pug Lund, Dale Rennebohm, Vern Oech, Ed Widseth, John Roning. Second row—Whit Rork, Art Clarkson, Milt Bruhn, Dick Smith, Stan Kostka, Bill Proffitt, Selmer Anderson. Third row—Glenn Seidel, George Roscoe, Leslie Knudson, Bud Wilkinson, Jay Bevan, Bill Freimuth, Bud Smith, Frank Dallera, Ray Antil, Dick Potvin. Fourth row—Julius Alfonse, George Svendsen, George Rennix, Babe LeVoir, Sheldon Beise, Head Coach Bernie Bierman, Athletic Director Frank McCormick, manager Paul Berggren, equipment manager Oscar Munson.

"Coach Bierman," said the man who himself would become a collegiate coaching legend at Oklahoma, "and (because) our players really wanted to play."

What was Bierman like?

"Very brilliant," LeVoir said. "And very intelligent. You knew if you followed what he wanted you to do, you'd have success. Bierman would pick up the opponent's best play and perfect it. If Michigan had a great play, we'd use it against Iowa. And if Iowa had one, we'd use it against Wisconsin. And do a better job of executing it than anyone."

Kostka recalled Bierman as a coach "who insisted on precision. If he wanted you to run a step and a half, that's what he meant. If you ran two steps, you'd end up circling the field for a few punishment laps.

"But Bernie was also a gentleman. After you graduated, he treated you on an equal basis and was as friendly as could be. I'm just glad I had the opportunity to play for him. It's astounding, but I don't recall a single player who played for Bernie in our era that didn't make a success of himself."

Were the Minnesota Gophers really "Destroyers," as Grantland Rice had written?

"I don't know about that," Pug Lund said. "But we were a fine, fine college football team."

Bierman thought so, too.

"Football is a better game in some ways today," he allowed grudgingly before his death in 1977. "There are more boys to choose from, and statistics prove that they have gotten bigger from one decade to the next.

"But I have not seen a team anywhere—in person, on film, on television—that is better than my 1934 team."

Minnesota, 1934-35

ROAD TO GREATNESS

1934 RESULTS (8-0)

Opponent	Score	Opp. Record	Opp. Bowl Game
North Dakota State	56-12	5-3-2	
Nebraska	20-0	6-3-0	
Pittsburgh	13-7	8-1-0	
Iowa	48-12	2-5-1	
Michigan	34-0	1-7-0	
Indiana	30-0	3-3-2	
Chicago	35-7	4-4-0	
at Wisconsin	34-0	4-4-0	

1935 RESULTS (8-0)

Opponent	Score	Opp. Record	Opp. Bowl Game
North Dakota State	26-6	7-1-1	
at Nebraska	12-7	6-2-1	
Tulane	20-0	6-4-0	
Northwestern	21-13	4-3-1	
Purdue	29-7	4-4-0	
Iowa	13-6	4-2-2	
at Michigan	40-0	4-4-0	
Wisconsin	33-7	1-7-0	

FACTS AND FIGURES

Minnesota's teams of 1934 and 1935 contributed 16 victories to the Golden Gophers' 28-game unbeaten streak, a string of success that began with the season opener of 1933 and ended in the fifth game of the 1936 campaign. During that stretch, only three opponents could dent the Minnesota defense for more than seven points in a game and 11 foes were shutout victims. . . . The Gophers attained elite status against some formidable opposition. Teams on Minnesota's 1934 schedule compiled a 33-30-5 record (.522 winning percentage), and those on the Gophers' 1935 slate posted a 36-27-5 mark (.566). . . . If the Gophers appeared a cut above in the X's-and-O's department, there probably was good reason. Besides an astute coaching staff headed by Bernie Bierman, Minnesota had some coaches-to-be in the trenches as well. Included in the playing ranks of the 1934 Gophers were Charles (Bud) Wilkinson, Milt Bruhn, Phil Bengtson and John Roning. Wilkinson went on to coach Oklahoma to a record 47 consecutive victories, while Bruhn directed Wisconsin to two Rose Bowls. Bengtson served as both an assistant and head coach in the pro ranks, and Roning coached at the University of Denver before that school dropped football after the 1960 season.

STATISTICAL LEADERS

PASSING

	Att.	Comp.	Yards	TD	Pct.	Int.
George Roscoe (1935)	54	15	344	4	27.8	7
Pug Lund (1934)	19	7	151	2	36.8	2

RUSHING

	Att.	Yards	Avg.	TD
Stan Kostka (1934)	111	665	6.0	10
Pug Lund (1934)	111	621	5.6	5
George Roscoe (1935)	138	592	4.3	5
Tuffy Thompson (1935)	85	368	4.3	5

RECEIVING

	Rec.	Yards	Avg.	TD
Babe LeVoir (1935)	8	168	21.0	1
Maurice Johnson (1934)	4	115	28.8	2
Ray King (1935)	4	70	17.5	2

SCORING

	TD	FG	PAT	Points
Stan Kostka (1934)	10	0	0	60
Sheldon Beise (1935)	7	0	1	43
Pug Lund (1934)	6	0	0	36
Tuffy Thompson (1935)	6	0	0	36

KEY CHARACTERS

The Conductor

COACH: Bernie Bierman.

Record: 93-35-6, 16 years at Minnesota.

Bierman succeeded Fritz Crisler as Minnesota coach in 1932 and earned his way into the College Football Hall of Fame. . . . He was a soft-spoken person, quiet by nature but a leader with few peers. . . . He successfully kept the Gophers among college football's elite teams, a position Minnesota fans had come to expect. . . . He guided the Gophers to five unbeaten seasons (1933, '34, '35, '40 and '41) and coached three national champions as selected by the Associated Press—in 1936, '40 and '41. . . . His teams compiled a 28-game unbeaten streak that began in 1933 and ended in the fifth game of the 1936 campaign—a 6-0 loss to Northwestern. . . . He coached 12 consensus All-Americas and 1941 Heisman Trophy winner Bruce Smith. . . . He began his head coaching career at Montana in 1919 and gave up coaching after the 1921 campaign and an unspectacular 9-9-3 record. . . . He returned to the coaching ranks as an assistant at Tulane and took the Mississippi A&M (now Mississippi State) reins for two seasons (1925 and '26) before taking over at Tulane. . . . His Mississippi A&M teams compiled an 8-8-1 mark in two seasons and his Green Wave teams were 36-10-2 in five years. . . . He led Tulane to an undefeated (9-0) 1929 season and his 1931 unit compiled an 11-1 mark, losing to Southern California, 21-12, in the 1932 Rose Bowl. . . . He coached in the 1936 College Football All-Star Game. . . . During World War II, he coached a Navy Pre-Flight team at Iowa State for two seasons. . . . Bierman was a captain in the Marine Corps during World War I and a lieutenant-colonel during World War II. . . . His overall college coaching record was 146-62-12 over 26 seasons. . . . He was known fondly around football circles as "The Gray Eagle." . . . He died in 1977 at the age of 82.

Personal Data:

Born: March 11, 1894, near Springfield, Minn.
High School: Litchfield High in Litchfield, Minn.
College: Minnesota.

The Supporting Cast

GUARD: Bill Bevan.

Bevan was a 1934 consensus All-America. . . . He was an effective defender who also handled kickoffs and placements for the Golden Gophers. . . . He was known as a rugged player and furthered that reputation by playing without a helmet. . . . He supplemented his unusual strength with outstanding speed and was without doubt the Gophers' quickest lineman and most ferocious blocker and defender. . . . He received his first letter in 1933.

Personal Data:

Born: March 26, 1913, in Toronto.
High School: Central High in St. Paul, Minn.

END: Stan Kostka.

Kostka played a significant role in the Gophers' 1934 national championship, even though he was a second-string player. . . . The talent-laden Golden Gophers were so deep that the bulldozing Kostka was relegated to reserve status, but he made the most of his opportunities and still led the team in rushing (665 yards) and scoring (10 touchdowns and 60 points). . . . That was his only collegiate season. He was declared ineligible for 1935 and chose to move into the National Football League. . . . He was nicknamed "Hammer of the North."

Personal Data:

Born: July 8, 1912, in St. Paul, Minn.
High School: South St. Paul High.

FULLBACK: Frank Larson.

Larson was a consensus All-America in 1934. . . . He was a solid player on both sides of the ball and a top-notch downfield blocker. . . . That was pretty much the limit of his role in Coach Bernie Bierman's single-wing offense. . . . He received his first letter in 1932.

Personal Data:

Born: 1913 in Duluth, Minn.
High School: Densield High in Duluth.

HALFBACK: Francis (Pug) Lund.

Lund was the team leader and most talented player. . . . He was an excellent all-around athlete who excelled in all phases of the game and had the knack for coming through when a big play was needed. . . . He was named the Golden Gophers' most valuable player in both 1933 and '34 and was a 1934 consensus All-America. . . . When a finger that he had injured years earlier continued to bother him on the football field, Lund had the digit amputated because he felt it restricted his play. . . . He was captain of the 1934 Minnesota team and the man Bierman chose to build his program around. . . . He earned his first letter in 1932 and eventually won election into the College Football Hall of Fame.

Personal Data:

Born: April 8, 1913, in Rice Lake, Wis.
High School: Rice Lake High.

Horses, Mules And Shock Troops

Notre Dame, 1924
By Bill Bilinski

In posting a career winning percentage that has never been surpassed, Knute Rockne became the collegiate coach by whom all others are measured. But if any coach today used the same strategy Rockne employed at Notre Dame in the 1920s, he'd be committed.

Imagine a coach having Tim Brown suited up but not putting him into the game until the second period, or ordering Vinny Testaverde to scout the opposing defense for a quarter before going in. The team's fans would be calling for the men in white coats before the media even had time to crucify him.

But football was a much simpler game in those days, and most fans didn't know enough about coaching strategy to be critical anyway. And besides, the Rock knew what he was doing.

In 1924, his seventh year at Notre Dame, Rockne had probably his strongest and most seasoned team. He had the Four Horsemen—quarterback Harry Stuhldreher, fullback Elmer Layden and halfbacks Jim Crowley and Don Miller—in his all-senior backfield, not to mention the Seven Mules up front. Those 11 players were so good "that the Holy Ghost couldn't have broken into that lineup," said Harry O'Boyle, a kicker and reserve halfback on that team. And yet Rockne seldom put them into the game until the second quarter. He usually started his second-stringers.

"The second team acts very much in the capacity of shock absorbers," Rockne explained, spawning the "shock troops" label handed the backups on many of his teams, particularly his 1924 club. "We know by experience that two football teams generally hit the hardest in the first quarter."

Rockne liked the idea of his "varsity sitting on the sidelines, becoming keyed up unconsciously" while the other team's starters began to tire. It was an odd strategy, but one he could get away with since he had the luxury of a second unit that was pretty talented in its own right.

"We were madder than hell we weren't on the first team," O'Boyle said. He and his fellow second-teamers channeled all that pride and determination into their performances, thus making the shock troops all the more effective.

By the time the first-stringers came in, Notre Dame's opponent generally was primed for a knockout punch. That happened 10 times in 10 tries in 1924, when the Fighting Irish earned accolades as the Helms Athletic Foundation's national champions.

Even that long ago, Notre Dame football success was nothing new. From 1887 through 1917, the year before Rockne became coach, Notre Dame compiled a 147-36-14 record. In Rockne's first six years the Irish had never lost more than one game in a season, and his 1919 and 1920 squads were undefeated. The only team to beat Notre Dame in the two years preceding the 1924 season was Nebraska, which had won in both '22 and '23.

Without question, Notre Dame football was big. Rockne just made it bigger, expanding interest in the Irish to the national level.

Rockne's teams played a national schedule, the first to do so on a regular basis. The Irish played only four home games in 1924, traveling to the Polo Grounds in New York, Princeton, N.J., Madison, Wis., Soldier Field in Chicago and Pittsburgh for their other five regular-season contests.

This national exposure increased Notre Dame's popularity, especially among the Catholic popula-

The famed Four Horsemen of Notre Dame were (left to right) halfback Don Miller, fullback Elmer Layden, halfback Jim Crowley and quarterback Harry Stuhldreher.

tion. "If you were Catholic," O'Boyle said, "it was sacrilegious to be against us. Generally, we were treated royally.... We were accorded a lot of esteem, maybe more than we were entitled to."

The media also treated Notre Dame well, largely because of Rockne. Knowing that a favorable press could help market his team, the coach was gracious and accommodating with reporters.

"Rockne was a bright, personable man," Crowley told a reporter years later. "He was what the sportswriters today would call 'good copy.' He could be funny, caustic, controversial. Hardly a day went by when he wasn't quoted somewhere.

"When we arrived in town for a game, there were always photographers waiting on the train platform. Notre Dame had always been in the paper, but Rockne put the school on page one."

Notre Dame's national following helped Rockne by steering a number of outstanding athletes in his direction. Rockne, a brilliant motivator and innovative strategist, took care of the rest.

Ironically, Knute never graduated from high school, perhaps because he spent too much time playing sports. But after four years of working in

Chicago, where he had lived since immigrating from Norway with his family as a youngster, he enrolled at Notre Dame and became a fine student, graduating magna cum laude. He also made his mark as a thespian, a writer for the student newspaper and yearbook and a flutist in the school orchestra.

Despite that busy schedule, Rockne played football for four years, earning third-team All-America honors as a senior end in 1913. He and quarterback Gus Dorais formed one of the earliest successful passing combinations, and his love of the aerial game later was reflected in his coaching.

Rockne was named the Irish coach in 1918, less than five years after his graduation from Notre

The man who lifted Notre Dame football into national prominence was Coach Knute Rockne (left), who had served as captain of the 1913 Fighting Irish (above). He was esteemed for his ability as a teacher, which included both verbal instruction (below right) and visual demonstration (above right).

Dame. He had spent the intervening four seasons as a graduate assistant in chemistry and assistant football coach. It wasn't much training for such a big job, but he learned quickly and then applied his own ingenuity to create many of the country's strongest teams.

One of Rockne's most successful tactics was the "Notre Dame shift," in which all four backfield men were in motion at the snap. It was so unpredictable—and unstoppable—that the NCAA eventually enacted a rule requiring a one-second stop before the snap, effectively wiping out the maneuver.

The use of shock troops and new blocking techniques were among the many other wrinkles Rockne added to the game. Other coaches were free to borrow Rockne's ideas and institute them at their schools, and many ultimately did, but never with as much success as Notre Dame. The Irish always seemed to execute better, largely because Rockne taught them so well.

"Rock always said football was a game of wit and intelligence, not brute strength," Crowley said.

It also was a game of emotion, and Rockne used that to his advantage. His famous locker-room speeches tapped his players' emotions, giving the Irish the motivational edge they sometimes needed to win.

"He was effervescent," O'Boyle said. "And he was quite an actor. He could really get you worked up. We never went into a game flat."

Even if it meant telling a white lie to inspire his troops. For example, Rockne thought his squad needed a shot in the arm to beat a superior Georgia Tech team at Atlanta in 1922, when the Four Horsemen were sophomores. As Joe Doyle recounted in his book "Fighting Irish: A Century of Notre Dame Football," Rockne supposedly broke into tears before the game when he read a telegram to the team about the serious illness of his son, Billy. The players made it their mission to win for little Billy. They succeeded, getting pretty banged up in the process, and returned triumphantly to South Bend, where one of the first fans to greet the team was, you guessed it, Billy Rockne.

"Not only did we win the game," Crowley said, "but we effected a miraculous cure in the process."

Notre Dame didn't need any tricks to beat its first two opponents in 1924, Lombard and Wabash. In winning those games easily by a combined score of 74-0, the Irish roared into New York with a full head of steam for their first big test of the year—Army, which was considered their strongest opponent on a formidable schedule.

This October 18 game at the Polo Grounds became famous, but it was more the power of the pen than the power of two football teams that made it so. If not for the colorful prose of New York Herald Tribune sportswriter Grantland Rice, this game and its star players probably would be long forgotten. Rice forever etched the identity of four backs into the mind of a nation, making them larger than life in their own time. His often-related account, considered a bit melodramatic by some, stuck like no other then or since:

> *Outlined against a blue-gray October sky, the Four Horsemen rode again.*
>
> *In dramatic lore they are known as famine, pestilence, destruction and death. These are only aliases. Their real names are Stuhldreher, Miller, Crowley and Layden. They formed the crest of the South Bend cyclone before which another fighting Army team was swept over the precipice at the Polo Grounds this afternoon as 55,000 spectators peered down on the bewildering panorama spread out upon the green plain below.*

All that for a 13-7 victory that wasn't secure until center Adam Walsh, who was playing with two broken hands, intercepted a pass late in the game. The backs played a superb game—Miller rushed for 148 yards, Crowley 102 and Layden 60 while Stuhldreher ran the offense masterfully—but their performances hardly seemed worthy of lasting fame.

In fact, Rice's account might have dissolved into history like any other game story had it not been for Rockne's student publicity aide, George Strickler, who later became sports editor of the Chicago Tribune. He was responsible for assembling the players shortly after their return to South Bend, posing them on horses and getting the photograph out to the wire services. The picture was reproduced across the country and provided a lifetime identity for the four young men.

"After that, we said a prayer for Granny (Rice) almost every night because we knew we weren't that great," Miller said modestly. "We have always felt that there were other backfields at Notre Dame superior to ours, such as the 1930 unit, but they never had a Grantland Rice for a press agent and we did."

Said Crowley: "The Four Horsemen thing really made us. There have been a lot of great backfields, but they didn't get that identity. I never expected it. I read the (Rice) story after the game. I thought it was very nice, but that's all. I didn't say, 'Wow, this is going to make us famous.' "

The novelty never seemed to wear off, causing at least one minor annoyance for one of the Four Horsemen. "Next to flying, about which I remain a devout coward, I like riding a horse least," Layden once said. "Yet it always seemed that whenever Stuhldreher, Crowley, Miller and Layden got together, someone wanted to put us on horses."

Layden, the fastest Horseman, was no more excit-

The Seven Mules were (left to right) end Ed Hunsinger, tackle Edgar (Rip) Miller, guard Noble Kizer, center Adam Walsh, guard John Weibel, tackle Joe Bach and end Chuck Collins. They protected quarterback Harry Stuhldreher, fullback Elmer Layden and halfbacks Jim Crowley (left) and Don Miller (right).

ed about playing fullback than he was about riding horses when Rockne first proposed that he switch from halfback late in the '22 season. The team's starting fullback had been felled by an injury, but Layden, who weighed only 162 pounds, squawked at the idea because he considered himself too light.

Rockne's response was quick. "Elmer," he said, "with you we are going to revolutionize fullback play. We are going to give it speed. You are a track man, the ideal type for my purpose. Man, you will go down in football history as the first of the new-style fullbacks."

Layden bought the line and went on to become a consensus All-America as a senior, earning much of his praise for his defensive work. He rushed for 423 yards that season, but his offensive statistics suffered from his own modest nature.

"Elmer could have been even a better player, a better scorer, if he hadn't been so unselfish," Crowley said. "He never failed to block for the rest of us. He was always a first-class gentleman."

And, in O'Boyle's recollection, the greatest overall talent. "He was as good as any I had seen," O'Boyle said. "There wasn't anything he couldn't do—block, kick, punt, pass—and besides that, he was a heck of a nice guy."

While Layden had the best speed, Miller had the best moves of the foursome. Rockne considered the 160-pound halfback the greatest open-field runner he ever coached. That was quite a compliment for Miller, who was so lightly regarded when he came to South Bend that he practically had to beg Rockne to give him a uniform, and he might not have gotten that had his three older brothers not played for Notre Dame before him. But he was the first of the Horsemen to earn a starting spot as a sophomore in 1922, and he led the 1924 Irish with 763 yards rushing and 297 yards receiving. Ironically, he was the only Horseman not to be named a consensus All-America as the last backfield spot was filled by Illinois' Red Grange.

Opposite Miller at left halfback was Crowley, another shifty runner. Called by Rockne the "nerviest back I've known" and "the greatest interferer for his weight (162 pounds) I've seen," Crowley rushed for 739 yards and led the team in scoring in '24.

Noting Crowley's drowsy-eyed look, Rockne dubbed him "Sleepy Jim" early in his Notre Dame career. "Rockne said he felt I had a great future as a tester in an alarm clock factory," Crowley recalled. Despite that appearance, however, the fun-loving Crowley became known as the wittiest of the Four Horsemen.

"Jimmy kept us from getting tense and taking ourselves too seriously," Rockne once said. "He was a reminder that college and even football should be fun. If anything, he was our team's unofficial spokesman."

The team's official leader was Stuhldreher. At 5-foot-7 and 151 pounds, he was the smallest member of Rockne's diminutive backfield, but he was tough and feisty.

"Harry was the cocky sort," Crowley said. "He oozed confidence, which was good for a quarterback, but he was small."

Nevertheless, he was an effective passer and punt returner, a surprisingly good blocker and a tremendous field general. "He was really a master of sound quarterback play," Rockne wrote in a 1930 Collier's magazine article. "He could read through another team's strategy without a key to the code."

Besides the Four Horsemen, the only Irish player who attracted much media attention was Walsh, the team captain. The scribes covering the Army game praised his ability to open huge holes in the Army line despite starting the contest with a broken bone in one hand and breaking a bone in the other during the game. But Walsh, like the other linemen, was generally lost in the shuffle of excitement over the backfield stars.

"We are just the seven mules who do all the work so that these four fellows can gallop into fame," Walsh told a reporter.

Thus was born a legendary line to protect a legendary backfield. The Seven Mules, who were more widely known for their collective nickname than their individual identities, consisted of Walsh at center, guards Noble Kizer and John Weibel, tackles Joe Bach and Edgar (Rip) Miller and ends Chuck Collins and Ed Hunsinger.

"There wasn't a game we played for three years, with one or two exceptions, where we weren't outweighed 10 to 30 pounds a man," Walsh once reflected about the Seven Mules, whose average weight of 176 pounds was only 17 pounds more than the backfield's. "We were quick, though. It's like the black flies they've got in Maine. One stings you on the nose, and by the time you reach up to swat him, he's got you on the seat of your pants."

The linemen generally accepted their low-profile roles without complaining, while the Horsemen did a pretty good job keeping their egos in check. But on a rare occasion when the backs started letting their chests swell a bit too much, Rockne had a quick remedy. He pulled out the Seven Mules and let the Horsemen take a few licks while running behind the second-string line. "See?" Rockne said. "Without the Mules, you Horsemen are just turtles."

The members of the shock troops also settled for second-fiddle status, so dissension never was a serious problem on the team. But O'Boyle said he sometimes bristled at all the attention being focused on the Four Horsemen.

"I think they could have spread around the achievements (glory) a little more," he said. "We (the shock troops) played an important part on that team and never got much credit."

Actually, the Horsemen sometimes got tired of being in the spotlight. They were besieged by flocks of reporters from around the country, all of whom wanted a new angle on the Four Horsemen theme. Before one practice, a female reporter from a major newspaper was especially persistent in her attempts to get something new out of Crowley.

"Who was she?" a teammate asked Crowley after the woman finally left.

"That was the Second Horsewoman: Pestilence," he replied.

Despite the distractions, the Irish kept winning. After a 12-0 conquest of Princeton, they recorded three straight easy victories, including 34-6 over Nebraska to avenge the previous two years' defeats.

Northwestern then made a run at the Irish on a muddy November 22 afternoon in the first game ever played at Soldier Field, which at that time was called Municipal Grant Park Stadium. The game story in the Chicago Herald and Examiner raved of the defensive work of Weibel and backup guard Dick Hanousek, who were "insurmountable mountains to the Purple (Northwestern) offense." Touchdowns by Stuhldreher and Layden gave the Irish the edge in a 13-6 victory.

A week later, Notre Dame traveled to Carnegie Tech and struggled to a 13-13 halftime tie. But the Irish ran away in the second half as the Horsemen "proceeded to give the most sensational exhibition of forward passing ever seen on any gridiron," the Pittsburgh Post reported. "Twelve straight passes were completed and, incidentally, two more touchdowns scored in the third quarter, and still two more in the last period. Stuhldreher was at his best. (Backup fullback Bernie) Livergood, who was playing in the place of Layden (who was injured), was unstoppable."

The 40-19 victory capped a perfect 9-0 regular season, Notre Dame's first since 1920. The Irish were selected to take on undefeated, once-tied Stanford and its legendary figures, Coach Pop Warner and fullback Ernie Nevers, in the Rose Bowl on January 1, 1925.

It was Notre Dame's first postseason game, and the Irish would not appear in another until the 1970 Cotton Bowl. For years, university officials ruled out bowl games because they conflicted with exam schedules. But Rockne convinced the administration to accept this bowl bid on the condition that Notre Dame's share of the proceeds be used for a new basketball court. Rockne was no big fan of basketball, but the school needed a new court and as athletic director, he saw a way to finance it. The trip to Pasadena was approved.

Among Rockne's primary concerns was his players' stamina in the warmer temperatures on the West Coast, where Notre Dame was making its first appearance. So, he arranged a slow, somewhat indirect cross-country train trip that would include stops in Louisiana, Texas and Arizona, thus giving the Irish time to both prepare for Stanford and get used to the weather.

The extra game provided the media with another opportunity to dote on the Four Horsemen. By that time, some of the other players were beginning to notice a distinct difference in the way they and the celebrated backs were being treated.

"We stopped in New Orleans to work out," Collins, the left end, recalled years later, "and the linemen rode on a leaky bus while the backs rode in Cadillacs."

As the train chugged westward, Rockne could see a potential problem developing. "We stopped off at Tucson," left tackle Bach once said, "and Rock was worried about all the publicity the backs were getting. He was afraid the teamwork would suffer. So

Irish fullback Elmer Layden was blessed with the ability to do anything—block, kick, punt or pass.

The 1924 Fighting Irish: Front row (left to right) —Harry Stuhldreher, Bill Cerney, Don Miller, John Weibel, Jim Crowley, Adam Walsh, Edgar Miller, Ed Hunsinger, Elmer Layden, Joe Bach. Second row—Head Coach Knute Rockne, Clem Crowe, Noble Kizer, John McMullan, Joe Boland, John McManmon, Chuck Collins, John Wallace, Charles Glueckert, Ward Connell, Bernie Livergood, Luther. Third row—Sutliffe, Eddie Scharer, Wilbur Eaton, Harry O'Boyle, Dick Hanousek, Gene Edwards, Joe Maxwell, Joe Harmon, Tom Hearden, Vince Harrington, Lieb.

he called us all together and he said we would take a vote to see which was more important, the line or the backs. The linemen won, 7-4."

Rockne, whose many contributions to college football included the art of downplaying his team's strength, also expressed concern about his club's physical condition. "Nobody on my squad is in shape to play a hard game," he said upon arriving in Tucson, where the Irish practiced again. "I will be satisfied with 3-0."

After the practice, however, the coach was more optimistic. "The men are in better shape than I thought," he said. "If the change in climate isn't too great, we may be able to cope with Stanford's powerful attack."

They were, but it took some big plays to do it. The Irish yielded 17 first downs while getting only seven themselves, yet still recorded a convincing 27-10 triumph.

The hero of the game was Layden, who ran three yards for Notre Dame's first touchdown and returned interceptions of Nevers passes 78 and 70 yards for two more scores. Notre Dame got another touchdown when the Indians fumbled one of Layden's deep punts and Hunsinger picked up the ball and ran to the end zone from 20 yards out.

Though the Irish gained only 186 yards while surrendering 316 and were bested in almost every other offensive category, they kept Nevers and Co. at bay most of the afternoon. They forced eight turnovers and came up with a critical goal-line stand in the fourth quarter to hang on after the Indians had moved inside the Notre Dame 1-yard line.

The game, played in 89-degree heat, took its toll on Crowley, who wound up in the hospital with heat exhaustion, and Stuhldreher, who had played with a broken bone in his foot. But they could enjoy the leisurely trip home—as national champions.

"That would always be my favorite team," Rockne once said. "I think I sensed that that backfield was a product of destiny. At times they caused me a certain amount of pain and exasperation, but mainly they brought me great joy. I suppose they'd been brought together by accident, but it was no accident that had made them into great players and a great unit. That was design and hard work."

And it wasn't just four backs who sparked the Irish to greatness. It was a team effort that would have fallen short without the tremendous performances of the Seven Mules and the shock troops.

"For real athletes, you must hand it to the old Four Horsemen team," Rockne said shortly before his tragic death in a 1931 plane crash. "Somehow they seemed able to go to town whenever the occasion demanded. I've never seen a team that had more poise, mentally and physically. In their senior year, they had every game won before they played it."

Notre Dame, 1924

ROAD TO GREATNESS

1924 RESULTS (10-0)

Opponent	Score	Opp. Record	Opp. Bowl Game
Lombard	40-0	5-4-0	
Wabash	34-0	5-4-0	
*Army	13-7	5-1-2	
at Princeton	12-0	4-2-1	
Georgia Tech	34-3	5-3-1	
at Wisconsin	38-3	2-3-3	
Nebraska	34-6	5-3-0	
†Northwestern	13-6	4-4-0	
at Carnegie Tech	40-19	5-4-0	
ROSE BOWL			
Stanford	**27-10**	**7-1-1**	

*New York City. †Chicago.

FACTS AND FIGURES

The 1924 Fighting Irish set numerous school records, including fewest yards allowed per game (72.3) and fewest total yards (651) and first downs (42) allowed in a season. . . . A good example of the stingy Irish defense was the Wabash game, in which the visitors failed to record a first down the entire game and were forced to punt 13 times. . . . Notre Dame posted three shutouts, and only two opponents reached double-digit scoring. . . . The Irish foes had a combined record of 47-29-8 (.607 winning percentage). . . . Eight of 10 opponents had winning records. . . . The Irish's 1925 Rose Bowl appearance against Stanford marked their first bowl game ever and their last until the 1970 Cotton Bowl. . . . The '24 Irish still hold numerous school bowl-game records, including longest rush (27 yards, Jim Crowley), most interceptions (two, Elmer Layden), most interception yards (148, Layden) and longest interception return (78 yards, Layden). . . . Layden also holds Notre Dame bowl-game marks for punting average (48.5 yards) and longest punt (80 yards). . . . Layden's three-touchdown performance against Stanford was not matched by an Irish player in a bowl game until the 1978 Cotton Bowl. . . . Layden intercepted a pass and returned it 40 yards for a touchdown against Northwestern in 1924. . . . Coach Knute Rockne was in the first class of inductees to the College Football Hall of Fame, and six of his players on the '24 team—the Four Horsemen, tackle Edgar (Rip) Miller and center Adam Walsh—are enshrined with him. . . . The '24 squad was the third of five undefeated teams under Rockne. . . . The only team that beat Notre Dame during the Four Horsemen years was Nebraska, which inflicted a 14-6 loss in 1922 and a stunning 14-7 upset that ruined an otherwise perfect '23 season for the Irish. Both games were played in Lincoln. . . . The Irish also were tied once in that span, a 0-0 stalemate with Army in '22. . . . Except for Nebraska and Army, no opponent held the Irish to less than 12 points in the Four Horsemen era. . . . More than 265,000 fans watched Notre Dame play in 1924, including capacity crowds at the Polo Grounds, the Rose Bowl and two games at Cartier Field, home of the Irish.

STATISTICAL LEADERS

PASSING

	Att.	Comp.	Yards	TD	Pct.	Int.
Harry Stuhldreher	33	25	471	4	75.8	2
Jim Crowley	26	14	236	2	53.8	1

RUSHING

	Att.	Yards	Avg.	TD
Don Miller	107	763	7.1	5
Jim Crowley	131	739	5.6	6
Elmer Layden	111	423	3.8	5

RECEIVING

	Rec.	Yards	Avg.	TD
Don Miller	16	297	18.6	2
Jim Crowley	12	265	22.1	3

SCORING

	TD	FG	PAT	Points
Jim Crowley	9	0	17	71
Don Miller	7	0	0	42
Elmer Layden	6	0	4	40

KEY CHARACTERS

The Conductor

COACH: Knute Rockne.

Record: 105-12-5, 13 years.

Rockne is widely considered the best college football coach ever. . . . His .881 winning percentage is unsurpassed in NCAA history. . . . He coached such legends as George Gipp and the Four Horsemen. . . . He coached quarterback Frank Thomas, who became a highly successful coach at Alabama. . . . Rockne and 16 of his players are members of the College Football Hall of Fame. . . . He succeeded Jesse Harper as coach after the 1917 season. . . . He coached five unbeaten Irish squads, and eight of Rockne's teams won nine or more games. . . . Only two of his 13 teams lost more than one game. . . . The Irish lost consecutive games on only one occasion under Rockne. . . . His teams had unbeaten streaks of 22 games (1918-21), 19 games (1929-30) and 17 games (1921-22). . . . He coached six teams that received national championship acclaim (1919, 1920, 1924, 1927, 1929 and 1930). . . . Rockne, who was considered a tremendous motivator, announced at halftime of a 1925 game against Northwestern that he was so upset with his team's performance, he wouldn't coach the second half. The score was 10-0, but by the time he returned in the third quarter, the Irish had taken a 13-10 lead that stood the rest of the game. . . . He often pushed his players to extremes in an attempt to get the most out of them. . . . Rockne was born in Norway and immigrated to the United States as a youngster. . . . He played only one year of high school football but excelled as a runner and pole vaulter. . . . He dropped out of high school after missing too many classes. . . . He was admitted to Notre Dame four years later after scoring highly on an entrance exam. . . . He lettered at Notre Dame from 1910-13, serving as team captain his senior year. . . . The Gus Dorais-to-Rockne passing combination stunned a powerful Army team, 35-13, in 1913. That performance revolutionized college football by showing that the forward pass was a legitimate offensive weapon. . . . Rockne served in numerous capacities at Notre Dame, including athletic director, business manager, trainer, track coach and ticket manager. . . . A popular speaker, Rockne was en route to Los Angeles to make a football demonstration movie when he died in a plane crash on March 31, 1931.

Personal Data:

Born: March 4, 1888, in Voss, Norway.
High School: Northwest Division High in Chicago.
College: Notre Dame.

The Supporting Cast

HALFBACK: Jim Crowley.

Crowley was known for his shifty moves and quickness. . . . He was one of the famous Four Horsemen and, like the other Horsemen, is a member of the College Football Hall of Fame. . . . He was a consensus All-America in 1924. . . . He led the Irish in rushing in 1922 with 566 yards and in passing in both '22 and '23. . . . He also led the team with four interceptions in 1923. . . . He lettered from 1922-24. . . . Crowley had successful coaching stints at Michigan State and Fordham, compiling a 78-21-10 record in 13 years. . . . At Fordham he coached the Seven Blocks of Granite, a powerful line that featured Vince Lombardi. . . . Future Notre Dame coach Frank Leahy was an assistant to Crowley at Fordham. . . . Crowley served as commissioner of the All-America Football Conference in the mid-1940s. . . . He died in 1986 at the age of 83.

Personal Data:

Born: September 19, 1902, in Chicago.
High School: Green Bay High in Green Bay, Wis.

FULLBACK: Elmer Layden.

Layden was the fastest of the Four Horsemen. . . . He excelled on defense as well as offense and handled the punting chores skillfully. . . . He was a consensus All-America in 1924. . . . He lettered from 1922-24. . . . Layden later returned to South Bend as coach, posting a 47-13-3 record in seven years. He was replaced by Frank Leahy. . . . He also coached at Columbia (Ia.) College, which now is called Loras College, and Duquesne. . . . His career record was 103-34-11 in 16 years. . . . He served as the first commissioner of the National Football League from 1941-46. . . . He died in 1973 at the age of 70.

Personal Data:

Born: May 4, 1903, in Davenport, Ia.
High School: Davenport High.

HALFBACK: Don Miller.

Miller was the team's breakaway threat. . . . He led Notre Dame in receiving from 1922-24 and in rushing in '23 and '24. . . . He holds the Notre Dame record for career average per rushing attempt (6.8 yards). . . . He lettered from 1922-24. . . . Miller is the only one of the Four Horsemen who did not become a college head coach, but he did serve as a part-time assistant at Georgia Tech and Ohio State. . . . He died in 1979 at the age of 77.

Personal Data:

Born: March 30, 1902, in Defiance, O.
High School: Defiance High.

QUARTERBACK: Harry Stuhldreher.

Stuhldreher was considered the team leader. . . . Feisty and arrogant, he led by example as a passer, blocker and punt returner. . . . He was a consensus All-America in 1924. . . . He was Notre Dame's leading punt returner in 1923 and '24. . . . Stuhldreher set school records for career punt-return yardage (701) and career kick returns (91). . . . He lettered from 1922-24. . . . A year later he was named coach at Villanova, where his teams went 65-25-9 over the next 11 seasons. . . . He then served as athletic director and coach at Wisconsin. He had a record of 26-45-4 in 13 years, the longest stint of any Badger coach. . . . He died in 1965 at the age of 63.

Personal Data:

Born: October 14, 1901, in Massillon, O.
High School: Kiski Prep in Massillon.

A Renaissance At Old Nassau

Princeton, 1933
By Phil Axelrod

When Art Lane was told that the 1933 Princeton Tigers were picked as one of the all-time great college teams, he grinned.

"A very smart pick," said Lane, a senior tackle and captain of that squad. "That was an awfully productive team."

Yes, outscoring opponents by a 217-8 margin while posting a 9-0 record certainly was productive. But many of the rating systems used before the days of wire-service polls considered Michigan, which had posted a 7-0-1 record that year, the No. 1 team in the land. Only the Davis system, which was simply the personal selection of noted football historian and Princeton alumnus Parke H. Davis, had the Tigers No. 1, and even then they were tied with Michigan.

Be that as it may. Princeton was undefeated and untied, and no other major college, including Michigan, could make that claim.

"Generally, we were considered in line to be the Number 1 team," Lane said. "Some thought Michigan was, some thought Princeton was. When we were at our peak, I don't think anybody could have beaten us, but we weren't always at our peak."

The Tigers, however, didn't have any valleys. "We merited the ratings we got," said Ken Fairman, a senior end on that team. "The Eastern schedules were not considered as tough as the Big Ten, but I think we were about the same."

Princeton and Michigan did not play each other and had no common opponents, so it is impossible to determine which team was better. But Princeton's almost-overnight rise from patsy to power-

Fritz Crisler learned the nuances of football under Amos Alonzo Stagg as an end at the University of Chicago.

house left a lasting impression on football fans. If improvement and character count for anything in the rating of college teams, then the '33 Tigers certainly deserve a spot among the all-time greats.

Lane, Fairman and the other seniors on that team were well aware how far the Tigers had come in a short time. They were sophomores in 1931, when their only victory was over lowly Amherst in the season opener. When they suffered a 33-0 defeat to Cornell in their third game, it marked the most lopsided loss in Princeton history. But the Tigers got whipped even worse a few weeks later when Yale romped to a 51-14 victory.

"We were pretty bad," Lane said of the '31 club. "We were absolutely swamped by Yale. We had some good players, but we didn't seem to be organized. We were all going in different directions."

Princeton football was behind the times. After nearly six decades of dominance, the Tigers had suffered three straight lean years (2-4-1, 1-5-1 and 1-7) as other schools pushed them aside using new techniques and strategies. Coach Al Wittmer did the best he could in '31 with the system that had worked so well for years under Bill Roper, but it was clear to Old Nassau fans that a change was in order.

The change, as it turned out, was more drastic than expected. For the first time, Princeton hired a non-alumnus as coach: Herbert O. (Fritz) Crisler.

Crisler had studied the game under the legendary Amos Alonzo Stagg at the University of Chicago, where he was a second-team All-America end in 1921. He then served as one of Stagg's assistants until 1930, when he became Minnesota's coach. After two years there, he accepted Princeton's offer to turn around its demoralized football program.

Crisler wasted no time chucking the Tigers' old offense and installing the single wing. The double wing was in vogue back then, but Crisler preferred the simpler formation, which he then spiced up with numerous variations that kept defenses off-balance.

Charlie Ceppi (left), a 5-11, 195-pound senior tackle, was a Princeton veteran in 1933, while Garry LeVan was a 5-9 sophomore halfback who doubled as a sprinter on the Tiger track team.

"He brought a terrific amount of offense that we didn't really absorb until late in the season," Fairman said. "The basic offense was called the Minnesota single wing, with the strong-side end split about six to eight feet, as much as a couple of yards. The wingback was back deep in the slot. It was a great setup for reverses. We didn't shift the line over.... There was an awful lot of stuff, a lot of exact timing. The ball changed hands quite a bit, particularly on the buck lateral."

Crisler also instituted many new blocking techniques. "He put in reverse cross-body blocking, trap blocking, and he had the ends slip the tackle to give us another blocker," Fairman said. "He gave us the mechanics of it; you could see it. Before that, the alumni coaches used to borrow plays from the opponents.

"This was a system that tied the plays together. You could see this on the charts. It was an intellectual experience for the Princeton players."

Crisler was a patient coach who spent long hours drilling the Tigers on fundamentals. But he also was a skillful teacher.

"We were getting coaching for the very first time," Fairman said. "He taught us things that we had never known."

The immediate result in 1932, his first season, was a 2-2-3 record that included a 14-7 loss to national power Michigan. But the Tigers gave the Wolverines an awful scare.

"We had gone out to play Michigan at Ann Arbor, and we were damn unlucky not to beat them," Fairman recalled. "They blocked a punt for a touchdown and they completed only one pass, late in the game for a touchdown. We felt we were on the way after that."

Lane's junior season was cut short by a broken collarbone against Columbia in the second game. Though he watched the rest of the season from the stands, he witnessed the impact Crisler made that first season. "We became respectable," he said. "He brought us back."

Crisler established himself as boss from the first day of practice. There never was any doubt that Crisler's word, usually delivered softly, was final.

"He was very much in charge," Fairman said. "He knew what he was doing. He was very calm, very positive."

Said Lane: "He was a great, able coach. He was highly respected. Although he was a quiet fellow, he had the ability to inspire the boys. He was a little austere. We held him somewhat in awe, but we had a lot of affection for him."

Crisler always was looking for ways to give the Tigers an edge, both physical and psychological. In those days of the single platoon, he kept his players

Garry LeVan breaks through the Dartmouth defensive line for a substantial gain in Princeton's 7-0 victory in 1933.

in good physical shape by making practices easier as game day drew near.

"The conditioning was sound," Fairman said. "They didn't overdo it. You rested after Wednesday. You didn't hit too hard on Thursday, and we had a lot of fun at practice on Friday. We practiced in old canvas pads, then wore knit, tight-fitting pants, lightweight jerseys and lightweight shoes instead of hard-toes in the games. We felt like track sprinters."

Said Lane: "Most of us played for 58 minutes. The only time he took you out was at the end of the game so you could get a hand from the crowd."

To give his players a psychological boost, Crisler trumpeted every opponent as the best team Princeton would play that year.

"He always held a towel to give you the idea that he was nervous, that his palms were sweaty," Fairman said. "I don't know if he was nervous, but he made us believe that he was worried all the time."

Before the biggest games, Crisler would pull out his time-honored inspirational speech and animatedly deliver it to the players, who hung on each word, each syllable, each inflection of his voice.

"He would usually give us a Knute Rockne speech," Lane said. "He was terrific. He was awfully good at it."

Even if he was a bit repetitive. "After you heard him for two or three years," Fairman said, "you realized that he tended to repeat his psychological messages. But they still were effective."

Especially in his first season at Princeton, where the players were unaccustomed to winning. "He turned us from boys into men," Fairman said. "He gave us our pride back."

As a result, optimism flowed freely on Princeton's campus when the football team assembled for practice in the fall of '33.

"We were enthusiastic about that season," Lane said. "We knew we had a chance to be pretty good."

Said Fairman: "We thought there was going to be a great difference (from the year before). We had good football kids. We knew that."

In addition to the return of a number of talented veterans, the Tigers were bolstered by a superb sophomore class that had gone undefeated and unscored upon in a four-game freshman campaign.

"Our main strength was our sophomore class," Lane said. "We gave them a good deal of friendship, a good deal of counsel."

The sophomores gave Princeton a new injection of talent and spirit.

"We didn't really know how good they were—at least I didn't know," Fairman recalled. "I was still playing lacrosse, avoiding football in the spring, but word got around that we had some pretty good boys coming up. That was a special class; seven or eight of the boys were sons of Princeton alumni."

The standout sophomore on the '33 team was 5-foot-9 halfback Garry LeVan. A sprinter on the track team, LeVan was a threat to go all the way every time he got the ball.

"He was a speedy little halfback whose nickname was Spook," Fairman said. "He was a very shifty open-field runner."

But LeVan had more than just moves. "He was terribly strong," Lane said. "Oh, sure, he was the fastest player on the team. He was just colossal."

Nevertheless, LeVan started only one game that year. He usually came in as a substitute for Chick Kaufman, another sophomore halfback, but LeVan played about twice as much.

Sophomores constituted almost the entire backfield as Crisler alternated LeVan, Kaufman, Les Kaufman (Chick's younger brother), Homer Spofford, Hugh MacMillan and Paul Pauk at the two halfback spots and Pepper Constable and Ippy Rulon-Miller at fullback. Spofford led the team in scoring with eight touchdowns, followed by LeVan with seven.

John Weller and Robert Kopf, who shared the left guard spot, and end Gil Lea were other sophomores who played a lot that year.

"We knew (the sophomores) had a strong nucleus, but they didn't take over the whole roster," Fairman said. "They sorted themselves out. They had a lot to learn."

As did the veterans, who still were mastering Crisler's new system. "It was a complicated offense," Fairman said.

The top returning veterans were Lane, Fairman and Charlie Ceppi, a 5-11, 195-pound senior tackle who was considered Princeton's most ferocious blocker and pass-rusher.

"He was a true All-America," said Fairman, who recruited Ceppi and roomed with him for four years. "He was quick, like a cat, and was an All-America in lacrosse, so you know he could move. He was a great all-around athlete. I knew he was going to be good. That's why I talked him out of taking a scholarship to New York University."

Fairman called Lane "a great, great talent. We had so much confidence in him. He was a fellow you could count on."

Lane, insisting that his best sport was hockey, said he was a "solid football player."

"I was not tremendously big by today's standards, but back then I was considered big at 205 pounds," said Lane, who later became a judge on the New Jersey state bench and still practices law in Princeton. "We weren't big at all. Nobody played at 260 pounds in those days."

In fact, Princeton listed Lane at 6-2, 190 pounds. Fairman checked in at 6-2, 173 pounds.

"I was a tall, skinny basketball player playing football," said Fairman, who was considered one of the top basketball forwards in the East. "I had a certain amount of speed. . . . Yes, I could say I had good hands. I did make All-East, and I was mentioned for All-America. One dummy picked me on his first All-America team, but I don't think he knew a thing about football."

Fairman and Lea were the favorite targets for 5-8 quarterback John Kadlic, a little guy with a big arm.

"We threw quite often—not as much as today, but we threw the ball," said Fairman, who later became Princeton's athletic director from 1941-72, with time out for duty in World War II. "Kadlic was an excellent passer from 15 to 20 yards. He had a good, hard spiral that was easy to catch. He was quite accurate. We did quite a lot with the pass when we needed it."

Which wasn't often. "We made so much damn ground grinding it out—I don't mean one or two yards and dust—that we didn't have to rely on the pass," Fairman said. "We had a fascinating short punt formation that was perfect for the buck lateral series."

Guard Frank John, who kicked most of the extra points, and center Elwood Kalbaugh completed Crisler's most common starting lineup.

"We were a subdued bunch, a modest team," said Lane, who was president of his class all four years at Princeton. "We had a quiet confidence, a quiet determination. There was no braggadocio. We had a good deal of unity. Everything came together; everybody worked for it."

Princeton kicked off the '33 season with a pair of easy victories over Amherst (40-0) and Williams (45-0). Though it had been six years since the Tigers had opened with consecutive wins, the small stature of their opponents caused few heads to turn. Princeton's big test—Columbia—was a week away. The Lions had gone 7-1-1 the year before and had another strong club in '33. If Princeton was to regain its spot among the national powers, this was the game to do it.

"We had our minds set on the Columbia game from the first day of practice," Lane said. "We hadn't won a major game in quite a while, and we really were keyed up for Columbia."

An inspired Princeton squad jumped on Columbia with 13 points in the first quarter on Spofford's seven-yard touchdown run, John's extra-point kick and LeVan's 52-yard punt return.

"Columbia had an All-America safety, Cliff Montgomery, who had a shot at LeVan," Fairman recalled. "But LeVan went down the sideline and left him out of bounds with a little hip toss. LeVan cut back and went for the touchdown."

The Tigers led, 20-0, at halftime. They did not

As Charlie Ceppi (69) looks for a defender to block, Garry LeVan breaks away from the pack en route to a 30-yard touchdown run in Princeton's 1933 opener against Amherst.

score again, but their defense made the lead stand up. Old Nassau had registered a stunning upset, one that became even more impressive as Columbia completed its regular season without another loss and then shocked Stanford, 7-0, in the Rose Bowl.

"That win re-established us as a pretty fair football university," Lane said. "Everything we did that fall pointed to that game."

Crisler later wrote that the triumph over Columbia "was one of the finest clutch performances during my years at Princeton. It was a game in which every member of the team bore down. The blocking especially was of a high order."

The next week, however, Princeton stumbled past Washington and Lee, 6-0.

"We worked so hard for the victory over Columbia," Lane said, "that we struggled the next two or three games because we had a great physical and mental letdown after that great buildup."

After playing its first four games on its own turf, Princeton traveled to Providence, R.I., to play Brown. The night before the game, the managers for both teams enjoyed a couple of beers at a local saloon.

"Our manager came back and told us that Brown was going to surprise Princeton with an eight-man defensive line," Fairman said. "Fritz got us up in the hotel room and made changes with our plays. He started the game with the second team in there to perform for five minutes to give us a look. They came out with it (an eight-man line), but they gave it up in a hurry."

Crisler used four complete squads as the Tigers thrashed the Bears, 33-0. It was Princeton's first win on the road since 1927.

In the next game, Fairman scored the only touchdown on a 20-yard pass to spark a 7-0 victory over Dartmouth. LeVan's school-record four interceptions then helped the Tigers beat Navy, 13-0. Princeton was 7-0.

And that wasn't all. For 28 quarters, Princeton's defensive slate was unsoiled. Its goal line had yet to be crossed as all seven opponents had been held scoreless. As if the Tigers' sudden resurgence wasn't enough to keep the sportswriters busy, they also had a shutout streak going.

"It was a big deal," Lane said. "We never said so, but we had hoped to go the whole season without giving up a point."

Said Fairman: "We thought it was possible. You'd like to say nobody scored, but we knew that all it would take would be for somebody to hit a lucky pass."

Princeton carried its streak into the Rutgers game, which marked the last game for the seniors at Palmer Stadium, home of the Tigers. After his team

Sophomore Chick Kaufman breaks loose for a big gain as Columbia defenders give chase during Princeton's crucial 20-0 victory over the Lions, who went on to complete their season without another loss.

When Brown came out with an eight-man defensive line in its 1933 meeting with Princeton, Crisler and Co. were ready with a solid passing attack (above) and a controlled offense that helped produce a 33-0 victory.

scored 13 points in the first quarter and six more on the first play of the second period, Crisler decided to give his first-stringers a rest. But when a bad snap led to a fumble that Rutgers recovered on Princeton's 12-yard line shortly before halftime, Crisler hustled his starters back into the game. Three rushes netted little and a pass fell incomplete in the end zone on fourth down to keep the streak alive.

In the third quarter, however, a play that will remain frozen in the hearts of all Princeton players and fans put an end to the streak. The Tigers were comfortably ahead, 19-0, and the second unit was on the field when Rutgers halfback Arnie Truex threw 20 yards downfield to Walt Winika. The Scarlet end hauled in the pass on the Princeton 40-yard line and kept running with only one Tiger defender in position to stop him short of the goal line.

"Les Kaufman, safety man, came diagonally across the field to head off the flying figure in Scarlet," A.J. Murray Jr. wrote in "Going Back," a review of Princeton's '33 season. "Forty thousand hearts beat madly, eighty thousand hands clenched nervously, as the two converged in the southeast corner. Kaufman's strategy was sound, but he overplayed his hand, was too cautious. Coming slowly and deliberately, bearding his prey as a cat stalks a mouse, Les hoped to knock him on the 5-yard line. . . . Fearful lest Winika should cut in on the 10, if he sprang too soon, Les withheld his tackle, bided his time. But that hesitancy proved fatal; with a last burst of hidden power, Winika dove for the goal line as the Tiger made his bid. You could hear the rasping wham of that deadly tackle all over the stadium. But Les' overcautiousness was a deathblow to the Nassau hopes; the momentum carried them both over. And over on the western (Rutgers) side of the stadium, it seemed as though all hell had broken loose."

Crisler was not floored by the rare defensive lapse. "When the touchdown occurred, Fritz told us, 'It's almost impossible to go the whole season and not be scored on,' " Lane recalled.

Nor did the Princeton players let the end of the streak ruin their day. "You laughed it off afterward," Fairman said. "They scored on the second team. That's why they were on the second team."

Princeton's first team never did give up a touchdown in 1933. A week after their 26-6 victory over Rutgers, the Tigers capped their perfect season with a 27-2 triumph over rival Yale. Princeton got a pair of touchdowns from Spofford and one each from LeVan and, of all people, Ceppi.

That touchdown by his tackle roommate is Fairman's most cherished memory of the '33 season. He recalls huddling with Ceppi in their hotel room the Thursday night before the game, plotting a way to block a Yale punt.

"They had a left-footed punter, and we always laughed about how we were going to block one of his kicks," Fairman said. "The coaches never mentioned it, but we had our own plan. Ceppi and I got

The 1933 Tigers: Front row (left to right)—John Gill, Donald Stewart, D.S. Hinman, Elwood Kalbaugh, Art Lane, Charlie Ceppi, John Bales, John Smithies, William Halton. Second row—Managor Gardncr, Homer Spofford, Paul Pauk, Garry LeVan, John Kadlic, Chick Kaufman, C.W. Wardell, Fielder Dudley, S. McPartland, head Coach Fritz Crisler. Third row—Lou Haggin, Ippy Rulon-Miller, Layton Schoch, William Cruikshank, Frank John, Robert Kopf, Les Kaufman, D.R. Chamberlain, Ben Delaney. Fourth row—Ken Fairman, Hugh MacMillan, Gil Lea, Adrian Fisher, Wilmer Gosnell, Henry Nelson, Pepper Constable, John Bliss, Edgar Rulon-Miller, John Weller.

together and placed chairs to design the play. I was the left end and Ceppi was the left tackle. I would cross in front of Ceppi—we knew there would only be a single blocker on our side because he was a left-footed kicker and the extra blocker would be on the other side—and Ceppi would take a step outside of me."

The strategy worked perfectly. Ceppi blocked the punt and picked up the bouncing football 35 yards from Yale's end zone.

"With the help of a few people, he scored," Fairman said, smiling. "I always told him that play made him an All-America."

Despite their 9-0 record, the Tigers stayed home for the holidays.

"It was rumored—there was some basis to it—that we had received an informal bid to go to the Rose Bowl, but the administration turned it down," Lane said. "There was a lot of emotion that year and we were all tired out. Emotionally, we were exhausted. There was no dissent."

In some quarters, there was relief. "I was ready to go play basketball," Fairman said. "I was a little torn between the two sports, but we were told that we weren't allowed to go (to Pasadena), so there was no use sweating it out. There wasn't much disappointment. We had already accomplished everything that we wanted to."

Few teams in the history of college football can say as much.

Princeton, 1933

ROAD TO GREATNESS

1933 RESULTS (9-0)

Opponent	Score	Opp. Record	Opp. Bowl Game
Amherst	40-0	4-3-1	
Williams	45-0	3-4-0	
Columbia	20-0	8-1-0	Rose (W)
Washington and Lee	6-0	4-4-2	
at Brown	33-0	3-5-0	
Dartmouth	7-0	4-4-1	
Navy	13-0	5-4-0	
Rutgers	26-6	6-3-1	
at Yale	27-2	4-4-0	

FACTS AND FIGURES

The 1933 Princeton team was greater than the sum of its parts. Not one player earned consensus All-America honors, although tackle Charlie Ceppi did get some All-America acclaim.... Center Elwood Kalbaugh, a junior in '33, received All-America notice in 1934.... Guard John Weller, one of Princeton's outstanding sophomores in '33, was a consensus All-America in 1935 and later was elected to the College Football Hall of Fame.... Fullback Pepper Constable, another talented sophomore in '33, finished fourth in the voting for the inaugural Heisman Trophy in 1935.... Two years after the sophomore-dominated Tigers went undefeated and untied in 1933, the senior-laden '35 squad posted another 9-0 season.... Some fans of Old Nassau consider the '35 team even better than the '33 club.... The Tigers suffered only one loss between those perfect seasons, a 7-0 upset by Yale.... The Tigers did not convert a field goal in 1933.... Princeton's rugged defense forced 17 punts and held Amherst to zero first downs and 25 total offensive yards in their 1933 contest.... Linemen Ceppi and Frank John scored touchdowns for the '33 Tigers. John found his moment in the spotlight in the Navy game when he pounced on a teammate's fumble in the end zone. Ceppi blocked a punt against Yale, picked up the ball and ran for a touchdown.... Seven players scored two or more touchdowns for the Tigers in '33—and all seven were sophomores.... The highest-scoring senior was Ceppi with one touchdown and one extra-point kick.... Princeton's opponents compiled a record of 41-32-5 (.558 winning percentage).... Seven of nine foes had non-losing records.... Through their first seven games, the Tigers had outscored their opponents, 164-0.... Princeton's average margin of victory was 23.2 points.... Sophomore halfback Hugh MacMillan played on the Princeton basketball team with seniors Ken Fairman and Ceppi in 1933-34. He served as team captain two years later.... Quarterback John Kadlic, a vocal leader in the huddle, was a good scrambler with an accurate arm up to 25 yards.... Kadlic also was described as a "lethal tackler."

STATISTICAL LEADERS

SCORING

	TD	FG	PAT	Points
Homer Spofford	8	0	0	48
Garry LeVan	7	0	0	42
Gil Lea	3	0	1	19
Pepper Constable	3	0	0	18
Les Kaufman	3	0	0	18
Frank John	1	0	10	16
Chick Kaufman	2	0	0	12
Paul Pauk	2	0	0	12
Charlie Ceppi	1	0	1	7
Ken Fairman	1	0	0	6
Lou Haggin	1	0	0	6
Hugh MacMillan	1	0	0	6

KEY CHARACTERS

The Conductor

COACH: Herbert (Fritz) Crisler.

Record: 35-9-5, 6 years at Princeton.

Crisler was dubbed "Fritz" by his coach at the University of Chicago, Amos Alonzo Stagg.... It was not meant as a compliment. Stagg was upset with Crisler's play and decided to call him Fritz because his last name resembled that of world-renowned violinist Fritz Kreisler, whose coordination and agile hands provided a stark contrast with Crisler.... Nevertheless, Crisler earned second-team All-America acclaim as a senior end in 1921.... He spent eight years as an assistant under Stagg before taking his first head coaching position at Minnesota, where he also was athletic director.... He compiled a 10-7-1 record in two seasons with the Golden Gophers.... He then moved to Princeton after the 1931 season, succeeding Al Wittmer, who resigned after his only season as football coach.... Crisler also succeeded Wittmer as basketball coach, directing the 1932-33 and '33-34 Tiger cagers. Both teams had winning records, including a 19-3 mark the first year.... Crisler was hired by the Tigers on March 1, 1932, the same day as the Lindbergh baby kidnaping in nearby Hopewell, N.J. Police arrested Crisler early the next morning when they found him driving a car that didn't belong to him. The car was a loaner from a Princeton alumnus, but Crisler was not released until the alumnus visited police headquarters and explained the situation.... Crisler's '33 club was his first of two undefeated teams at Old Nassau.... He later had one more undefeated team in his last year at Michigan, where he directed the Wolverines to a record of 71-16-3 from 1938-47.... Crisler is a member of the College Football Hall of Fame.... He died in 1982 at the age of 83.

Personal Data:

Born: January 12, 1899, in Earlville, Ill.
High School: Earlville High and Mendota High in Mendota, Ill.
College: Chicago.

The Supporting Cast

TACKLE: Charlie Ceppi.

Ceppi was a big man with great mobility and agility... He was a ferocious pass rusher and an excellent special-teams player, usually arriving downfield first on kick coverage... A columnist once wrote that Ceppi "knocks down trees along Prospect Street to keep in trim."... He lettered from 1931-33.... Ceppi played in the Shrine East-West Game in San Francisco after the 1933 season.... Ceppi earned All-America notice in '33 but was not a consensus pick.... He also played basketball and lacrosse for the Tigers.

Personal Data:

Born: May 8, 1912, in Fair Haven, N.Y.
High School: Central High in Syracuse, N.Y., and Dean Academy in Boston.

END: Ken Fairman.

Fairman was a big-play receiver with sure hands and speed to burn.... He was a good blocker as well.... He lettered from 1931-33.... He also played basketball and lacrosse at Princeton.... He was captain of Princeton's 1933-34 basketball team, which posted a 13-8 record under Fritz Crisler.... Fairman won the 1934 B.F. Bunn Trophy, which recognized his contributions to the Princeton basketball team that season.... He later coached the Tiger basketball team for three years (1935-36 through '37-38).... He served as Princeton's athletic director until he retired in 1972.

Personal Data:

Born: February 23, 1912, in Spring Valley, N.Y.
High School: Central High in Syracuse and Manlius Prep in Manlius, N.Y.

TACKLE: Art Lane.

Lane was an effective player on both sides of the ball.... He was a solid blocker on offense and a devastating hitter on defense... A charismatic leader, Lane was captain of the '33 squad.... He missed most of his junior season with a broken collarbone... He lettered in 1931 and 1933.... He also played hockey for the Tigers.

Personal Data:

Born: December 26, 1910, in Arlington, Mass.
High School: Exeter Academy in Exeter, N.H.

HALFBACK: Garry LeVan.

LeVan was a breakaway runner who combined terrific speed with elusive moves.... Though he started only one game as a sophomore in 1933, he quickly made his mark as the most electrifying player on the Tiger roster, both running the ball and catching passes.... He also was brilliant on defense as a safety.... One writer described him as a "twinkle-toed broken-field runner."... He also was a member of Princeton's track team.

The Authors

Phil Axelrod (Pittsburgh 1980-81 and Princeton 1933) covered the Panthers for the Pittsburgh Post-Gazette from 1974-81. A graduate of Duquesne University, Axelrod joined the Post-Gazette in 1972 and has been covering college football and basketball for the last 16 years.

Bill Bilinski (Notre Dame 1946, 1966 and 1924) covers Notre Dame football for the South Bend (Ind.) Tribune, where he began working in 1983 and now doubles as assistant sports editor. Except while attending college and working for four years at two other Indiana newspapers, Bilinski has lived in South Bend his whole life. The graduate of Hanover (Ind.) College was reminded how deep his South Bend ties run when he researched the 1924 team and discovered a letter written to his grandfather by Knute Rockne. The 1920 letter, reprinted in Jerry Brondfield's "Rockne," was intended to drum up civic support for the Irish football program.

Al Browning (Alabama 1979 and 1934) was sports editor and columnist for the Tuscaloosa (Ala.) News when the '79 Crimson Tide won the national championship. After 10 years at the News he became a free-lance writer and then moved to the Knoxville News-Sentinel, where he again served as sports editor and columnist. Browning, an Alabama graduate, returned to free-lancing in 1987. He has written two books concerning Alabama football—"Bowl, 'Bama, Bowl" and "Third Saturday in October." He is now writing a book on a criminal case in Nashville that will be published in 1989.

Ronnie Christ (Penn State 1968-69) has been covering sports for the Harrisburg (Pa.) Patriot News for 26 years and Penn State football since 1967. He also covers other important college football matchups as well as college recruiting, professional golf and some basketball.

Bill Connors (Oklahoma 1974-75) has been sports editor and columnist for the Tulsa World since 1964. The Oklahoma State graduate began working in Tulsa in 1953 and has shared the Oklahoma and Oklahoma State football beats ever since. He has averaged about six Sooner games a year.

Tracy Dodds (UCLA 1954) has been covering UCLA football and basketball for the Los Angeles Times since 1982. The Indiana graduate previously worked for the Houston Post, where she covered Southwest Conference football for two years, and the Milwaukee Journal, where she handled the Milwaukee Bucks beat from 1973-80.

Jack Ebling (Michigan State 1965-66 and 1952) has won several sportswriting awards since assuming the Spartan football and basketball beat at the Lansing State Journal in 1983. A Michigan State graduate, he taught English and coached football and track in Lapeer, Mich., before joining the Journal in 1979.

Joe Gergen (Syracuse 1959) is a sports columnist for Long Island-based Newsday. The Brooklyn native and Boston College graduate has concentrated on baseball and pro football in his 20 years at Newsday, with side trips into just about every other sport imaginable. Gergen, who began his journalism career 25 years ago with United Press International in New York, has written four books, the most recent of which, "The Final Four," was published in 1987 by The Sporting News.

Charley Hallman (Minnesota 1934-35) has been covering Minnesota football off and on since 1979. He began his journalism career as a correspondent for Leatherneck magazine while serving in Vietnam. He then spent two years as night city editor for the Associated Press in Minneapolis before moving across the river to the St. Paul Pioneer Press & Dispatch, where he has been a sportswriter for the last 19 years. Now the Golden Gophers' beat reporter, Hallman also covered the National Hockey League for 14 years.

Bob Hersom (Oklahoma 1955-56) covers college sports and minor league baseball for the Daily Oklahoman in Oklahoma City. The Mount Mercy (Ia.) College graduate began his newspaper career in 1973 and worked for the Cedar Rapids (Ia.) Gazette for five years before coming to Oklahoma. He has covered college sports for the last eight years, concentrating mostly on Oklahoma football and basketball.

Paul Hornung (Ohio State 1968) covered Ohio State football for 37 of his 41 years with the Columbus (O.) Dispatch. He began working part time with the Dispatch while attending Ohio State in 1938 and then took over the Buckeye beat when he joined the paper on a permanent basis two years later. Hornung, who spent the last 23 years of his career as columnist and sports editor of the Dispatch before retiring in 1981, covered 319 consecutive Ohio State football games at one point.

Steve Kornacki (Michigan 1947) is a sportswriter and occasional columnist for the Ann Arbor (Mich.) News. The Eastern Michigan graduate has been covering Michigan football for the last nine years and spends the better part of his summers covering the Detroit Tigers.

Jim Martz (Miami 1986-87) is a regional sports editor and columnist for the Miami Herald, where he has worked since 1971. He covered Hurricane sports for several years and is the author of "Hurricane Watch," a historical look at the school's football program, and "Hurricane Strikes," which examines Miami baseball.

Mike McKenzie (Nebraska 1971) is a free-lance writer and teacher living in the Kansas City area. The Westmar (Ia.) College graduate has worked for six daily newspapers in a career that spans 24 years. Two of those years were spent with the Atlanta Journal and the last nine with the Kansas City Star and Times, for which McKenzie was a sports columnist (two years) and a special-assignments feature writer (six years). He has been free-lancing since January 1988.

George Morris (Louisiana State 1958) has been covering LSU football and basketball since 1984, two years after he started working for the Baton Rouge (La.) State-Times. The South Carolina graduate previously worked for the Tampa Times from 1977-82.

Dave Newhouse (Southern Cal 1972) is an author, a sports columnist for the Oakland Tribune and a sports talk-show host on radio station KNBR in San Francisco. The San Jose State graduate has written three books—"Rose Bowl Football Since 1902" (with Herb Michelson), "The Jim Plunkett Story" and "Heismen, After the Glory." Though his only stint as a college football beat writer was spent covering the California Golden Bears from 1966-69, he has covered numerous Southern Cal football games in Northern California and at the Rose Bowl during his 24-year sportswriting career.

Ernie Palladino (Army 1944-45) has been covering sports for the Gannett Westchester-Rockland Newspapers in Westchester, N.Y., for the last 13 years. About 10 of those years have been spent covering college football, including the 1984 and 1985 Army football seasons. Besides covering those Cadet teams, he researched many of the older Army squads and interviewed former Cadets for a number of historical articles. Palladino, a graduate of Fordham University, has written a weekly column on college football and now covers baseball as well as college and pro football.

Nick Peters (Southern Cal 1967) covered Pacific-10 Conference sports for more than 20 years. He has been covering the San Francisco Giants for the Sacramento Bee since coming to the publication in February and will cover college basketball over the winter. He spent nine years with the Oakland Tribune before moving to Sacramento.

Scott Pitoniak (Pittsburgh 1976) spent seven years covering college football for the Utica (N.Y.) Daily Press and Observer-Dispatch before switching to pro football when he moved to the Rochester (N.Y.) Democrat and Chronicle in 1985. The Syracuse graduate has won several sportswriting awards while covering college basketball and minor league baseball as well as college football during his 11-year career.

Mark Wangrin (Texas 1969) has been covering Longhorn football since joining the Austin (Tex.) American-Statesman in 1985. The Northwestern graduate previously worked as a sportswriter for newspapers in Arlington, Tex., and Tyler, Tex.